Introduction
to Perception

S. Howard Bartley
MEMPHIS STATE UNIVERSITY

HARPER & ROW, PUBLISHERS, New York

Cambridge, Hagerstown, Philadelphia, San Francisco,
London, Mexico City, São Paulo, Sydney

1817

In gratitude to all those who have so loyally and devotedly supported and helped to produce this book and the findings and ideas in it. The list is not short.

Sponsoring Editor: George A. Middendorf
Project Editor: Eleanor Castellano
Senior Production Manager: Kewal K. Sharma
Compositor: Kingsport Press
Printer and Binder: The Maple Press Company
Cover Design: Helen Iranyi
Art Studio: J & R Technical Services, Inc.

Library of Congress Cataloging in Publication Data

Bartley, Samuel Howard, Date—
   Introduction to perception.

   Based on the 2d ed. of the author's Principles
of perception.
   Includes bibliographical references.
   1. Perception. I. Bartley, Samuel Howard,
1901–   Principles of perception. II. Title.
BF311.B289   153.7   79–20538
ISBN 0–06–040514–7

Contents

Preface

The second edition of *Principles of Perception* took some advantage of the idea of perceptual systems developed by J. J. Gibson. The present text involves a full expression of this idea and embodies further innovations. As an introduction, the book is not simply an enumeration of various so-called theories of perception that had accumulated up to the time of writing but substitutes in the first chapter a framework for viewing cause and effect and for eliminating the average person's reliance on the causal pairing of mind and body. Basic scientific items are put into two classes: those involving the cause and effect of the energistic system and those called emergent phenomena which arise from patterns in the energistic system and in themselves are not causal, although traditionally they have been given causal efficacy.

The second chapter portrays the relation of perception to other aspects of psychology and shows its bounds and nature. Throughout, the chapter depicts perception as the comprehensive active interrelation of the organism and the environment, assuming the individual as a part of Nature rather than apart from it.

The third and several subsequent chapters describe the perceptual systems, adding one not previously identified and placing it along with the familiar five. This is the *homeostatic perceptual system*, which deals with the sense mechanisms that help to maintain organic equilibrium.

The remaining chapters, excluding Chapter 17, pertain to certain features of response, such as space perception and the perception of movement and what is generally called constancy on the one hand and illusion on the other, that cut across the systems already depicted. The final chapter discusses certain special perceptual states.

These changes or innovations, although unusual, are incorporated in this text in order to round out the overall domain and portrayal of perception.

I thank Mrs. Jean Conley for her unflagging devotion and enthusiasm. Without her help, this book would have been impossible.

S. Howard Bartley

Chapter 1
Introduction

THE INDIVIDUAL AND THE ENVIRONMENT

This is a textbook that concentrates on one aspect of human behavior, namely, the relation of the organism to the energies in its context—the environment. It is helpful to examine psychology as a whole briefly to see where this study fits.

PROBLEM AREAS IN PSYCHOLOGY

Tasks and objectives in psychology as a science can be put into five major categories or problem areas as follows:

1. *Action and its direction and goals.* We need a way to explain why anything takes place and, furthermore, why it happens in the way or direction it does. This was not a problem in psychology first but rather one in physics and then one pertaining to very simple biological organisms. Usually, we do not spend time on this problem in the same manner as the physicists and biologists do. We deal with it at a higher level

of complexity, that is, by dealing with *motivation* and *goals*. But it is appropriate that we relate what the organism does to the basic foundations set forth by the physicists and biologists.

2. *Humans in relation to the physical world.* We already have much detailed information relating the organism to the physical energies, such as the gravitational field, thermal activity, chemical activity, photic radiation ("light"), and range of mechanical vibrations known as acoustic energy. These are the energies that by their intrinsic nature and pattern form what we call *stimuli* for our sense organs.

3. *Forms of change the organism manifests in overall behavior.* As a function of time and the influences of the environment. These changes include maturation, learning, acclimatization, addiction, tolerance, development of physical fitness, and aging.

4. *Internal organization and conflict.* Some portions of the nervous system are reflexive and seem to pertain to homeostasis and survival, whereas others have to do more directly with overt skeletal reactions and awareness. Recently, Miller (1971) and his associates have experimentally dispelled some misconceptions regarding differences between the two portions but there are ways in which the two may *conflict.* Some of this conflict comes to the surface in human awareness.

5. *The ability of the organism to meet demands.* Some of these demands are ordinarily couched in experiential (personalistic) terms, others are describable in terms of what happens in the nervous system. Fatigue, impairment, work decrement, and boredom are some of the end results accruing from inadequacy to meet demand.

All of the concerns in psychology can be placed in one of these problem categories. Perception, pertaining to relations to our surrounds, falls into the second.

THE HUMAN AS A PART OF NATURE

There are several other considerations in becoming properly oriented and in making an appropriate start in the study of psychology—in this case, the study of perception.

People, in general, make a dualistic description of humans. They say humans are bodies and minds, or perhaps *have* bodies and minds, which they have been told since childhood. We shall discuss this in more detail later.

Secondly, the typical person has been taught that the human is *apart from* Nature rather than *a part of* Nature. This provides for all kinds of cause and effect. In fact, many make these up as they go along. Our society has been a maze of such descriptions, each with its believers and adherents.

In science, the human is a biological organism and *is* a part of Nature.

THE CAUSAL AND EMERGENT FEATURES OF NATURE

Another matter is, how is Nature to be described and understood? A very effective way is to consider Nature as having two aspects— energistic and phenomenological. The *energistic* aspect is one wherein there is quantitative cause and effect. Units such as grams, meters, calories, feet, pounds, and the like are used, and forms of mathematical systematization are applicable. Nuclear physics, astronomy, and chemistry dealing with the most basic features of this aspect of Nature.

The *phenomenological* aspect is the feature of Nature that has many kinds of qualitative descriptions. This aspect of Nature contains what are called *emergent* phenomena. These phenomena are not cause-and-effect units or complexes.

An example of an emergent phenomenon is given by Miller (1962) when he says a *lap* is an emergent phenomenon. When a person sits down a lap emerges. When the person stands up, it disappears. Laps themselves are not to be described quantitatively in cause-and-effect terms.

Even in elementary chemistry the student is taught partly in emergent terms. When the chemical elements are described they are described as either solids, liquids, or gases. They are described as to color, taste, and then finally the describer gets closer to cause-and-effect terms when atomic weight is mentioned. Energistic descriptions are given in molecular, atomic, and subatomic terms.

Our job here in dealing with the human is to recognize the various categories that are used and to apply concepts appropriate to these categories. *Human awareness is an emergent phenomenon.* Our experiences emerge from certain neural and other tissue conditions. We as scientists have to fashion a logical scheme with appropriate vocabularies to handle the energistic conditions and the emergent phenomena that pertain to humans relating to Nature (which includes other people).

It is crucial to know when to use energistic descriptions and when to use phenomenological descriptions and not to get these intermingled in unwitting ways.

SENSATION AND PERCEPTION

Traditionally, perception was not dealt with alone but always in connection with sensation. The relations between the two have been a basic problem. Psychology, taking its cue from physics and the atomistic thinking of the times, sought psychological *elements.* The physical domain had them, psychology could be expected to have elements too. They would be building blocks for consciousness. Thinkers in this area sought hard for these building blocks, and sensation was taken to be one of them. This was an error of atomism.

Atomism is the assumption that to arrive at an understanding of something complex, one must discover its elemental components. Moreover, it is the technique of *beginning* with elements ("atoms") and supposing that one can predict complex consequences from combinations of these elements. This view failed to realize that complexes possess properties that are not inherent in the elements themselves. For example, four equal lines may be put together to make a square, but the square possesses properties that did not exist before—there are corners, there are angles, and there is area.

The view that has differed from atomism is called *organicism.* Organicism starts with the chosen complex whole and notes its properties. It is only then that the determination of the roles of the parts can be seen. We shall choose organicism in portraying perception.

The result of stimulation is perception, a form of information, a discernment of the nature of objects, their position, shape, size, distance, and other features, including higher order meanings.

Titchener and his laboratory, at the turn of the century, assuming the elemental (building-block) character of sensation, carried out persistent experiments to gather data showing this. When he used a stylus to touch the forearm of a blindfolded subject instructed to describe sensation, the subject typically would say "something touched my arm." Thus the subject did not *describe* a sensory quality or an elemental tactile experience at all. Actually, Titchener never got any of his subjects to achieve this. What was always reported amounted to being a perception of some sort rather than a sensation.

The atomistic and oversimplified and even erroneous definition of perception that was taught 50 or 60 years ago was that "perception is sensation plus meaning."

Now our outlook on sensation and perception is much more sophisticated. We can begin by remembering that for a very long time there were thought to be five classes of sensations, emerging from the functioning of five classes of sense organs. As time went on additional kinds of sense organs were found. This did not, however, change the thinking of the average person, as evidenced by the fact that even today one hears about *the five* senses. The traditional view was that perception is based on sensation. As stated, we are now beginning to recognize that perception need not be based on sensation. Perception can occur without intervening sensations.

Strictly speaking, sensation is a *conscious* result from external input mediated by sense organs. Nevertheless, many illustrations show that input to sense organs can eventuate in perception (meaningful response) without evoking the kind of consciousness we call sensation. Perception, however, *cannot occur* without the *activation* of receptors in sense organs. Perception cannot be "extrasensory," so Gibson affirms, if to be "extrasensory" means being without any input. He says there can be sensationless perception, but not informationless perception.

In using the term *information* here, we face the same problem as we shall see later in using the word *stimulus*. Should we attach the word information to the thing delivered (input) or to what the organism derives from receiving the input?

PERCEPTUAL SYSTEMS

Today's thinking about perception progressed when it was realized that we do not have five senses but rather five *perceptual systems*. J. J. Gibson (1966) was the first to state this matter clearly and to deal with perceptual systems. He says that there are five modes of external attention—looking, listening, smelling, tasting, and touching. Along with these there is the basic orientation of the organism to the gravitational system that does not have a *specific* mode of attention but may be said to have a broad general one—being awake, upright, and alert. Thus we seem to have a sixfold classification. However, since tasting and smelling are so intimately intertwined, they form a single class called the savor system.

As mentioned above, more than five kinds of sense organs have been found. They are those of vision, audition, touch, taste, smell, temperature, pain, muscle sense, vestibular sense, and a common chemical sense. This latter sense does not provide an easily identifiable experience, so we shall ignore it for the present.

The human organism relates to certain basic energistic features of the environment. In other words, the human extracts information from the impingements on its sense organs. The most pervasive energistic feature is the gravitational system. The vestibular mechanism in the ear is the definitive sense organ used in this case. But this sense organ does not act alone—the posturing muscles of the body are also involved. Furthermore, the eye (the visual sense organ) is likewise involved. With these three mechanisms functioning cooperatively, individuals can orient themselves successfully to gravity. This ability is called the *basic orientation perceptual system* and will be further discussed later.

Another feature of the environment is the mechanical, wherein there is contact (touch), push, pull, lift, and so forth. This form of relating to the environment involves more than the sense organ of touch. It involves the muscle sense organs, the pain sense organs, and those for temperature. These work together to give the end result that superficially has been called touch but is much more than the resulting action of the touch sense organs. This group of cooperating sense organs is called the *haptic perceptual system.* Haptic comes from the Greek word meaning to "lay hold of."

The third aspect of the environment to which the human organism is sensitive is the chemical. The taste buds and the olfactory (smell) receptors in the nose respond to this aspect. In many ways it is difficult for a person to tell whether it is taste or smell that is experienced in a given situation. Even here the overall result is not solely produced by the action of these two sets of sense organs. The taste, for example, is dependent on activation of the temperature sense and the tactual sense in the mouth. Crisp material tastes different from mushy material of the same chemical composition. So again, we have a system at work—the *savor perceptual system.*

The fourth feature of the environment to which we are sensitive is vibration (over a certain range of frequencies). We call this range of air vibrations the *acoustic* range. The cochea of the ear is sensitive to it. So we have an *auditory perceptual system.* With the posturing of the head, we can locate objects at a distance and can detect the kinds of sound sources.

The range of electromagnetic frequencies called *photic radiation* is the fifth aspect of the environment. These frequencies are the energies to which the eye is sensitive, but the eye does not function alone. The vestibular mechanism in the ear is also involved. This, for example, provides the individual with the information of right side up and upside down. So with the eye and the vestibular mechanism and some of the other sense mechanisms, the individual is able to detect a number of things about the environment not otherwise observed, that is, to see objects, their color, their textures, position and distance away, and so forth. This is the *visual perceptual system.* Table 1.1 on page 8 summarizes the perceptual systems.

THE NATURE AND GROWTH OF SCIENCE

It is appropriate that the student be aware of the general nature of the development of science. This suggestion applies very well to the area of perception. In examining what has happened in the science of perception, we shall see that the remarks of T. S. Kuhn (1970) on the nature of the growth of science are cogent here. Accordingly, the following is somewhat in line with T. S. Kuhn's model of the development of science and its revolutions.

Proclaimed knowledge, or shall we call it science, does not evolve by mere accumulation of bits of data. It, or subareas within it, such as the sciences of perception, are characterized by a series of crises. The resolution of which are literally scientific revolutions.

During the period prior to a crisis the activities within a named discipline are characterized by a customary pattern or a paradigm. This *paradigm* is a body of rules, practices, and consents that constitute the framework within which the "normal science," or "textbook science" exists.

A paradigm as expressed in textbook science fixes research directions, supplies research methodology—acceptable instrumentation—decides relevant facts and problems and the necessary means for their solutions, and involves a number of quasi-metaphysical presuppositions.

The task of normal or paradigm-controlled science is to solve puzzles. It works on problems for which a solution is certain when the thinking and the tools provided by the paradigm are used. The object of normal science is not to produce unexpected or novel results but to join the parts of paradigms together—that is, to improve the match between the paradigm and Nature by making more and more precise measurements and by reaching known solutions in different or new ways. Paradigms are not explicit formulations. They are learned not so much by formal statements as by practice and education and by *doing* research.

In time, the paradigm, as exemplified in normal science, leads to increasing specialization among individuals and to narrowing conceptual perspective and concern. It also fosters increasing precision of measurement. Paradigms are not easily relinquished, and unexpected outcomes in experiments are not easily recognized for what they are.

However, an accumulation of unexpected results within a paradigm may lead to a crisis. One symptom of a crisis at hand is an accumulation of unlike versions of a given general theory. The awakening to a crisis eventuates when a set of persisting anomalies occur

Table 1.1 PERCEPTUAL SYSTEMS

NAME	FOCAL ACTION	PRIME SENSE ORGAN	IMPINGEMENTS	INFORMATION RESULTING
The visual system	Looking	Eyes and ocular muscles	Photic radiation	Size, shape, location, distance, color, texture, hardness, softness
The auditory system	Listening	Cochlea, middle ear	Air vibrations	Nature and location of acoustic sources
The savor system	Smelling	Nose	Chemical composition of inspired air Pain stimuli	Characteristics of volatile sources
	Tasting	Mouth	Chemical composition and thermal state of ingested material Pain stimuli	Palatable attributes of ingested material Detection of noxious substances
The haptic system	Touching Handling Pushing Pulling Lifting etc.	Skin, muscles, joints, ligaments, tendons	Deformation of tissue Action and position of joints Stretching of muscles Thermal and painful stimuli	Contact with ground or floor Mechanical encounters Object shapes Material states, softness, hardness, wetness, dryness, coldness, hotness

NAME	FOCAL ACTION	PRIME SENSE ORGAN	IMPINGEMENTS	INFORMATION RESULTING
The basic orientation system	Posturing and locomotion	Vestibular organs Kinesthetic receptors Visual sense organs	Static gravity and acceleration	Direction of gravity, pushes, pulls.
The homeostatic system	Maintenance of internal equilibrium	1. Carotid sinus receptors. 2. Depressor sensory endings in walls of intrapericardial vessels and pulmonary veins. 3. Pressor sensory cells in the vestibular nuclei. 4. Thermal-sensitive neurons in hypothalamus. 5. Receptors in the tracheobronchial tree.	Temperature, pressure, CO_2	Comfort, well-being, avoidance of overheating and chilling.

that the accepted problem-solving routine cannot solve. New theories at such times will get a hearing when the anomalies just alluded to are recognized, if the theories are suited to one of these trouble spots.

The transition from an existing paradigm to a new one is not just a matter of adding something new, it must be reconstructed, using new fundamentals. As a consequence, a radically new understanding of the matter emerges. Naturally, the old and the new paradigms are conflictive because the meanings of some of the most basic concepts have changed.

The foregoing states the way even the most sophisticated human understanding (called science) evolves. A grasp of this should be one of the means whereby the reader can begin to appreciate and evaluate the textbooks and articles read in scientific journals.

Chapter 2
The Problem of Perception

The problem of perception lies (1) in deciding on an appropriate definition, (2) in distinguishing it from sensation, the concept usually paired with it, (3) in examining its production, and (4) in providing various examples. We shall follow Gibson (1966) in distinguishing cases in which perception is evoked without the emergence of conscious sensation. Traditionally, sensation was thought to be the basic component in perception. Sixty years ago perception was defined as "sensation plus meaning." Sensation had to occur if perception were to result. Now we know that this is not the case.

Perception is the immediate discriminatory response of the organism aroused through activation of sense organs. Forgus and Malamed (1976) define perception as "the process of information extraction." McBurney and Collings (1977) say, "It is probably impossible and certainly fruitless to define perceptual behavior as if it were distinct from say, cognitive, emotional, or some other supposed category of behavior. For this reason we will define the field of perception . . . as the study of the process by which an organism responds to features of the environment with regularities in its behavior."

In other words, perception is the complete immediate relation of the organism to its surrounds, thus it includes something that can be called action as well as simply receipt of, or formulation of, information. Note that McBurney and Forgus include *response* in their definition.

From the beginning we should understand that perception is not restricted to consciousness. It is the immediate action on the organism's part elicited by sense organ activity. This action runs the gamut from some restricted chemical or neural adjustment all the way to the emergence of some extremely subtle experience. This broad range will be apparent when the perceptual systems are more fully described. An activity must possess the aspect of completeness at the personalistic level to be labeled a perception. Many local reactions are simply components of this overall response. For example, in Chapter 9, we shall see that some of the "complete reactions" are basic adjustments to the thermal aspect of the environment. While seemingly "low level," reflexive, or what not, they are presided over by the higher levels of the brain and represent the organism as a person.

The intent of the foregoing statements is to steer the reader away from the ordinary dictionary definitions, among which are synonyms such as "knowledge" and the like, and from restricting the understanding of perception to conscious activity.

One of the approaches of today is the *experimental,* in which beliefs and conclusions are arrived at by concrete laboratory experiments and procedures are those in which the demands of statistics are met.

Much that is now called *behavior* is far from the category we call conscious. The human organism relates to the environment from moment to moment in surprising ways, particularly when we consider how it reacts to temperature, humidity, barometric pressure, and wind velocity. Earlier teachings led us to put many such reactions in a category by themselves, but if we want to be consistent and regard the human organism as a unity rather than a loose and nebulous cluster of unlike components, we must discover the lawful interrelations among components even though descriptively quite different. On the other hand, we may discover that we have become unrealistic in postulating some of the entities in which we usually believe.

In this book we shall avoid using the term perception for dealing only with what can be called conscious reactions. However, we shall also avoid using the term perceiving as a synonym for *judging, thinking, knowing, believing,* or *understanding.* While not shunning a discussion of perception in relation to cognition, we shall consider perceiving in the realm of immediate response to environmental energies. Perceiving is our only process of direct contact with our natural context.

A full understanding of perception rests on the realization of the process components that are involved. They are: (1) the energy system we call Nature, or the environment with its impingements on sense organs; (2) the individual as an energy system governed by the same ground laws as the rest of Nature—we are unique only as being specially organized constellations of Nature; and (3) the interaction of the individual with the environment. This interaction can be viewed from either of two standpoints, namely, from the organism as a reference or from the reference of the environment. In psychology these two references are used. Stimulus–response psychology generally describes activity as originated by something outside the individual, even when the focus of psychology is largely on descriptions of awareness. Experience or consciousness belongs to the class called emergent phenomena. To account for experience, we have to ascertain the underlying bodily activities. This is a very different outlook on human behavior from what we have inherited from earlier times, with mind treated as one of the two cause-and-effect systems.

Only energy that impinges on receptors is potentially stimulating. The language of psychology in some quarters has implied a different state of affairs. The term *distal stimulus* has been used, which implies that something at a distance affects the organism. What we call the impingement was called the *proximal stimulus.* However, the organism, even through its impingements and associated reaction, *is* aware of events at a distance, by reason of what has been called *eccentric projection.* That is, it projects outward existence to what is imaged on the retina. It is only under special input conditions that acoustic inputs are localized within the head. The stimulus is never something that fails to reach the sense organ in a physical (energistic) sense. This is the marvel of perceiving: the organism can utilize an impingement to ascertain "what is out there," that is, can achieve a relation to a world that extends into great distances from it simply by using the impingements it receives.

THE SENSE ORGAN

What is a sense organ? We speak of sense organs on many occasions, but despite this, very seldom is a sense organ defined. However, having a definition of a sense organ will help to clarify the matters we shall be discussing. A sense organ is a tissue system sensitive to energies generally applied from the environment but also sensitive to those applied within the body. This tissue system consists of two parts: the tissue directly sensitive to the energies just mentioned—receptors—and the tissue that supports this specialized tissue. The supporting tissue has various functions, among which sometimes is the orienting of the sensitive tissue toward the impinging energy as in the case of the muscles of the eye.

According to this definition, the skin is part of the tactual sense organ. The receptors are located within the skin. For example, the skin plays a multiple role for it is the immediate supporting tissue for several types of receptors, each of which is the basis for a separate sense modality.

WORDS PERTAINING TO ORGANISM–ENVIRONMENT INTERACTIONS

Since many of the words used to depict the relation of humans to their surrounds have different connotations from those the reader already has, it is appropriate to consider them here.

First, three terms are used to label what lies outside the human individual. When using the word, *environment,* we shall mean the *energistic environment.* The human exists within and as a part of the energistic universe described by physics and chemistry. We shall avoid using the term environment when something *phenomenological* is meant. The *"social environment"* is the third meaning. Our use is a greater restriction in meaning than is common but has certain intended advantages.

Two other words that will appear in our discussions are: *context* and *surrounds.* The term context tends to be quite neutral and will be used to mean any broad context. It may include the environment or what is social. The term surrounds pertains to what lies outside of and around a focal experimental presentation such as in a visual experiment. In many cases it is the ground in a figure-ground arrangement—simply a term used in a specific experimental situation.

Not all data used in the scientific study of perception have arisen from planned and intellectually executed experiments. In the cases in which the data came from incidental situations, the organism–environment relationship can be called an *encounter.*

When the situation is a planned one, the material or event can be called a *presentation.* When this term is used the description does not intimately deal with the question of what is *energistic* and quantitative but rather with what is *phenomenological.*

In visual experimentation the description of what is being done is generally given in phenomenological terms. We often speak of circles and other geometrical forms. What reaches sense organs is some pattern of energy, so it is obvious that we are dealing with two domains—the visual (phenomenological) and the energistic. The uninformed person starts out by failing to recognize this two-domain involvement when language is used.

The most widely used class term for the presentation to the subject is *stimulus*. Even among technicians, stimulus has had a number of different connotations, and thus there has been much confusion. The form of psychology that we are studying here is, in the broad sense, what is called *stimulus-response* psychology. J. J. Gibson (1960) devoted his entire presidential address to the Eastern Psychological Association to showing the many connotations of the word stimulus.

Our concern with all the words we use technically relative to behavior shoud be organism centered rather than environment centered. This helps us in the present case to define the word stimulus. We would expect a stimulus to stimulate, but at the same time we know that a label is needed for the energy that reaches sense organs and does not stimulate. Nevertheless, this has been called a stimulus. So we have a contradiction that has not been consistently handled by all concerned. I would say that a stimulus is that which stimulates. The word is loaded. That is, a *result* is implied. We need a neutral word, and it is not hard to find. *Impingement* is a word labeling what touches on (reaches) sense organs without necessarily producing an end result in the category studied. In psychology that category is personal behavior. So an impingement is the word we shall use to specify the energy reaching a sense organ. If the end result we call a response occurs, then that particular impingement stimulates and can be called a stimulus. Thus *a stimulus is a species of impingement.*

Of course, when in broad generalizing certain energies that potentially may stimulate are discussed, we can call them *stimuli*. Here we are not pinned down to specific cases. But when describing specific cases, we give our language a great deal more precision by distinguishing between stimulus and impingement. Causes without effects, or effects without causes, are not to be conceived.

Psychology is so varied in its tasks that the preceding discussion need not apply to all of them. In a social situation, psychologists may not be *specifically describing physical energies* when dealing with intended cause and effect. Thus they are only talking about some condition described in social terms as the cause of the result in question. However, this takes the matter out of the context of strict experimental psychology.

A number of years ago I began using the word *target* for the presentation given the subject in a visual experiment. Here, again, a neutral term was chosen, which did not specifically make the presentation phenomenological or energistic. But it probably did not clarify matters in the intended way for the person unfamiliar with the subject.

In dealing with perception, we find that the term *information* has become prominent. The word information like others has several meanings and these lead to confusion if some explanation about them is not given. The word in common speech implies the communication or reception of knowledge. That is, the knowledge lies in the item communicated. But in the study of stimulation and response, which is the study we are pursuing here, we need two words—one for what impinges on sense organs and the other for the result. So it would seem that information is (in one sense) not what impinges on sense organs but what the organism makes out of it—the impingement. Thus information is the interpretation or use made, not the energy pattern supplied. However, the same data may result in being information of one sort to one person and of a different sort to another.

We should become acquainted with the second meaning of information, since it is in vogue in psychophysics, which will be discussed in the next chapter.

ATTENTION

Current texts in perception vary widely in the treatment of attention, ranging from the absence of the word, even in the index, to subordinating it within *information processing*, to dealing with it more in accord with the traditional manner.

The topic of attention must by discussed in order to achieve a better understanding of the conditions both external to the organism and within it making for and against response to impingements on sense organs.

Traditionally, attention referred to the matter of awareness. All psychology then pertained exclusively to consciousness, that is, to something mental. Accordingly, the problem of attention involved several aspects: (1) levels of clearness, (2) factors in arousing this clearness, and (3) kind of stimuli evoking awareness in the first place. In the days of traditional psychology the question of which factors were attributes of the stimulus and which pertained to the human subject were both discussed and studied, although stimulus factors seemed to be preferred. Early investigators were also interested in whether the subject would attend (response clearly) to more than one thing at a time.

Attention was divided into two forms—voluntary and involuntary. This was the same as saying that organismic factors would in some instances determine attention and, in others, some sort of stimulus prepotency determined what was experienced or, as we say, responded to. Viewing attention as an agency as well as an end result of the operation of that agency is not logical, even though we speak of both of them.

According to the definition of perception most appropriate today, all mechanisms involved in formulating the immediate interaction of the organism with the environs mediated via sense organs contribute to the overall perceptual response. This is where attention comes in—it is a word to be helpful in dealing with the selective features of perception. It is an attempt to deal with the conditions under which response will or will not occur. In turning our interest toward the qualitative features of immediate responses, we are turning away from attention to matters given other labels.

Just before the turn of this century, attention was a major topic in psychology. William James opened his discussion of attention by pointing out the narrowness of consciousness. He said that "the sum total of our impressions never enters into our experience, consciously so called, which runs through this sum total like a tiny rill through a broad flowery mead. Yet the physical impressions which do not count are there just as much as those which do, and affect our sense organs just as energistically." James pointed out that there is voluntary attention and involuntary attention and that "there is no such thing as voluntary attention sustained for more than a few seconds at a time."

Following James' day, experimental psychology came along, with such problems as: (1) determiners of attention, (2) shifting and fluctuations of attention, (3) distraction, (4) divided attention (doing two things at once), and (5) span of attention.

The study of attention was a basis for the study of eye movement. In such studies the attention-getting effect of size and position of an item on a page was determined. It was found that doubling size increases the attention value by only 40 to 60 percent, not 100 percent (Rudolph, 1947).

So-called ambiguous figures such as the outline cube, staircase, and other figures of reversible perspective were studied. The shifts in what the subject would see were considered shifts of attention (see Figure 2.1). Average rates of reversal were reported by Tussing (1941).

More recent studies of attention have been reported by Berlyne (1951, 1973). Using ten subjects who were first given some practice in perceiving the perspective reversals in a line cube and then re-

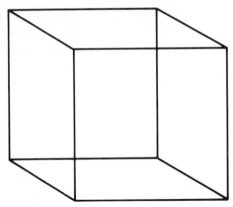

Figure 2.1   Reversible cube. The lower vertical face or the upper face can be seen as near, but not at the same time. This shift is typically called a shift of attention.

cording them by pressing a key, he found the rate to vary all the way from 3.7 to 47.5 per minute, with a median of 15 per minute. When the subjects tried to increase their rates, the median was doubled. When they attempted to slow down the rate, the median was reduced to one half. In general, the subjects increased their eye movements as registered by the eye movement camera when they attempted to increase the shifts in perspective and decreased them when they attempted to slow down the shifts. Those who saw more reversals were those who made more eye movements. But there was no one-to-one relation between eye movements and reversals, however.

Dealing with eye movements brings in the concept of "scanning." What is called scanning is not a matter of successive eye fixations. This is ruled out as a conclusion by the use of tachistoscopic presentation. Bryden (1961) and Crovitz and Daves (1962) recorded the direction of eye movements *after* the presentations. A definite trial-by-trial correlation occurred between the part of the target most accurately reported and the movements of the eyes after the presentation. The latency of these movements ranged from 150 to 200 milli-seconds. In the second study, 85 percent of the movements were in the right direction.

Whatever known as in neural terms, the process seems to be identification. This requires foveal vision when dealing with what we see. Forgus and Malamed (1976) talk about the organism's *decision* concerning the direction of subsequent eye movements, which depends on the material ("information") located on the retinal periphery. Neisser (1967) suggests that an object cannot be identified until it is first segregated from a background or context. This, he calls a preattentive process. When the "figure" once becomes segregated, focal attention can ensue, typically by a shift of the eyes.

Sanders (1963) supposes that there are three attentional fields, or ranges, differing by the visual angles they cover: (1) the *display* field—what is covered in central and peripheral vision during a single fixation; (2) the *eye* field—which in addition includes the area covered by saccadic movements; and (3) the *head* field—which covers the visual space provided by head movements. To investigate the head field Sanders tested his subjects both with the head free to move and with the head fixed.

From the foregoing paragraphs it should be apparent that as yet there is no standard use of many of the terms involved in describing the processes of perception.

MODES OF PERSONAL EXISTENCE

The organism is not in a uniform overall state as a function of time, but varies in ways that can be labeled. These differ in respect to what any given momentary environmental condition will cause the organism to do or fail to do. I shall call these periods, *modes.* Modes are mentioned simply because they are differences in the organism's manner of dealing with impingements on it. The first is the *appreciative* mode, which is the general state that characterizes the individual at a symphony or at an opera or at an art gallery. The various patterns of impingement are reacted to with a disposition of extracting pleasure and appreciation. The organism is in a state of searching for understanding and pleasure.

A second mode is called the *motoric* mode. This is exemplified by players in a game of football. The major responses to all that affects eyes and ears are motor. The players run, pause, pivot, avoid other players, and so forth. These motor responses are perceptual responses according to the definition of perception that we have adopted, because they are immediate forms of interaction with the environment.

The third mode is the *meditative.* The individual is preoccupied with thoughts, memories, and so forth. In this state, one does not respond to what reaches the sense organs in the same way as in other modes. It is as though one does not hear nor see what is going on around him or her. A salient difference among these modes is describable in terms of differences of attention.

Response bias, discussed in the next chapter, has some connection with attention inasmuch as attention describes something about the contribution of the organism in determining thresholds or responses to minimal energies.

Several *unusual* states of awareness will be considered in Chapter 17. While these states have never been described simply as different states of attention, they do express a different relation of individuals to their surrounds.

THE NATURE OF PERCEPTUAL ENCOUNTERS

Gibson (1966) states some observations about perception that are relevant and helpful here. The *encounters* of the organism with its surrounds are of two sorts—*obtained* or *imposed*. Thus some are *active* and some *passive*. Of the active sort, there are two kinds— *exploratory* and *performatory*. This complicates how the encounters are to be studied and what may be said about them or expected of them. Perception as identification, as appreciation, and as quantification are affected by these conditions.

BROAD NAMED APPROACHES IN STUDYING PERCEPTION

There are several present-day approaches to understanding and depicting perception. The matter is so complex that no single approach is able to deal satisfactorily with the activities within and without in relating the organism to its surrounds. Three prominent approaches are: (1) the information-processing approach, (2) the cognitive stage, and (3) the so-called integrated approach. Other writers depict perception in ways that they leave unnamed.

The *information-processing approach* has come mainly from the concepts involved in the development of today's computer. These have been applied to perception. A computer receives input, which in our analogy would be sensory input. The computer does things with this input (processes it). Comparing the way the human organism does things to some instrument with which we are familiar is not new. At one time, we compared human perception to the activity of a telephone switchboard. Even Freud's concept of motivation was comparable to our hydraulic model.

It is difficult to depict information processing briefly because it is complex rather than simple. The typical case is the flow of data from one stage to the next, shown in flow charts. The model is analogous enough to what seems to be going on in the human nervous system so that we can expect to see information processing utilized in a great deal of perception research.

The *cognitive stage approach* recognizes the category of cognition. Cognition pertains to all the processes by which input to the sense organs comes to be transformed, changed, elaborated, retained, retrieved, and used. Cognition is involved even when these processes occur in the absence of concurrent input to the sense organs. In such cases the experiences are called imaginings and in others, hallucinations. A number of terms are used to indicate hypothetical stages or aspects of cognition. Among these are sensation, perception, imagery, recall, thinking, and problem–solution.

Some psychologists use *motivation* as an origin for their discussion, others use *sensory input* as the original. That is, one group starts with a *personalistic concern*, the other with the organism's *relation* to the physical environment. The cognition psychologist begins with concern for the individual's goals, needs, or features of inherited nature. Thus he or she begins at the opposite end of the matter, commencing with processes that do not rest on specific stimulation but instead are a part of the organism's more nearly permanent resources. This allows the cognitive stage adherent to deal focally with matters that are not specifically connected with stimulus input at a specified moment.

The *integrated approach* is an approach in one of the current textbooks on perception. It does not present specific procedures that identify the approach in easily describable terms that distinguishes it from the more usual approaches. In this connection, we mention the outlook and procedures that have been named under the title of "Adaptation Level Theory" by Helson (1964). It is an attempt to recognize more fully and to evaluate the organism's participation and contribution to what we observe and measure as perceptual response. Helson calls it the *adaptive state*. He shows how to deal with the adaptative state in psychophysical experimentation, but the general idea of what he describes as adaptive state goes further. Although I consider Helson's contribution to the study of perception very valuable, it is impossible to describe briefly.

SENSORY CODING

Another significant concept is that of *sensory coding*. The word, coding, has been used in communication theory, in cryptographics, and in present-day studies of the representation of genetic traits by large molecules. Throughout there has been a somewhat constant meaning. It is the material that pertains to *representation*—pertaining to the question of how signals or symbols from one area of discourse represent kinds of information in another. Uttal (1973) points out that the major idea underlying coding theory is that there are invariants of organization, pattern or meaning, that can be conveyed from origins to destinations although represented by different symbols and in unlike kinds of energies as this is performed.

We cannot go into the ramifications of the theory and use of sensory coding here, but the idea itself must become a part of our thinking when dealing with the problem that we have in perception. The problem is age-old—how one set of processes or one set of appearances or one set of events relates to another that is seemingly essentially different. Perhaps the old mind–body problem is a good example, wherein some of today's understandings about coding would be helpful.

However, the concept of sensory coding is involved clearest when the transformation (transduction) from photic energy to neural energy is considered. The coding that occurs in the central nervous system is the specific locus where coding has not yet become explicitly understood. The locus is the basis for controlling the emergence of "mind" from patterns of body conditions. It is the area with regard to which the average person has minimal understandings and concerns and where mysticism has long been the substitute. For an extended treatment of sensory coding you are referred to Uttal.

CONCLUSIONS

The purpose of this chapter has been to state the operations and major concerns regarding the organism that are to be included in perception. No experiment or line of investigation is to be thought of as belonging to perception just by naming it that. The experiment or investigation is only part of perception if its focal purpose is to elucidate the immediate relation of the organism to the environment as mediated through sense mechanisms. Modern science has plunged into obtaining so much detail and concern for reliability and validity that the loci of experiments in psychology's overall framework is often overlooked.

Perception is not only a functional aspect of behavior, but is also a major area label. It so happens that many experiments and experimental problems are only obscurely connected with elucidating perception until their purpose and role is made explicit. Failing this, the resulting information only clutters the journals and textbooks. The failure to clarify the purpose of accumulating data is the factor that often makes many interest areas in psychology so unrelated.

To round out our understanding of perception, we should recognize the several kinds of information that are obtained. In general, one has to deal with several categories of action in order to relate humans to their environment. Terminology often cuts across categories if one is not careful. These categories are: (1) body structure and function facts; (2) facts about impinging energies known as stimuli; (3) facts about transduction, that is, those relating what goes on in sense organs to what impinges on them; (4) facts regarding immediate response of the organism as a total—some response is experiential (conscious) and some is motor; and (5) facts regarding the involvement and role of change made in the nervous system by past encounters of the organism with its surrounds.

With such complexity, we can expect experimentalists in psychology to get involved in extremely diverse kinds of activity in attempting to answer a great array of questions. From the onlooker's standpoint the relevance of much of this activity is not always obvious. Also, it is true that the enticements of specific questions that come to experimenter's minds often bypass the question of their importance in the overall advancement of the understanding of human behavior (psychology).

In examining the literature found in psychology journals, one will be impressed by the variety of endeavors that are carried on and may conclude that it is impossible to report much of this activity in a textbook. An extreme amount of culling is necessary.

In this chapter we have portrayed the outlook and subject matter of perception and have emphasized that the popular outlook does not appropriately encompass nor comprehend this area. It is very important that the needed shift in the reader's understanding of perception take place and become a basis for dealing with specific studies in the various aspects of perception to be discussed in the remainder of the text.

Note that not all branches of psychology have been applied to an explicit definition of perception and so the situation within psychology in this matter is not unitary and homogeneous.

Note

Here and at the end of some chapters dealing with the perceptual systems, there will appear a notation regarding concrete examples of the way the perceptual system in question functions. These will be found in *Perception in Everyday Life* (Bartley, 1972), a paperback devoted primarily to interesting actual examples of perception in action.

Chapter 3
Experimental Methods—
Psychophysics

Since perception is the name for the immediate interaction of the organism with its physical surrounds, the attempts to become acquainted with all classes of these interactions and the mechanism whereby they are made possible are fundamental. One approach is the study of sensitivities of the organism to the various energistic impingements on it. These have been derived in terms of thresholds.

Another group of the procedures was to scale the organism's responses in relation to suprathreshold magnitudes of impingement. For over a century various workers interested in this matter have developed a number of procedures for obtaining data. This group of procedures tests specific responses to limited aspects of the environment. In vision, at least, the presentations to the observer have been called *targets*. The experimenter controls these targets in intensity or in duration, or in other respects, and requires some form of response from the observers to indicate what they see. While the response being studied need not be the perception, it bears a usable relation to the perception. In practice, in psychophysical experiments the response is often called a judgment.

The justification for giving the response the label of judgment rests in the fact that the response may be a delayed, one in which case more than one perception has actually occurred. Eye movements and various things occur that are forerunners of the response being measured. Hence the response in a laboratory experiment is not an instantaneous cross section of action and thus better fits the definition of judgment. Even so, dealing with judgments is no admission that the experiment is not some device to get as close as possible to ascertaining features of perception.

THE THEORY OF SIGNAL DETECTION

The concept of sensory threshold has been with us for a while, but now several alternative connotations or understandings are apparently being urged to supplant it. If the value called the threshold is presumed to be determined exclusively by a receptor, receptor groups or a sense organ, or other pinpointed functions, then the move to discard the idea of sensory threshold is perfectly valid. If the sensory threshold is defined as the least energy that is required to evoke a measurable perceptual response, then we still can use the term. What the threshold is thought to be makes the difference.

The *theory of signal detection's* rejection of the idea of sensory threshold is based on the traditional idea just stated that the sense organ is being measured. We can, however, recognize the virtue of signal detection theory and practice without holding to the exclusive receptor-senseorgan basis for requiring a new concept. It is nothing new to recognize, at least in an implicit way, that there is more involved in determining perceptual response than merely the action of a sense organ.

Let us look at what is involved in signal detection theory (TSD). First, let us realize that psychophysical experiments are not all of one kind. There is a model of experimentation on which TSD is based and there are other models as well.

The model for TSD is based on situations such as the following. Let's say it is your job to listen for a certain signal and to make a response when you hear it. The signal is very weak and there is also some sound in the background. Therefore sometimes you will not hear the signal when it does occur and sometimes you will feel certain it occurred when it actually did not. In such a task you will try to form a notion of the likelihood of the signal really occurring. If the signal is to occur frequently, you will hear it more often than if you think it will occur only infrequently. In this situation you will attempt to differentiate between the kinds of things to be heard.

However, sometimes when no signal occurs, the sound you hear will be exactly as though no signal occurred. But at other times the background noise will sound exactly like the signal you are set to hear. There is no way of telling which is which. What has just been described is common for those who must detect weak signals when other sounds can also be heard.

There is still another factor in the situation we have just described, namely, how important it is not to miss any of the signals. Or in other cases, how important it is not to hear signals when they do not occur. This is true, for example, in submarine warfare.

We are indebted to Green and Swets (1966) for the introduction of the theory of signal detection into psychophysics. As stated, signal detection theory does not utilize the concept of threshold. It assumes that events constitute a continuum e. The experimentation, of course, is divided into trials, any of which can contain noise alone. That is, they do not all contain the stimulus in question. Likewise, any trial can contain both the stimulus and the noise. All that the subject knows is that a trial has occurred but does not know whether it contained only noise, or contained both signal and noise.

The theory of signal detection recognizes the features in the foregoing description and so introduces a term to cover what goes on in the subject—and calls it *response bias*. Response bias is one way of taking into account that the central nervous system makes a contribution, in addition to the sense organ sensitivity and activity already involved.

The situation in the TSD model is a forced choice one. This new procedure, like classical psychophysics, attempts to find out how weak an input can be and still evoke a response.

If only a single factor were operating, namely, the quantitative value of the impingement, then a single curve would represent the outcome, that is, the relation of response to the impingement value. The simplest outcome would be pictured by the curve in Figure 3.1(a). All inputs below a given magnitude would evoke no response. As intensity is raised, a magnitude would soon be reached that would evoke a response. And every time a presentation of that magnitude or greater is involved a response would be elicited. Figure 3.1(a) shows this. But this is not the actual situation. No result such as that in Figure 3.1(a) occurs. As impingement values shown in the abscissa are varied, the response that indicates experiencing the signal occurs in 0 to 100 percent of the trials. The value of the impingement that results in a "yes" response on 50 percent of the trials has traditionally been taken as the threshold value. It is sometimes called the *absolute* value (see Figure 3.1(b)).

No "noise" is included in this procedure, so that there are sup-

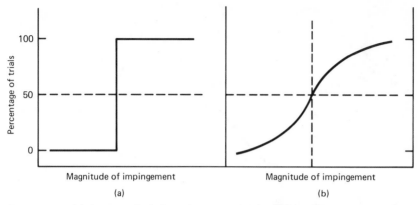

Figure 3.1   (a) An unrealistic but often supposed relation of response to stimulus (impingement) values. (b) Actual relation. The signal value responses 50 percent of the time are considered the absolute threshold.

posedly only two response relations to the presentation. Each trial contains a presentation that is either perceived or not perceived. So the curve in Figure 3.1(b) is simply a result of the probabilistic nature of response. This model has been used in the older psychophysical methods.

However, in signal detection theory two determinants—the *observer's sensitivity* and *response bias*—are assumed; the response bias being the factors within the observer other than simple sensitivity. The response bias is largely represented by what the observer decides will have to be experienced to call it a trial containing the signal. This would naturally be different for careful observers and for those not taking the task so seriously. Thus signal detection theory makes assumptions about response bias as well as about sensitivity.

To put the matter to test, the experimental procedure has to be different from those in the traditional psychophysical methods. The situation involves not only a signal, but a background continuum, called noise. A single value for the signal is chosen and the trials presented to the observer are of two kinds, one with noise only and the other containing noise plus the signal. When the results are plotted separately for the two trials, we have two hypothetical curves of normal distribution. These curves overlap as shown in Figure 3.2(a), (b), and (c). It will be noted that the extent of overlap is different in each. If the overlap were to be complete, both noise and noise plus signal trials would be shown by a single curve. This would mean that the observer could not tell the difference. If the curves do not overlap, then a very different interpretation is needed. It would mean that every trial with no signal would be responded

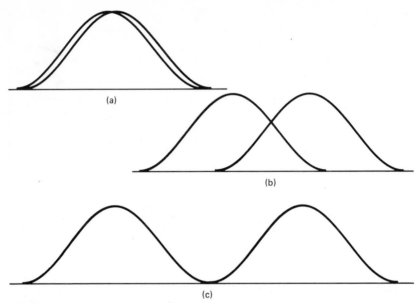

Figure 3.2   (a) Case in which noise and noise plus signal could not be distinguished. (b) Case in which some distinction is possible. (c) Case in which full distinction occurs, thus signal too strong for test purposes.

to by "no" and every trial containing a signal would be responded to by "yes." This would mean that the experimenter had chosen such an intense signal that there was no chance of it being undetected. The conditions satisfying the observer's criterion would always be met.

Now if we inspect Figure 3.3, in which the usual results are labeled, it is obvious that some of the "no" trials will be cases in which the rejections are correct, and some incorrect ("misses"). Also, we shall see that some of the "yes" trials will be correct ("hits") and some will be "false alarms."

In Figure 3.3 the abscissa is the *decision* or *observation* axis. The measure d is distance between the mean of the "noise" distribution and the "signal plus noise" distribution. According to theory, the observer decides what the criterion will be for responding with a "yes." When the sensory effect is above the criterion, the observer reports "yes" and when below, he or she says "no." Once the criterion is established, the probabilities of four possible outcomes mentioned earlier are determined.

The two curves overlap. Whereas the left-hand curve represents the frequency distribution of the "no" responses and the other represents the frequency distribution of the "yes" responses with respect

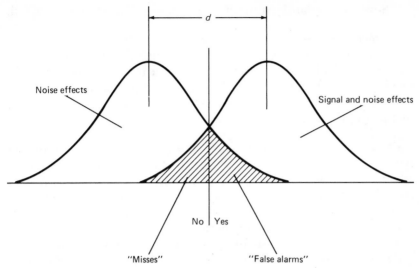

Figure 3.3   Usual results from using a series of randomized signal and signal-plus-noise trials.

to a fixed value of the signal, some of the "no" responses occur when the noise plus signal is presented while most of them occur when noise is presented. For the right-hand curve, two results also occur. Most of the "yes" responses occur when the signal is given, whereas some of them occur when only the noise is presented. The observer's criterion was placed where the two curves (in this case) overlap. It may occur elsewhere on the decision axis. The fact that the criterion does not bear a fixed relation to the two curves depends on the observer's response bias, for example, whether he or she is prone to detect or reject.

TRADITIONAL METHODS

Psychophysical methods have included a number of essential *procedures* which are indicated below.

    A. Naming
    B. Rating and ordering
    C. Composing
        1. Equating and matching
        2. Fractionating
        3. Multiplying
        4. Bisecting; trisecting
        5. Preferring
    D. Evaluating single stimuli—absolute threshold

Several standardized methods for proceeding were developed.

• *The method of average error.* Also called the *method of reproduction.* It consisted of a large number of trials in which the observer manipulated the variable. For instance, an observer may be presented with two lighted rectangles in a darkroom and required to match them in brightness. The value of one is fixed and the other is manipulated by turning the knob on a rheostat.

• *The method of limits.* Sometimes it is called the *method of minimal change.* In this method the experimenter rather than the observer adjusts the variable. It is also a procedure of comparison. In one trial the experimenter begins with the variable greatly different from the standard and slowly reduces this difference until no difference between the two is detectable by the observer. In the next trial the variable is too slight to be detectable and is made more and more different until the difference is detectable by the observer.

Figure 3.4 The relation between the percentage of correct responses and the difference between standard and comparison stimulus magnitudes. With two possible kinds of response, threshold is at 75 percent; with three kinds of response, three curves are involved and threshold is at 66.7 percent.

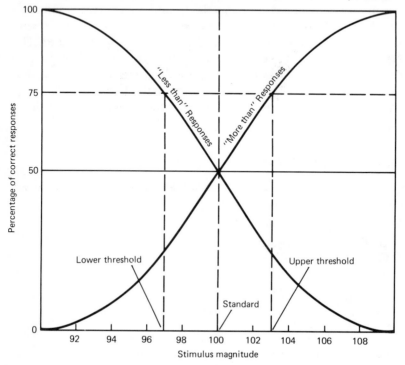

• *The method of constant stimuli.* In this procedure the experimenter chooses a fixed number of values for the variable (so-called "constant stimuli"). These range both above and below the value of the standard. The observer is only asked to indicate which of the two presentations possesses more of the property in question, for example, brightness, redness, smoothness, or some other one in question. In this method the observer does not know which of the two presentations is the standard or the variable. The results are plotted as in Figure 3.4, where the "less than" and the "greater than" the standard responses are indicated in the percentage of the correct trials. A variant of this procedure is provided by allowing the observer to make one or the other of three responses—less than, equal to, or greater than—rather than the usual two (see Figure 3.5.)

• *The method of paried comparison.* In this procedure the members of groups of things are judged pair by pair. Whereas in many of the psychophysical methods all items are compared to a single standard, in the present method every item is compared with every other one, one or more times. There is a random order in doing this.

FECHNER AND FECHNER'S LAW

Fechner lived from 1801 to 1887 but the starting point for experimental psychology is considered to be 1860 when Fechner's *Elementes der Psychophysik* appeared. The first experimental laboratory founded by Wilhelm Wundt was founded 19 years later. Fechner coined the term *psychophysics.* Weber, before him, had investigated the ability of subjects to perform discriminations and, as a result, concluded that discrimination is a relative rather than an absolute matter. In other words, the amount of increase or decrease in a stimulus needed to detect it as different is proportional to the magnitude of the stimulus. If the magnitude of a stimulus is, say, 60 units, and the addition of one unit is just appreciable, the addition of one unit would not be appreciable if the magnitude of the stimulus were 120 units. The addition of two units would be required for the change to be appreciable. Expressed as an equation:

$$\frac{\Delta I}{I} = k$$

Where *I* is the magnitude of the stimulus intensity (presentation magnitude) and ΔI is the differential threshold, or the increment added to the *I*, that produces a *just noticeable difference* (jnd), and

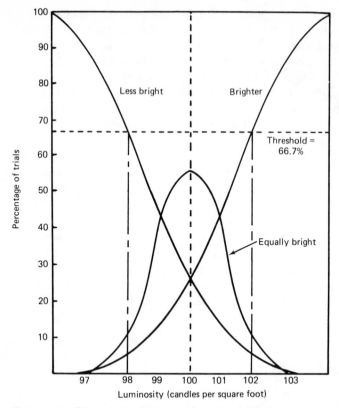

Figure 3.5 The relation between the value of the stimulus variable (in relation to the standard) and the percentage probability of making a correct judgment when one of three responses is allowed. The responses in this case are "less than," "equal to," or "greater than" the standard. (Source: S. H. Bartley. *Beginning Experimental Psychology.* New York: McGraw-Hill, 1950, Fig. 5. Copyright © 1950 by Howard S. Bartley. Reproduced with author's permission.)

k is the resulting proportionality. This proportionality *(k)* differs for the various sense modalities.

In 1860 Fechner proposed that the jnd described by Weber be used as a unit to measure the subjective magnitude (sensation). The jnd does not possess the overall validity supposed, since the constant ratio k does not hold at *all* levels for a given sense modality. k holds reasonably well in the middle ranges, but breaks down for intense and weak levels.

Fechner began with the assumption that for a given sense modality all jnd's represent psychologically equal units. That is, as far as *sensation* is concerned they are equal, though the energy taken to evoke them is not.

As the jnd's grow arithmetically, stimulus intensity increases geometrically. This is a logarithmic relation so that the equation is now $S = k \log I$.

This equation is an expression that has been known as Fechner's law. However, this law, like Weber's ratio or law, is only an approximation of the relation of experienced magnitude to physical magnitude.

STEVENS' POWER LAW

The doctrine of Fechner's law prevailed for a long time, but recently S. S. Stevens (1960) developed a relation—called *Stevens' power law*—that has superseded it. According to Stevens' power law, subjective magnitude grows in proportion to the magnitude of the presentation ("stimulus") raised to some power. This can be stated as follows:

$$S = kI^b$$

where k is a scale factor that takes into account the class of units used. Various sensory modalities function differently. That is, they

Figure 3.6   Stevens' power law, shown when impingement intensity and response magnitude are plotted in logarithmic terms.

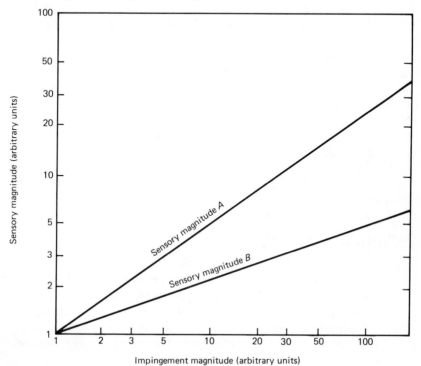

are represented by a different power (a different *b*). When the response (subjective) magnitude and impingement intensity are plotted against each other in logarithmic terms, the result is a straight line (see Figure 3.6).

Although numerous impingement–response relations have been shown to obey the power law, some do not. For example, at low levels of luminesce, the brightness function departs from luminosity plotted as just indicated. Reason for such deviations have been sought and attempts have been made to modify the power law to accommodate for this. However, these will not be described here.

The power law, of course, accommodated to cross-modality matching, as we shall see later.

SENSORY SCALING

While a number of psychophysical methods have been devised to deal with the subject's lower limit of sensibility (originally called the absolute threshold—or absolute limen—AL) or the smallest differences detectable between two presentations (DL), already spoken of as jnd's, these do not constitute the whole gamut of methods for measuring sensibility. There are times when the magnitudes of suprathreshold presentations become involved. The experimenter wants to know something about the sensitivity to members in a range of such magnitudes. This has led to procedures of *scaling.*

Fechner made an approach to this problem. He assumed that it is impossible to measure sensory experience directly. He built a scale of sensation indirectly by using Weber's law (the Weber fraction). For example, if one were to start with a presentation value of 100 units and finds that the smallest addition that would be detectable was 10 units, the next standard would be 110 units and the expected smallest detectable increment would be 11 units. Adding this to 110 units, we have 121 units. The increment would be 12.1 units, and so on. A difficulty at arriving at the scale in this manner, was the controversy as to whether the jnd was an appropriate unit of sensation.

MAGNITUDE ESTIMATION

In more recent years Stevens developed a direct procedure for scaling. In it the subject is given a series of presentations differing in actual physical magnitude. One of these presentations, a standard, is given an arbitrary value, say, 100. The other presentations are to be estimated in magnitude by the subject who is to assign the magnitude as a ratio of the standard. This ratio scaling method, known as *magnitude estimation,* is a direct procedure. Some experimenters proceed by not giving the subjects a standard number to apply to a given presentation, but by allowing them to build their ratio scales from scratch. The subjects may choose any range of numbers that suits them.

CROSS-MODALITY MATCHING

By this procedure, presentations (stimuli) from more than a single modality may be compared with each other. This is called *cross-modality matching.* For example, Stevens and Marks (1967) used the signal from a white noise generator in such an experiment in studying the relation of the perception of warmth to intensity of heat application.

In each trial the subjects, instead of assigning a number to represent the experimental intensity of warmth, adjusted the intensity of the white noise they heard. The white noise generator was calibrated so that the experimenter obtained a numerical value for the white noise level. The subjects were told to set the noise first too loud and then too soft and to "zero in" on the setting they felt represented the warmth intensity. Surprisingly, this kind of procedure gives reliable results. While to the uninitiated person it may seem that comparing modalities in this manner would not be possible, the subject can make such comparisons with consistent results. For example, the subject can find a temperature that is as hot as something is salty.

KINDS OF SCALES

Stevens (1936) has pointed out that his theory of measurement provides for numbers assigned to subjects, objects, and events, each forming scales. There are several kinds of scales such as nominal, ordinal, interval, and ratio. A number of assumptions he made with regard to the uses of these scales has been criticized recently by Prytulok (1975) in an extensive review. This review is too extensive to discuss meaningfully here, but knowing of its existence is worthwhile.

However, one should be familiar with the definitions of the various scales just mentioned. Nominal scales are those in which numerals are assigned only as labels. The numbers only *denote.* When we rank order a number of items, an ordinal scale emerges. In such a scale, ordinal numbers like first, second, third, and so on are used. Interval scales imply rank order and also equality of intervals between classes or ranks. When cardinal numbers are used, the scale possesses nearly every property allowing use of common statistical operations. The property of a true zero point is absent, however. The ratio scale is usable for counting, while the other scales already mentioned are not. Prytulok criticizes Stevens' implication that some scales are inferior to others.

FOURIER ANALYSIS AND SYNTHESIS

The study of the relations between the human organism and the physical environment does not always stop at dealing with the over-all magnitudes, as implied in the preceding sections, but delves into mechanisms that are at work within and result in the expressions of these relations. Certain concepts and devices originating in mathematics and physics and engineering are employed to do this.

One of these is *Fourier analysis.* Another is *information processing* which has recently come into use or at least has come up for consideration in psychology. We shall not discuss these in detail since we are not dealing with what is ordinarily called the mechanisms of sensation but rather with those closer to depicting perception itself. Nevertheless, we should call attention to them.

Fourier analysis is a procedure that provides the separating of a complicated function of time or space into simple functions (components). More specifically, Fourier's theorem says that it is possible to analyze any periodic function into a set of sine waves (see Figure 3.7). Most vibrations in Nature are complex. For example, a person uttering a simple vowel sound such as "ah" produces a complex acoustical pattern and when recorded on a receiving instrument, the pattern will look very complex. Although it does not look like a sine wave pattern or a complex of them, it can be analyzed into a number of sine waves.

The problem in this case is what the ear is able to do about such an impingement. The frequencies (sine waves) put into the receiving system (ear) will either be lost or faithfully reproduced. The process can be called one of *transfer.* This transfer function can be taken as a measure of the system's limitation in following (reproducing) input. This transfer function can be pictured as a frequency-response curve, in which the ratio of input to output is plotted against frequency.

Naturally, the reproduction in the receiving mechanism (sense organ) is not complete at all frequencies. This drop from completeness is called *attenuation.* Attenuation is thus the percent by which the input is reduced as it is represented in the receiving system.

Whereas Fourier analysis is a mathematical procedure, the determination of a transfer function is a concrete experimental task.

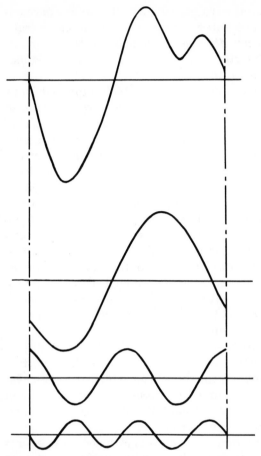

Figure 3.7   A complex wave at the top, analyzed into its sine wave components as the three lower waves.

The virtue of the transfer function is that, for a given receiving system, it permits one to predict the system's behavior for any chosen input (impingement). The use of the Fourier principle in this way is called *Fourier synthesis*. Fourier analysis and synthesis are applicable not only for understanding temporal activity in response mechanisms but for analyzing spatial patterns as well.

INFORMATION PROCESSING

Psychophysics is not confined to the procedures we have just considered. So far, we have been describing the way the organism reacts to a single presentation, or a comparison of two items per trial.

Psychophysics also includes the study of the way the organism reacts when trains of items are presented. These experiments have come to be called studies of *information processing*. Since this term has become so widely and eagerly used, rigidly specifying the bounds for its appropriate use is now difficult.

Information processing is any or all the techniques whereby response activity within the organism is followed through some or all the stages of its natural course. Sometimes this procedure is conducted at the neurophysiological level, and sometimes it is conducted by making manipulations in a complex stimulus pattern to see how the organism reacts to them, by noting the characteristics of perceptual response. Various mismatches eventuate between input and output and work toward gaining a picture of how the organism operates. It is at the perceptual level of response that experimentation can be called psychophysics. In such experiments the environmental input is related in a more direct way to perceptual response by a procedure that discloses some of the stages of internal action often described in terms more "psychological" than neurophysiological. Here is where perceptual and cognitive studies tend to intertwine or lose some of their indentity. This is not always describable from the experimenter's standpoint.

Analysis always involves some degree or kind of artificiality so that what we understand about what we are doing can have certain flaws. We have moved away from the era in which response was studied as if a single almost nontemporal process. We are beginning to follow effects from periphery to center and to overt response. In such cases we see them as number of stages.

We have come to studying certain stimuli as space–time events and see that these presentations produce a variety of input–output mismatches. In spite of the responses being mismatches, there is lawfulness to the mismatches, and peering into them enlightens us in ways no other procedures can do.

Intermittent Stimulation

A major forerunner of some of the present-day research labeled information processing is the work that used trains of stimuli. This was called *intermittent stimulation* and was carried on principally in vision. Thus the factor of time was being introduced.

Trains of repeated short visual stimuli ("flashes," but better called "photic pulses") were used and comparisons made between outcomes and the outcomes of presenting extended uniform illumination of the same intensity.

Talbot's law was formulated in such experiments. More popularly the experiments were known as "flicker" experiments. One of the essential underlying variables was the degree to which the visual system could match its response to the input. As rate of presentation of the members of the train was increased, mismatch increased to the point at which the perceptual result was a steady continuous experience, instead of a series of light flashes or a string of undulations of light. This point was called the *critical flicker frequency* (CFF). Numerous studies of the factors making for CFF have been conducted.

Talbot's law was to the effect that the brightness of the target at and above CFF was equal to the ratio of photic pulse length to the stimulus cycle (PCF—pulse to cycle fraction). This meant that if the pulse duration and the period between pulses were equal, then the brightness was half that seen when the pulse filled the whole cycle, that is, when the stimulus input was continuous. The ratio of photic pulse to cycle was not used but rather the ratio of the pulse to the interval between pulse, called the light-dark ratio (LDR) that was used. However, since this is labeling input in output terms, it is not advisable to use.

Attention to some information-processing studies at the neurophysiological level, however, provided the data and understanding for further progress in the flicker-type studies. Hence we shall give a brief description of one type before describing space–time investigations,—advanced forms of psychophysical information processing.

From 1931–1942 Bishop and Bartley devoted themselves to electrophysiological studies of the optic pathway. They excluded retinal complications and stimulated the optic nerve with trains of electric shocks (stimuli) varying in intensity and rate and observed the results in the cortex on a cathode ray tube display. The authors were considering the optic nerve as a bundle of parallel pathways (channels). By varying the shocks in intensity, they thereby varied the number of the pathways responding because the pathways differed in their threshold sensitivity.

From these studies, Bartley later evolved the *alternation of response theory*. This was a description of the relation between the input and the number of pathways responding. The theory stated that maximal shocks activated all the channels simultaneously. However, when such shocks were repeated at too high a rate, not all channels would respond to each shock, since such a rate exceeded the rate at which all channels would recover between shocks. Successive shocks activated only those that had recovered at that time. The first few members of the shock train produced a resorting of the channels active so that each shock activated the same number thereafter. This would account for the fact that the first maximal photic stimulus would produce a perceptual brightness greater than the uniform brightness produced by a train of maximal stimuli at and above CFF.

The studies of Bartley, Nelson, and Ball (see Chapter 8), based on the alternation of response theory, constituted a program of information-processing studies that brought out a number of novel outcomes.

Space–Time Studies

Space as well as *time* may be manipulated as a stimulus factor. As trains of photic items are presented, they may be presented at differing points in the visual field. So what is being presented and responded to is a space–time configuration. Such experiments constitute an advanced form of information processing.

Mayzner and his associates have conducted a number of information-processing studies at the psychophysical level which involve not only temporal but spatial manipulations, made possible by a computer-based cathode ray display system. (Mayzner and Tresselt, 1970.) With such a system, various luminous points on the face of the tube can be manipulated in desired sequences. In some cases one or more of the usual points, for example, in a square or grid, can also be omitted or displaced to see what the perceptual reaction will be. The number of different space–time configurations such an instrumental set up can provide is amazing.

Whereas manipulations of timing in trains of inputs produce input–output mismatches, space–time configurations used as inputs may produce many more input–output mismatches. Mayzner (1972) lists six kinds of mismatches; (1) failures of some inputs to be detected, (2) inability to detect the input stimulus order, (3) distortions in various features of stimulus input, (4) inaccuracies in the spatial features in stimulation, (5) inaccuracies in the relative brightness produced by the inputs, and (6) various experiences of apparent movement and the like.

Still another aspect has resulted from some studies in information processing. These seem to be manipulations that have led to investigators hypothecating stages in the utilization of stimulus inputs. Some of this is called the "cognitive stage" study of perception. In this endeavor, various "flow charts" indicating the interrelation and timing of processes within the brain, but spoken of in more or less experiential terms rather than specific neural terms, are constructed. This sort of endeavor is not to be classed as clearly psycho-physical.

Information processing has also come to be the label for endeavors that were studied earlier simply under other and more specific labels such as masking, for example.

Chapter 4
The Basic Orientation
Perception System

The most pervasive and forceful environmental factor with which the human organism has to reckon is the gravitational field of the earth. Objects are held onto the surface of the earth by this force field unless certain energies are spent to lift them. Likewise, the force field pertains to motions along the earth's surface, which occur only by the expenditure of energy—in an organism this is spent primarily by muscles.

The human organism faces a number of problems in connection with this force field, such as the maintenance of upright posture, execution of body motion, and coping with gravity when the body is transported from place to place. All this includes the ability to identify the upright position of rods and poles, and other objects, perceptually and to judge what is level. The organism must be able to distinguish between motion and static position and between various rates and kinds of acceleration in body motion.

The human has a special kind of sense organ that has a primary function in enabling the organism to cope with these problems. Although this organ, the vestibular mechanism, is sensitive enough in detecting motion and changes (acceleration) and directions, it does not function alone in providing the fine abilities the human has in coping with the dictates of the gravitational field. Two other sense modalities that come notably into play are vision and the kinesthetic sense. Performing most adequately in the gravitational system involves these three modalities.

THE VESTIBULAR MECHANISM

The vestibular mechanism is quite different from other organs in that its operation is not ordinarily accompanied by any form of awareness. Certain unpleasant forms of awareness emerge only when coping with gravity is not going well.

The bony labyrinth of which the cochlea, the auditory mechanism, is a part has two kinds of structure, each containing the sense cells for the vestibular modality. The semicircular canals, the more familiar structures, are three canals lying at right angles to each other. These form a sort of three-dimensional coordinate system so that acceleration in any of the three dimensions will affect one of the canals. Within the canals is a fluid called *endolymph* that circulates in accordance with the direction and amount of acceleration. At the base of each canal is an enlargement called the *ampulla,* which contains the endings of the nonauditory part of the VIII cranial nerve—the vestibular nerve. Hairlike fibers of the nerve extend into a gelatinous mass, which is disturbed by accelerations and sets up impulses that are conducted up the nerve to the brain. Aside from the normal stimuli incident to acceleration, the *ampulla* with its hair cells is affected by thermal impingements. If hot or cold water is put into the ear, the result will be a series of nystagmoid movements of the eye, and the perceptual end result will be dizziness. The water put into the ears possibly becomes effective by setting up convection currents in the endolymph. Two other forms of impingement also induce vestibular responses: direct pressure and electricity (see Figure 4.1).

Another portion of the vestibular structure is the *utricle,* which also contains sensitive hair cells and constitutes what is sometimes called the *otolith organ,* sensitive to static posture. Some believe this organ is slower in action than the semicircular canals. It is very difficult to isolate the actual functions of the canals and the otolith organ, for the various operations intended to produce stimulation may not only stimulate both of these organs but may also include muscular stresses and tensions in the rest of the body that contribute to the overall sensory effect.

For example, if we wish to study the effect of posture, how

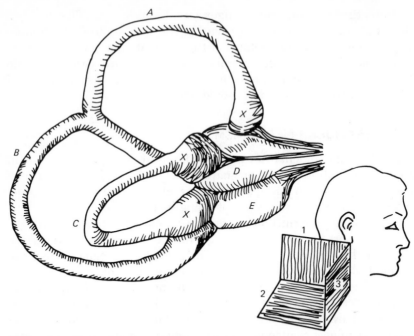

Figure 4.1 The vestibular apparatus. *A, B,* and *C* are the semicircular canals for the right ear. They lie approximately in the three planes of space. *A* is in the vertical (superior) plane, *B* in the horizontal (posterior) plane and *C* is in the lateral plane. These are exemplified by the planes 1, 2, and 3 in the schema. *D* is the utricle, and *E* is the saccule. *X, X,* and *X* ampulla.

should it be done? If we tilt the subject on a tilting board to which the subject is strapped, the whole set of mechanical pressures and pulls on body tissues is altered by each manipulation intended to affect the vestibular organs, thus complicating the matter considerably. One of the best ways would be to put the subject in a tank of water, for when a subject is immersed in water the pressures on the body are equal in all directions. But this is not so easy in practice. We would have to fill the tank completely and put a lid on it so that tilting would not churn the water. If the tank was not full, the water would be disturbed by the movements of the tank and the subject would be moved within the water. This, of course, would disturb the equality of pressure in various directions and would violate the conditions for which the water support for the body was sought originally. This description begins to show how difficult it is to study vestibular function in the most precise way.

The perception of motion of the body is mediated by vision, kinesthesis, and the vestibular sense. The retina is totally insensitive to forces such as acceleration acting on or with the body, but the semicircular canals and otolith organ are very sensitive to forces such as gravity and acceleration that act on the body. These same mechanisms are, on the other hand, insensitive to conditions not involving force. *But only when displacement and force are linked in certain ways do they operate to produce the experience of motion.*

Very peculiar end results sometimes occur, depending on how the two forms of stimulation are coupled. Take, for example, the case in which a person drives into an angled parking place and just after the car has come to a stop another car pulls into the space alongside. A possible result for the first driver, if the visual field is restricted to glancing at the second car, is to feel as though he or she is in motion. A mere instant before, that person supposed that he or she had come to a dead stop. But at the instant of viewing the second car in motion there is relative visual displacement between his or her car and the car alongside. This relative displacement gives rise to perceived motion but not in an ordinary way. The experienced motion occurs without any application of force on the vestibule that is characteristic of all acceleration. The acceleration-force factor is lacking, and its absence distorts the usual sensory input to the central nervous system. The usual innervations contain vestibular and kinesthetic components. Perhaps because these are absent, the experience of visual motion of oneself is very peculiar in such a case. In fact, the experience contains a definite aspect of uneasiness. One might call the experience a twinge of sickness. The main twinge is over within a second or two, but the aftereffects may last for some time. It may be said, then, that not all motion sickness is brought about by contributions form the vestibule but that some may result when usual contributions that should occur are absent.

A bit of the same momentary uneasiness may occur when sitting in a stopped train and seeing a train on the next track begin to move. One appears to see his or her train moving instead. Here again there is some uncertainty. The experience carries at least a kind of ambiguity. Once more, the usual sensory component is lacking—the kinesthetic stimulation that vibration of active motion would set up. Since one's train is motionless, there is no basis whatsoever for the usual muscular factor underlying the motion one sees. Without the usual jolting, vibrations, and so on, the movement is fantastically smooth and a bit "unreal." One quickly looks around in various directions to ascertain which train is moving. The answer to the question of how one came to see visual movement in the first place lies in the structure of the visual field. The railroad car viewed through the window is seen as a portion of overall stable externality, whereas one's car is considered a restricted portion of the environment more or less identified kinesthetically with oneself.

NYSTAGMUS

The vestibular mechanism plays a role in the control of eye movements, along with the control mechanisms of vision, the neck muscle receptors, and the cerebral cortex.

One method of isolating vestibular effects is to move the subject in a rotating chair with the head fixed so as to avoid tonic neck reflexes. Vision is also excluded so that visual reinforcement or inhibition are excluded. In a small arc of passive head-body-chair rotation, the eyes manifest slow compensatory drifts interrupted by fast return movements. This is one form of nystagmus. The total compensatory movement is short of complete return so that the net effect is a rotation of about 60 percent of the head-body-chair rotation. The eye drift extends in time a little beyond the head-body-chair rotation, but its deceleration is more abrupt. If one eye is open during rotation, the total slow phase is increased from 60 to 80 percent. If visual fixation is made on an object that rotates with the chair, the drift is reduced to about 5 percent.

If the subject is rotated at 180 degrees per second, the shift from the stationary condition to steady rotation induces nystagmus. This consists first of a *primary nystagmus* and then of a *secondary nystagmus* in the opposite direction. The slow phase of the primary nystagmus lasts longer than the duration of the head-body-chair acceleration, usually for about 35 seconds, during which time it slowly decreases. (This is called *post rotational nystagmus.*) After this (the normally described nystagmus), the inverse or secondary nystagmus sets in and increases for about 80 seconds until the amplitude of the slow phase reaches approximately 5 degrees per second. This nystagmus may not totally disappear for as long as 10 minutes. (For more details regarding nystagmus, see Dodge, 1923; Fischer, 1928; and Wendt, 1951.)

INVESTIGATION WITH THE HUMAN CENTRIFUGE

A number of studies have been made on human subjects by using a merry-go-round or centrifuge. Several large experimental centrifuges exist in this country for this purpose; they are very heavy and run with extreme smoothness. The accelerations and decelerations are smooth enough so as not to be detectable through the muscle and pressure senses as are roughness or jarring.

A large part of the study of the vestibular sense consists in

obtaining thresholds. Thresholds for angular acceleration, for example, have been worked on quite carefully and have been obtained
with the body in various positions—prone, upright, head down, and
so on. Finding out just how sensitive vestibular and related mechanisms are provides a beginning understanding of perceptual response to gravity. Another important kind of study is ascertainment
of limits of tolerance for extreme accelerations. Part of the effects
produced in such cases, of course, go far beyond effects on the vestibular mechanism to sheer mechanical effects on tissues and blood
circulation.

Several centrifugal studies on vestibular function will serve to
illustrate the sort of work that has been done in more recent years.
One is Graybiel, Kerr, and Bartley's (1948) study on the thresholds
for angular acceleration. Some kind of criterion had to be used.
The "common-sense" criterion for a subject's sensitivity to speeding
up or slowing down while riding on a centrifuge at or near its center
would be the minimal feeling of being revolved very slowly. Various
earlier investigators had used this direct experiential criterion. Graybiel and his colleagues instead used what has been called the "oculogyral illusion."

To explain this "illusion," let us say a subject is revolved while
in an upright position (a sitting position, for example) with the axis
of revolution through the center of the body and head. If this is
done in the dark so that there are no visual landmarks, then the
following effect can be produced. If the platform on which the subject is revolved carries a tiny light source that the subject fixates,
the light will not only revolve with the subject but will be perceived
to lie straight ahead no matter at what speed the subject is revolved.
But let the rate of body movement be suddenly changed and the
light will appear to move to the right or to the left, depending on
whether the change has been one of speeding up the revolution
or of slowing it down. This visual effect is known as the oculogyral
illusion. We prefer to call it simply the oculogyral effect.

The problem of Graybiel and his colleagues was to determine
how much the slowing down or speeding up of the rate of movement
of the centrifuge had to be before the illuminated target appeared
to move to the right or to the left. The authors not only controlled
the rates of accelerations, positive and negative, but interposed uniform motion for necessary lengths of time between test periods
for the canals to regain equilibrium. They controlled the lengths
of test periods in order that they would be long enough to produce
effects at minimal accelerations. The investigation disclosed that
angular accelerations of 0.12 degrees per second per second were
necessary to reach human threshold detection.

There is a phenomenon in connection with riding on centrifuges that is both significant and interesting. You will recall that when you rode on a merry-go-round you leaned "inward," toward its center of rotation, once the merry-go-round went into motion. You gained the sensory impression that if you did not, you would lose your balance and fall outward. Of course, the act of leaning inward was not a consciously calculated one; it was automatic or "reflexive."

If you were strapped into a chair fastened to the merry-go-round and were facing the center of rotation, you would feel as though you were being tilted backward when the merry-go-round went into motion.

If the merry-go-round is in the dark and all you can see is a light, the source of which is fastened at eye level to the axis of rotation, the light will appear to rise as the merry-go-round accelerates. To get a better understanding of this, consult Figure 4.2. The forces acting on the subject are indicated by *CF* and *G*, and the visual target is indicated by 1 and 2. Note that *R* is on a tilt from

Figure 4.2 Human centrifuge (merry-go-round), in which the posture of the subject is held upright while he or she is given a visual target to fixate in darkness. Rotation produces centrifugal force, *CF,* active in a horizontal direction. This and gravity, *G,* form a resultant, *R.* The visual target is perceived to be in position 2 during rotation. Also, axis of body seems to be tilted from position 1 to position 2.

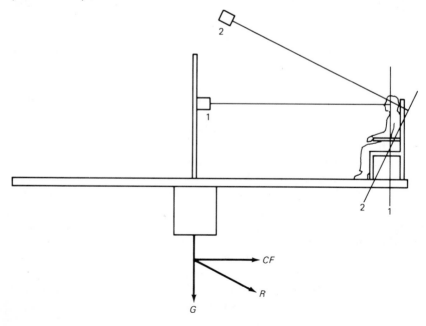

the perpendicular. This new direction of force is the perceptual "straight down" direction. Hence if this is straight down, then the subject must be tilted back of "straight down." Consistent with the experience of being in a tilted back position, the subject sees the light as above the old horizontal direction perceived at the beginning.

EXPERIMENTS WITH A WAVE MACHINE (VERTICAL MOTION)

Various sorts of motion, such as pitching, rolling, and yawing (sidewise movement) of vehicles, may be imparted to the body. Among all the possible motions, the up-and-down or vertical motion is one of the most effective forms on the organism. Aside from revolving chairs and centrifuges and swings, up-and-down moving platforms resembling elevators have been used for experimental purposes.

An arrangement used for imparting various rates and amplitudes of vertical motion to experimental subjects was employed by Alexander and his colleagues (1945). The device resembled a common passenger elevator and could be raised and lowered automatically by merely setting certain prearranged controls. It was called a *wave machine* because the motion looked like an up-and-down wave motion. The investigation consisted in varying the amplitude of the vertical excursions from 4 to 10 feet (perhaps even more in certain experiments) and in varying the rate of motion from 200 to 400 feet per minute. Variations were also made in the rate for reaching maximum motion—that is the pattern of the wave was varied. Figure 4.3 gives some indication of what certain of the wave characteristics were.

Healthy young subjects were used, and the criterion for the effectiveness of the wave motion was whether or not sickness was produced within a limited time by riding in the wave machine. No subject was used for more than one trial, and so numerous subjects were required. The relation of motion sickness to time of day and to prior history of motion sickness of various kinds in the subjects were also studied. Finally, the question of whether manifesting motion sickness in the wave machine bore any relation to performance deficits in subsequent military tasks was also examined.

The subjects were blindfolded during the ride and clothing was reduced to confine sweating to that induced by motion. Some of the subjects became sick during the tests and others did not. The degrees of sickness produced were distinguished by three categories, 1, 2, and 0. Those who vomited within the limited time allowed on the machine were in category 2. Those reporting definite nausea

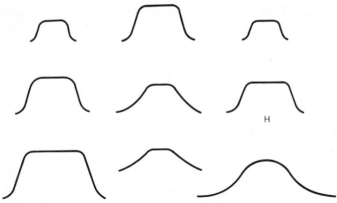

Figure 4.3   Various patterns of vertical motion used by Alexander *et al.* to study motion sickness in a wave machine. (Source: S. H. Bartley. *Beginning Experimental Psychology.* New York: McGraw-Hill, 1950, Fig. 68. Copyright © 1950 by Howard S. Bartley. Reproduced with author's permission.)

or manifesting profuse sweating were in category 1. All other subjects were in category 0. Subjects assigned to 0 were not necessarily entirely unaffected. Some reported dizziness, headache, or slight nausea. Even pallor and a slight amount of sweating showed up in some cases.

The wave patterns used were not equally effective in producing sickness despite the fact that they all possessed the same energy content and that, at the midpoint of the excursions, the velocity was the same, namely, 400 feet per minute. Figure 4.3 shows that wave *H* was most effective, although it did not involve the most abrupt transitions from one rate to another throughout the excursion.

MOTION SICKNESS

Motion sickness is made up of one or more of the components, headache, cold "sweating," feelings of muscular weakness, and experiences of malaise referable to various general parts of the body and head. The discomfort produced does not tend to cease with the termination of body motion and in some cases may last several days. It is reported that deaf persons who show no other signs of vestibular sensitivity do not become motion sick. Apparently, some separation of acceleration and deceleration of movement is highly effective in producing sickness. Short rapid phases of movement do not seem to be so effective. Such movements more nearly simulate ordinary head movements. Rotation in several planes at once or in sequence is most effective. Vertical motions, such as those studied on the wave machine and which occur in rough airplane travel or in ships or in the rear seats of automobiles, are among the most usual causes of motion sickness. Lateral motion is believed to be quite ineffectual in producing sickness.

Obviously, the general attitude of the subject is a large factor. Unfavorable past experiences or convincing descriptions of the effectiveness of certain motions tend to induce genuine uneasiness in subjects, which can very easily be enhanced by the imaginative processes that accompany stimulation in present situations. One of the outstanding observations has to do with the slightness of the physical motions that may induce sickness in the passively moved subject, in contrast to the many varied and energetic motions that do not result in this way when the subject is in active motion. It would seem that no movement carried out by the subject is taken to be threatening at all, whereas movements induced by vehicles do carry a potential threat to the subject. Habituation to motion may occur in many cases: the rough motion of high-speed passenger trains becomes an insignificant feature in the everyday experiences of train personnel.

Once the reader grasps the details of the situations that produce motion sickness, he or she should understand that externally induced motion imparted to the human individual is a potential hazard with which the organism through its evolution has had to develop means to cope. Motion had to be detected and adequate and appropriate kinds of adjustment had to be possible in response to such motion. Of all the forms of external impingement that the organism encounters, none is more compelling than motion due to loss of support from beneath or massive violent tossing. Such forms of mechanical disturbance might mean violent death, and the organism does not accept such forms of impingement with comfort and passivity. Even lesser forms have their untoward experiential effects and seem to call for avoidance. Passive submission comes only after a learning period, which may have, as one of its aspects, familiarization wherein the given motions are discovered not to be harmful after all.

Recently, Pitblado and Mirabile (1977) divided 24 male subjects into three groups according to their susceptibility to motion sickness. Their task was to adjust a luminous line to an apparently vertical position. The subjects were first given a standard test of susceptibility by being rotated at each of several speeds in a rotating chair, while their heads were in each of several directions of tilt and their eyes kept closed. The subjects were to report the occurrence of any symptoms and were to order the session to terminate if they became too uncomfortable to continue.

In the test situation a luminous rod 30 inches long and 1 inch wide in an otherwise totally darkened room was to be placed in a true vertical position. The subjects viewed the rod from a reclining position on a laterally tilted table at an angle of 70 degrees from the upright. The subjects lay on their sides the full length of the table. They were classified into high, intermediate, and low susceptibility to motion sickness from the tests. A significant relationship was found between susceptibility to motion sickness and the errors in judging the vertical. The study suggested that the use of perceptual responses may have potential value in the study of motion sickness and allied conditions.

VISUAL VERSUS POSTURAL FACTORS IN PERCEIVING VERTICALITY

It has long been supposed that when a subject is asked to adjust a visual target to the perceived vertical, kinesthesis and the vestibular sense play a dominant role. If centrifugal force is combined with gravity, the subject would then use the somesthetic factors as determined by the resultant of the two forces mentioned earlier. Mach (1914) made this conclusion many years ago.

Koffka (1930) believed that when the visual and the somesthetic frames of reference are brought into conflict, subjects use the visual in their perceptions. Wing and Passey (1950) believe that Witkin and Asch's (1948a and b) findings point toward a compromise between the two frames in the behavior of their subjects. Passey and Guedry's (1949) subjects tended to set the perceived visual vertical in line with the true, or gravitational, vertical in all cases.

Mann and his colleagues (1949) have shown that when a subject is tilted away from the perpendicular and is not allowed to use vision, the subject will not readjust to the true vertical if held in the tilted position for a number of seconds. The error in readjustment depends on both the time in the tilted position and the angular value of the tilt. The amount of tilt that is most effective seems to be in the neighborhood of 35 degrees and, up to this point, error increases with degree of tilt. Error increases with time in tilt, up to about one minute.

Mann and Dauterive (1949) found that the uncertainty of a subject in perceiving the true vertical in posture is greatest when he or she is tilted only a few degrees. This range on both sides of the vertical was called the "arc of uncertainty." The reduction of proprioceptive cues tends to increase the arc of uncertainty.

Many years ago Aubert (1886) found that when a subject viewed an upright visual target with head tilted, the target seemed to be rotated away from the perpendicular in the direction opposite to head tilt. Subsequent refinements in observation have shown that when the head is tilted only slightly, the apparent tilt of the visual target is in the same direction as the head tilt, but when the head tilt is great, the effect noted by Aubert occurs.

Mann and Berry (1949) found that the mean error and variability in perceiving the visual horizontal are greater when the subject is in a tilted position than when vertical.

Witkin and his colleagues (1954) performed a number of experiments in which visual and postural factors were pitted against each other. One of the chief devices for making such studies was a tilting-room-tilting-chair combination. A small room, about 7 feet in each dimension, was fixed so as to be rotatable around a horizontal axis (Figure 4.4). The axis was through the center of the room and the subject's chair was pivoted on the same axis. This provided for lateral tilts of the subject to the left or the right when sitting facing the

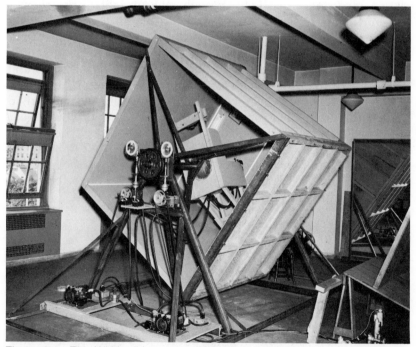

Figure 4.4   The Witkin tilting-room tilting-chair apparatus. In this photograph the chair is tilting to the left of vertical and the room is tilting to the right of vertical. Little of the far wall of the room is visible. This and the floor, sidewalls, and ceiling constitute the subject's total visual field. (Source: From Psychology Laboratory, State University of New York, by permission of Herman A. Witkin.

wall of the room, which could include tilts of both room and subject in the same direction, in either equal or unequal amounts. Both male and female subjects were used and found to behave differently.

The results that are relevant here pertain to the relative weights of the visual and postural factors. One might suppose that even in the dark, where there is nothing involved but postural stimuli (those involving kinesthesis, vestibular activity, touch, and pressure), the subject would be certain of being tipped when actually placed a number of degrees from the vertical, but this is not always the case. When a subject is confined in a chair whose arm and shoulder supports are adjusted snugly against him or her and the subject is tilted, the tactual and pressure experiences may simply mean pressure is applied laterally (horizontally) rather than perceived as indications of pressure due to tilt. Actually, such pressure resembles that induced by being squeezed against other persons in a crowd and, in line with this, these experiences evoke social connotations. In fact, they may have curious, affective flavors.

The room in the Witkin experiments provides, of course, an all-encompassing visual field. Visually, the upright of the room is the convincing upright of the earth. If a plumb line is suspended from the ceiling of the room, it naturally conflicts with the expected positions that a plumb line should assume when the room is tilted. The plumb line appears different. In other words, whereas a plumb bob ordinarily looks as though it hangs by its own weight, the plumb bob does not look that way when the room is tilted. It looks rigid, in deviating from what is perceived to be the vertical. This appearance is, of course, an immediately and directly perceived one. Incidentally, this example is one of the many kinds that indicate the close parallelism between perception and what would be expected to occur through "reasoning." Both processes seem to follow the same logic, the same self-consistency.

RIGHTING REFLEXES

In connection with the activity of the vestibular mechanism, considerable reflex activity is evoked. This is made most apparent in animal experiments in which *righting reflexes* have been studied. Four sorts of righting reflexes are distinguishable.

A decerebrate mammal such as the rabbit, when held head downward will, even when blindfolded, put its head in the same position as when its body is horizontal (normal position), exhibiting the *labyrinthine-righting* reflex. Changing the body in various positions still produces reflex movements whereby the head is put into the normal position. Such reflexes do not occur if the labyrinth is removed. One can faintly demonstrate these righting reflexes in the neonate.

They develop in the very young human infant and are part of the child's ability to position head with reference to gravity.

Neck-righting reflexes, a second group, have to do with orienting the body with reference to the head. The body and the head can obviously assume a number of different positional relations to each other, and it is equally clear that the body must assume certain positions in the gravitational field to be effective. Hence only certain combinations of head and body position will be effective, and reflex mechanisms sort out the effective combinations from the ineffective. These reflexes change body position so as to orient the body properly with the head in certain positions with reference to gravity.

A third class is called the *body-righting reflexes.* If an animal with labyrinths removed is lowered to a surface while in a lateral position (on its side), the animal brings its head into a normal position with reference to the surface. The asymmetrical activation of tactile receptors on the two sides of the animal supposedly elicits body-righting reflexes. If an animal lying on its side is given symmetrical pressure stimulation on its two sides by pressing a board against the upper side, its head will have the "normal" position and will assume the lateral position in line with the body.

There are also *optic-righting reflexes.* In the higher subhuman species the orientation of the head can be shown to be greatly controlled by vision. In such labyrinthinectomized animals freely suspended in air the head is disoriented (may hang down) while the eyes are closed or blindfolded, but as soon as the animal is allowed to see, it fixates on items in the visual field and positions its head in relation to the field.

These righting reflexes are utilized by animals (a cat, for instance) in quickly righting themselves with reference to gravity either in a fall or in cases where they are forcefully put into an ineffective position with gravity and the floor or other surface.

Whereas the reactions just described are called reflexes, they are forms of perceptual response since they fit the definition of perception that we have been using. These reflexes are similar to reactions ordinarily called perception except that they are somewhat "automatic." This automaticity does not remove them from the perception category, nor does it mean that the term reflex is to be discarded.

For some excellent examples of basic orientation perception see Bartley's *Perception in Everyday Life.*

RETROSPECT

In the foregoing you have been given a discussion and a sampling of basic orientation perception.Thus it has been demonstrated that several sense modalities work together in a way that accomplishes a single end, namely, the organism's effectual relation to the gravitational field. The orientation perceptual system is peculiar inasmuch as the accomplishments do not evoke awareness ("sensation") unless the demands of the situation become excessive or some deficit exists in the body mechanisms themselves, as in disease. Even some activity in this form of perception is reflexive, but to admit it is reflexive is not to exclude it as part of the nature of some perception.

Chapter 5
The Haptic Perceptual System

As indicated in Chapter 1, the organism is equipped with a perceptual system that has to do with mechanical contacts and exertions and the appreciations associated with them. This is the haptic perception system. Early understandings of the human organism did not recognize system behavior and so dealt with *touch* as a single label for mechanical contact and overlooked some of the features now recognized.

Even mere touch involves more than cutaneous contact. People can touch or can be touched therefore it is evident that touch can be active or passive. Touching involves the appreciation of a complex of qualities, such as smoothness; roughness; hardness; softness; warmth or cold; wetness; dryness; and, at times, pain.

When one intentionally touches (contacts) an object, one employs muscle action that engages the kinesthetic sense with its receptors. Many times touching involves grasping—at other times, pushing, pulling, lifting, caressing, snuggling. It is easy to see why this system is called *haptic* for the word comes from a Greek word meaning "to lay hold of."

In this chapter we shall deal with all of the sense modalities that interplay to constitute the haptic system.

THE STRUCTURE OF THE SKIN

The skin has arbitrarily been divided into three layers: the *epidermis*, the *dermis* or corium, and the *subcutaneous tissue*. Each is far more complicated structurally than the average person would suppose and an extended description would only emphasize their complexity.

The specialized sensitive structures in the skin may be divided into (1) *free nerve endings*, branching nerve fibers that end on epithelial cells; (2) *hair follicles*, whose bases are supplied with nerve endings; and (3) *encapsulated end organs* of various types, in which the nerve fiber ends within a shell-like structure, of which there are several types. Encapsulated end organs differ greatly in size and structure and consequently have been classified and named. Best known are the Meissner corpuscle, Pacinian corpuscle, Ruffini cylinder, Krause end bulb, and Golgi tendon organ and Merkel's cell. Some doubt exists as to how clear-cut the distinctions implied in the naming of some of the structures can be.

In the early decades of the study of skin sensitivity there was an attempt to relate forms of sensitivity to specific structures. It appeared that tactile sensitivity was mediated by Meissner corpuscles, since at first these structures seemed to be frequently seen in body regions where tactile sensitivity was the greatest. On the same basis, Krause end bulbs were identified with sensitivity to low temperatures and Ruffini cylinders were identified with high temperature sensitivity. Free nerve endings were most frequently identified with pain experiences.

These earlier identifications were made on a gross basis. Later studies involved more precise attempts to connect structure and function. Studies using carefully controlled sensory data and slices of skin (biopsies) for examination of the structures actually present in the localized skin region stimulated have led to the conclusion that no fixed relation between particular types of encapsulated end organs and sensory experience can as yet be stated. There is often no encapsulated end organ found in the biopsy of a sensitive spot determined by stimulation.

What is known as the Oxford group interpreted the findings as follows. Different cutaneous experiences (perceptions) are produced not as a result of selective activation of special receptors, but as a result of different impingements affecting given neural elements in a different way. Thus the internal neural elements in the pathway from skin to central nervous system produce different discharge patterns, rather than there being a selective effect among them whereby some discharge and others do not to provide the various sensations of cold, warmth, pain, and touch pressure.

The basis for this conclusion is that experimenters are unable to relate specific neural endings with specific modalities of experience. In fact, all modalities of experience have been elicited from the cornea of the eye in which the only known ending is the simple *free nerve ending.* The Oxford group said that careful histological evidence shows that all the specialized endings are essentially alike, for they arborize into the same fine filaments. The evidence shows that there is a range of intermediate structures extensive enough so that we need not accept the classification of specialized structures of the types generally found in the literature. This would mean that, as far as the sense organ is concerned, there would be no such thing as four sense modalities. The separateness of modalities would arise first as separate neural *pathways* from the skin leading to different projection areas of the cerebral cortex.

Not all workers seem willing to interpret the findings in quite the way just indicated, however. Some credence still is retained in the significance of the diversity of structure as a condition for difference in sensory experience that results.

A view proposed some time ago by Head (1920) was that there are two kinds of sensations as a result of a dual sensory mechanism in the skin. One is a more generalized and more primitive system; this he called the *protopathic system.* The other is a more specific and more advanced one, called the *epicritic system.* This idea did not gain general acceptance, although it did gain considerable attention. Even so, some workers think there is a possibility that a protopathic system may exist, since the activity set up by tactile stimuli, for example, is conducted up the spinal cord in at least two independent pathways. For a more extensive discussion of the topic see Bishop (1946) and Rose and Mountcastle (1959).

THE NATURE OF THRESHOLD CUTANEOUS SENSITIVITY

One of the outstanding features of threshold sensitivity of the skin is its pointlike nature. This is also true for touch, temperature, and pain. A slightly suprathreshold stimulus applied to the skin is not effective on all portions of the skin surface but only at certain points. At intermediate positions no sensory result is obtained unless more energetic impingements are applied. As soon as contact is made more energetic, the pointlike nature of sensitivity is lost and all portions of the skin, when contacted, result in sensation. The density of the distribution of "touch spots," "cold spots," "warm spots," and "pain spots" is not the same for all portions of the skin, nor are the different kinds of spots the same in concentration in any single region. This depends on at least two factors: variation in skin structure and variation in density of distribution of neural structures that give rise to the spots.

Although at times there seems to be some variation in the locale of these sensitive spots, their anatomical stability has been reported by various authorities. Dallenbach (1927) has relocated certain pressure and cold spots after an interval of more than a decade. The pointlike nature of threshold sensitivity of the skin was discovered independently by three men at about the same time: Blix in 1884 and Goldscheider and Donaldson in 1855 (see Goldscheider, 1911, 1917). The method of von Frey (1897)—the use of manually applied horsehairs—long ruled as the technique for investigating tactile sensitivity. In more recent years several different investigators constructed electromechanical devices called *kinohapts*, whereby tiny styli could be raised and lowered on the skin with more or less uniform impact and with precise timing. Bishop (1943) has used tiny electric sparks as cutaneous stimuli. This form of stimulation avoids the production of momentary distortions of skin tissue.

Another use of electrical stimulation is the application of brief shocks to a nerve trunk such as below the surface on the volar aspect of the arm. Here one can insert an electrode close alongside the nerve trunk and thereby be able to stimulate it. In doing this, one is not selecting out the fibers that carry impulses for a single cutaneous modality; instead the analysis is carried on by varying impingement intensity and rates of repeated stimulation. Thus this is not a mode of studying touch, thermal sensitivity, or pain solely or separately, but a mode of making comparisons among them on the basis of simple impingement variables. Therefore if it is found that the experiences of touch are evoked with a weaker impingement than those of temperature, then that is one important datum. If pain experiences relate differently to repeated impingements, then that, too, is important in building an understanding of the differences in the underlying mechanisms. For example, it was found that the first shocks of a certain intensity might not elicit a pain experience, but if the same value of shock were repeated at a given rate, a pain experience would emerge. At first the pain would be weak, but then it would build up as the shocks are repeated. This kind of result did not occur for repeated stimulation of the touch fibers. The analysis also disclosed that different qualities of touch are dependent on impingement level and rate of repetition.

METHODS OF DISSOCIATING THE CUTANEOUS EXPERIENCES

Whereas cutaneous receptors have not been well identified, the separateness of the experiences and the pathways that subserve them have been demonstrated. In fact, there are six ways by which the dissociation is brought about.

1. Local anesthesia is accomplished in several ways. Sometimes it is done by nerve block. To understand this sort of dissociation, as accomplished by Heinbecker, Bishop, and O'Leary (1934), one must first be acquainted with their analysis of cutaneous modalities. They have disclosed, to their satisfaction, four forms of superficial cutaneous sensibility: touch, pricking touch, warmth, and cold. Pain is the experiential quality arising from suprathreshold stimulation of pathways of the pricking-touch modality. Perceptions of hot and burning arise from strong stimulation of warmth pathways. Deep cutaneous sensibility is made up of two modalities, pressure and pressure pain. Dissociation brought about by local anesthesia begins with effects on the smallest nerve fibers and ends with effects on the largest. The cutaneous sensibilities are obliterated in the following order: cold, warm, pain, and touch. Deep pain goes along with superficial pain, and deep pressure goes along with touch. Of course, on the return of sensibility as the anesthetic wears off, the reverse order is shown.

2. Complete loss of sensibility through injury or through asphyxiation (mechanical pressure block) is involved in the second form of dissociation. In asphyxia the first experience obliterated is light pressure, or touch. Thenceforth, the order is somewhat different from that obtained by the use of anesthesia by cocaine and procaine block.

3. Dissociation is also produced by removing thin slices of skin. This layer-by-layer technique provides for the disappearance of certain sensibilities before others, touch being the first to go.

4. Reliably different *chronaxies* for warmth, cold, touch, and pain have been obtained.

5. Spinal anesthesia produces some dissociation of the cutaneous senses. Likewise, nicking the spinal cord (i.e., severing certain portions of it) may stop pain and spare touch.

6. Various pathological conditions result in dissociation, one of the outstanding being *syringomyelia,* a lesion that begins in the central gray matter of the spinal cord and moves to-

ward the periphery. Pain is the first to disappear, while the other sensibilities are still intact. Warm and cold experiences go next and finally the sense of touch. That is, of course, because various sensory tracts are separate and one is reached by the disease before the others.

TOUCH

Kinds of Tactile Experiences

The experience aroused by mechanical contact with the skin, usually called touch or pressure, is not always the same, and consequently a number of terms have arisen to label the variations. Among them, we have "contact," a lively and bright experience. "Deep pressure" is another, dull and heavy. Some pressure experiences are pointlike, some dense, some diffuse, and some even granular. One of the differentiating features that stands out is the degree of superficiality versus the degree of depth. Sometimes pressures emerge abruptly: others well up slowly. Apparently few kinds of cutaneous perception are simple in composition. Aside from mere touch and contact, there are special experiences we call *tickle, itch, vibration, creep,* and so on. Impingements that are displaced along skin surfaces give rise to the experience of tactual movement. Properly timed sequences of momentary stationary impingements also give rise to the experience of movement (or apparent movement).

For tactile experiences the most common stimulus is, of course, mechanical. Tiny masses (disks, styli, and the like) that are placed on the skin deform it to some extent. This deformation requires time. Gradients of skin deformation may be produced not only by applying the kind of impingement just mentioned but, for example, by immersing one's finger in a vessel of quicksilver (mercury). Everywhere but at the juncture of the air and mercury the pressure on the finger will be uniform. It is at the juncture that the greatest changes in pressure occur as the finger is moved. And that is where the experience of contact will be felt.

What a Tactual Stimulus Is

A most enlightening investigation on the fundamentals of the pressure or tactile sense was done by Nafe and Wagoner (1941). They constructed a precision instrument (Figure 5.1) whereby pressures could be manipulated and minute differences in the amount of deformation of the skin measured. Their stimuli consisted in a series of disks of various areas and of different masses. Their instrumentation

Figure 5.1   Apparatus to study tactual response in relation to depression of the skin by styli of various areas. (Photograph by Paul Berg, *St. Louis Post Dispatch*, Sunday Pictures.)

measured and recorded the rate at which these disks sank into the skin by force of weight or by instrumental determination. Their subjects were instructed to indicate, by pressing a key, when they felt or did not feel the pressure of the disk. It was found that as long as the disk's "rate of fall" into (i.e., depression of) the skin was above a certain value, the subject felt the disk's pressure. When this critical rate no longer was being maintained or exceeded, no experience of contact was produced.

The commonsense viewpoint makes stimulation the mere contact of the disk with the skin. Nafe and Wagoner had to substitute for this the idea that stimulation consists in deforming the skin. Without the deformation process no stimulation occurs. They found that not only was the process of deformation necessary, but the process had to occur at or above a critical rate to constitute stimulation.

It is customary to speak of *adaptation* as the cessation or reduction of activity of a sensory mechanism, while supposed stimulation is held uniform. The final failure of the disk to be felt has long been considered an example of tactual adaptation. Nafe and Wagoner had to attribute "adaptation" not to a sense organ failure while stimulation was held constant but rather to the termination of conditions that in themselves could be called stimulation. Hence it could be said that what is ordinarily called tactile adaptation is not a sense organ failure. The subject simply ceases to feel the disk when the process of stimulation ceases. On the other hand, if we must adhere to the older definition of adaptation—namely, that it is partial or total failure of the sense organ to be able to respond to stimulation—then our present tactile example is not one of adaptation at all. Nafe and Wagoner's concept of the stimulus and why the disk finally ceases to be felt, avoids the curious paradox of talking about a stimulus that does not stimulate. For that reason, among others, it seems to be a very fortunate way of envisaging the situation.

Nafe and Wagoner's interpretation also coincides with the general notion we have expressed in several earlier places—namely, that sense organs are made up of two sorts of tissue, neural and nonneural. Adhering to this concept, we could say that the skin that surrounds the free nerve endings and other sensory endings is a part of the tactual sense organ. Tactile stimulation consists, then, in doing something to the nonneural part of the tactual sense organ. Accordingly, the skin does not become exhausted by "stimulation" (the presence of the disk). We simply do not keep the disk moving and thus are failing to deform the skin continually at a sufficient rate. This fails to produce some consequent effect that is the condi-

tion for setting up nerve impulses. When this is the case we do
not feel the disk.

Guilford and Lovewell (1936) made a study of the tactile spots
on the skin based on the fact that the more forcefully a stylus is
applied to the skin, the more dense the distribution of the skin
spots becomes. This relationship was implied earlier in this chapter.

Guilford and Lovewell's nine styli ranged from 0.01 gram to
1.60 grams. Each was applied to 200 equally distributed locations
on a one square centimeter area on the back of the hand (Figure
5.2). As pressure was increased, a greater and greater percentage
of all the spots responded. This sigmoid shape of the curve represented the relation between impingement intensity and density of
spots. To some, this suggests that any unit area of the skin possesses
some probability of responding to a given impingement of a given
intensity.

Various calculations have been made concerning the minimal
energy required for eliciting tactual experience. One author reported that 0.026 erg on the end of the thumb and 0.037 erg to
1.09 ergs on the tips of the fingers were threshold values. Comparing

Figure 5.2   Relation of pressure on the skin to probability of response. (Source:
J. P. Guilford and E. M. Lovewell. "Touch spots and the intensity of the stimulus," *J. Gen. Psychol.,* 1936, 15, 149–159, Fig. 1.)

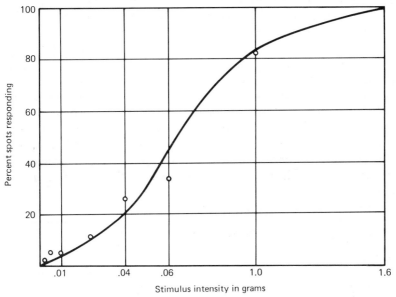

threshold tactual values with visual and auditory thresholds, we may say that 100 million to 10 billion times as much energy is required by touch as by the other two senses.

Von Frey (1897) reasoned that if there are two separate senses, touch (or pressure) and pain, then they ought to have separate thresholds. He believed that the threshold for the pressure experience should be lower than for pain. Accordingly, he carefully explored a restricted area of the skin on the subject's leg. In this area he found about 15 points with a threshold of about 33 grams per square millimeter or less. He gradually raised the stimulus pressure and did not find any additional pressure spots. When a pressure of about 200 grams per square millimeter was reached, von Frey began to elicit a pricking and painful experience. He also found that the distribution of the spots was different for the two experiences. From this he concluded that the separateness of pressure and pain modalities had been demonstrated. Table 5.1 provides a few examples of thresholds for pressure and pain; it indicates that the relation among thresholds for the two experiences is not simple: In some, but not all, cases there is a wide distinction.

Our interest does not lie solely in where on the skin tactual impingements can be felt but also in where these impingements are perceptually localized. Do subjects feel the contacts in the location where they are made? Renshaw and Wherry (1931), among others, have addressed themselves to this problem. They studied the ability of subjects to localize spots on the back of the nonpreferential hand and the flat surface of the volar forearm throughout a daily practice period ranging from 7 to 32 days, depending on the subject. The subjects ranged from 8 to 65 years of age. Renshaw found rather large practice effects in both the young and old subjects. The children were not only more accurate than the adults but showed a more rapid reduction in magnitude of errors. During the first two days the children localized the stimulus more accurately on the forearm than on the hand. The adults did just the opposite.

Renshaw suggested that the poorer performance manifested by adults may be due to the fact that adults were handicapped more than the children by using blindfolds in the experiment; the

Table 5.1 CUTANEOUS THRESHOLDS

	PRESSURE (gm/mm²)	PAIN (gm/mm²)
Fingertip	3	300
Calf of leg	16	30
Forearm (back)	33	30
Forearm (front)	8	20

supposition was that the adults' behavior is more dominantly visually controlled than the children's. This idea was tested by using a procedure different from that in the first experiment. Four subjects were chosen: two adults 28 and 58 years of age and two boys 12 years of age. Two methods of reporting where the subjects had been contacted were used. One was the tactual–kinesthetic method of having the subjects quickly touch the spot thought to be felt. The other, the visual method, was simply to look at the skin surface on which a grid had been marked and to answer as to which square in the grid had been contacted. The adults did better by the visual method, and the children did better by the tactual–kinesthetic one. This was in the direction of a confirmation of Renshaw's idea that the dependence on contact for tactual localization in children is substituted, as time goes on, by visual control of the performance. He suggests this substitution might occur near the age of puberty.

Renshaw, Wherry, and Newlin (1930) studied tactual localization in congenitally blind children and adults in comparison with sighted young and old. They found that blind adults are superior to blind children in tactual localization; blind adults are likewise more accurate than sighted adults; sighted children are superior to sighted adults; sighted children are superior to blind children; initial performance is better on the forearm than on the hand for sighted children, but the opposite is true for all others. When the results of the blind are plotted agewise, the results of the adults are a projection of those of the children.

The inferiority of the sighted adults with reference to sighted children is thought to be due to the shift in the adults to dependence on distance receptors in localization—that is, to vision. Renshaw and Wherry (1931) studied a group of subjects over an age range of 6 to 16 years to determine when ocular dominance in tactual localization sets in. They concluded that tactual–kinesthetic localization is superior to visual from the eighth to the twelfth year, at which point the difference vanishes. At puberty, there seems to be an increase in the accuracy for both methods. Between the thirteenth and fourteenth years, the visual method becomes superior and continues to become greater as age increases. The workers pointed out that when the children use the visual method (their poorer method) and the adults use the tactual–kinesthetic method (their poorer method), there is no true difference between the results. This would nullify the Rivers–MacDougall law that states that sensory discrimination is inversely proportional to age and degree of civilization of a population.

The findings of Renshaw and his colleagues bear on the findings of Bartley (1953, 1955) and his colleagues obtained on children compared to adults. In the study of whether children perceive block size in relation distance from the eye, it was found that children did the same at all distances and made smaller or fewer errors than adults. When we put all the available information together, it seems to indicate that the children did not use visual imagery, at least to the same extent as the adults, and that visual imagery was responsible for the size-distance effect found in adults.

Body Loci and Tactile Form Perception

A great deal of form perception is visual, but haptic perception also provides for experiencing form. In haptic perception, form is apprehended in one of two ways. The individuals either blind or under blindfold or with eyes closed may actively come to experience the forms of objects by manipulating them while they are held, or the subjects may run their fingers around the forms while the forms are stationary. Secondly, a flat object or outline may be placed on the skin, with the subjects trying to determine the object's form. Some workers have said that accuracy of form recognition is a function of the sensitivity of the body surface. (Gibson, 1962; Schwartz, Perey and Azulay, 1975; and Zigler and Barrett, 1927.)

Heller (1977) studied the question of the relative perceptual ability to determine forms when they were placed on three different locations on the skin. The forms used were a square, a triangle, a closed arch, a circle, a teardrop, and a peanut. These were drawn on the palms of the hands, on the forearm, or on the biceps of 42 subjects, with the use of vision excluded. For this purpose templates were used. Heller did not find a simple relation between the skin surface as an information transducer and cutaneous sensitivity. He found no significant difference in the accuracy of form perception on the palm of the hand and on the biceps.

Bach-y-Rita (1972) found that recognition with a "tactile–vision" substitution system was better on the abdomen than on the back. Of course, this form of experimentation uses vibrating stimulation which is not fully passive.

Sinclair (1967) published a taxonomy of the somato-sensations and concluded that, in general, the concept of associating axon diameter with specific experiences is not justifiable at present.

The Tau Effect

The tactile sense may be used to demonstrate one of the most fundamental principles in the process of stimulation—that *both time and place are involved in defining or specifying stimulation.* Tactual impingement reaches the skin not only at some *place* but at some *time*. It makes a difference, then, both in terms of time and place, what the end result will be.

Helson and King (1931) performed experiments on a phenomenon they called the *tau* effect, because they did not want its name confused with those of other phenomena. The tau effect was demonstrated by contacting the skin three places in a straight line in temporal succession. The investigators used an instrument called a *kinohapt* (Figure 5.3) to make contact with the skin at *A*, *B*, and

Figure 5.3   A Bartley kinohapt, an electromechanical device for contacting the skin with tiny styli with precise pressures and time relations. Item 1 is the knob for adjusting the whole carriage vertically; 2 is one of the solenoids activating a stylus; 3 is a solenoid carriage adjustable horizontally; 4 is a knob adjusting a single solenoid vertically; 5 is the arm rest, adjustable in all directions; 6 is the armrest lock.

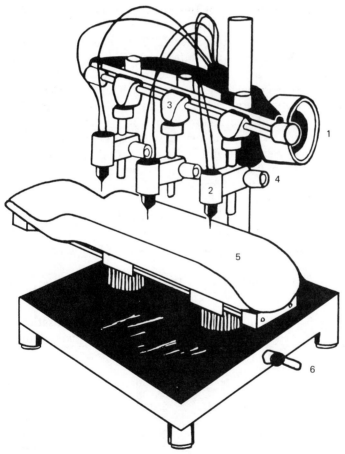

C. There were, of course, several possibilities with regard to both spacing and timing. A and C could be equidistant from B lying between them, or A could be nearer to or farther away from B than C was. The same possibilities held true for the timing of the contacts. A, B, and C could be presented with an equal interval between A to B and B to C. Or the first time interval could be longer or shorter than the second. Furthermore, the timing and spacing would be related to each other in various ways.

Let us assume that space intervals 1 and 2 are equal and time interval 1 is longer than interval 2. The subject is likely to report that space interval 1 is the longer. This effect can still be maintained when space interval 2 is made longer than 1. The procedure is to determine how much longer than time interval 2 time interval 1 must be to have the space intervals appear equal. As the time intervals are made unequal, the space intervals must also be made unequal in the opposite direction.

We can now turn to some of the findings of Helson and King (1931), summarized in Table 5.2 in which the first column shows time interval 1 divided by time interval 2. In the third column, space interval 2 is divided by space interval 1. The ratios of columns 1 and 3 are given in the second and fourth columns. The ratios are the ones found necessary by Helson and King to make space intervals 1 and 2 appear equal. For time intervals of 500 and 200 milliseconds the space intervals were 30 and 50 millimeters, respectively. That is, while the time intervals were to each other as 2.5 to 1, the space intervals were not quite the actual reciprocal, but rather 1 to 1.67. To make the two spaces appear equal required time compensation and in milliseconds it was greater than would be expected in simple reciprocity.

According to the common outlook, the tau effect is a *time–space illusion*. But it is to be recognized that the results were perfectly according to law and depended on the operation of time and space factors in neural activity.

To see how certain variations of the procedure work, we turn

Table 5.2 TIME AND SPACE INTERVALS

t_1/t_2 (msec.)	RATIO	s_2/s_1 (mm)	RATIO
500/200	2.5	50/30	1.67
500/250	2.0	45/30	1.50
500/300	1.67	40/30	1.33
500/350	1.43	35/30	1.20
500/400	1.25	30/30	1.00

again to Helson and King. Instead of contacts *A, B*, and *C* lying in a straight line, they were now the corners of an equilateral triangle. With this new and very different arrangement the manipulation of timing, as the contact sequence was followed through, changed the apparent shape of the triangle to nonequilateral. Also, the investigators contacted the two points instead of three in the order *A, B, A*. When the timing in going from *A* to *B* was different from going from *B* back to *A*, it did not seem as though *A* was being contacted on return. This result showed that a given point on the skin does not possess, in itself, some unique property whereby it is localized. The point lies in a cutaneous field, controlled by both spatial and temporal factors.

Helson and King's investigation was a demonstration of the fallacy of Lotze's theory of *local signs,* in which it is asserted that every point on the skin possesses its own unique and sufficient characteristics for being localized when stimulated.

We should remember that space and time are operants of two sorts. On the one hand, they are concepts applicable to operations performed or processes observed. In introducing the tau effect, we said that stimulation involves places on the skin and places in the nervous system at which processes occur. We said that the processes that occurred, occurred in time, and that the relative timing of several neural processes controlled the perceptual end result.

Space and time are also to be looked on as something *perceived.* There are spatial and temporal features of perception. Helson and King's study involved space and time in both ways. Once we understand how space and time are involved in neural processes, it is not so surprising to see them involved in perceptual response (experience).

WARMTH AND COLDNESS

A feature of haptic perception is the experience of warmth and cold. The surface of the body is the contact region between organism and environment, and so it is the skin that contains one set of receptor elements for our temperature experiences. There are receptor elements *within* the body that are thermally sensitive and have to do with internal body temperature regulation. We shall deal with these briefly in the chapter on the *homeostatic perceptual system* (Chapter 9).

Certain intensities of thermal stimuli produce pain, and such cases will be considered in discussing pain, its nature and production. In recent years the John B. Pierce Foundation Laboratory has worked extensively on temperature perception. Only a brief report of the extensive findings (Stevens and Marks and associates, 1969) is possible here.

Stimulus Conditions

In principle, the stimulus conditions for the experiences of warmth and coldness arise out of the fact that the human as a warm-blooded organism maintains a fairly constant internal body temperature but the skin temperature is quite different. Skin temperature is not nearly so constant and its mean level is lower; it depends partly on the level of outside temperature and partly on the moment-to-moment nature of the blood supply to the skin. Generally, there is a temperature gradient downward from internal body temperature to skin surface temperature. The temperature of whatever contacts the skin may differ from the skin surface temperature up or down and thus may add or subtract heat from the skin. Various factors converge toward producing what has long been called a *physiological zero*. If the temperature of the impingement, whatever it may be, is higher than physiological zero at the time, a feeling of warmth is generally produced; if lower, a feeling of cold ensues. This is not always the case, however. Under certain specified conditions paradoxical results can be produced in the laboratory and can be expected in everyday life.

Paradoxical Results

When impingements with a temperature higher than physiological zero produce a feeling of cold, the result is called *paradoxical cold*. When impingements below physiological zero produce a feeling of warmth, the result is *paradoxical warmth*. However, the paradoxes exist only as long as one has no understanding of how they are produced.

Paradoxical coldness is produced not by activating "warm spots" by "warm stimuli" but by activating "cold spots" by "warm stimuli," and for this it was found that a stylus at 33 degrees C (33° C) [91 degrees F (91° F)] is usually high enough to elicit warmth. The stylus usually must not contact much skin surface to obtain paradoxical coldness; with extensive contact, "warm spots" are also activated, giving the experience of warmth. If, however, the skin is first well heated, say up to 45° C, and then a stylus at 48° C is applied, coldness will be the first experience elicited, with warmth following a little later.

Paradoxical warmth is less commonly elicitable. One experimenter believed that slight warmth could be elicited by a stylus at about 0.1 to 1.5° C below physiological zero. Another put the range for paradoxical warmth at 6 to 10° C below physiological zero. The conditions for producing this form of warmth have not been well established.

In recording from peripheral nerves in the tongue, Hensel and Zotterman (1951) found a group of *mechanoreceptive fibers* also activated by cooling. Their response to cooling differed from that of true cold-mediating fibers, however. The mechanoreceptive fibers could be activated only by extremes in cooling and terminated their discharge when thermal conditions were made stable. In the radial nerve, Hensel and Bowman (1960) found fibers that responded to mechanical stimulation and manifested a steady discharge when the temperature of the skin was in the indifferent range, even when no mechanical impingement was involved. Cooling increased the discharge slightly. Witt and Hensel (1959) discovered the same phenomenon in the cat. These results might explain the so-called Weber illusion of pressure, produced by cooling. Lippold, Nichols, and Redfearn (1960) found that some of the muscle spindles they studied in the cat responded to thermal ("cold") stimuli quite like specific "cold" fibers while maintaining a normal response to stretch.

This overlapping or cross-modality response probably accounts for a number of the everyday sensory effects, such as people feeling cold when they have extensive aches in their muscles. In some cases, there is a nebulous kind of discomfort interpreted as feeling cold, but the feeling may not mean that the person is cold in the usual sense of the word. Kenshalo, Nafe, and Brooks (1961) found that at somewhat extreme temperatures sudden thermal changes produce two readily distinguishable sensations, the occurrence of each depending on the size of the change.

The Heat Grill

A unique way of producing the experience of heat is a synthetic method involving the use of a "heat grill," which consists of a set of small copper tubes in which alternate parallel tubes carry water at different temperatures. One set of tubes used alone would elicit the experience of warmth; the other would elicit coldness. This arrangement tends to produce first an experience of coldness, then one of hotness, and then a possible return to coldness. Heat is produced by this method without the use of high temperature stimuli.

Woodworth and Schlosberg (1954) pointed out that paradoxical cold and synthetic heat are by no means the most frequent results elicited when making thermal explorations of the skin. Only two out of Jenkins' (1938) four subjects reported paradoxical effects at all and then only 27 times in 9000 observations. Geldard (1953), on the other hand, stated that paradoxical perceptions of cold are produced commonly enough in mapping warm spots.

The explanation for divergence in effects when several observers place their wrists on a metal grid in which alternate rods are of different temperatures of suitable values, has to do with the observers' sets and with their quickness of responses. There are those who retract their hand quickly as though burned. Others are slower. The time required for the experience to emerge is shorter for cold than for warmth, and warmth emerges before pain. For observers who draw their hands away quickly, all that should be experienced is coldness and warmth, but they report hotness. For those who keep their wrists on the grid a little longer, the distinctions between cold and warm are more likely to be experienced for what they are.

Contact and Radiant Stimulation

So far we have been reporting results from thermal stimulation through contact. Thermal effects can also be transmitted to the skin by radiation. The two methods lead to different results. It seems that warmth cannot be experienced at all when restricted areas of radiant impingement are used. When skin areas of less than 700 square millimeters are radiated, pain is experienced at the time radiation is strong enough to elicit any experience. When contact styli are used, areas as small as a single square millimeter or even less may be efffective in eliciting warmth. Whether this distinction has some meaning in the economy of the organism is not known.

In line with the fact that large areas are required for the effectiveness of thermal radiators, it can be said that spatial summation is characteristic for this form of stimulation. The energy needed per unit of skin area to produce threshold results is much less for two regions than for one. Summation is marked enough to show up when the two areas are represented by the backs of the two hands. It is not equivalent for all portions of the skin, as shown by the fact that two regions, one the hand and the other the forehead, will not summate to the same extent as if the two test regions were on the two hands.

Until recently the receptive area on the skin for a single nerve fiber conducting thermal information was thought to be a small spot less than one millimeter in diameter. Kenshalo, Decker, and Hamilton (1967) found that the discharge in a fiber is augmented when any of eight different spots are cooled. In other fibers tested, numbers varying from two to six spots were involved. The activity in the fibers increased in a summative fashion as additional spots were added to the first one cooled. Since psychophysical experiments had shown that areal summation occurs in the production of the experience of cooling, the present experiment would seem to demonstrate one neural factor that works in that direction.

Stevens and Marks, over a period of years, have concentrated on the study of the perception of warmth. In 1967 they reported on apparent warmth as a function of thermal irradiation. The subject's back was periodically exposed to radiant heat. The method of magnitude estimation was used. In other experiments, using the same levels of thermal irradiation used in a previous experiment, they matched the loudness of white noise to warmth. Both experiments showed that warmth is related to absorbed irradiance by a power function whose exponent is about 0.7.

In 1968 they reported on the correlations among the degrees of perceived warmth, the level and duration of irradiant flux on the skin. For a constant *duration,* perceived warmth increased as a power function of the difference between the flux and the flux approximating the absolute threshold for warmth. The power function for a duration of from 2 to 6 seconds was about 0.87, rising to 1.04 for a duration of 12 seconds. For a constant level, perceived warmth changed only slightly with duration. But surface skin temperature and inferred temperature of deeper layers rose continuously and markedly with duration. Neither this *change* in skin temperature nor the *rate of change* nor the *thermal gradient* tallied consistently with level of perceived warmth. Stevens and Marks supposed that sensory adaptation at the site of the receptors mediating the warmth could account for this lack of correlation. In 1969 these authors and associates found that discomfort followed the power law.

In 1971 Stevens and Banks examined the relation between the perceived magnitude of warmth and simple reaction time to warmth stimulation. They found that the degree of warmth depended nearly as much on the extent of skin surface involved as on the level of stimulation. Two questions were asked: (1) does the quickness of reaction to radiant stimulation depend on the areal extent and the flux density in the same way as perceived warmth and (2) will the principle whereby area and flux density trade to preserve the perception of constant warmth predict a constant reaction time? Previously, Wright (1951) indicated that reaction time does show spatial summation. The present study confirmed this.

In another study, Stevens and Marks (1971) showed that power functions for the back and the forehead extrapolate to a point of convergence near the threshold for pain and actual tissue impairment.

In 1972 Marks and Stevens performed experiments bearing on four questions: (1) does perceived cold conform to a psychophysical power law when duration is constant; (2) do the constants of the power equation depend on duration; (3) what is the nature of the growth of cold perception over time; and (4) are experiences of cold simple and derived functions of skin temperature? They concluded that for a constant duration the terminal cold experience grew as a power function of reduction in heat irradiation in cold air. For any constant reduction, cold, unlike warmth, increased continuously and markedly with duration. Perceived cold at low levels of heat reduction, but not at high, correlated strongly with changes in skin temperatures.

In 1974 Marks wrote on spatial summation in the warmth sense. In the same year, Stevens, Marks, and Simonson dealt with regional sensitivity and spatial summation in the perception of warmth. In this study they used the cheek, forearm, calf of the leg, and the back as sites. They found that some regions of the body are far more responsive than others to low-level amounts of heat, but all regions react more or less the same when heating is high enough.

In 1973 Marks and Stevens wrote on spatial summation of warmth stating that spatial summation of warmth experience occurs primarily in the central nervous system and that summation can occur over large skin areas up to at least several hundred square centimeters.

In 1975 Taus, Stevens, and Marks dealt with spatial localization of warmth. The forearm was the site used. The subject had to tell on which side of a tactile reference line the warmth was localized. Correctness improved as gradient intensity increased as well as with increasing distance from the reference line. Apparently there is an inverse relation between accuracy of localization and spatial summation. At low levels, both intensity and area are large factors in perceiving warmth and localization is poor. But as intensity increases, area contributes less and less to sensation and localization is better.

FUSION IN USING THERMAL STIMULI

In 1971 Ladan and Nelson used an intermittent radiant stimulus on the upper back of three subjects. Eight pulse-to-cycle fractions (PCF's) were used while area and intensity were held constant. Their results showed an increasing phase for short PCF's, as in Kastorf's study, but TFF's (thermal fusion frequencies), declined as PCF was varied, in cases where radiant flux per unit time was increasing.

Recently (unpublished results), .Ladan and Nelson extended their previous experiments, varying more factors than they had formerly used, including the following: PCF, intensity (I), stimulus area (A) and body location, to ascertain the effect on TFF. Stimuli were applied to the forearm and to the subject's back. Four subjects were used.

The results were similar to those obtained with similar parameters in studying vision. TFF rises to a peak as PCF is varied, and then declines as in vision. TFF increases in a nearly linear fashion as area is increased as in vision. The range over which TFF increases is large, though it was not tested at extreme intensities, so as to avoid producing pain. The results suggest that despite the structural differences in the receptors in the two modalities, the same type of neural integration may occur in the thermal system as is expressed in the visual system in the "Alteration of Response Theory" in *The Journal of General Psychology,* January 1971.

THERMAL ADAPTATION

The skin adapts to thermal conditions. That is, to say, thermal conditions felt as warm or cold cease gradually to feel either way with an elapse of time during which the impingement condition exists. The course of this thermal adaptation is a negatively accelerated curve (Hahn, 1930).

At temperatures close to the usual skin temperatures, adaptation is short. Hensel (1950) reported that at temperatures outside the range of 20° to 40° sensation does not disappear. When single small spots are tested, adaptation is rapid even at temperature extremes. To adapt to a thermal level is not only to become sensationless for that level, but to shift in the experience produced by thermal levels just above and below. Those below feel cold.

It is known that fiber response to thermal conditions does not increase uniformly as temperature changes but instead shows one or more peaks of sensitivity. That is, fibers are activated maximally at certain levels throughout a range. The explanation of this fact is quite different from explaining the activities of fibers as monotonic functions as temperature changes. Certain central inhibitory functions are suggested: reciprocal inhibition would provide for adaptation (Deutsch and Deutsch, 1966).

Kenshalo and Scott (1966) undertook new measurements of temperature adaptation because the literature reported various results of, for example, changes in sensation with concomitant thermal changes in the skin and because at the terminal stages of adaptation, sensation waxes and wanes, making judgments of the end point of adaptation quite difficult. The older methods of ascertaining temperature adaptation involved exposing the skin to an extreme temperature for a period such as that provided by cold water and then ascertaining the temperature of a bath at which a warm sensation was induced. In another method, the course of temperature adaptation was ascertained, including the determination of its limits by exposing the skin to specific temperatures and asking the subject to report when he or she no longer felt warmth or cold. Kenshalo and Scott felt that these methods were undesirable because (1) it is difficult for a subject to attend to a sensation even for a single minute, let alone for 40 minutes and (2) it is extremely difficult, if not impossible, to determine the instant of no sensation, thus the second method fails to produce a clear-cut end point.

Hence Kenshalo and Scott undertook a different method— namely, a variation of the method of average error, in which the subject controls the temperature of the stimulator to maintain a given level of sensation. The device they used was able to control the temperature within $\pm 0.01°$ C. At the end of a 20-minute period, the dorsal surface of the forearm of the subject was measured by a thermocouple. The stimulator was adjusted by the subject so that a just-detectable experience of warm or cold was maintained throughout a period of 40 minutes. At 5-minute intervals the experimenter changed the temperature toward neutral and instructed the subject to adjust it until a just-noticeable sensation was produced. This technique produced a range of complete adaptation much smaller than ranges reported by previous investigators. Complete adaptation was 8.2° C in one subject and 4.5° C in another, whereas values of 23° C, 27° C, 21° C, and even 40° C were obtained by four other investigators, respectively. Adaptation was completed in from 10 to 20 minutes in Kenshalo and Scott's study.

Theories of Temperature Sensitivity

Since this book is not as much concerned with bodily mechanisms as physiological psychology textbooks or textbooks solely on the senses are, we shall discuss the theories of temperature sensitivity only briefly. Our concern is more with the personal behavior that stems from stimulation of sense organs.

The classical theory of temperature sensitivity rests mainly on the supposed correspondence between distribution of sensitivity and distribution of certain end organs. Attempts to correlate structure and function have not been very rewarding. At present, we cannot say for sure which form of specialized ending subserves the function of the temperature experiences.

One theory of thermal sensitivity is that of Nafe (1938), which can be called a neurovascular theory. He believed that the smooth muscle walls of the blood vessels of the skin—arterioles, for example—are responsible for thermal experience. In the walls are free nerve endings, button-formed endings, and terminal loops. It is supposed that contraction and relaxation of the vessel walls activate these endings in appropriate ways. The resulting neural activity is utilized by the central nervous system to provide the ultimate experiences of warmth and cold. In other words, temperature perceptions are a form of kinesthetic or muscle-induced experience. Nafe rested his case on the reports of various investigators to the effect that smooth muscle is thermally sensitive, relaxing in certain upper temperature ranges and contracting in lower temperature ranges. Much of what is proposed in Nafe's neurovascular theory is quite convincing; nevertheless, his theory does not at once tell us why the two kinds of temperature spots are distributed differently. At present, we can only say that the understanding of the mechanisms responsible for temperature sensitivity leaves much to be desired.

Geldard (1953) suggested that nerve tissue is directly sensitive to thermal conditions and thus no specialized nerve endings would be needed for mediating temperature experiences. The generality seems too broad, however.

Kenshalo and Nafe (1963) made simultaneous measurements of changes in the threshold for "cool" impingements and of cutaneous vasodilation as a function of the temperature to which the skin was adapted. The changes in the two measures occurred in close correspondence, suggesting to these investigators that the cutaneous vascular system may be valuable as a temperature detector model and thus may contribute to a theory of temperature sensitivity.

Detection of Thermal Conditions in the Surrounds

One function of the temperature sense is to "inform" the organism of the thermal nature of its surrounds, which are made up of three kinds of thermal conditions. One is the set of conditions that involve *radiation*, either to or from the organism. Sources of radiant energy such as fires, lamps, stoves, and the sun radiate *to* the body. Other situations involve radiation *from* the body when its temperature is higher than the surrounds. The second thermal impingement to which the organism is obviously sensitive is the process of *convection*, for example, in air currents. The third process is *conduction*, the transfer of heat by contact.

All three conditions are encountered by the organism in its moment-to-moment activities, and when near equilibrium thermal conditions exist, the organism has no conscious realization of temperature. Generally, only as these optimal or equilibrium conditions are departed from does awareness of warmth or coldness arise.

Whereas pointlike radiation to the skin is ineffective in producing perception of warmth, large skin areas are extremely sensitive to radiation. Only a trivial radiation playing onto the forehead produces the experience of warmth. An increase in radiation intensity of only 0.0014 calorie per square centimeter per second, inducing a rise in skin temperature of only 0.003° C was felt as warmth.

Solids with which the body comes in contact vary widely in their property of conducting heat. We experience the difference in the way common solids feel to the touch. A stone bench is colder in winter and hotter in summer than a wooden bench because of the difference in thermal conductivity. Metals are among the coldest and hottest of objects. The conductivity of silver is about 18,000 times as great as that of the air. Cotton is about 7 times as conductive and glass is about 44 times as conductive as air. Hence the way these substances feel could be expected to be quite different in various circumstances.

PAIN

Pain was originally studied experimentally as one of the three perceptual responses to threshold stimulation of the skin. The other two perceptual experiences were, of course, touch and warmth. Thus pain was an identifiable uncomfortable experience at the threshold levels. But this was and is not the only connotation that the word, pain, possesses. Various things can happen both to the body's surface and its interior that produce uncomfortable reactions. These reactions, although called pain do not have as simple a basis as might be supposed. In fact, the meaning (cognitive) factor looms large in producing pain. Therefore it would be better to have another name for pain. *Anguish* might be appropriate. Some very good examples showing the two kinds of discomfort are found in Beecher's *Measurement of Subjective Responses* (1959). Before dealing with what might be called anguish, let us look at some studies that tie the pain experience to definite body structures at least in the skin.

The stimulus for pain may be thermal, mechanical, chemical, or electrical. Laboratory experimentation on pain has employed several distinct kinds of stimuli, among which have been: (1) mechanical impingements, to discover thresholds and distinguish between points on the skin mediating pain and touch; (2) thermal radiation, as applied for example to the forehead; and (3) electrical shocks applied by electrodes inserted under the skin alongside a nerve trunk.

Among the questions that have arisen is, how specific must a form of impingement be to evoke pain? That is, might not a variety of forms of impingement, if intense, evoke pain? Certain questions regarding the close connection between tactile and painful sensations arise in using certain stimuli.

Electrical Stimulation

We shall begin by reporting on certain findings brought out by Bishop (1943, 1944, 1946, and 1949) using electrical stimulation. One of Bishop's investigations (1944) disclosed what he called a "peripheral unit for pain" conceived of as the tiny skin area served mainly by a certain branching nerve fiber. Anywhere within this skin area a weak impingement will elicit a kind of sensation, depending on actual intensity. The threshold will be lower in the center of the area than at the periphery. The skin area does not correspond, however, to any well-defined describable anatomical nerve-ending distribution to which a specific pain experience can be assigned. Peripheral units overlap, and it takes careful exploration to detect any behavior that has led to the concept of the peripheral unit.

The sensory experiences resulting from the activation of this unit vary depending on the nature of the stimulation applied. Bishop's stimulation consisted in trains of tiny electric shocks that he could vary in intensity and in rate of delivery. These factors determined various rates and durations of afferent neural discharge to the central nervous system. The perceptual experiences that resulted differed, accordingly, in both qualitative and quantitative properties.

At the lowest threshold, an "inconsequential" touch experience was elicited; at a little higher threshold, a pricking experience was elicited; with certain specifications of impingement, itch, or pain ensued. If two skin units are stimulated concurrently or by alternate bursts of electric shocks, a two-point discrimination between them is possible. That is, the two separate loci, each being stimulated, do not summate into pain. Some adjacent points when stimulated, result, in a modified effect. That is, they neither summate nor are recognized as two separate spots.

The electrical threshold for the prick endings is lower than for touch endings, which precludes complicating the experiment by stimulation of the true tactile sense, at least at threshold. However, shocks strong enough to induce pain may elicit nonpainful touch. Touch is more sharply localized than pain. Even so, one might ask whether or not pain and touch are unavoidably confusable. Bishop (1943, 1944, and 1946) pointed out that the two are distinguishable by differences in their temporal characteristics. Touch is "deadbeat"—that is, a separate brief experience occurs to each shock. Prick and pain, in contrast, are persistent and rise gradually rather than abruptly to maximum. A 10-per-second rate of administration of shocks to a touch spot will not summate or induce a fused sensory end result. On the other hand, pain from such stimuli will rise to its maximum only after five or six shocks have been delivered. Pain also persists for almost a second following the cessation of stimulation. Thus shocks at a 10-per-second rate are, in a way, a single continuous stimulus rather than many separate ones. The maximally sensitive skin areas for pain and touch are generally not identical in location. If a maximally sensitive spot for pain is stimulated, touch will generally not be aroused by the range of stimulus intensities used.

It can be seen, then, that pain spots are identifiable and the results of stimulating them are distinguishable from the results of using similar stimuli on nearby skin areas identified as touch or temperature spots.

Experiences elicited by activation of the mechanisms giving pain are, at their lowest thresholds, not painful but have a pricking quality by no means as describable as pain. Pain is elicited only by more intense or longer trains of stimuli.

The analysis of pain mechanisms, pain qualities, and pain thresholds by this electrical method gives somewhat different impressions to experimenters from those they receive from mechanical or other methods. In all cases, however, investigators conclude that they are dealing with a different mechanism from that involved in producing tactile and thermal experiences.

Are There Two Pains?

It has been concluded that the fibers carrying information from pain-producing impingements are of two types: A fibers that conduct impulses at high velocity and C fibers that conduct impulses much more slowly. We know that there are two main qualitative sorts of pain, the prick pain (a bright, relatively short pain) and dull pain (longer lasting and more diffuse). Some have argued that the bright pain is mediated by A fibers, dull pain by C fibers. One evidence for fiber mediation comes from the results of differential fiber blocking produced by cocaine. This affects C fibers first and A fibers last. When only A fibers are conducting, pain is of the brief, pricking sort. By another form of differential block—pressure that halts circulation—A fibers are blocked first and C fibers last. When only C fibers are conducting, the pain is dull.

As early as 1892 Gad and Goldscheider, and then Thunberg in 1902, reported that there are two pains rather than the expected single pain to certain stimuli. These were identified by the time interval separating their onset.

Zotterman (1933) showed that when A fiber conduction is blocked the pain that predominates is the second pain. Although this double effect is not too hard to demonstrate, Jones (1956) claims that it need not be interpreted as an essential duality but as only due to certain kinds of impingements reaching different fibers at different times by differential penetration of different depths in the skin. He demonstrated that some kinds of stimuli do not produce two pains.

Stevens, Adair, and Marks (1970) also reported on a study of perceived warmth produced by infrared irradiation in relation to its density, duration, and distribution over the body. This irradiation can produce three types of experience: *pain, discomfort,* and *warmth,* all three of which obey the power law of S. S. Stevens. Pain from brief, intense irradiation of tiny spots on the forearm or forehand grows as a power function of the differences between the flux used and the threshold flux. The function is 1.0. Discomfort produced by exposing the whole front surface of the body grows as a power function of the increase or decrease in temperature from that which feels comfortable. Warmth discomfort involves a power function of less than one-half that involved in cold discomfort.

PAIN AND ANGUISH

Much of the pain the average individual suffers is localized *within* the body. This noncutaneous pain possesses the greatest significance in the life and economy of the individual. Looked at from one standpoint, the study of pain is just a consideration of one of the several forms of body sensitivity that have been investigated in the laboratories of sensory physiology and psychology. Not too much is known about it yet except those facts already mentioned. From another viewpoint, pain is one of the most important subjects in all psychology, for through pain and anguish most bodily derangements are expressed. In this manner such troubles are made known to the individual. Also, much medical diagnosis is made possible through the nature and location of pains. Moreover, pain is a kind of personality expression. Some individuals experience pain for which medical personnel can find no bodily correlate. So it behooves psychologists to give serious attention to pain.

There are times when what seems to be rather moderate tissue involvement results in a very distressing personal state. What one feels is out of proportion to what one might expect. It has been difficult to account for this under the old concepts of how the organism functions. But when we realize that in all cases the sensory experience is an expression of the way the central nervous system utilizes peripheral input, we begin to make sense of the results. A quotation from Bishop (1946) is relevant:

> Pain is unique in the degree to which its arousal overflows into affective or emotional protest, although other senses also share this capacity, which may be accentuated or depressed in abnormal mental conditions. Below a certain intensity, whose level varies both with mental and emotional states and under anesthetics and analgesics, pain may be perceived without significant affective reaction. Below the intensity of stimulation required for pain, activation of pain endings induces sensations qualitatively different from pain, as prick, itch, etc., depending on the pattern of stimulation. These non-painful "pains" fused with touch and temperature may contribute to the complex sensations of casual experience not recognized as partaking of the character of pain.

The four specific kinds of distress that constitute the topics for this section are called *headache, spontaneous pain, referred pain,* and pain spoken of as due to *neuritis* (which includes neuralgia, although at times it seems to be partially a form of spontaneous pain). Spontaneous pain, sometimes called *central pain,* is distinguishable from other forms by the fact that its origin does not seem to be in the stimulation of sense organs. In fact, it is attributed to lesions in the central nervous system. Referred pain is still another kind of phenomenon inasmuch as its origins generally lie in the activation of peripheral tissue though the localization of the experience is at some site removed from the point of stimulation. Neuritis involves a form of pain presumably originating from an abnormal condition of the nerve sheath.

Headache

One of the commonest and most distressing forms of pain is headache. All that can be said about headache is based on its distinction as intracranial pain. Nevertheless, the origins of headaches are so complex and so poorly understood that headaches possess something in common with other forms of pain we are discussing.

Headaches can be dealt with from the standpoint of what apparently causes them. They arise not only from malfunctioning body mechanisms but also from nondisease origins such as personal conflict. This is tacitly recognized in the everyday use of the word "headache" as a symbol for nuisance and other forms of personal trouble. Our first task is to discover the body mechanisms that most immediately underlie headache. One of the most direct attacks of the problem consists in determining what intracranial structures give rise to pain.

Penfield (1935) found that the dural sinuses[1] are particularly sensitive to pressure, traction, heat, and electrical stimulation. Disturbance of the middle meningeal artery and its dural branches likewise gives rise to pain. Cerebral vessels in general are insensitive except for an occasional vein near a dural sinus or low in a brain fissure. The skull and the brain are themselves insensitive to cutting and to electrical stimulation.

Regardless of the types of stimulation used, the only forms of experience that can be elicited from within the cranial cavity are pain or pressure. The individual usually calls the experience headache. Pain elicited from adequate disturbance of the meningeal arteries is usually sharp and fairly restricted in locality. Pain elicited by action on the dural sinuses is generally referred to another part of the head.

Clark, Hough, and Wolff (1936) produced headaches by administering histamine and measured both the cerebrospinal fluid pressure and the blood pressure within the cranium. They concluded that the headache following the giving of histamine is produced by the difference in the behavior of the blood vessels inside the cranium and elsewhere in the body. Systemic blood pressure is raised, but the cerebral blood vessels dilate and consequently are less able to absorb pressure changes of the arterial pulse. These mechanical changes are thus left to affect the sense organs in the vessel walls more intensely. The authors suggest that the same mechanism operates when various vasodilators—such as amyl nitrite, carbon monoxide, and foreign proteins—are taken into the body. Clark, Hough, and Wolff found that raising the arterial pressure or lowering the cerebrospinal pressure during headache intensified the pain. Like-

---

[1] The brain is covered by two connective tissue sheaths, one of which is the *dura mater*, generally called dura. Sinuses are pockets or cavities in the organism and dural sinuses are formed at the junctures between the medial and transverse partitions in the dura mater. These dural sinuses are part of the venous circulation system and are thus filled with blood that ultimately empties into the internal jugular vein. The sinuses thus drain the blood from the brain. They represent portions of the dura that would mechanically be most likely to be subject to stress owing to variations in blood pressure and to the fact that they lack the solid masses of brain tissue on both sides as exists elsewhere along the dural partitions.

wise, raising the cerebrospinal pressure or lowering the arterial pressure decreased the pain. From this, it would seem that the adjustments that returned the relationships between the pressures on the two sides of the arterial walls toward the normal balance reduced pain. This seems to be true regardless of whether the vessel walls dilated.

Central or Spontaneous Pain

In most cases, spontaneous pain has been attributed to lesions in the thalamus. Early in the century, Head (1920) believed that the thalamus was responsible for the feeling tone that accompanies visceral and somatic sensation. This doctrine has since become quite widespread. More recently, however, other evidence has indicated that lesions in the spinal cord, cerebrum, medulla, or even in peripheral regions, as well as those in the thalamus, can cause spontaneous pain.

It has been reported that cranial nerve lesions produced "burning sensations" localized along the distributions of the nerve. Certain spinal cord lesions were accompanied not only by central pain but also by vibratory sensations and distorted thermal sensations (cold being called hot). In two cases, without thalamic lesions but with lesions in the parietal cortex, central pain existed. This was associated with the impairment of deep pressure and tactile sensations. In most of the cases reported, spontaneous pain was associated with lesions involving incomplete destruction of the spinothalamic tract.

It would seem, then, that lesions in a variety of locations might be expected to result in central pain. further study may tend to show, however, that although central pain and distortions in sensation may result, lesions in the thalamus result in effects somewhat different from lesions elsewhere.

Referred Pain

We have already seen that in the conditions producing headache, the principle of *referral* (discrepancy between locus of stimulation and locus of sensation), is at work. When the dural sinuses are mechanically disturbed, the pain is felt not in the sinuses but elsewhere. Part of this apparent reference could possibly be brought about by mechanical effects transmitted to tissue distant from the point of application. This is not the general interpretation in these cases, however.

Referred pain as commonly spoken of has to do with pains felt in the body wall when the disturbance lies in the visceral organs.

One of the most marked origins of this form of pain is the heart, as in the production of *angina pectoris*. In this affliction, pains are not localized in the heart but include intermittent pains ranging from dull oppressive sensations to severe intolerable pain about the sternum, often radiating to arms, throat, and face. Many "heart pains," however, have no relation to the heart or its blood supply but are common phenomena in high-strung, overworked individuals and may be related to the vague state called nervous hyperirritability.

The neural pathways for referred pain have not as yet been delineated with satisfactory certainty. Among the routes suggested are:

1. Visceral and somatic impulses may lead into a common neuron in the spinal cord. The combined innervation would tend to make many subthreshold excitations from the body rise above threshold. When this occurs, the location the pain is referred to is the skin and skeletal muscles, for example, rather than the viscera.
2. Visceral afferent impulses may set up reflex actions on blood vessels of muscles, skin, meninges, and so on by causing release of chemical substances or indirectly through vasomotor changes. The ultimate result would then be activity in somatic fibers leading to the cord and sensations of disturbance in the skin or muscles.
3. Visceral afferent impulses may conduct in the reverse direction (antidromically) along certain branches of their axons, either before or after they have entered the spinal cord. The antidromic impulses act on blood vessels, and effects such as suggested in (2) take place. The pain that results is, of course, referred to skin, skeletal muscles, and so on instead of to visceral structures.

Whatever the exact mode of transmission of effects, referred pains are an indubitable phenomenon and must be taken into account in interpreting painful sensations.

Neuritis

Neuritis in peripheral nerve trunks is of two sorts: inflammatory and degenerative. Whatever the disturbances are, nerve tissue is stimulated and the result is pain in the somatic members involved, particularly when there is muscle movement. Some physiologists suggest that since mechanical and vascular influences are involved in the former and chemical and toxic in the latter, a closer study of disturbances of pain, tactile, and temperature modalities might help distinguish the type of neuritis existing in any case. Physiologists point out, however, that most of the pains usually attributed to neuritis do not arise from changes in nerves but rather as referred pain from joints. Thus they may be arthritic rather than neuritic.

Anguish

What began in the experimental laboratory as a cutaneously localized sensation has grown to something far more pervasive and involving the experience of threat or harm. Thus it should be apparent that our terminology has become inadequate to mirror reality. Pain as a sensation evoked by local tactile stimulation at threshold and slightly above is one thing. Pain felt in everyday life is another, for it can be felt when no known stimulation exists and in all cases includes the appreciation of threat or harm. I have already suggested that this be called *anguish*. Anguish then would be the name for the form of personal discomfort localized in tissue as a form of sensation but involving an evaluative (emotional) component and sometimes devoid of actual tissue disturbance discoverable to account for it. This definition incorporates the fact that the discomfortable experience can occur when very little bodily disturbance can be found and even absent when extensive bodily mutilization and injury exist and can occur as localized in *phantom limbs*. Phantom limbs are the limbs that have been amputated but are still experienced by the amputee.

Let us recognize the peculiar nature of the experiences we are considering here by feeling free to call them anguish. Of course, in everyday speech, anguish also has to do with distress completely apart from specific tissue stimulation. The dictionary defines anguish as "extreme distress of body or mind."

Phantom Limbs

Phantom limbs are limbs that exist in perceptual experience after removal from the body. One might expect that once surgery has removed a limb it would be gone as far as sensation is concerned. But this is not the case. The patient continues for a very long time to experience its existence. One of the major experiences is what we have just called *anguish*. Phantom-limb anguish is not exceedingly rare. The fact that this occurs has occasioned much scientific curiosity and some attempts to account for it. That it does exist speaks for the central determination of pain, including the role of anxiety and the like in the matter.

Melzack (1970) says that phantom-limb anguish is more likely to occur in a patient who had anguish in the limb prior to amputation. The pain in a phantom limb such as from bunions can be felt after amputation. Melzack says that phantom-limb anguish continues for more than a year in 70 percent of patients, thus long after the stump has healed and is itself not sensitive or painful.

Sometimes *trigger zones* form. These are spots that when touched evoke intense anguish in the phantom limb. These zones may develop not only in the stump but also in distant regions such as the head or in the opposite limb.

Many things that one might expect to help, do just the opposite. On the other hand, salt solution injected into the tissue around the spine has been known to produce dramatic relief for hours, weeks, or indefinitely once the initial sharp pain produced for about ten minutes is gone. The variety of findings and the attempts to generalize or account for phantom-limb anxiety are legion. We cannot survey all of them.

Placebos

The role of placebos is a pertinent topic here, for they have long been used in medicine to relieve distress and have been quite effective in many cases. Physicians use drugs and chemicals that they have reason to believe will relieve distress. In some instances the use of drugs does not have the desired effects, or the drugs may come to produce undesirable side effects. One of the procedures resorted to is prescribing medicines, which although unknown to the patient, were actually placebos. Such medicine is described to the patient as having curative powers, whereas it really is a neutral substance. At times remarkably favorable results ensue from the placebo prescriptions. Thus the question of how this occurs arises. The result demonstrates that the patient himself or herself plays a crucial role in his or her own relief. Remember, however, this is not "mind over matter," for matter constitutes the only causal system, "mind" being what emerges from body process.

An extended discussion of placebos here is not possible. You are referred to H. K. Beecher's *Measurement of Subjective Responses* (1959), a work easy to read, but written by one of the highest authorities in the area of anesthetics, analgesics, and the like.

"SEEING" WITH THE SKIN

White, Saunders, Scadden, Bach-y-Rita, and Collins (1970) studied the ability of subjects given tactile patterns on their backs to identify three-dimensional presentations (displays). For this they used a vision substitution system pictured in Figure 5.4. It consists of a television camera that can be manipulated by the subject. The zoom lens of the camera can be aimed at any part of the room enabling the S to localize and identify objects and persons. The target area is a back-lit screen on which items can be presented by a motion picture projector or by slides. The material thus projected is transformed and sent to a grid of solenoids (20 × 20 or 400) mounted on the back of a stationary dental chair. There the specific pattern of the visual presentation is copied on the grid and given to the back of the subject as a tactile pattern. Thus a tactile impingement pattern can be given to the blind or the blindfolded.

The presentations given the subjects consisted of a grouping of 25 complex items, for example, such things as a telephone, a stuffed toy animal, a coffee cup. These were viewed obliquely at an angle of 20 degrees from the horizontal. Naturally, the view of some of the items was partially occluded. In this experiment the tactile subjects were able to identify the objects and to describe their arrangements. This, of course, suggested that three-dimensional information was provided by the tactile image. One of the cues for object location in the third dimension was provided by

Figure 5.4 Schematic drawing of the visual substitute system. (Source: B. W. White, F. A. Saunders, L. Scadden, P. Bach-y-Rita, and C. C. Collins. "Seeing with the skin," *Perception & Psychophysics*, 1970, 7(1), 23–27.)

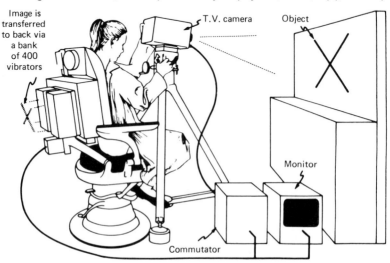

the vertical position in the cutaneous image. Overall, the results obtained were truly remarkable.

More recently, Apkarian-Stielau and Loomis (1975) studied the possible similarity between tactile form perception and visual form perception when the visual target was blurred. This was done by using the vision substitution system described above. The presentations given the visual subjects were produced by a 400-point photic display. In front of this, a sheet of white Plexiglas was placed to produce blur. The subject viewed the target monocularly through strong spherical lenses to produce further blur.

The general purpose of the study was to test hypotheses concerning the degree of a tactile resolution in comparison to the visual as a factor enabling response. Two of the comparisons between tactile and visual response supported the hypothesis that limited resolution in the tactile sense was responsible for its being inferior to the visual sense. But a third comparison did not, and possible reasons for this were offered.

Chapter 6
The Savor Perceptual System

As we all know, the environment contains myriads of molecular combinations called chemicals. The human organism is related to this chemical world in several ways, the most basic being food, air, and water. The organism has ways of selecting between food and other substances, many of which are definitely harmful or fatally poisonous. The two major forms of perception involved here are the senses of taste and smell. These have traditionally been placed among the lower senses relative to vision and hearing, but a more unbiased consideration gives them more significance. These two sense modalities are in a common perceptual system mainly because they are both chemical sensors and because the experiences evoked are often so similar that human perceivers are not always sure whether they are tasting or smelling a given substance, or doing both. So by the logic that has been used in recognizing the other perceptual systems, a single perceptual system is assumed here. It is the *savor perceptual system.*

As a selection system protecting the organism and for a form of appreciation, the savor system is associated with the haptic system already dealt with in the previous chapter. The haptic factors involved are temperature, surface texture, and the consistency of the substance taken into the mouth, as well as shape, bit size, specific gravity, and granularity. Gibson (1966) points out that the mouth is probably more acute than the hands as a haptic organ. The haptics involved include not only the lining of the mouth but the surface and muscles of the tongue, lips, muscles and joints of the jaw. All of these are supplied with receptors and although in separated anatomical regions they are all parts of a single system.

Pure air is made up of about 78 percent nitrogen, nearly 21% oxygen, and the remaining 1 percent of carbon dioxide, argon, and helium and the other "insert gases." Water vapor in the air varies in amount, but never exceeds 5 percent by volume. When some additional substance appears, it is a potential stimulus and something to be detected.

Among animals, there exist several classes of substances to be smelled. These are: substances favorable for eating, others that are offensive, and those that emanate from other animals. Each animal is the source of an unseen cloud of vapor which is specific not only to its own species but to it as an individual. In everyday life the air is full of intermingled clouds of the substances mentioned.These can be detected, isolated, and identified in olfaction. Hence it is obvious that the olfactory sense is of great significance in biological economy.

TASTE

Taste, of course, has to do with the selection and enjoyment of food. It too, has a defensive role, because many things that might be taken into the body are censored by the effect produced in the mouth. So owing to our relation to and dependence on the chemical world for our existence, we have this savory perceptual system.

Beidler (1961) points out a distinction between taste and flavor, which is in line with our attempts to have a clear terminology. He says *flavor* is the experience resulting when material is placed in the mouth and activates the temperature, pain, and tactile and taste receptors. Included, of course, are the odors released during mastication when the gases from the material reach the olfactory region of the nose. *Taste* is the sensations resulting solely from the activation of the taste receptors. Commonly four fundamental tastes have been isolated, but other taste qualities may exist. Some authors speak of water as a fifth taste quality.

Taste Receptors

Taste receptors are located primarily on the tongue and give rise to four perceptual qualities; salt, sweet, bitter, and sour. The areas of greatest sensibility are the tip, sides, and rear of the top surface of the tongue. The middle of the top surface is quite insensitive for taste production.

The receptor organs are called *taste buds.* They are made up of a group of cells, one to two dozen in a cluster. The sensitive cells are spindle-shaped. The receptor cells are constantly degenerating and being replaced by new ones (Figure 6.1). Taste buds are grouped in papillae of four forms: *fungiform, foliate, circumvallate, filiform.* The circumvallate papillae are surrounded by a "moat" into which the taste pores open. The papillae contain many buds.

The gustatory receptors (the cells in the taste bud) serve only to generate the impulses sent to the central nervous system. Nerve fibers arborize and terminate on the receptor cells: these fibers carry the impulses to the brain. Since the receptors change chemical energy supplied by the impinging substance to neural excitations, they are said to be *transducers;* the nerve fibers are called gustatory afferents.

The tongue and mouth are supplied by four cranial nerves. The facial (VII nerve), the glossopharyngeal (IX nerve), and the vagus (X nerve) are involved in the sense of taste. The trigeminal (V nerve) is concerned solely with skin functions; even so, the trigem-

Figure 6.1   A taste bud. It is made up of two sorts of cells: the sense cells (shown in black) and the supporting cells (shown striped). The sense cells terminate in hairs that project into a slotlike cavity or "moat."

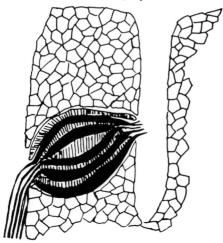

inal is involved in taste, since it has to do with the tactual patterns we have already said are a part of the overall "taste" experience. Taste is not represented in the cortex by a special primary receiving zone (or projection area) with exclusive gustatory functions.

Pfaffmann (1959) stated that it is certain from neurophysiological evidence in animal experiments that taste receptors are not always classifiable into the four basic types corresponding to the taste qualities of sour, salt, bitter, and sweet. Individual fibers are differentially sensitive to substances probably, he suggested, because of functional differences at different places on the cell membrane. Thus the overall resultant pattern of sensitivity stems from a cluster of separate sensitivities. This cluster differs from cell to cell.

Species differences in response to gustatory stimuli have been shown by differences in recorded neurophysiological responses. Afferent discharges were found to be quite similar for HCl in the cat, rabbit, and rat, but marked differences showed up for NaCl (table salt). The lesser magnitude of response to quinine and sucrose may indicate fewer sensitive fibers in the animals. The cat shows the best response of the three to quinine and the poorest to sucrose. This is the opposite with the rabbit, while the rat responds equally well to both.

Since Pfaffmann's records were obtained from nerve fibers rather than from receptor cells, it is appropriate to ask whether individual fibers may serve several receptor cells, each of which subserve different taste qualities. This is possible anatomically, since two or three fibers generally serve a single taste bud. The question seems to be answered by the work of Kimura and Beidler (1956), who recorded from single receptor cells and obtained the same results as those of Pfaffmann. Therefore it is likely that the patterns of sensitivity depicted by Pfaffmann represent receptor cells.

Békésy (1966) concluded, contrary to electrophysiological evidence that taste papillae are specific for single chemical stimuli. Harper, Jay, and Erickson (1966) got results that contradicted this, which they explained on the basis of differences in methodology. O'Mahony (1972a and b, 1973a, b, and c) has pointed out variables in addition to those already alluded to, one being adaptation variation.

Taste Stimuli

In order to be tasted, usually a substance must be soluble in water. Regardless of the physical state of the substance to begin with, if it dissolves to some extent in saliva, the substance is effective. The effectiveness of the impinging substances depends on several factors, such as degree of solubility, concentration, ability to ionize, temperature, and chemical composition. From all the variables we know, there are still only the four elemental taste effects, if we keep to the activation of taste buds.

Common table salt (NaCl) is the standard stimulus for saltiness, and all other substances are compared with it for that quality. Both of the ions (Na^+ and Cl^-) are responsible for saltiness. The chloride ion (Cl^-) can, of course, be combined with other elements and positive ions, such as potassium, ammonium, calcium, lithium, and zinc. All the resulting compounds taste salty but not qualitatively the same, indicating that the positive ions as well as the chloride ion must be factors.

In addition to stimulating taste buds as such, some substances have effects; some are astringents and thus produce *peculiar mechanical effects on tissue and activate the cutaneous sense.* The salts, such as sodium and potassium, are molecularly light. With heavier elements the salty taste tends to shift to bitter. Cesium chloride, a substance with high molecular weight, is sweet. Not all heavy halides (the group of elements that includes chlorine, fluorine, bromine, and iodine) are sweet but tend to be bitter. Hence what we know about chemicals and the tastes they produce does not form perfectly simple relationships.

Sourness is a result of ionization, too. The substances that produce sourness provide acid dissociation and liberation of hydrogen ions. The common inorganic acids such as sulphuric acid, hydrochloric acid, and nitric acid are similar in taste when matched in concentration. Organic acids do not resemble each other completely in their sour taste, and thus it is deduced that the concentration of the hydrogen ion is not exclusively responsible for their tastes. Perhaps such chemical compounds affect more than a single sort of taste receptor and in that way bring about a taste complex.

The stimuli for bitter and sweet usually do not seem to be ionic. Among the most common bitter taste producers are the alkaloids, such as nicotine, strychnine, quinine, and brucine. These seem to be effective in molecular rather than ionic form. The commonest ionic solutions that give rise to bitterness are magnesium, iron, silver, and iodine.

The sweetest-tasting substances are the complex molecules of the sugars and similar compounds used as sugar substitutes, such as saccharine. Some substances are supposed to be thousands of times as effective as ordinary cane sugar, but reactions to them are not as constant and predictable as they are to cane sugar.

There is a close connection between bitter and sweet, as evi-

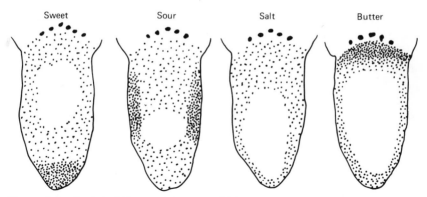

Figure 6.2   A plot of the gustatory sensitivity of the tongue, using Hänig's and Henning's findings combined.

denced by the result of slight changes in chemical composition needed to shift the sensory effect from sweetness to bitterness.

The complex tastes of many substances can be duplicated by combinations of other substances that elicit the four elementary tastes. The salt-sour-bitter quality of potassium chloride, for instance, can be duplicated by a certain mixture of sodium chloride, tartaric acid, and quinine.

Pointlike stimulation of areas of the tongue indicates that sensitivity to stimuli producing the salty quality is greatest on the tip and sides, that sour is better evoked along the sides than at the tip, that sweet is easiest to evoke on the tip, and that bitter is best evoked with the appropriate stimuli on the back of the tongue. It seems that in some of the various papillae there are combinations of the four elemental types of taste buds (see Figure 6.2).

Individual nerve fibers have been found to supply more than one taste bud. Certain fibers isolated in the cat respond to the application of only a single substance, for instance, an acid, whereas two other types of fiber were also found by Pfaffmann (1955). One of these responded to acid and salt stimuli, and another to acid and quinine (bitter). He did not find any responsive to sugar.

Taste Thresholds

Not all individuals taste the same qualities from a substance put into the mouth. In general, there must be considerable likeness, but in some cases there is an unquestionable difference. First of all, some people are virtually "taste-blind" to such substances as phenylthiocarbimide while others taste it as bitter. Insensitivity seems to be inherited. The differences in threshold for the tasting of other substances may be based on differences in the acidity of the taster's saliva. It has been reported that during pregnancy certain taste thresholds are raised. This is often true for sodium chloride and for acid-tasting substances.

As mentioned earlier, temperature has considerable influence on taste end results. The best extensive work on the effect of temperature was performed by Hahn and Günter (1932). Using a particular device, they brought the tongue area under investigation to the temperature of the taste stimulus to be used and maintained there. The experiment started with a temperature of 17° C (about 63° F). Raising the temperature of a weak solution of dulcin (a sweet-tasting substance) caused the threshold for it to drop until a temperature of about 34° to 35° C was reached. At about 36° or 37° C (95° F) the threshold began to rise again, indicating that the sweet taste could be detected more easily as the temperature rose from around 17° C to 37° C.

Sodium chloride at about 17° C had initially a lower threshold than the acid solution just mentioned, but the threshold rose in a virtually linear fashion up to the limit of the range tested (42° C, or 107.6° F). Hydrochloric acid remained about the same in taste-producing effect over the entire range tested.

Quinine sulphate, which at the lower end of the temperature range tested was the most effective of the solutions used, soon rose slowly in threshold, then more rapidly as temperature was raised, and ended at being about as effective as sodium chloride at the upper limit of the temperature range.

Pfaffmann (1951) pointed out that such complex effects cannot be interpreted as simple chemical reactions between substances and taste cells, for most chemical reactions are magnified as temperature rises. Some of the end results just given run in the exact opposite direction. Of the four substances mentioned, dulcin alone behaved this way, and only over part of the range.

The sense of taste adapts quite fully. Adaptation has been studied by Dallenbach (1927) in precise experiments on restricted portions of the tongue. Adaptation is proportional to the strength of the solution used. A large number of salty taste-producing substances tested were found not to interfere with each other in their adaptations. That is, adaptation to one substance of the group did not affect sensitivity to the others. This poses the question of whether there is more than one type of salt receptor. All acids were found to affect each other, that is, to cross-adapt. Certain sweet and bitter tastes cross-adapted, but others did not. A possible conclusion from the failure of cross-adaptation is that adaptation and stimulation are two separate processes. This was suggested on the assumption that there are not as many kinds of salt receptors as salt-producing stimuli that do not cross-adapt. There were 24 such substances in the experiment. On the other hand, if stimulation and adaptation are two separate processes, one cannot deduce the nature of stimulation from adaptation findings.

Taste Scales

Understanding a process is promoted by success in scaling the end result in relation to the quantitative features of the stimulus. Lewis (1948) worked on the scaling of the elemental tastes somewhat in the manner of those who have scaled loudness and pitch of sounds in sones and mels and weight-lifting in wegs. He found that the classical scale units (jnd's, just-noticeable differences) differed in size in different portions of the stimulus scale.

Beebe-Center and Waddell (1948) made cross-comparisons between salt and sweet. This was possible because the subjects were able to select a solution of salt stimulus that would be as salty as sucrose was sweet. The scales for all four elemental tastes were

Figure 6.3   Relation of gusts to concentration of solution. Curve *A* is for quinine sulphate, *B* for tartaric acid, *C* for sodium chloride, *D* for sucrose. (Source: J. G. Beebe-Center and D. Waddell. "A general psychological scale of taste," *J. Psychol.*, 1948, 26, 517–524, Fig. 3.)

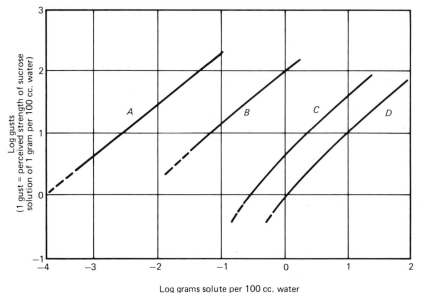

Log grams solute per 100 cc. water

integrated. The investigators then defined the unit of taste as a *gust,* the taste strength of a 1% solution of sucrose. Gusts applied not only to strength of sweetness but also to strengths of sourness, bitterness, and saltiness.

In Figure 6.3, gusts, in logarithmic terms, are plotted against the concentration of the taste-producing solution (log grams per 100 cubic centimeters of water). It will be seen that the strength of taste production of quinine (bitter) is greater than the strength of tartaric acid (sour) and that the acid is stronger in taste than sodium chloride, the standard of saltiness. In turn, sodium chloride is stronger than sucrose, which is sweet-tasting. The slope of the curves for each quality is nearly the same.

Beebe-Center (1949) went further and examined common food substances with the gust scale. The scale data were obtained by the fractionation method There is some doubt as to the full validity of what was used as "half-value." Also a suggestion has been made that adaptation might have distorted the results. Despite these criticisms, the scale, as a standardization, has some value.

Other Psychophysical Studies of Taste

Although not much success has resulted from efforts to relate taste qualities to chemical structure of substances, certain psychophysical investigations have succeeded in scaling tastes such as sweetness. For example, two sweet-tasting substances—sucrose and crystallose—were scaled in terms of concentrations of solutions needed to give a series of jnd's in sweetness between the two substances. It was found that equal numbers of steps above threshold were not equally sweet. For example, a concentration providing for six steps (jnd's) above threshhold for sucrose required nine steps to match it in sweetness with the other substance. As concentrations of the two substances were made greater, the crystallose became relatively less effective than sucrose in producing sweetness when applied to the tongue. This was true also for certain other substances. Some substances increased slightly in relative sweetness as concentrations were increased. Investigations studying the possibility of scaling sweetness have indicated that jnd's for sweetness vary in their magnitude as concentration increases.

Acids are generally thought to taste sour. When hydrogen ion concentration is equaled, organic acids taste more strongly sour than inorganic ones. Strangely enough, all acids do not taste sour. For example, amino acids and sulphuric acids taste sweet. Furthermore, some substances that are not acids, taste sour.

Generally, chemicals called salts, taste salty, but cesium chloride is sweet. Alkaloids are bitter, so are other chemicals such as potassium iodide and magnesium sulfate. In the case of some inorganic salts, taste changes with concentration. These inorganic salts taste sweet in low concentrations and change to sour and salty as concentration increases (Dzendolet and Meiselman, 1967). Some tropical fruits containing no carbohydrates taste intensely sweet (Cagan, 1973).

Foods, Personality, and Status

It appears that tastes (and odors) involve stronger effective aspects than perceptions in other modalities, excepting pain. The four taste qualities are not alike in the direction of their effects, as indicated by strong bitterness being unpleasant and strong sweetness being generally pleasant. Of course, psychophysical findings must be tempered with everyday observations contradicting them, for these sense impressions are open to much variation through learning. It is possible that taste and smell are open to wider variations in conditioning than any of the other sense modalities.

Food aversions and cravings are used for diagnostic purposes in certain modes of professional psychotherapies. High-anxiety subjects have been found experimentally to have a greater number of food aversions than low-anxiety subjects.

Cross-Modality Experiences

Kristian Holt-Hansen (1976) reported on some extraordinary experiences during cross-modal perception. His nine subjects were required to perceive together the taste of beer and a rhythmic sound whose pitch could be manipulated. The acoustic frequencies at which harmony between the taste and sound occurred was noted. Under this condition, the subjects reported that the beer was optimally pleasant. The subjects experienced rhythmic sensations in the head, tickling sensations in the jaws and mouth. Three of the nine subjects reported experiences like those reported by individuals after they had taking such drugs as mescaline, psilocybin, LSD, and cannabis. We can suspect here much suggestibility and thus do not know how the effects were dependent on this factor and possibly the factor of memory images of those times of drug indulgence.

It is possible that numerous studies in social perception could be made by using taste substances as stimuli.

THE TASTE OF WATER

We can say a great deal or can be curious about the taste of water. Commonly, the various tastes experienced in water are attributed directly to something foreign that is in the water.Water is said, for example, to contain iron or sulphur, as it comes from the earth, or something that has entered in storage, as from tanks and pipes.

The question now entertained and studied by those technically interested in water tastes is whether or not some of the tastes are inherent in water itself and may be brought out by various experimental manipulations, such as adaptive effects produced by prior exposure to other substances, for example, NaCl. In the case of detecting NaCl thresholds in water, it may be that the threshold measured is a water threshold. Bartoshuk (1974b) cites the work of several investigators in which this issue has arisen.

Distilled water tastes flat, or as some would say, it is tasteless. All of the remarks we could quote would imply that pure water should not have any taste that one could describe. Water is just a fluid vehicle for something else that may impart a taste On the other hand, when water is distilled and supposedly rendered free from foreign material, it is said to *taste:* to taste flat.

SMELL

Since the olfactory sense cells in the nose are often involved when substances are taken into the mouth, the senses of taste and smell function in indistinguishable combination in many everyday situations. We often ascribe to the sense of taste the functions that belong, at least in part, to the sense of smell. Substances evoking one of the four elemental taste qualities do not alone involve the sense of smell. But the situation is very different when common food substances are to be rightly identified and fully appreciated. The full flavor of butter, fruits, coffee, meats, and so on depends greatly on the sense of smell. It is startling to learn that the individual cannot detect taste differences between raw potato and apple when the nose is stoppered and the eyes are not used. The chief differences are mechanical, that is, dependent on the hardness and textural qualities of the substances rather than on the taste. Many other substances fail to produce their usual tastes and instead provide only weak sweet, sour, or bitter tastes when the sense of smell is prevented from functioning. Substances such as peppermint, onion, cinnamon, all of which are thought to be quite strong in taste, elicit little taste when smell is precluded.

A good substance for gauging three major kinds of effect on oral and nasal tissue is ethyl alcohol. The modalities of smell, taste, and pain can be tested with varying concentrations of this one substance. For example, smell can be evoked by concentrations *20,000 times weaker than needed* to evoke taste. Concentrations three times as great as needed for taste produce a "cutaneous" burning effect.

Smell Receptors

The sense cells for smell are contained in two small patches of epithelium, the *olfactory epithelium* high up in the nasal passages. The cells are not in the main passageways for the air used in breathing. The air must be deflected to reach them. In reaching the receptors, the air is moistened and cleaned of dust.

The substance reaching the sense cells must obviously be airborne and in a gaseous state. Not a great deal of the substance need reach the cells, as is indicated by the fact that only four one-hundred millionths of a milligram of ethyl mercaptan in a liter of air is enough for it to be perceived. While this sounds like a miniscule amount, a single sniff of the air so diluted will contain several million molecules. The olfactory epithelium is so inaccessible that research is extremely difficult.

The matter of methodology has always been a problem in the study of olfaction, and a series of methods has developed. One of the better known devices in the early days was Zwaardemaker's olfactometer. The curved end of a tube was placed in the nostril. A larger-bored tube containing the odor-producing material was fitted over the opposite end of this tube, and a hypodermic syringe leading to a tube reaching to nearly the bottom of the bottle forced a known amount of added air into the bottle. Two tubes leading to the nostrils were held shut by a pinch clamp until the extra air was added to the bottle. When the pinch clamp was released, air went into the nostrils.

Wenzel (1949) used a still different stimulus system. The subject's head was placed in a Plexiglas chamber into which a constant stream of purified air was blown. Odorous material of known amount was added to the flow system so that the concentrations could be specified in molecules per unit volume of air. Still other devices are being used, but those described indicate the most common methods. Wenzel (1973) estimated that there are about ten million olfactory cells in humans.

Classification of Olfactory Qualities

The elemental gustatory qualities are few and definite. The same is not true of smell qualities. Investigators have attempted to discover natural classifications to provide some rhyme and reason to the very complex situation. The oldest classification we know about was made in the middle of the eighteenth century by Linnaeus. It had seven categories: aromatic (carnation), fragrant (lily), ambrosial (musk), alliaceous (garlic), hircine (valerian), repulsive (certain beetles), and nauseous (carrion).

Zwaardemaker (1925) studied odors for 30 years. He expanded this classification, by adding ethereal and empyreumatic as a result of the expansion of organic chemistry with its many new substances. Zwaardemaker also divided the nine classes into a number of subclasses. His contemporary, Henning (1916), during the later part of the Zwaardemaker period, developed a very different classification of only six categories, occupying the corners of a prism (Figure 6.4). These were: fragrant, ethereal, resinous, spicy, putrid, and empyreumatic (burned smell).

The findings that gave rise to Henning's prism ran somewhat as follows. A group of substances that seemed to belong together according to smell were examined carefully for the quality complex that each presented, and a sort of progression emerged. Starting, for example with sassafras, he might have come next to nutmeg, then pepper, then cinnamon, with a seeming progression in spiciness in the order mentioned. But as other substances of this general group were examined, a new quality emerged and the spiciness receded. Expressed geometrically, it was as if a corner had been reached and turned. Cassia, cloves, bay, and thyme seemed to represent a new progression. A corner was again reached, and since there were now four corners and the progression turned on itself to make a closed cycle, the geometrical form taken to represent the progres-

Figure 6.4 Henning's odor prism.

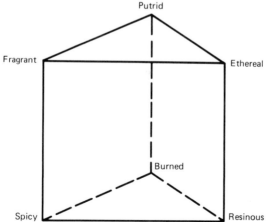

sion was a square. It could have been a rectangle or some other quadrilateral figure instead. When odors that did not seem to belong in the progression, or loop, were found, they had to represent dimensions (or progressions) running off at angles to the first one. Some odors studied did not belong in the surface just mentioned, so the geometrical figure had to be three-dimensional. Henning finished with a five-faced prism along whose edges, he believed, all odors would find a place. Pure odors lying between two other odors along an edge might resemble them but cannot be synthesized by combining them. Experts as well as lay persons have taken some cognizance of this fact.

MacDonald (1922) and Findley (1924) independently attempted systematic investigations to test a number of odors on the basis of Henning's prism. The stimuli they used for Henning's "primary" odors were (fragrant) oil of jasmine; (ethereal) citral and oil of lemon, respectively; (resinous) eucalyptol and turpentine, respectively; (spicy) anethole and cinnamon, respectively; (putrid) thiophenol and hydrogen sulphide, respectively; (burned) pyridine and oil of tar, respectively.

The procedure was to present one standard or primary substance to the observer, then one of the many secondary substances to be perceived, and then one of the other standard substances. The task of the observer was to tell which of the two standards the secondary or comparison substance smelled more like. The report was presumably to be based on odor rather than on intensity or some collateral quality such as coldness or bitiness. Each of the many comparison substances was compared to all six primary or standard substances during the overall procedure. It happened that, even in this attempt to be systematic and orderly, the comparison odors were highly variable in their perceived similarities and tended to be like various standards in turn. This sort of result might be interpreted as requiring the placing of substances *within* the prism instead of only along the edges between the primaries at the corners. Henning had insisted, on the contrary, that the prism is empty and does not contain internal positions representing odor relations to each other. He declared that the prism was an odor prism and not a stimulus prism. Various odors do change—that is, any given substance is likely to be smelled differently from time to time—but this was not to lead to the use of the space within the prism for odor designations.

MacDonald (1922) used only the four primaries contained in the FERS face of the prism, the *f*ragrant, *e*thereal, *r*esinous, and *s*picy-smelling primary stimuli. He used eleven stimuli and asked his observers to place the separate odors where they seemed to belong in the square or along its edges. The comparison stimuli used supposedly had no resemblance to the putrid or burned odors. For some stimuli, the placement could be accomplished but with difficulty. One curious result was that a given odor might seem to belong in the square but not resemble all the corners well. Some odors seemed to lie along the diagonals of the square. Nutmeg and geraniol lay along the ES diagonal, for example, while not always resembling E or S. The logic of the prism would require that the middle of the ES diagonal would also be the middle of the FR diagonal. Anything at this point would resemble F and R. It turns out, then, that the actual olfactory results do not fit the prism either as used by Henning or MacDonald, who allowed the interior to be used.

Substances may smell somewhat the way they taste, once the perceiver realizes that he or she is smelling instead of tasting. For example, substances may smell sweet or sour; others may smell prickly, warm, or cold. This is not surprising, because the nose is supplied not only with olfactory epithelium but also with the cutaneous senses of touch, pain, and temperature. Sharp, prickly, or biting odors obviously involve the sense of pain: ammonia and chlorine evoke pain, whereas menthol stimulates cold receptors.

Woodworth and Schlosberg (1954) stated that the presence of nonolfactory sensations neccesitates the revision of the classification of odor qualities or at least an experimental reexamination to factor out the nonolfactory components. The whole FERS face might coalesce into a single class if pungency (pain sense), freshness (cold sense), and sweetness (taste) could be eliminated. The system of odor qualities might be simplified, or certain fundamental odors that fail to stand out when blended with nonolfactory components might be disclosed.

Hermann (1926) found in trying to use Henning's prism that his observers balked. Some of them declared that the Henning choices as fundamentals were no more primary than certain other substances that could be given other labels. Among the items in this category were camphor and mint.

Perhaps a reworking of primaries would still accomplish the end result expected of Henning's six groups. Actually, all faces would not need to be quadrilateral. Some might be three-sided, some five-sided. It cannot be said that the idea of using a geometrical figure to represent systematic relations among odors (not stimuli) has been tried to the point of logical discard. The idea that all faces need not be of the same number of sides is borne out by the fact that at present some odors have been found not to belong at all to Henning's prism. In Hazzard's study (1930), for example, various dimensions of olfactory experience not commonly brought out were examined. These were heaviness-lightness, looseness-tightness, smoothness-roughness, softness-hardness, dullness-sharpness, liveliness-inertness, thinness-thickness, brightness-dullness, surfaceness-deepness, and smallness-largeness. It was found from Hazzard's observers that spicy odors tended to be sharp, lively, and bright. Putrid odors were dull and inert. Burned odors were hard, tight, and heavy. Fragrant odors were light, soft, and loose. Woodworth and Schlosberg reported that the texture components reported for odors suggest the participation of the cutaneous sense in "smell."

Thresholds: Individuals, and Gender

It appears that thresholds for certain odorants are affected by hormonal state and gender. For example, the threshold for the musklike synthetic lactone odorant used as a constituent of perfume varies in the human female with her reproductive stage and the menstrual cycle. For example, Le Magnen, mentioned in Vierling and Rock (1967), found that most sexually mature women found the odor of Exaltolide quite intense while immature females and all males found it barely perceptible or could not smell it at all. For the mature females the intensity of the odor peaked 17 days and 8 days before menstruation, namely, just before the ovulation phase and during the lutein phase. This suggested that the presence of estrogen influenced the sensitivity, which was supported by findings on women with ovariectomies.

It is common to find that equal amounts of perfume on some women cannot be easily smelled, whereas on others the perfume is quite noticeable.

Even though very small concentrations of *odors* can be smelled, there is no fine discrimination among concentrations. This discrimination does improve with practice. (Desor and Beauchamp, 1974.)

Interaction of Olfactory Stimuli

It is very often said that one odor may mask another. If taken literally, the statement would assert that one sensory experience may mask another. We should remember that a masked experience is no experience at all. It is gratuitous to infer that the masked experience exists but is simply covered up. Instead of implying that there are two experiences, one entirely covered up and the other not, we should recognize that there is only one experience. All this means that two olfactory impingements, each of which produces an experience when operating alone, may, when operating concurrently, interact to produce the experience expected of only one of them. The illogic of common speech shows up in its usual connotations. Something is implied to exist that does not exist. If there is any case in which this does not work, it is sensory experience. Sensory experience, to exist, must be an experience. That which is not experienced does not exist.

When two olfactory stimuli are presented together in time, any one of six results may ensue.

1. Two odors blended together—the production of a single odor having some properties of both and, possibly, some new characteristic—is the most frequent. In what is called a blend, one may detect the resemblances to the separate odors produced by the same two stimuli when they are presented independently in time. Substances that produce end results more nearly alike—that is, in which it is most difficult to isolate one or the other of the two components—produce the best blends. Possibly increasingly precise experimentation will find this conclusion not strictly true in all respects.
2. Two odors are both produced, first one and then the other being the center of attention, when stimuli yielding very dissimilar odors are presented together.
3. Two odors are smelled in alternation. When one odor is presented to one nostril (dichorhinic stimulation) and another to the second nostril, the results are somewhat as in binocular rivalry. Whether this is a compelling result from some basic perceptual standpoint or merely a shift of attention is not certain. Some declare it is the latter and should not be called rivalry.
4. Two odors may be experienced simultaneously and yet separately. They may appear, according to Woodworth and Schlosberg (1954), as a chord of musical tones or as two separate but unrelated odors. Henning (1916) declared that this last result is possible only with dichorhinic stimulation, whereas Skramlik (1925) stated that it can occur with either one or two nostrils. In fact, Skramlik stated that all so-called dichorhinic effects can be obtained with a single nostril.
5. One odor may "mask" the other entirely, an effect already discussed.
6. One odor may neutralize another. This, too, must be an effect taking place below the level of consciousness so that nothing appears in consciousness as an odor. There has not been complete agreement as to whether neutralization can occur, but

the authorities who have declared it possible include those given to careful experimentation.

Pheromones

The olfactory system in some species receives from the environment—including other animals—certain inputs that provide information we have not yet mentioned (Marler and Hamilton, 1966). One form of chemical communicants or signals, is called *pheromones* (from the Greek words meaning "to carry," and "to excite"). These are chemical substances secreted to the environment and passed back and forth among members of the same species by way of special glands or in the urine. Pheromones are used for sexual interactions, for signaling danger and for territorial marking.

While we have no experimental data to offer pertaining to humans having to do with pheromones, we can certainly say that perfumes and body odors are factors of human attraction and repulsion. (See relevant description in *Perception in Everyday Life.*)

RETROSPECT

Here again we have seen, in this chapter, the demonstrations of a perceptual system, where the common everyday results and also the less well-known perceptual end results are products of interactions among a cluster of sense modalities functioning together in a way that merits a single class label. The savor perceptual system scarcely deserves the low status given the separate sense modalities in the traditional outlook.

Chapter 7
The Auditory Perceptual
System

We have just dealt with the human organism's response to certain chemical energies resulting in taste and smell. In this chapter we deal with response to *mechanical* energy in the form of vibration, which results in hearing. In Chapter 8 we shall be discussing a range of *radiant energy* that provides for seeing. Both forms of energy are reflected from surfaces and are thus manipulatable after they leave the sources that generate them. Both types of energy can be focused, and there are sound shadows as well as visual shadows.

This vibratory energy carries information concerning external events. It indicates: (1) their nature, thus permitting identification; (2) their direction; and (3) their distance. The hearing mechanism responds to vibrations made by the individual himself or herself, particularly in vocalization. The hearing of one's own voice, for example, permits the control of temporal patterns of acoustic output. Gibson (1966) calls special attention to the fact that this "vocal-auditory loop" is well fitted as a vehicle for social interaction between organisms.

A number of terms need to be defined. We shall use *audition* as a synonym of hearing; it is a generic term covering all that pertains to hearing. *Acoustics* pertains to the transmission of vibrations in the frequency range resulting in hearing. Thus the first term pertains to response and the second to the impingement or the stimulus for hearing. *Sound* is what is heard. It is not the appropriate name to give the vibratory energy producing sensation; it keeps things clearer to speak of the *acoustic stimulus* or acoustic impingement for this. *Pitch* is a response term pertaining to a quality of the sound heard, which is designated as high or low. *Frequency* is the impingement feature most closely related to pitch. *Loudness* is also a response term and is most closely related to the energy content of the impingement. Thus one can say a sound is loud and that the acoustic input is intense.

THE ACOUSTIC STIMULUS

Within certain frequency limits, any vibratory motion that can be made to impinge on the auditory mechanism is able to evoke the experience of sound. Stimulation most usually occurs by way of acoustic waves in air, but also by way of vibrations in the bones of the head. Acoustic sources intermittently compress and allow for expansion of the air as they vibrate and thus set up the traveling waves that reach the ear.

Most vibration is not confined to a single frequency of compression–expansion alternation but is a mixture of frequencies. All such patterns can, however, be analyzed into a group of simple frequencies, each with its own amplitude, by Fourier analysis. All the component waves that result from this analysis are sine waves (see Figure 3.6).

Békésy (1959) pointed out that there are at least six ways that hearing can be produced: (1) airborne vibrations, (2) mechanical vibrations applied to the skull (bone conduction, (3) electrical stimulation of the ear, (4) electrical stimulation of the acoustic nerve, (5) electrical stimulation of the auditory cortex, and (6) without any intentional stimulation whatsoever. The latter case is exemplified in *tinnitus,* the temporary or chronic "ringing" in the ears.

THE EAR

The ear has three major components—the external ear or *pinna,* the inner ear, and the middle ear, a canal reaching to the inner ear. We are mainly interested in the inner ear as a sensitive mechanism.

The middle ear ends at the tympanic membrane or ear drum

(Figure 7.1). To the inner surface of this, one of the three tiny bones (the ossicles) is attached. To this bone is attached a second, which in turn is articulated with the third, the *stapes.* The overall structure of the auditory part of the inner ear is called the cochlea, a coiled tube of 2¾ turns. The vibration of the ear drum is relayed to the oval window at the base or beginning end of the cochlea. Were the cochlear helix uncoiled, we would have a straight tube. This tube is partioned into three longitudinal compartments, each of which is filled with fluid. Two of these are of major importance in our description.

One compartment, the *scala vestibuli,* is in effect continuous with the second compartment, the *scala tympani* (Figure 7.1), because the partition does not reach the whole length of the cochlea but ends in the opening called the helicotremia. Mechanical effects imparted to the fluid in the scala vestibuli are transmitted, of course, to its walls and ultimately clear around to the base end of the scala tympani. The partition between the two compartments involves several layers, one of which is the *basilar membrane* (Figure 7.2).

Along the basilar membrane there are four rows of external or outer hair cells and a single row of internal hair cells. These initiate the physiological response that feeds into the fibers of the auditory nerve attached to them. The hair cells and the fibers of the auditory nerve constitute the neural portion of the ear. The mechanical disturbance of the hair cells constitutes the immediate event that sets up the process ending in impulses being propagated along the auditory nerve.

Figure 7.1   Schematic drawing of the inner ear. The components significant for our purposes are labeled.

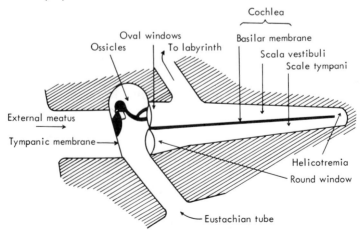

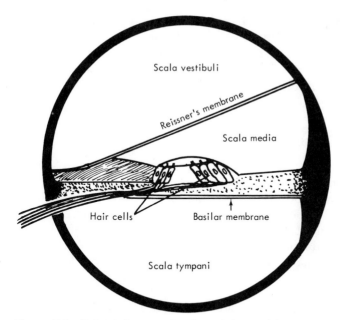

Figure 7.2   Schematic cross section of the cochlea.

AUDITORY SCALING

The Decibel

For measurement of the energy of the acoustic impingement there is a very convenient and appropriate unit called the *decibel*. The decibel is proportional to the general magnitude dealt with. This characteristic is quite appropriate, since sensory reactions are themselves proportional to the energy levels involved. A decibel is specified as

$$db = 10 \log \frac{E_1}{E_2}$$

when E_2 is the threshold energy for activating the hearing modality and E_1 is the energy in use at the time. Both measures are in absolute energy units.

The use of the decibel provides for plotting on the same graph amounts of energy near threshold and huge amounts near the upper end of the usable range. Acoustic sources such as airplane motors and thunder are at the upper limit. Above this range definite discomfort and even pain is produced. The acoustic energies generated in a boiler shop are of about 100 decibels. Those of a busy street in traffic are at about 70 decibels. Conversation is rated at 60, the typical office at 40, and a whisper is probably 15 decibels. These figures sound very unrealistic, for one tries to relate them in a simple fashion to the loudnesses of the various situations specified. The decibel does not refer at all to loudness but rather to the energy involved in the pressure vibrations set up.

The Sone

In order to have a unit that pertains to loudness, Stevens (1936) applied ratio scaling in obtaining the relation between experienced loudness of a tone and the energy that produced it. To begin with, however, a unit of loudness had to be chosen. All sources of the same energy content do not sound equally loud. Some of the higher frequencies sound louder for the same energy involvement. Therefore a frequency had to be selected for use as a standard, and the

Figure 7.3 Curves showing the relation between loudness in sones and the acoustic energy input in decibels. Each curve is for a different vibration frequency. (Source: S. S. Stevens and H. Davis. *Hearing: Its Psychology and Physiology.* New York: Wiley, 1938, Fig. 43.)

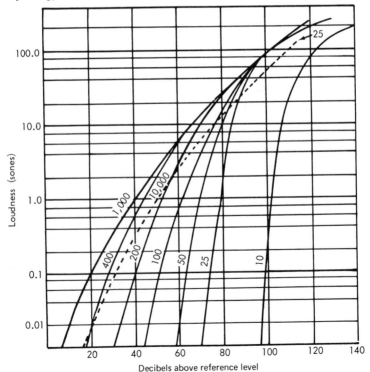

frequency chosen was 1000 cycles per second. With this, a given energy content had also to be chosen. This was an energy of 40 decibels. *Thus a sone is a unit of loudness and is the loudness of a tone produced by a source of 1000 cycles per second and an energy content of 40 decibels.* The sone is simply the loudness heard under such conditions. Two sones are the loudness of a sound twice as loud as one sone. The curves in Figure 7.3 show the relation of sones to decibels. It will be seen that sones are plotted in logarithmic terms. Decibels are already logarithmic units.

The family of sone curves, one curve for a given frequency, shows that when the stimulus has a low energy content, loudness varies most with energy. In the region of 100 decibels a great shift in decibels varies loudness only slightly. The curves for many of the various frequencies tend to converge as loudness increases. It turns out that a loudness of 100 sones is produced by an energy of little more than 100 decibels for most of the frequencies shown.

A scale for Pitch in Mels

In essence, the same procedure was used by Stevens, Volkmann, and Newman (1937) to construct a scale for pitch. Figure 7.4 shows

Figure 7.4   The relation between frequency and pitch in mels. (Source: S. S. Stevens, J. Volkmann, and E. B. Newman. "A scale for the measurement of the psychological magnitude: Pitch," *J. Acoust. Soc. Amer.,* 1937, 8, 185–190.)

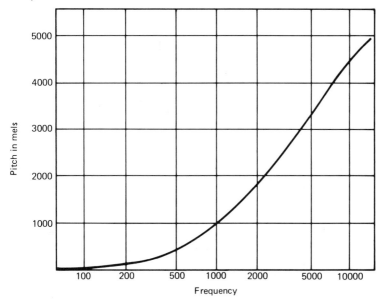

a curve relating pitch and frequency. It will be noted that except for tones produced by sources having frequencies of less than 1000 cycles per second, the relation of pitch to frequency is almost linear. The unit of pitch used by these investigators was the *mel. It is so defined that the pitch heard is 1000 mels when the energy level is 60 decibels and the frequency is 1000 cycles per second.* In other words, a source had to be chosen that was considerably above the one that would produce the pitch unit of the convenient size. A 1000-cycle source was chosen. The pitch heard could not be called one mel, for that would reduce the whole frequency scale to production of a range of only 5 mels. So the 1000-cycle tone was called 1000 mels, and the scale was worked out for sources both lower and higher in frequency, using 1000 cycles as a standard.

Auditory Thresholds

The measurement of the thresholds for hearing at a series of representative frequencies is called *audiometry* and is generally done by use of an instrument designed especially for the purpose. Such instruments are electronic devices consisting in audio-frequency os-

Figure 7.5 Audiogram of a case of high-tone deafness. The solid line on top is for the right ear, and the solid line below it is for the left ear. (Source: S. S. Stevens and H. Davis. *Hearing: Its Psychology and Physiology.* New York: Wiley, 1938, Fig. 20.)

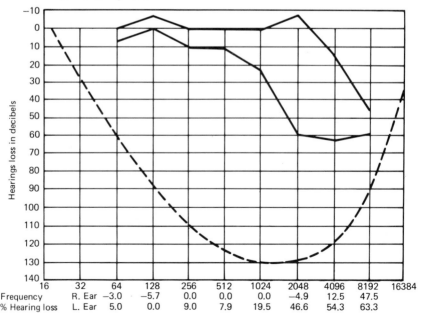

Frequency		16	32	64	128	256	512	1024	2048	4096	8192	16384
% Hearing loss	R. Ear		−3.0	−5.7	0.0	0.0	0.0	−4.9	12.5	47.5		
	L. Ear		5.0	0.0	9.0	7.9	19.5	46.6	54.3	63.3		

cillators constructed to generate eight or more fixed frequencies. These relate to each other as octaves from, let us say, 64 to 8192 cycles. This instrument is calibrated in "sensation units," for which the decibel scale is used; its zero point being the average threshold for the normal ear. The intensity in decibels that the energy at the given frequency must be stepped up above zero is stated as the hearing loss for that frequency. When all the frequencies have been tested, a profile or audiogram is constructed (Figure 7.5). The dotted line in Figure 7.5 is a curve showing the losses defining the "total loss of serviceable hearing." Some large-scale studies have shown that in males age has no impairing effects for frequencies below 1000 cycles but that considerable losses do occur at high frequencies, that is, at 4096 and 8192 cycles. The average loss was about 31 decibels. Females manifest material loss for low frequencies but less for higher frequencies. Curious as it may seem, the sex differences are marked. One feature of this is that men show more frequent partial loss for high frequencies than do women.

HEARING LOSS

Some hearing loss is such that the impaired ear provides for hearing less well at all acoustic energy levels. In another form of hearing loss, hearing is as good as normal for acoustic energies well above threshold. In the third type of hearing loss, hearing improves relatively as intensities are increased but never reaches normal. This is, of course, a case intermediate between the other two. In the first type of hearing loss, it may be assumed that the effects are reduced somewhere in the auditory pathway before reaching the cerebral cortex; this type of hearing loss is the common result with defects in the middle ear.

The second type of hearing defect is as if there was the same absolute loss in terms of sones for all intensities. This would be expected if there was a deficiency in the total number of neural elements involved; we might call it a case of "nerve deafness." In dealing with this sort of deficiency, we could subtract a given constant amount of "loudness." Thus as intensity is increased and the relation between loudness in sones and the decibels of energy in the stimulus shifts, such deaf persons could "catch up" with the normal individual. (Refer to Figure 7.3, which gives the relation of sones to decibels.)

Threshold Differences in Onset

One problem that has both theoretical and practical significance is the question of how different two sources may be in time of onset and still be perceived as beginning simultaneously. Bürck, Kotowski, and Lichte (1935) determined this. It seems that the time intervals involved are fairly similar to the time needed to recognize the tonal quality of sound. In the first source begins long enough before the second source begins so that the first produces a sound whose tone is recognized, then the second source will produce a second tone; that is, two successive tones will be heard.

PITCH

Pitch and Loudness

In our definition of a sone, we recognized that loudness depends not only on energy input but also on the vibration frequency; a frequency of 1000 cycles per second was chosen as a standard. We can now ask what the relation is between loudness and frequency, which in effect is asking for the relation between units pertaining to response and a characteristic of the input. The direct way of answering this experimentally would be to vary the frequency and determine the change in pitch. Since pitch is expressed quantitatively in mels, we would be plotting mels against frequency. But because the human observer cannot respond by reporting directly in terms of mels, experimentation has to proceed in some other way.

One method is to vary the frequency of the stimulus and determine whether or not pitch changes; least change in frequency that will produce a change in pitch can be determined. The result is *jnds*, or just-noticeable differences. If we choose a series of standards throughout the entire frequency range, we can determine the *jnd* at each point, which would provide data for a plot of *jnds* against frequency.

Another way to proceed is to vary intensity (not loudness) and find the change in frequency required to maintain a constant pitch. In Figure 7.6 the change in frequency is expressed in percent. The intensity level ranges up and down from a midvalue. From the figure we note that for frequencies ranging between 1000 and 3000 cycles per second little change in frequency is required to maintain constant pitch as intensity is varied up or down. For higher frequencies greater percentage shifts in frequency are required with concomitant intensity changes. Or, stated another way, as intensity is varied, greater shifts in frequency are produced. For frequencies lower than 1000 the same thing happens, but whereas increase in intensity raises pitch for the high frequencies when frequency is held constant, the opposite happens for low frequency standards. Thus pitch is lowered as intensity is raised.

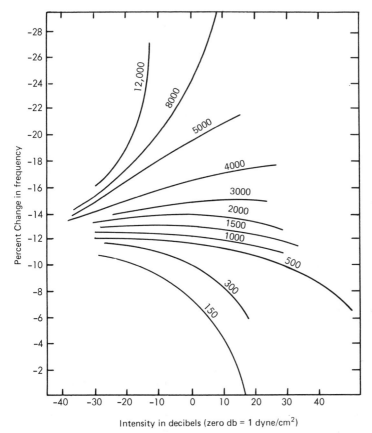

Figure 7.6   The relation between frequency and intensity to maintain a constant pitch. (Source: S. S. Stevens and H. Davis. *Hearing: Its Psychology and Physiology.* New York: Wiley, 1938, Fig. 23.)

Pitch and Duration

When an acoustic source lasts for less than one second, the phenomenal (or perceptual) effect is a click rather than a tone. One might suspect that a click would have no pitch, but this is not strictly the case. Some clicks sound higher than others. The ear acts as an analyzer, even for short acoustic stimuli; thus some clicks sound sharp and others sound dull and lower in pitch. Stevens and Davis (1938) discussed how this analysis takes place. Figure 7.7 indicates the relations Ekdahl and Stevens found between duration of a tonal source and pitch. (See Stevens and Davis, 1933.)

Bürck, Kotowski, and Lichte (1935) studied the relation between the minimum duration of a sound stimulus and its frequency in order for the listener to experience a definite pitch. A source with a frequency of 50 cycles per second must last for 60 milliseconds,

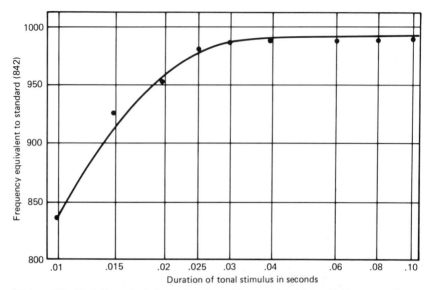

Figure 7.7   Relation of pitch to duration. (Source: Ekdahl and Stevens. Cited in S. S. Stevens and H. Davis. *Hearing: Its Psychology and Physiology.* New York: Wiley, 1938, Fig. 36.)

whereas a source with a frequency of 1000 cycles need last only a little longer than 10 milliseconds. Obviously, the latter source will involve 12 pressure waves in that time, whereas the first source would produce about 3 waves in 60 milliseconds.

Pitch from Complex Wave Forms

When a complex tone is produced by frequencies differing by a constant value of, let us say, 100 cycles or more, the pitch is not the pitch expected from a frequency represented by the mean of the frequencies acting, but rather the pitch produced by a source whose frequency is equal to the constant difference between the frequencies. Let us say that the component frequencies of the complex acoustic source are 800, 900, 1000, and 1100 cycles. Such a source produces a perceived tone expected from a stimulus of 100 cycles. By the same principle, a complex source composed of frequencies of 500, 700, and 900 cycles produces a pitch expected from a source with a frequency of 200 cycles. Furthermore, if to a complex acoustic source composed of frequencies of 400, 600, 800, and 1000 cycles the additional frequencies 500, 700, and 900 are added, the pitch seems to drop a whole octave, namely, from a pitch produced by 200 cycles to one produced by 100 cycles.

This principle was reported many years ago by Fletcher (1934) at the Bell Telephone Laboratories. In addition to these findings, certain very unexpected results in connection with filtering out certain frequencies of a complex sound source were obtained. The common understanding with regard to the pitch produced by a complex source is that the pitch depends on the frequency of the *fundamental* component, the component with the lowest frequency. The other frequencies, being all higher, are called the overtones and are expected to affect timbre but not pitch.

Let us say that the complex source with which we are dealing contains a fundamental of 300. The first overtone will be a frequency of 600; the second overtone will be a frequency of 900. Thus there is a common frequency difference between the component tones, and the sound produced will be a tone that is expected from a frequency of 300 cycles. This allows us to eliminate the fundamental, just as long as the remaining components still possess the constant frequency difference. All this means that, usually, in order to get a set of frequencies differing by a constant frequency value, a wave of this very frequency is one of the components produced by the source. The physical characteristics of the acoustic source are such as to vibrate at a given rate and at any one of several higher rates that are multiples of the lowest rate, the fundamental. If certain overtones are somehow left out or greatly reduced, we may expect a rather indefinite tonal effect.

LOUDNESS

Loudness and Duration

Just as in the experience of pitch, the experience of loudness depends on the duration of the acoustic stimulus. When it is very short, the loudness is at its minimum. As duration increases, the loudness grows, finally reaching a maximum. With further increase of duration, the loudness diminishes to a stable value. This is reminiscent of the brightness produced by a photic stimulus, and therefore helps to unify our understanding of the way the organism operates. According to Békésy (1933), acoustic stimuli lasting less than one-half second are heard less loud than those that are longer.

One hypothesis covering the relation between loudness and duration, stated by Licklider (1951), is the *diverted input hypothesis,* according to which a constant portion of the acoustic input (power) is diverted from the excitation process and therefore is not integrated in producing the sensory end result. The threshold function can be stated by

$(I - I_0)t = \text{constant}$

This means that the impingement minus a certain fixed fraction multiplied by the duration of application is a constant. These relationships apply not only to the absolute threshold but also to differential thresholds.

MASKING

If two acoustic energies of different frequency and different intensity impinge on one ear, the weaker energy may not be effective at all. This is called *masking*. The weaker source may, of course, be made to be heard by intensifying it. *Masking is measured by determining the amount by which the threshold of one acoustic source is raised by the presence of another.* The masking effect extends over considerable ranges of difference in frequency but is greatest for tones of nearly similar frequencies. One frequency will mask a higher frequency more easily than one of a lower frequency.

The language used in the literature has varied and it has not always been clear as to what the term masking refers. Masking may refer to input (the impingement or stimulus), in which case it would be said that one acoustic source may mask another. That is, the listener would hear only one of the two acoustic sources, although it is known that the vibrations from both reach the ear.

Masking may refer to some operation (or activity) in the mechanical or neural mechanism of the ear, in which case it would be implied that one activity masked (covered up) the activity of the other, although both activities would actually be there.

Masking may refer to the sensory experience (the sensation) itself, in which case it would be implied that there are actually two experiences but one covers up the other. It should be obvious that no such result is possible, for by definition a sensation is something experienced. There could be no such thing as an unexperienced or nonexperienced experience.

Wegel and Lane (1924) depicted the various auditory effects of using two acoustic sources, one of which is called the primary source, the other, the secondary source. The primary source was at 1200 cycles and 80 decibels in intensity. The secondary source varied both in frequency and in intensity. Figure 7.8 shows the effects produced. At first glance the figure looks forbiddingly complex, but we can make it intelligible and significant by describing examples of various source combinations and by indicating the auditory results produced.

Let us begin by noting the solid curve at the bottom left of

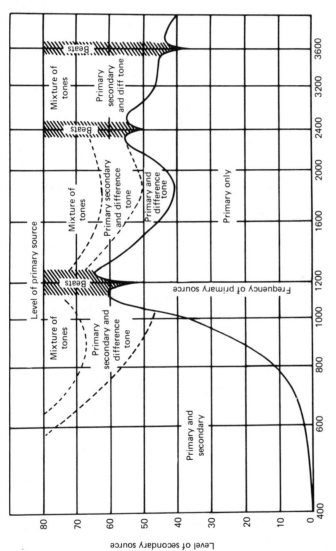

Figure 7.8 Auditory effects from using primary and secondary acoustic sources. The primary source is held at 1200 cycles per second and at 80 decibels. The secondary source is varied both in frequency and intensity. (Source: R. L. Wegel and C. E. Lane. "The auditory masting of one pure tone by another and its probable relation to the dynamics of the inner ear," *Phys. Rev.*, 1924, 23, 266–285, Fig. 5.)

the figure, keeping in mind that the primary source is at a fixed frequency of 1200 cycles, as indicated on the horizontal axis, and at 80 decibels, as indicated on the vertical axis of the diagram. If the secondary source is below 1200 cycles and is increased from a subaudible level to a value that is just audible, it is first heard as a separate tone in addition to the primary tone. The area of the diagram below the dotted line indicates the level at which the tone can be raised and still be heard as a separate tone. When the intensity of the source is raised further, a difference tone emerges, and with still higher intensities the overall effect is spoken of as a mixture of tones. However, if the frequency of the secondary source is close to 1200 cycles, either slightly below or above, *beats* are heard.

A very different effect is produced as the frequency of the secondary tone is raised somewhat above 1200 cycles. Unless the secondary source is quite intense, only the primary source is heard (masking). In the range from 1200 to 2400 cycles, an octave, if the secondary source is raised enough, both sources will be effective. The secondary source will be effective to the extent that it will participate in producing a difference tone. Thus the primary tone and a difference tone will be heard. If the intensity of the secondary source is raised still further, a primary, a secondary, and a difference tone will be heard. With still more energy put into the secondary source, a "mixture of tones" will be heard. When the secondary source approaches 2400 cycles, beats will be set up as in the octave below. When the secondary source ranges from a little above 2400 to close to 3600, the effects are as labeled in the diagram.

Directional Effects

Alexeenko (1970) manipulated the direction of a sound heard by variations in intensity and duration of input. The subjects were given bursts of "white noise" from 5 to 25 *db* above threshold. At first the bursts to each ear via head phones were equal in duration and intensity. They produced a single sound perceived as from straight ahead. After a few presentations the duration of the burst to one ear was either increased or decreased. This caused the subjects to hear the sound as originating to one side or other of the midline (straight ahead). This shift in locus of what was heard could be compensated for by increasing the intensity of the shorter burst.

Relative duration was found to be a more effective factor in the binaural interaction than relative intensity. Nevertheless, the effectiveness of the duration factor in changing localization was found to terminate at 1.5 milliseconds. A masking aftereffect occurred with durations of 4 to 10 milliseconds.

EXAMPLES OF AUDITORY PERCEPTION

For examples of auditory perception, see *Perception in Everyday Life*, units 27 to 32 inclusive.

TONAL QUALITY

Tones, Overtones, and Timbre

The acoustic sources producing single frequencies are called *tonal*. The sources that produce groups of waves that relate to each other according to simple whole numbers are also called tonal. Other acoustic sources are *atonal*, or noise-producing sources. The waves of the tonal sources are of two classes: the lowest frequency is the *fundamental* and the others are *overtones*.

Obviously, there are several primary variables involved—wave frequency, wave amplitude, and degree of simplicity or complexity of the wave pattern. Insofar as a single frequency dominates, the result is a perceptual quality called pitch. The amplitude of the waves, insofar as the waves do not cancel, provides loudness. The complexity of the wave pattern provides for distinctions among tones, noises, and numbers of separate tones heard at once. Tonal sources can be distinguished from each other in terms of the number and relative strengths of the overtones. That is, a violin can, of course, be distinguished from a French horn or an oboe or a piano. This is on the basis of *timbre*.

Combination Tones and Beats

Combination tones are formed by two frequencies being presented simultaneously. Not only are the tones arising from each of the single sources heard, but also the tone that would be produced by a frequency that is the sum of the two frequencies actually generated as stimuli and the tone expected from a frequency that is the difference between the two frequencies of the stimuli. These two extra tones are called *summation tones* and *difference tones*, respectively. There may not only be a first-order difference tone and summation tone, but there may also be second-, third-, and possible fourth-order tones.

When two frequencies do not differ greatly enough to generate difference tones, a third phenomenon may occur. The difference in frequency may generate a low frequency variation called a *beat*, or low frequency waxing and waning of the loudness of the tones.

Consonance and Dissonance

Consonance and its opposite, dissonance, are not generally treated as a quantitative matter but nevertheless they are. When two frequencies are generated at the same time, the listener will hear either a pleasing or a displeasing sound. Some tones are heard as fusing and blending well. Others are described as jarring, rasping, or clashing. Perhaps this qualitative effect is nothing that can be considered stable and similar among all people. Sounds have meaning and can take on new meanings, and it is possible that what is called consonance and dissonance may have some basis in the listener's system of meanings and habits. In our society the frequencies that have long been considered consonant are those having a ratio of $2:1$ (the octave), $3:2$ (the major fifth), $4:3$ (the fourth), $5:3$ (the major sixth), $5:4$ (the major third), $6:5$ (the minor third), and $8:5$ (the minor sixth). The first three are better than the last four; it is with reference to goodness among these ratios that listeners differ even while calling them all consonant. Frequency ratios that are called dissonant are $9:8$ (the major second), $15:8$ (the major seventh), and so on.

Volume

Certain writers have referred to a characteristic of tones called volume. Low tones of an organ, for example, sound bigger and more space-occupying than the squeak of a mouse. Even when two sounds are equated for loudness, the difference called volume persists. Volume is used in another way, too. We should not confuse the two meanings. Radio sets have volume controls, and when volume is dealt with in this manner, it is intensity that is being manipulated. As far as the listener is concerned, of course, it is loudness that is consequently varied.

The property of volume as bigness has been studied by several workers. Volume was first studied as a function of stimulus frequency. Later it was studied as a function of stimulus intensity. The thinking behind these attempts was that if the difference limens for volume are different from those for pitch and loudness, then volume as an attribute of tones is different from either of the other two.

Stevens (1934b) established that volume is a tonal attribute. In his investigation the observer was given impingements of unlike frequency producing alternately different tones of different pitch. He varied the intensity of one stimulus until it matched the other in volume. This procedure established the fact that the two tones could be made equal in volume while being experientially different in pitch and loudness.

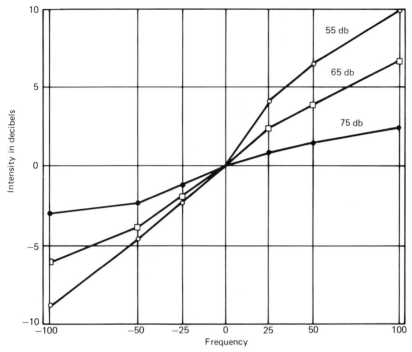

Figure 7.9 Equal volume curves showing how volume is kept constant by manipulation of intensity and frequency. Each curve is for a constant volume but a different intensity. (Source: S. S. Stevens. "The volume and intensity of tones," *Amer. J. Psychol.,* 1934, 46, 397–408, Fig. 1.)

The slopes of the curves in Figure 7.9 indicate that at low intensities the relative effectiveness of intensity is less than that of frequency in determining volume. At high intensities the opposite is true. The graph is so constructed that as the intensity and the frequency of certain sources are varied above and below a given common reference point, shown at the center of the diagram, the equal volume conditions vary as represented by the curves. Stepping up frequency of a source requires that its intensity be stepped up also if equality of volume is to be maintained between the two resulting tones. The slopes of the three curves, each curve representing a fixed intensity, show that this relation is more marked for lower intensities than for higher ones.

Tonal Density

Observers have declared that some tones have a fourth possible attribute, sounding denser, tighter, or harder than others. Stevens

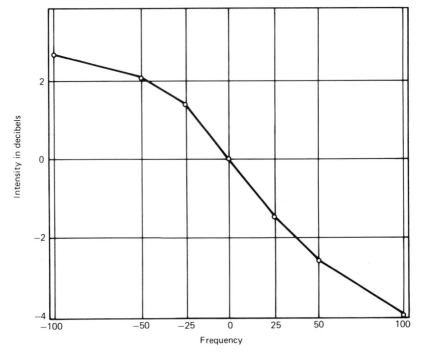

Figure 7.10   Equal density curve showing how a difference in frequency can be offset by a difference in intensity to keep density constant. (Source: S. S. Stevens. "Tonal density," *J. Exp. Psychol.,* 1934, 17, 585–592, Fig. 1.)

(1934a) obtained the differences of two stimulus values that would result in tones that were equal in density but not in loudness. In this way he showed that there was no confusion between density and loudness in the behavior of the observers. Figure 7.10 indicates the relation among density and frequency and loudness. Comparison between this set of relations and the behavior of volume can be made by turning back to Figure 7.9; the two functions run in opposite directions.

Brightness of Tone

A fifth term, *brightness,* has often been used by observers to describe the quality of the tones they hear. Again, several investigators addressed themselves to the task of finding the operations that had to be performed to manipulate the quality that the observers alleged. There is no doubt that many observers find the terms bright and dull to be quite aptly descriptive of the tones they hear. Some investigators identified, or at least closely associated, brightness with pitch.

This led, of course, to the assumption that the two characteristics had a single operational dimension.

Abraham (1920) thought he had demonstrated that pitch and brightness are actually independent by showing that, with a Seebeck siren, tones differing in brightness could be produced by the same frequency. Boring and Stevens (1936) examined the claim and found that the difference between Abrahams's tones was produced by a difference in the proportion of some of the higher overtones present. The observers also called the louder of the tones the brighter. Brightness was thus found to be a function of the combined operation of the dominant wave components of a sound source and its intensity. This does not make brightness a myth but since density seems to be a similar function of frequency and intensity, brightness and density may be two words for the same experience.

Observers can equate two pure tones (produced by a single frequency) in brightness, but they are unable to do so once brightness is declared to be something other than what they were calling density. There just do not seem to be two distinguishable characteristics amenable to this treatment.

THEORIES OF HEARING

The theories of hearing possess two main components. The first has to do with the effects of the vibratory impingement on the ear in a mechanical way. The second has to do with the relation of vibration frequency and the activities set up in the neural part of the ear. Békésy has had more to do with the clarification of the first component, and a series of other workers led by Wever and Bray have contributed to understanding and describing the second component.

The work of Békésy (1947) provides a description of the mechanics of what happens in the ear and demonstrates the fallacy of supposing the actual existence of a set of resonators. The ear accomplishes its analysis by a different method. The cochlear bulge produced at each compression phase of the impact on the oval window is a traveling wave in the cochlea. The bulge for high frequency inputs travels a short distance, produces a peak, and dies out. Vibration inputs of low frequency travel farther (depending on how low the frequency is) before peaking and damping out. Thus peaks can be mapped for different frequencies. This is a *place* factor. But for low frequency inputs the bulge is not so restricted as for those of high frequency. More and more of the cochlea is involved in the bulge and thus the principle of selective effect according to place fades as a simple factor. By depending on this selectivity, one does not explain how the ear provides for the individual's ability to hear low frequencies. Since we know that the listener can distinguish well between two frequencies in the low range, some other mechanism in the ear must be sought either to supplant or to supplement a place theory. This necessity has led to reliance on *periodicity* as a factor. It is generally assumed nowadays that both the place factor and the periodicity factor operate.

The periodicity factor is expressed by the fact that the neural elements, by reason of their own periodicities, can follow cycles of the input by being able to discharge and recover once per cycle. This can be expected to apply to any element just as long as input frequency does not become too high. While the input frequencies are low enough, individual neural elements can respond at the input rate, and thus the central nervous system is provided a differential neural input directly in terms of the neural discharge frequency itself.

With the realization that the maximal discharge rates of neural elements cannot keep pace with the higher ranges of input frequencies, the problem of explaining pitch is not fully solved by the description thus far. Wever and Bray (1930) formulated as a solution what is known as the *volley theory* to account for how the activity in the auditory nerve could be discriminatory although the single neural elements are unable to follow the highest stimulus input frequencies. This theory supposed that although none of the elements could repeatedly fire at rates required to follow the input frequency, one to one, they could fire to alternate or at every third, fourth, or nth cycle of the input. Thus if some fired to one cycle and others to different cycles, a fraction of the total neural element population would be firing at every cycle regardless of how high the input frequency would become.

This theory and Bartley's alternation of response theory describing the visual system's reaction to photic input are in many respects the same. While we can say that the auditory theory preceded the visual theory, the visual research and theory did not stem from it.

The theory involves another assumption similar to the one involved in the alternation of response theory in vision, namely, that the latencies and recovery rates of single neural elements are not totally identical. This variance is a factor contributing to the temporal staggering (or desynchronization) of elements in the overall response just described. (It may be well to point out that the same principle is encountered in the depiction of the tactual and the kinesthetic modalities.) (See Nelson, et al., 1971.)

SOUNDS AS SYMBOLS

Sounds do not refer to objects as directly as visual experiences do. Sounds are often more significant as symbols to the human being than as indications of the existence and location of objects at the moment. Sounds can be used independently of the reference to the world that perception provides the person at a given moment. That is, they can be used to convey ideas that may be independent of the momentary space field and temporal movement. This is not common for most visual objects. Although one may convey ideas by pantomime, it is not often done nor nearly so accurately and easily accomplished. Curiously enough, the communication of ideas by *signs* is called sign language. In broad principle, acoustic as well as photic sources of stimulation are signs.

In this connection it is relevant to point out that the synesthete is a person who uses visual items as symbols in a manner somewhat similar to the way that sighted nonsynethetes use sounds (i.e., words). Blind synesthetes as described by Cutsforth (1951) use visual experiences (or imagery) induced by acoustic stimuli for their thinking processes. Although these experiences are visual items other than written words, they are the blind synesthete's language. We are not certain as to the role and conditions of operation of synesthesia in the sighted person, but we can make some suppositions. For example, let us suppose that for given sighted individuals visual items rather than auditory items (words) are the symbols for their language. They would thus employ vision for their thinking in the way that normal sighted people use words. Sighted people must use vision to get around in their world; they make all kinds of visuomotor manipulations from moment to moment. If they had to use the visual modality for their thinking also, they would be forced into a double use of vision and thus into conflict. Sighted individuals could not well use vision for perceptual purposes relating to space and time concurrently with purposes divorced from time and space. They would have to stop and close their eyes in order to think. Otherwise, what they would need to "see" would not refer to what is taken to be out in front of them, and yet at the same time, they would need to refer quite directly to those very realities—the objects of space and their locations, sizes, and shapes. This difficulty is inherent in a small way when formalized movements such as those in ballet are to be taken as meaning what they do not literally mean when functioning merely as direct perceptions of people moving about on a stage.

In conclusion, then, although it seems in keeping with observation to disclaim any initiating role for audition in the production of perceptual externality, we can conceive for audition the prime role in dealing with abstract ideas. Hearing is divorced from spatial realities or from dealing directly and inescapably with the space domain, greatly enough that it can be used for abstract symbolism. Hearing is so space-free that it can play the role it does. Hearing gives us a mechanism that at one and the same time involves sensory processes with their means of transfer, or signaling, between persons and a relatively space-free tool for abstract symbolism in the parties involved. Vision could not carry on this function as well.

SPEECH PERCEPTION

In recent years speech perception has become of such widespread experimental interest that we shall devote some attention to it here. Although speech is primarily an acoustic affair, it is not exclusively so; lip-reading attests to the fact that speaking can be seen as well as heard. But since we are dealing with audition, we shall confine our attention to the acoustic part of speech.

Since sounds that are heard as speech and sounds that are not heard as speech are dealt with very differently by the listener, it is easy for descriptions of what is called the stimulus to become contaminated by descriptions of the listener's response itself. This is not a new problem for we have met it at every turn in the discussion of previous forms of perception, but it does involve much more complex ramifications than any case met so far.

Articulation

We immediately meet with the term articulation. Sometimes an acoustic product that is heard as speech is called an articulation because the perceiver hears it as something distinctive. On the other hand, articulation is used to describe the vocal processes whereby distinctive acoustic results accrue so as to be heard as speech.

Speech, then, is a form of acoustical input utilized by the auditory system. It is fundamentally a form of energy made to impinge on the ear. However, a description of the acoustic input, stated simply in terms of wave frequency and amplitude (the usual energistic description) is not in itself meaningful for purposes at hand. There must be an additional description of what actually occurs before the stimulus can be appropriately delineated. And this delineation has to do with the category of patterning called *articulation.*

Speech is a two-way affair. It is produced by the human organism as well as perceived by other humans. As the behavior of a vocal mechanism, then, articulation is viewable from two aspects: the motor mechanisms involved and the acoustic vibrations produced. The task for the researcher in speech perception thus is to discover what goes on in the production of what is heard as speech sounds. The necessary vocabulary is therefore a reflection of how the acoustics of speech is produced and a description of the product.

To the layman the units of speech are letters, syllables, and words, particularly words. But to those who study speech experimentally in a fundamentally scientific way, speech is broken into units finer than words, and the various pronunciations of letters become a matter to consider.

Since speech is an acoustical product, it can be copied, modified, stored, and imitated by mechanical and electrical means. With the aid of recorded pictures of the wave patterns accomplished by the use of present-day instrumentation, anyone is able today not only to hear something that has been said but to view the stimulus or the wave pattern of the acoustical product. Such records are subject to analysis to determine their characteristic components and whether what is heard relates in a constant way to these components or human perception displays certain unexpected variants in relation to acoustic patterns. It is thinkable from the very start that some features of the recorded wave picture may be more dominant or more inflexible in their effect than others in producing the perceptual end result. Also, it is possible that the components play very different roles in various sequences.

Speech described solely in acoustical terms would pertain only to the wave patterns as evidenced by instruments sensitive to acoustical energy. This would not in itself tell anything about how these complex wave patterns are produced, nor would it be a statement of the relation of wave patterns to the letters or words that form what we call language. The study of speech perception thus had to develop this relation by employing *phonetics,* the branch of linguistics dealing with the sounds of speech. It includes *articulatory phonetics,* which studies the physiological processes involved in speech production as well as the distinctive sounds that are heard.

Phonetic Alphabets

Phonetic alphabets are not familiar to most people; they have arisen to aid students of various language transliterate alphabets into a standard notation, necessary because certain letters (if not all of them) from language to language and even within the same language have more than one pronunciation (see Table 7.1). For example,

Table 7.1 SOME PHONETIC SYMBOLS

PHONETIC	DICTIONARY	KEY WORDS
f	f	*f*ig, i*f*
θ	th	*th*ick, ba*th*
s	s	*s*ew, ba*ss*
ʃ	sh	*s*ure, ra*sh*
tʃ	ch	*ch*ick, lat*ch*
v	v	*v*ow, lea*v*e
ð	th	*th*is, la*th*e
z	z	*z*ing, lo*s*e
ʒ	zh	le*s*ion, mea*s*ure
dʒ	j	*j*ab, hed*g*e
ŋ	ng	sti*ng*, wro*ng*
ɔ	ô	b*or*der, l*aw*

the vowel *a* in English is pronounced differently in the words *bathe, bath,* and *haunt.* Most vowels have a long and a short pronunciation, and some have others. A phonetic alphabet lists, by use of symbols, the various pronunciations (or sounds) of the various letters and letter combinations of the usual alphabet. A phonetic alphabet therefore is useful material in studying the perception of speech.

A second form of material is the classification that describes the way certain sounds are produced by the vocal apparatus—that is, *labials, dentals, nasals, palatals,* and so on. A third form of material has to do with temporal and intensive characteristics of articulations, such as stops, fricatives, and affricates. A *stop* is the acoustic effect produced by the complete momentary blockage of the breath stream (or implosion), as with the lips or tongue, followed by a sudden release (a "plosive," as in contrast to a "continuant"). In English the stops are *p, b, t, d, k,* and *g;* the nasals *m* and *n* may also be included. A *fricative* is a consonant produced by the passage of breath through a narrow aperture with a consequent audible friction such as *s.* An *affricate* is an acoustic effect consisting of a stop followed by a fricative release at the point of contact.

A way other than alphabets of talking about the material perceived as speech is to define another unit, the *phone;* defined in terms of (1) articulatory processes or (2) acoustic attributes. Classification of phones involves *phonemes, allophones,* and the like. A phoneme is a class of phonetically similar phones that substitute for each other according to the phonetic environment. A phoneme is the smallest contrasting unit in the acoustic system of language acting to distinguish utterances from each other. For example, the English phonemes *t* and *p* distinguish the words *tin* and *pin,* whereas the qualities of *t* in *top, stop,* and *pit* do not function in this manner and hence are all members of the same phoneme. An *allophone* is any of the nondistinguishing variants of a phoneme occurring in a particular context. For example, *k* of *coop* and *k* of *keep* are allophones of the phoneme *k*. An allophone is sometimes called a positional variant.

Another basic unit is the *morpheme* with its variant forms called *allomorphs*. A morpheme is the smallest meaningful unit in a language or a dialect. It is sometimes a word, sometimes a base, and at other times a prefix or a suffix. For example, *boy, egg, pro, -ing,* and *-ess* are morphemes.

Vowels and Consonants

The study of speech perception recognizes the familiar two-division classification of alphabet letters as consonants and vowels, which are different, both as acoustic stimuli and as something that is heard.

Consonants are divided into three classes according to articulatory criteria (Liberman, 1957) rather than on a strictly acoustical basis:

1. Acoustic effects produced by the consonant constriction are fricatives such as /f, s, u, z/ and the bursts of the stops /p, b, t, d, k, g/. The constriction sounds are produced only during or just after the most nearly closed part of the articulation of the consonant.
2. Acoustic effects originating from action in the voice box rather than at the point of consonant constriction. These actions must travel through the entire vocal tract before the result issues from the lips. Unlike the acoustic effects produced by constriction, these are affected by the articulatory movement involved in going from a consonant to the next phone. The first class involves *constrictions;* the second class has to do with *transitions.*
3. Acoustic effects that result from the on–off action of a *fixed resonator.* The nose is a fixed resonator and so nasal resonance is the acoustic feature of the nasal components /m, n, ng/.

Formants and Transitions

A *formant,* in acoustics and phonetics, is any of the acoustic vibration frequency ranges in which the partials of a vowel are strongest and determine its "acoustic quality" or "tone color." A partial in acoustics is a simple component of the combination of frequencies produced by the complex vibration of the acoustic source. Partials are either fundamentals or overtones.

Transitions are the acoustical phenomena produced in passing from consonants to vowels and vice versa. The perceptual effectiveness of the features involved in transitions are so important that it is difficult to exaggerate their significance.

Recording and Playback Instruments

Various instruments are used to record the acoustic outputs of speech (Pulgram, 1959). We shall only briefly describe the spectrogram, one kind of record that makes the essential features of acoustic output visible, picturing the characteristics of vowels and consonants and the transitions from one to the other.

Spectrograms as actually recorded are complex patterns of waves representing the vibration frequencies in the acoustic output of speech (Borst, 1956). They are then transformed and simplified into hand-drawn schematics. It is with these simplified forms that we shall be primarily concerned. No waves are evident in them; instead, what is painted are two or more broad solid bands representing the frequency locations and amplitude coverages of the original spectrograms (Figure 7.11).

The ordinate, or vertical, axis of the spectrogram indicates vibration frequencies of a vocal utterance. The horizontal axis represents time. A hand-painted spectrogram consists mainly of broad lines running from left to right in either a straight or a sinuous fashion. Among the briefest spectrograms are those picturing consonant–vowel combinations such as *bi, ba, bo, di, da, do, go.* In Figure 7.11 there are two lines or bands for each consonant–vowel combination. The lower band represents the *first formant,* the upper band

Figure 7.11   Simplified spectrograms of several consonant–vowel combinations. (Source: P. C. Delattre, A. M. Liberman, and F. S. Cooper. "Acoustic loci and transitional cues for consonants," *J. Acoust. Soc. Amer.,* 1955, 27, 769–773, Fig. 1.)

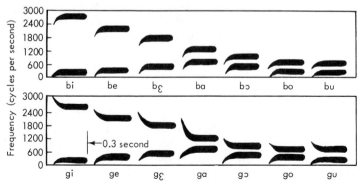

the *second formant.* Some spectrograms show a *third formant.* (A formant, it will be recalled, is a frequency range in which the partial or component frequencies of the overall output are strongest.)

In addition, note in the figure that the bands begin at single points and spread quickly into band widths. The beginnings of the bands thus represent what we have already defined as one class of consonants—the stops (called stops because the air stream is momentarily obstructed.) It is also evident that the formants for one consonant linked with each of several vowels are different and that the transitions are likewise different.

Another instrument in speech study is a device whereby a spectrogram can be used to produce an acoustic output, providing a playback. This instrument can utilize synthetic spectrograms or actual spectrograms that have been altered in certain ways so as to determine the effects of omissions or variations in the features already discussed. For example, a portion of the spectrogram representing the *b* part of *bi* can be spliced onto a portion representing an *a*. The consequent spectrogram is not heard as *ba* but instead is totally unrecognizable. In general, this procedure has one of two possible results: The result is either unrecognizable or the consonant becomes another consonant.

Speech study by such instruments thus becomes the analysis of the various components in the acoustic records to see how they function in providing the listener with the information found in spoken language. Some parts of the acoustic output are critical and emphatic for this purpose, others not nearly so much.

Some Findings in Speech Perception

Liberman, Delattre, and Cooper (1952) made experimental modifications in spectrographic displays and played them back as acoustic stimuli. These investigators found that they could produce reasonably intelligible sentences from greatly simplified spectrograms, affording a basis for additional study into stimulus essentials for individual units, whether phonemes, syllables, or words. They demonstrated that the irreducible acoustic stimulus is the pattern corresponding to the consonant–vowel syllable.

Liberman, *et al.* (1956) found among their other results that the transition tempo is enough to distinguish the stop consonant *b* from that semivowel *w* in connection with a number of vowels. The two factors considered in transition are rate and duration. The various vowels tested with regard to rate are not nearly so similar as when tested for duration. The authors concluded that duration was the potent factor of transition that they had been calling tempo.

Liberman, *et al.* (1961) measured various durations of silence involved within a speech sequence in which the variable elicited a phonemic distinction. When the same variable was used in a non-speech acoustic output, no distinctions were found. In the speech example the duration of silence divided two syllables of a synthesized word: the word heard was *rabid* when the silence was short and *rapid* when the silence was long. With acoustic factors equal, discrimination was more acute between *b* and *p*—that is, in *crossing* the phoneme boundary—than *within* either phoneme category. This tallied with the extreme assumption that listeners could hear these inputs only as phonemes, not discriminating any other differences between them.

With the nonspeech presentations, although the same durations of silence separated two acoustic bursts, matching the onset, duration, and offset characteristics of the speech signals, discrimination did not show any appreciable increase in the region analogous to the phoneme boundary. The discrimination of nonspeech inputs was also poorer than that of speech.

Assuming that the responses obtained with the nonspeech inputs represent the basic discriminability of periods of silence not influenced by linguistic training, one supposed that the peaks of discrimination in the responses to speech inputs stem from learning in perception. Learning was believed to serve to increase discrimination *across* phoneme boundaries.

O'Conner, *et al.* (1957) found that the direction and extent of second-formant transitions are potent factors for the listener in distinguishing with stop *(p, t)* and nasal *(m, n)* consonants. The same variables likewise operate in other consonant groups such as *w, j, r,* and *l.* Second-formant transitions are to some extent influenced by transitions of the third formant. First-formant transitions also help to distinguish among the stops, nasals, liquids, and semivowels. A liquid consonant *(l, r)* is formed without the usual friction in the vocal apparatus, making the consonant somewhat vowellike. A semivowel is a vowellike sound, such as *y, w,* and *r,* used as a consonant; these are also called *glides.*

Variations in duration and direction of second- and third-formant transitions provide for the perception of various consonants depending on the place (the frequency level) of production. Such variations in the first formant provide for the manner of hearing.

There are typical loci at which formant transitions begin or to which they are assumed to point. Thus transitions are movements of formants from their loci to frequency levels appropriate for the phone that follows.

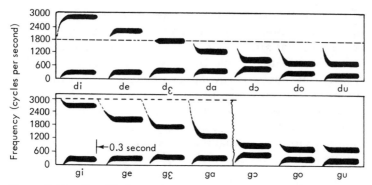

Figure 7.12   Simplified spectrograms representing the relation of various acoustic and articulation effects. (Source: A. M. Liberman. "Results of research on speech perception," *J. Acoust. Soc. Amer.,* 1957, 29, 117–123, Fig. 3.)

Proprioceptive Elements in Speech Perception

Liberman (1957) pointed out that the correspondence between articulation (a motor aspect of speech production) and the acoustic effect is not always one to one. When articulation and the acoustic effects "go their separate ways" (do not correspond), it may be asked which way the perception goes. Liberman says that the perception goes with the articulation.

Figure 7.12 shows the various transitions in the second formant of *d* and *g* needed to precede each of several vowels. In the case of *d* the direction and extent of the second formant changes with the vowel involved. Despite this, the perception of the consonant is always the same; the listener always hears *d*. The one feature of the acoustic basis for *d* that is constant in all cases is the locus of the *d* transitions for the various vowels; they all seem to originate from the same frequency, 1800 cycles per second.

The situation is different for *g*. The consonant makes a larger transition to the vowel as the vowels are varied from *i* to *a*. The locus, however, is always around 3000 cycles per second for some of the vowels. But for *go* it suddenly changes. This means that acoustically there is a real discontinuity in the acoustic product. Liberman states that he has not been able to find anything in acoustics by which to explain why *g* always sounds like *g* despite this sudden shift of locus.

This example and others suggest to Liberman that speech is perceived in reference to articulation. He suggests that articulatory movements and their sensory results mediate between the acoustic input and the end result called perception. In the extreme and traditional form of this view it is supposed that we overtly mimic the incoming speech sounds and then react to the proprioceptive and tactile stimuli that are produced from such articulatory movements. Liberman says that while this position is totally untenable, he believes the reference to articulatory movements and their sensory results must somehow take place in the brain without passing into the peripheral mechanisms. The question in connection with speech learning is not whether learning occurs but how it occurs. The answer seems to be that what is learned is a connection between acoustic inputs and certain articulatory processes in the listener.

Perceptual Restoration of Speech Sounds

When an acoustic input extraneous to those for speech occurs somewhere during a perceived speech vocalization and replaces a missing portion of the vocalization, the listeners "hear" the missing portion as if it occurred. Stated differently, if a cough, for example, occurs during a recorded sentence in which a word is missing, it is heard as though it were included. It does not seem to matter where during the sentence the cough occurs; the sentence is heard as being complete. However, if silence replaces a speech sound, the absence of the sound is perceived. Several investigators have reported this. (Ladefoged and Broadbent, 1960; Bever and Lockner and Kirk, 1969; Warren and Warren, 1970; Warren, 1970.)

This sort of paradoxical hearing is not the only example. Warren, Obusek, and Acknoff (1972) report impingement–response relations that are equally puzzling and actually important for people in general to know about. It is common, particularly among the older adult population, for people to misunderstand each other. One will declare that the other did not say such and such, while the speaker declares he or she did. Or the total pattern of what is uttered gets perceived clear out of context, with the result that such people tend to *blame* each other, or mistrust later declarations of what was said.

The above authors showed that it is not only speech sounds that can be "heard" when not present. They say that at least two other types of "perceptual synthesis" can be grouped as cases of what they want to call auditory induction (AI).

They discovered one of these by testing what was heard with a sequence of three levels of intensity of the same "sound," for example, when a 2000 Hz band input was presented through headphones at three levels of intensity. For instance, they used 60, 70, and 80 *db* above 0.0002 µbar, each of the levels lasting for 300 milliseconds. This sequence was repeated without pause, with the result that the weakest of the three inputs appeared to be *continuous*, that is, coexisting with the other two louder sounds.

A Theory of Speech Perception

Liberman, et al. (1962) have suggested a theory of speech perception based on a number of facts and requirements, the first of which is that the elements of a phonemic system must be identifiable in absolute terms. This means not that identification is perfect and the listener will make no mistake but that he or she will hear one phoneme or another at a given instant and not some sort of intermediate sound. For instance, the phoneme *b* must be heard as *b*, not as merely something more or less like *b* than the last sound heard. A second requirement is that the phoneme must accomplish its task quickly, although we do know that at times recognition is delayed.

The distinctiveness manifested in speech perception is not inherent in the acoustic input itself, as is shown by the kinds of responses obtained in comparing speech and nonspeech inputs. Acuteness in discrimination is shown only in response to the inputs heard as speech. The distinctiveness of response emerges at phoneme boundaries in spite of the fact that the acoustic signals (or inputs) for the stop consonants lie on a continuum. This poses the question of whether these peaks of discrimination are an inherent feature of the perceptual machinery or whether they are the result of learning. The answer at present seems to assign the responsibility to learning.

An examination of the way learning takes place has led to the belief that the articulatory mechanisms—motor mechanisms of the vocal apparatus—are involved and are a definitive factor in making the response to speech signals uniquely effective. It is recognized that response to speech inputs is quick. Hence all incoming signals cannot be "tried out" by articulatory mimicking before speech recognition actually results. Liberman and his colleagues, calling their theory a motor theory, attempt to obviate this and act in accord with the learning brought about by the feedback from the vocal machinery on previous occasions. It is apparent that this requirement is not yet well accomplished, being a most subtle task.

These theorists do try to take advantage of experimental evidence, for example, the fact that the correspondence between phonemes and articulation is more nearly one to one than that between phonemes and acoustic inputs themselves. That is, when articulatory "matching" responses are made by trying to mimic the sounds heard, the neural feedback from the articulatory movements is more distinctive than the acoustic inputs.

Liberman and his co-workers recognize a distinction between articulators (vocal mechanisms) and the neural commands needed to activate them. So they attempt to conceive of how the brain uses the results of learning without the use of actual articulation in the listening process, which is much more difficult than to conceive of how articulation by way of mimicking is brought into learning to sharpen the acuteness of speech production as trial and error proceeds. The problem here is not wholly unlike the problem posed in social perception in explaining the perceiver's ability to discriminate tabooed items from socially acceptable ones and to manifest a higher threshold for one class of items than the other. It seems fortunate, however, that the authors have seen fit to try to take into account the motor system in perceptual response.

REMARKS ABOUT PARTIAL DEAFNESS

In the first part of the chapter the usual textbook concerns about auditory perception, such as pitch, loudness, absolute threshold, masking, and the like were discussed. The second part described the way speech perception is studied.

However, what was said about speech was given in a technical vein, perhaps without due concern for providing the reader with a down-to-earth outlook or understanding of what is involved in hearing and what may be involved in partial deafness. Undoubtedly, the fullest understanding includes a detailed knowledge of how the hearing mechanism operates, but an understanding of hearing that is lacking among people in general can be given far short of this intimate detail. I say this because it seems that the common notion is that hearing deficiency consists in the inability of the hearer to detect *weak* inputs, on account of the weakness alone.

Those who have studied speech perception are aware of several factors in addition to the sheer energistic factor of input intensity that impair hearing. A discussion of these as well as of intensity follows.

1. The intensity factor is usually represented in the audiogram that is given in testing partial deafness. The common range of vibration frequencies runs from 20 to about 20,000 per second. Tests for hearing loss for frequencies within this range provide for picturing a curve called the audiogram. In aging, for example, the threshold intensities for certain

portions of the range rise. But this sort of departure from normal is not the only one.

2. The slowdown in the processing rate of the input is the second factor. Remember, what one is given is not an instantaneous, extremely brief signal, but something extended in time and varying throughout that time course. Although the overall input extends in time, the variations within the signal come and go very quickly. The processing has, in effect, to keep pace.

3. The variations in input may be of normal magnitude, or the speaker may "mumble." Those persons deficient in hearing ability may not tolerate these variations being less than normal. That is, they require maximal *articulation.*

4. Speech is an acoustic pattern or figure on a ground. The ground may be an energistically dead one, what listeners call *silence,* or it may involve (a) reverberation, that is, echoed or reflected inputs from the speech source and/or (b) inputs from other sources. These sources may become garbled with the first or may become dominant and therefore be the figure itself. Thus the intended signal gets lost.

5. The preoccupation of the potential hearer may actively preclude utilization of the signal, or it may be a strong bias in what is being produced by the signal. In such a case the hearer hears something that he or she considers sensible but may later see that it does not fit the context in which he or she intellectually involved.

6. The overrecruitment, or a kind of inherent bias in processing, may be involved. To understand this requires a knowledge of the way nerve circuits function.

While the foregoing list may not include all the terms that various workers have used to describe the inappropriate features of speech production and overall signal input and the inadequacies of the hearer or listener, they do help to show why shouting at a deaf person will not always be successful.

Chapter 8
The Visual Perceptual System

The visual perception system, like the other perceptual systems, constitutes a complex mode of interacting with the environment. Photic radiation (light) is the form of energy that is central for this system. How the eye, and the central nervous system, use photic inputs is of first concern, while why the world appears as it does is the ultimate concern. No other perceptual system relates to the environment in the same way as the visual. Through the visual perceptual system we are aware of a whole space domain that entirely surrounds us and that does not have to be apprehended bit by bit in the same way the environment is explored by the tactile sense in haptic perception.

Audition gives us a space world, too, whereby objects (sound sources) are localized and identified, but sound under special circumstances only can be said to fill all space around us at any one instant. However, sound provides for greater immediate symbolism and for emotional effects associated with it than vision. But vision provides for concreteness and experience of reality in its own way. In this chapter we want to discover the ways and means of how the visual perception system deals with energistic data and the information extracted from that data.

We shall discuss representative facts from the vast array on hand, which fall into several main categories: (1) structure of the eye and image formation in general, (2) photometry, (3) visual acuity, (4) visual acuity targets, (5) factors affecting visual acuity, (6) intensity effects, (7) local spatial effects, (8) temporal effects that are given under labels such as masking, metracontrast, inhibition, and effects called adaptation, (9) spectrum, color system and color experience, (10) nature of and effects from intermittent stimulation, and (11) effects of eye movements. The role of vision in space perception will be covered in Chapter 12.

From here on throughout the text it may become apparent that material will often have some aspects that could well be discussed within one or more of the other chapters. This is unavoidable: Nature is not compartmentalized but is a unity.

Although workers in experimental vision laboratories do not mainly study the same factors that are the primary concern of the opthalomologic and optometric clinics, we should begin by remembering that all people are not alike as far as the optical features of their eyes are concerned. Thus there are nearsighted (myopic), farsighted (hyperopic) and oldsighted (presbyopic) individuals. The eye is an image-forming (focusing) mechanism and the distance range for some people is from a little beyond arm's reach inward; for others, from beyond arm's reach outward; and still for others, the range is small and good image formation at any distance is poor.

THE STRUCTURE OF THE EYE

The eye is a hollow sphere held in position and moved by tissues around it. The movers (posturers) are the extrinsic muscles. The sphere is filled with liquids called humors. The photic input enters the eye through a window called the pupil, whose diameter varies roughly from about 2 to 8 millimeters depending on illumination levels and the intentional and emotional state of the individual. The inside back wall of the eye is the *retina*, the neural part of the eye (a kind of miniature "brain").

The retina is composed of several layers of cells, in one layer of which are the receptors (rods and cones). Figure 8.1 is a simplified schema of the retinal layers. The actual retinal is very much more complex. When the eye is directed toward a source of photic input (an "object"), the rays along the "line of regard" fall on the center of the retina, the *fovea,* a region made up of cones only. Surrounding the fovea, the retina contains both cones and rods. Further toward

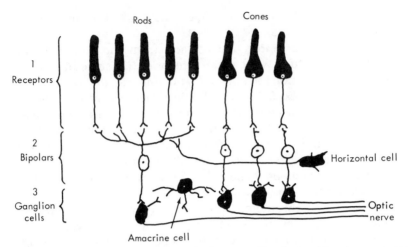

Figure 8.1   Principal elements of the human retina. Layer 1 involves receptors, layer 2 the bipolars, and layer 3 the ganglion cells. These constitute the three-unit chain to the lateral geniculate body and cortex. Other cells in the retina interrelate some cells laterally.

the peripheral, there are rods alone. The optic nerve entering the eye produces a disklike area called the *optic disk*. This is the region that does not contain rods or cones and that gives rise in vision to a *blind spot*.

The cones are sensitive to high, medium, and low-medium levels of photic radiation. The other receptors, called *rods*, are sensitive not only to high levels but to very low levels as well. Each group of receptors has other distinguishing characteristics. For instance, the two kinds of cells are not equal in speed of reaction. The cones respond differently to various parts of the spectrum and form the basis of our ability to see various hues and saturations. Rods do not possess this property. But these elements alone do not account for the neural activity that is conducted from the eye to the brain. Part of the eye is a complex neural system involving convergence, divergence, inhibition, and other processes characteristic of masses of neural tissue.

The receptor layer (rods and cones) is the first layer of the retina's responsive tissue, the layer acted on by photic radiation. The cells in this layer form the first in a chain of three (Figure 8.1). The second type of cell in the chain is the *bipolar*. The third is the *ganglion*. The axons of ganglion cells are fibers that constitute the optic nerve. Note from the figure that the axons of several bipolar cells converge on a single ganglion cell. This means that there are more receptors than fibers in the optic nerve. All the neural processes that occur in the eye are not yet known, but it is certain that neural effects converge and diverge and that the overall temporal grouping of impulses sent up the optic nerve is a result of considerable interaction in the eye. The eye plays a role in determining many of the basic features of vision.

In addition to the elements mentioned, which form an ongoing chain, there are cells directed at right angles to this chain that participate somehow in these interactions. Among these are the *horizontal cells* and *amacrine cells.* There are still others, the functions of which have not traditionally been thought of as neural, but in regard to which more recent evidence seems to point toward active participation in forming the neural message conducted to the visual cortex.

The Duplicity Theory

The duplicity theory, proposed by Schultze (1886), by von Kries (1895), and then by Parinaud (1898), details the roles played by the rods and the cones and indicates how these receptors differ and account for a number of well-known features of visual sensation. The different activities of the two kinds of receptors is reflected in the quantitative characteristics of many visual end results. At high luminances, cones provide for both color vision and seeing fine details (high visual acuity). Rods, acting at lower luminances, provide for vision without color.

Two different variables figure mainly in differentiating between rod and cone function. We have already mentioned luminance; the other is retinal position. It is known that the retinal distribution of the rods and cones differ. The cones alone populate the very central area of the retina, the fovea (a circular patch subtending about 1.5° (degrees) in the human eye). As areas progressively farther from the fovea are reached, the density of distribution of cones tapers off rapidly for the first 10°. From there on the density is almost uniform but is much lower than the population density of the rods. The rods, on the other hand, begin only at the border of the fovea and from there rise in population, so that from there outward there are many more rods per unit area than cones. Outward from about 10° the rod population density is nearly constant. Thus if the experimenter wants to study cone function, he or she uses targets whose images lie only in the fovea. If rods and cones are to be studied, the experimenter can move outward; for rod function study, low luminances can be used. Many manipulations on such bases have been made over the past nine decades, and the characteristics of rod and cone function have been disclosed from the results.

There are five major visual functions among those that display differences between rod and cone function. The first is adaptation, shown in the work of Hecht, Haig, and Chase (1937). The next is intensity discrimination in the work of Steinhardt (1936). The third is differences in critical flicker frequency (CFF) as demonstrated by Hecht and Verrijp (1933). The fourth and fifth functions are color vision and visual acuity.

PHOTIC RADIATION

Luminance, Radiance, and Brightness

The peculiar relation between the energistic features of photic radiation, the response of the visual system, and the ultimate response of the organism as a seeing person must be understood both to fully appreciate sight and to do basic work in visual perception. To begin with, we shall abandon the term *light* as the name of the energy that effectively stimulates the eye. We shall, instead, call it *photic radiation* and use the word light to indicate what one sees. There is no simple relation between amounts of photic radiation and the intensity of the visual experience we call *brightness*. Photic radiation is regarded as a wave phenomenon, composed of a combination of many wavelengths. The total of the combination is called a *spectrum*. Not all parts of the spectrum (not all wavelengths) are equally effective in producing brightness. Hence the first step toward defining the relation of photic input to the eye and describing the ultimate sensory result is to determine the relative effectiveness of all parts of the spectrum.

One way is to select a wavelength or a very narrow band of wavelengths as a reference. Other wavelengths are then compared by using a bipartite target in which one half is this reference source and the other half is the wavelength or narrow band of wavelengths to be compared to it. The energy level of the comparison half of the target is adjusted until the two target halves look equally bright. This principle of comparison is continued until all parts of the spectrum have been examined, providing a set of measures of the relative amounts of energy for all parts of the spectrum that will produce equal brightness. The part of the spectrum requiring the least energy for producing the brightness involved in the comparison is taken as unity. All other parts of the spectrum, being less effective, are assigned various values all less than unity. Once this conversion to values has been made, a curve can be plotted, as in Figure 8.2, called a *luminosity curve*. *Luminance* is defined as the ability of photic radiation to produce brightness. It used to be known as photo-

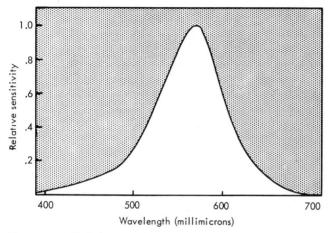

Figure 8.2   Relative sensitivity of the human eye to various parts of the spectrum.

metric brightness or simply brightness, but this confused the result with the cause, the input with the response.

Thus we have photic radiation in purely energistic terms, called *radiance,* and in terms of its ability under standard conditions to produce brightness; *luminance.* But this still does not tell the whole story, for seen brightness depends not only on photic energy per unit area applied to the retina but also on a number of other factors— such as the state of adaptation of the eye, the amount of retinal area involved in the image, the shape of the target, and the input to other parts of the retina, as well as the part of the spectrum involved. The psychologist's or the psychophysicist's job is to determine by experiment what the various factors are and to what extent they determine brightness.

Conditions for obtaining luminance are made as simple and as fundamental as possible. The two halves of the bipartite target are of equal size and shape. The duration of presentation is the same for both. Only a matching of brightness is required and this does not imply a measurement of absolute brightness but is simply a procedure for comparing various parts of the spectrum. Subjects with normal response (normal color vision) to all parts of the spectrum are used.

A step beyond designating *radiance, luminance,* and *brightness* can be taken, a procedure whereby a unit of brightness is chosen and the relation between a luminance scale and a brightness scale is ascertained. Brightness units have been called brils, but brils have not yet come into wide use: their existence as a theoretical and experimental achievement is important, however.

The unit of radiance is the *watt per steradian per square centimeter,* which is a little difficult to comprehend unless one works in photometry. It is mentioned here only to indicate that photic radiation can be measured in *watts,* a familiar energy unit in the everyday measurement of electricity. Luminance is measured in *candles per square foot* (or square meter or square centimeter or square inch or the like) or in *millilamberts* or in certain other units.

PHOTOMETRY

There are two ways of measuring effectiveness of the photic impingement: photometry and radiometry. In general, *photometry* is a procedure in which a human observer makes instrumental comparisons between an established standard intensity and the stimulus whose intensity is to be determined. There are other procedures for measuring intensity, in which an instrument not involving human observation is acted on by photic radiation and gives a quantitative reading. The "electric eye" or "photocell" is no doubt a familiar object. An application of the principle involved in the photocell can be used to measure photic radiation quantitatively. Photocells are somewhat selective in their sensitivity to the different wavelengths involved in ordinary photic radiation; some of them are very much like the eye in this respect, and for some purposes this is an advantage. For other purposes, however, it is a disadvantage, as when we wish to know the total energy in the impingement or stimulus without regard to wavelength. Measuring photic impingements without the intervention of a human observer is known as radiometry, and the instruments used are called radiometers.

The Photometer

You will have a much better idea of how photic radiation is usually measured if you understand the principle of the photometer. One of the most commonly used photometers is the Macbeth illuminometer (Figure 8.3). It consists essentially in a photic source whose effectiveness on the eye can be manipulated by varying its distance from the eye. The next essential element is a prism used to direct into the eye the radiation from both the source and the target to be measured. The prism (called a Lummer–Brodhun cube) is so constructed that the radiation from the instrument is visible as a ring, the radiation from the test target as a disk within the ring. The task of the user of the photometer is to adjust the intensity of radiation in the instrument so as to have the ring and disk match each other in brightness. The instrument is calibrated so that when the

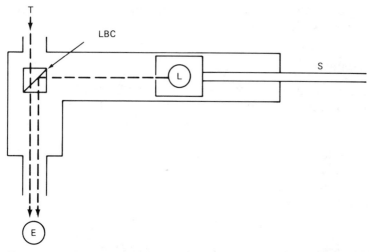

Figure 8.3   Schema of Macbeth illuminometer, a very common photometer. S is a stick that moves L, the standard source of radiation with respect to the Lummer–Brodhun cube, LBC. T is the test source; E is the eye. The eye receives radiation from both the test source and the standard source.

adjustment is made and the two fields match, the reading obtained can be transformed into any of the standard units for photic measurement.

When we want to know the value of illumination supplied to a working surface such as a desk, we place on the desk a disk of matte-white magnesium carbonate whose percentage of reflection is known. The disk usually reflects back to the photometer about 70 percent of the radiation falling on it. Thus when a reading is taken with the photometer pointed toward the disk, we know that the reading represents 70 percent of the radiation intensity falling on the disk, and the full intensity falling on the desk or table can be determined. If we pointed the photometer directly at the desk, we would not get the same reading, for the desk's percentage of reflectance is different from that of the disk and is unknown. Since we do not know what this percentage is, we would be unable to determine the level of illumination at the desk surface. The procedure just described measures *illumination,* and a common unit is the *foot-candle.*

When we want to know the luminance or the quantitative value of a target as viewed directly, we can point the photometer toward the target and translate our reading into units (luminance) that have to do with the effectiveness of the radiation as it directly strikes the eye. Very often, the targets we look at directly are translucent opal glass plates behind which is some form of original photic source such as incandescent lamps.

The Radiometer

Radiometers are instruments directly sensitive to photic radiation. Since radiation is made up of a number of different wavelengths, the question of whether the particular type of radiometer one uses or needs is equally sensitive to all wavelengths in the spectrum is of prime importance. Of course, we remember from Figure 8.2 that all parts of the human eye are not equally sensitive to all parts of the spectrum. It will be noted that the central region of the band of wavelengths called the "visible spectrum" is the portion to which the eye is most sensitive. Some radiometers, such as the exposure meters used by photographers in determining the proper camera settings for their pictures, possess sensitivity curves fairly close to the human luminosity curve; others are sensitive in absolute energy terms.

Sensitivity Range

The range of intensities to which the human eye is sensitive is enormous, covering about 12 logarithmic steps, that is, from somewhere in the neighborhood of 0.000001 millilamberts to 10,000 millilamberts. This range is divided into two major portions, the lower consisting of the levels at which only the rods are sensitive (the scotopic range) and the upper consisting of the levels at which the cones are also sensitive (photopic range).

The range can be labeled in several ways—in log millilamberts (throughout the whole range), millimicrolamberts, microlamberts, and lamberts in accord with the levels at which these units are most appropriate. The very bottom of the range is the level representing the least energy that will provide for any vision whatsoever; this point is called the *absolute* threshold.

VISUAL ACUITY

Definition of the Visual Angle

The visual angle is the solid angle formed by the target at the eye. From Figure 8.4 it will be seen that two factors enter into the determination of visual angle. The one is target size; the other is the distance of the target from the eye. Specifying visual angle precludes

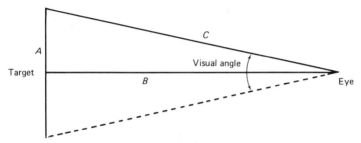

Figure 8.4   Use of the tangent in specifying the visual angle subtended by a target. (The tangent is a trignometric function that involves right-angle triangles.) The dimensions used are one-half of the dimension of the target and the distance of the target from the eye, which together form the right angle *AB* of the triangle *ABC*. The tangent is *A/B,* one-half of the target dimension *(A)* divided by the distance from the target to the eye *(B)*. This fraction put into decimal terms can be used to read from a trigonometric table the angular dimension of the angle *BC*. This value is one-half of the visual angle and is doubled to represent the full visual angle subtended by the target at the eye.

the need of specifying the two factors of target size and target distance.

This is not the only reason that visual angle is used. As a measure or unit, it relates to a great deal more that is known about the spatial features of the retina. For example, the two receptor populations are not homogeneously distributed throughtout the retina. The fovea, which is the central area of the retina, has a diameter of from 1½ to 2 degrees. Thus by using targets with visual angles well below this subtense, we know that an image is projected within the fovea, which is populated with cones alone. The distribution of both rods and cones over the remainder of the eye is pretty well known in terms of angular extents. The location of the optic disk, the retinal area devoid of receptors, as well as visual acuity, are known and designated in angular terms. Visual acuity is designated as the reciprocal of one minute of arc, for instance.

Normal vision is such that target elements separated by one minute of arc can be seen as separate. In other words, the visual system can *resolve* elements separated by one minute of arc. If more than this separation is required in any case, visual acuity is substandard. If smaller angles are sufficient, visual acuity is better than normal. Thus if one uses the reciprocal of the value found, based on one minute of arc, visual acuity is given a quantitative statement. The reciprocal of 2, being ½, would indicate that visual acuity is ½, or 0.5. Likewise, if only ½ minute of arc is required, visual acuity is the reciprocal of ½, or 2. Therefore the details of size and distance are not expressed but are only latent in stating visual acuity. This works only up to a certain point. Clinically, it has long been known that distance does count. Some people have good visual acuity for close targets and poor for distant ones; others are just the opposite. Thus visual acuity is usually tested for two different and unlike distances, at about 16 inches and at 20 feet, representing near vision and far vision, respectively.

To find visual acuity in angular terms—that is, in minutes—we use a trigonometric function, the *tangent*. In Figure 8.4 the tangent is *A/B:* we divide one-half of the linear value of the target by the distance of the target from the eye. This provides a decimal value that can be used in consulting a trigonometric table, which will show the angle corresponding to the decimal value. For example, let us say that the overall target size is 2 inches and that the target distance from the eye is 50 inches. $A = 1$ and $B = 50$; thus for *A/B*, or 1/50, the decimal is .02. The tangent of .02 is 1°9' (1 degree 9 minutes). But since this is only one-half of the target dimension, the full dimension subtends 2°18' of visual angle.

VISUAL ACUITY TARGETS

Laboratory Targets

For testing visual acuity in the laboratory, several different kinds of targets are used: (1) a grating, or a field with contrasting stripes of equal width; (2) a broken circle, or Landolt C; (3) a pair of parallel bars; (4) a single fine line on a homogeneous background; (5) a single area, such as a disk on a homogeneous field; and (6) an interrupted contour by which vernier visual acuity is studied (Figure 8.5). When single disks or single fine lines are used, the separations between the opposite borders of the disks and between the lines are the critical features. In the case of the single disks, visual acuity and threshold target size become identical.

Figure 8.5 Visual acuity targets. For parallel bars the separation between them is a critical feature. In the Landolt C the gap is the critical feature. In a grating the width and separation of the lines are critical.

In the laboratory, visual acuity is stated not in the terms described for the clinic but in terms of the minimal visual angle that the relevant elements in the target must subtend in order to be seen, or resolved.

Gratings and Broken Circles

Shlaer (1937) determined the relation between visual acuity over a background illumination range of about 8 log units for a grating and also for a broken circle, or Landolt C, with a background subtending a visual angle of 30°. Thus he was measuring the effect of a virtually nonluminous (or "black") test figure on a luminous field. Figure 8.6 shows the results. The grating provided for higher visual acuities under about 7 trolands[1] and lower visual acuities above this illumination.

The greatest acuity possible with the grating was 30 percent lower than the open circle. Shlaer showed that with an aperture of less than 2.33 millimeters the pupil is the limiting factor in the resolution of grating, whereas when the aperture is larger, the size of the central cones governs it. Various other workers studied this matter but did not use artificial pupils and failed to use a single viewing distance. These factors lead us to consider Shlaer's work as the standard for visual acuity for dark targets on light backgrounds.

Fisher (1938) measured visual acuity for a grating in a 2° foveal area when the intensities of the area were 0.193, 10.97, and 318 trolands. Monocular fixation, with a 2-millimeter artificial pupil, was used, while the other eye was confronted with a uniform field of low intensity. Annular surrounds varying both in subtended visual angle and intensity were also employed for the measurements. The radial widths of the annuli were 2.4, 4, 7.4, 12.4, and 20, while their intensities were 0.0566, 0.193, 10.07, 318, and 8560 trolands. Under these conditions the results were as follows. When the annulus was more intense than the test area, visual acuity became poorer with an increase in the size of the annulus. When the annulus was less intense than the test area, visual acuity became better with an increase in the size of the annulus. When the two were equally intense, changing the size of the annulus had no consistent effect on visual acuity. This last effect was similar in principle to one of Shlaer's experiments.

---

[1] A troland is a unit of retinal illumination that takes into account pupil size as well as target intensity. If the pupil aperture were one square millimeter and the target intensity were one candle per square meter, the retinal illumination would be one troland.

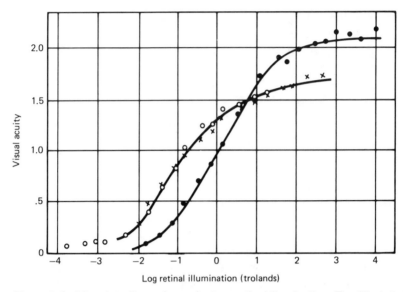

Log retinal illumination (trolands)

Figure 8.6 Visual acuity as dependent on retinal illumination. The filled circles represent the outcome with the C target. The open circles and crosses represent the outcome with the grating target. (Source: S. Shlaer. "The relation between visual acuity and illumination," *J. Gen. Physiol.*, 1937, 21, 185–209, Fig. 2.)

Parallel Bars

Wilcox (1932) used conditions quite different from those of Shlaer. He used light targets on dark backgrounds as well as the opposite and parallel bars instead of broken circles or gratings. His results are shown in Figure 8.7. The left-hand curve shows the results with dark bars; the right-hand curve shows the effects when the intensity (or luminosity) relations between bars and ground were reversed. It will be noted that up to a certain point, increase in illumination favored visual acuity, and beyond this a reversal set in.

Fry and Cobb (1935) found that broad and narrow bars do not produce like results when used to test visual acuity. They used two pairs of bars; the bars in the one pair were 1000 seconds in width; in the second pair, 168 seconds in width. The lengths in both cases were 2000 seconds. The results are plotted in Figure 8.8, in which it is shown that as the intensity of the bars is increased from a very low level up to 3-foot candles, visual acuity rapidly rises at first, but for the narrow bars it falls again very slowly. For the wide bars, visual acuity continues to ascend slowly after the first rapid rise. To explain this, the investigators used the Fry–Bartley (1935)

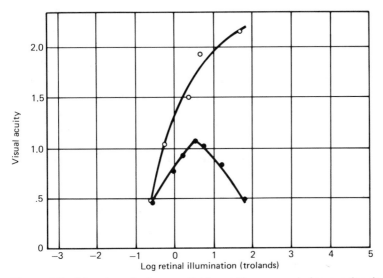

Figure 8.7   Visual acuity for parallel bars. The open circles are for dark bars on a light background. The filled circles are for light bars on a dark background. (Source: Modified from Wilcox, in S. H. Bartley, *Vision: A Study of Its Basis.* Princeton, NJ: Van Nostrand, 1941. Copyright © 1941 by S. Howard Bartley. Reproduced with author's permission.)

Figure 8.8   The effect on visual acuity of varying the luminosity of two bars on an unilluminated background. *W* is the result with wide bars (1000 seconds in width), *N* with narrow bars (168 seconds). (Source: Adapted from Fry & Cobb, in S. H. Bartley, *Vision: A Study of Its Basis.* Princeton, NJ: Van Nostrand, 1941.)

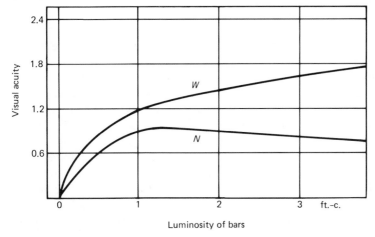

principle, namely, that physiological contour processes underlying the images of parallel target borders interfere with each other.

The production of threshold edges in perception is undoubtedly interfered with by the existence of two closely spaced parallel borders such as those of the bars. This makes the width of the bars a factor in the determination of visual acuity (see Figure 8.8). When the bars are wide, the opposite borders of the bars themselves are removed far enough from each other to interfere very little. When the borders are close to each other as in N, the contour processes responsible for seeing edges interfere with each other as much as or more than the smallness of the distance between the bars. But in W, the opposite borders of the bars in the target are far apart and do not elicit contour processes that interfere as much with each other as in the case of target N.

FACTORS AFFECTING VISUAL ACUITY

Retinal Mosaic

The relation of visual acuity to the retinal mosaic is of fundamental significance. The retinal mosaic is one of the limiting factors in determining the smallest angular separations that can be seen between target elements.

The results that Hecht and Mintz (1939) obtained went far beyond the expectations and findings of earlier workers. It was once thought that for two portions of a visual target to be seen as separate, their images on the retina had to be separated by at least one row of cones. Hecht and Mintz (1939) showed that this was not the case.

Pupil Size

Pupil size influences three features of visual function: sharpness or definition of retinal image, resolution of detail, and experience of brightness. The definition of a lens increases as aperture decreases; therefore as the pupil constricts, sharpness of image is increased. Resolution increases as lens size increases, and thus resolution improves as the pupil dilates. It turns out, however, that in the eye these factors just about offset each other over a considerable range of pupil size. Visual acuity, with constant brightness of the object seen and constant intensity of the retinal image, does not change greatly with pupil diameters ranging from 2 to 6 millimeters. This is actually most of the range over which the pupil varies in the usual day-to-day situations.

On the other hand, people may improve their ability to see

certain targets in low illumination by supplying themselves with an artificial pupil. For example, if we are viewing a projection screen in a weakly illuminated room, the material (tables of numbers, for instance) may not be legible. If we punch a small hole in a card and view the screen through it with one eye (the other eye being closed), we will likely be able to read the tabular material.

Stelmack and Leckett (1974) manipulated pupil size in a recognition study of neutral and taboo words with three subjects using an artificial pupil. They found that recognition improved as the artificial pupil decreased. Under a fully dilated condition without artificial pupils there was a slight decline in recognition. From their results the workers surmised the pupillery mechanism might be involved in perceptual defense, a concept dealt with in social psychology.

Age

In the literature we find various statements indicating that in older people a drop in illumination affects visual acuity, whereas in younger people no great effect is brought about in this way. Is it that the pupils of young and old behave differently to manipulations in level of illumination, or is some other factor responsible?

The following are representative values given by Luckiesh (1944) regarding the relation between visual acuity and age. Beginning with the age of 20 years, visual acuity is 100 percent (normal = 20/20); at the age of 40 it declines to 90 percent; at 60 it is down to 74 percent; and at 80 it is down to 47 percent. Obviously, such figures are only statistical and may not apply to any given individual but, on the other hand, they indicate that, in general, considerable decline is to be expected.

Taper or Blur of Retinal Image

The discrepancy between the visual target and its image on the retina must be considered in the matter of visual acuity. Ideally, the natural image is described as a copy of the visual target but is not in fact such a copy. Although targets may be said to possess abrupt borders, their images do not. The images are at best somewhat tapered or blurred. There are various optical reasons for this that involve the nature of the mediating tissues.

The laws of chromatic and spherical aberration are generally used to calculate the pattern or degree of blurredness, but such calculations do not take into account the slight oscillatory action of the eye itself, which introduces a blur factor of its own. Fry and Cobb (1935) took this into account by a direct measuring method. They assumed that the center-to-periphery intensity distribution

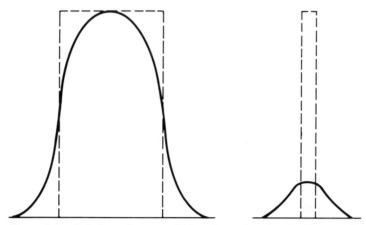

Figure 8.9 Relation of target width to intensity of retinal image. Broken lines represent distribution of radiation in target, solid lines, the distribution of radiation in image. (Source: S. H. Bartley. *Vision: A Study of Its Basis.* Princeton, NJ: Van Nostrand, 1941.)

in the image of a homogeneously luminous target would be a taper described by a well-known equation. To check on the matter, they obtained the intensity thresholds of bars *A* and *B* in a visual target. Bar *A* was made so wide that greater width did not reduce the intensity threshold. Bar *B* was made so narrow that intensity and width were made reciprocal in determining threshold. The investigation showed that any width greater than 224 seconds of arc was sufficient for bar *A* and any width less than 30 seconds of arc was sufficient for the latter. By comparing the results with what the ideal results would be if there were no taper and by using the equation, Fry and Cobb were able to calculate the magnitude of the taper.

It can be said that the threshold response to a long, narrow line used as a target depends not only on the intensity (or luminosity) of the line, but also on its width. Evidently, some spread of radiation forms the image. Fry and Cobb's study was taken to invalidate the assumption that intensity of the center of the image remains constant for various bar widths. In Figure 8.9 the center-to-periphery taper of the retinal image is shown. Reducing the *width* of the line, which is already very narrow, would be expected to lower the *intensity* at the center due to the tapering.

Stray Illumination in the Eye

In addition to the factors producing slight blur of the retinal image, stray illumination of the retina from dispersion of radiation at the junctures of the various media (the inside of the cornea, the vitreous humor, the aqueous humor, and the lens) occurs in considerable amount, so that even an image of a target subtending only a few degrees of visual angle provides a broad taper of general illumination, which when target luminosity is high, becomes an effective stimulus over large portions of, if not the total, retina. In fact, it may be that the existence of such a total, determines whether such phenomena as "autokinetic movements" occur. That is, this stray illumination and thus the activation of the whole retina may be the basis for the perception of a stable visual field. This idea has not as yet been put to a quantitative test.

Bartley and Fry (1934) were aware of the stray illumination in the eye and used an indirect method to study it. A luminous target was placed in the peripheral part of the visual field and the amount of stray illumination falling on the fovea was measured by the change produced in the differential threshold there. The differential threshold target was a ring-annulus. The change brought about by the peripheral target on the differential threshold at the fovea was compared with the effect on the threshold produced by a known level of illumination cast directly on the fovea. The peripheral target was placed at a series of distances from the fovea and the threshold effects for them were found. From this a curve was plotted, representing the relative amounts of stray illumination produced at various distances from a target of known size and luminosity.

Later, Bartley (1935) measured stray illumination in the eye by using excised eyes of albino rabbits. Such eyes were placed on a pedestal in a dark room facing a lamphouse with a luminous disk as a target, which was imaged on the retina of the eye. Thus the whole eye was also internally illuminated in addition to the image, which, of course, shone more brightly through the translucent wall of the eye. The level of luminosity of the eye wall was measured from the outside at various distances from the image itself. Likewise, the factors of image area and intensity in producing the luminosity of the eye wall were measured.

Much later, Boynton, Enoch, and Bush (1954) also measured stray illumination in excised eyes. Their equipment and technique were considerably more precise than Bartley's, but the study confirmed his findings in general.

INTENSITY EFFECTS

Stimulus Variables at Threshold

Brightness depends on a number of factors, among which are area of the retinal image, luminance, and impingement duration. Classically, each was studied one at a time with the others held constant. But added understanding of visual mechanisms is to be gained by determining how two or more factors vary in relation to each other in producing a constant end result, such as threshold brightness. Some earlier workers were concerned with relations between target area and photic intensity to produce threshold brightness.

Riccó (1877) found that the product of area and intensity (or luminance) is constant for threshold excitation. This has been called *Riccó's law* and holds when the image of the target covers the fovea as well as in the periphery if the image subtends an angle no greater than 10 minutes. Piper (1903) also stated a rule, which says that in peripheral vision the product of intensity and the square root of the area is a constant for threshold. *Piper's law* has been found to hold in the periphery for visual angles lying between 2° and 7°.

Much more recently, Graham, Brown, and Mote (1939) extended the examination of the retinal area-luminance relations to cover greater visual angles. These investigators believed they could control the experimental conditions more precisely than earlier workers had. For targets involving visual angles of from 1.86' to 1° for the fovea, and from 1.86' to 25° for the periphery, the results were as follows: When the logarithm of luminosity is plotted against the logarithm of the target radius, the curves for both fovea and periphery are nonlinear but increase in slope as area is increased. The increase is consistent and becomes asymptotic for the largest areas.

Bloch (1885) suggested that for short photic pulses the sensory effect depends on the product of luminance and pulse duration. This is known as *Bloch's law* and results have been confirmed for threshold sensation for durations exceeding 1 millisecond. Blondel and Rey (1911) showed this for peripheral stimuli, and Karn (1936) for the fovea. What happened with pulses briefer than 1 millisecond was left in doubt. Brindley (1952) reduced his photic inputs to about 4×10^{-7} seconds and found a satisfactory reciprocity between luminance and duration for suprathreshold effects. It is supposed that this would hold for threshold as well.

Recently, Dwyer and White (1974) reported finding that the trade-off between impingement area and intensity for reaction time could not be accounted for by the traditional theories of spatial summation. For example, Graham, Brown and Mote (1939) believed that threshold response of retinal elements contribute to brightness in inverse proportion to some power of their distance from the center of stimulation. Dwyer and White's work showed that for small targets, area has a greater effect than intensity for determining latency of response. Edmonds and Dwyer (1977) extended this work in an attempt to establish which, if any, of the theoretical formulations on hand could account for the nature of area-intensity relations operating at scotopic levels. Their results showed that traditional theories did not account for the reciprocity relations they found in reaction times.

Brightness Discrimination and Target Diameter

Figure 8.10 (Steinhardt, 1936) shows a number of curves, each of which represents the relation between $\Delta I/I$ and level of retinal illumination (both in logarithmic terms) for a given target size (disk). The diameters of the disks vary from 23.5' of arc to 24°. That would be roughly a range of from 1 to 60. The largest target would have 60 times as great a diameter as the smaller one. All the disks were looked at directly; hence their images were centered on the fovea. When the succeeding targets were used, they included retinal areas

Figure 8.10 Human intensity discrimination as dependent on illumination and size of target. Each curve is for a separate target; the visual angles subtended are as follows, reading from the upper to the lower curves in order: 23.5', 31', 56', 2°14', 5°36', and 24°. (Source: J. Steinhardt. "Intensity discrimination in the human eye. I. The relation of $\Delta I/I$ to intensity," *J. Gen. Physiol.,* 1936, 20, 185–209, Fig. 2.)

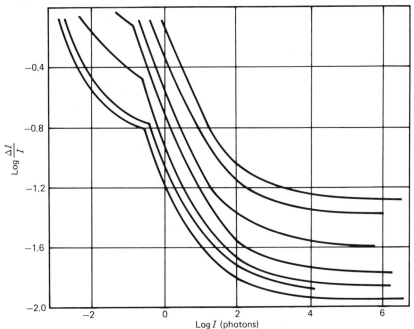

farther and farther from the fovea and thus activated many rods.

It is possible to separate intensity effects and spatial effects. In some experiments the purpose is to study one effect and in other experiments, the other.

SPATIAL EFFECTS

The Ganzfeld or Homogeneous Field

By far the most work on the nature of visual perception is done with test fields that are inhomogeneous. The effect of components of structure giving rise to the experience of objects and bounded areas has involved the most experimentation. The full understanding of visual perception is not gained without studying the consequences of using unstructured targets—broad homogeneous fields of illumination. These are called by their German name, *Ganzfelden.*

A *Ganzfeld* may be provided by any one of several means. Hochberg, Treibel, and Seaman (1951) used halves of Ping-Pong balls over their subjects eyes. Cohen (1957) made a *Ganzfeld* by using two intersecting hollow spheres painted white on the inside. The subject looked into the first sphere through a peephole. The opening that formed the intersection of the two spheres could be used to provide a central area (figure) when the illumination of the two spheres differed in level (see Figure 8.11). Gibson and Waddell (1952) had their subjects look into a translucent globe.

Figure 8.11   The Ganzfeld, a uniformly illuminated, visually unstructured field, achieved by having a hollow sphere with a hole for monocular viewing. A second sphere is conjoined and can be differently illuminated when one wishes to produce a figure on the otherwise uniform field. Spheres are used because any restricted source of radiation (light) will produce uniform illumination in all parts of the sphere.

What one sees under *Ganzfeld* conditions appears to be a dense fog. Cohn reported that if the *Ganzfeld* is uniformly illuminated with photic radiation producing a highly saturated hue, the color gradually fades. In about 3 minutes the field becomes gray, with the impression that the grayness is nearer than the hue.

To maintain the original color of the *Ganzfeld,* the worker had to introduce structure, for example, a gray disk when the *Ganzfeld* was seen as red. This gave the disk a blue-green color, the complementing color of the *Ganzfeld* itself, and was more saturated than the *Ganzfeld.*

Another way to produce structure (heterogeneity) was to make the second sphere's luminance level different from the first. This produced a disk where the spheres intersected as indicated.

Brightness Contrast and Induction

Although the effects of stimulating separate areas on the retina can be determined, there are many situations in which the level or areal extent of stimulation of *adjacent* areas has a very marked effect on the observed brightness of the area in question. Contrast pertains not only to brightness but also to color effects. That is, there are both *brightness contrast* and *color contrast.* We shall concern ourselves only with brightness contrast here.

In dealing with contrast as with other phenomena, we should be careful to distinguish between the phenomena themselves and the conditions that produce them. For example, contrast is a perceptual phenomenon and the factors that are manipulated should not have "contrast" for a label. If we are concerned with differences in intensity between the impingements on two portions of the retina, the difference can merely be called a difference or a ratio, thus retaining the term "contrast" for what is seen.

Purdy (1935) pointed out that, in general, the brightness of any visual area is lowered by raising the brightness of nearby areas. He continued by indicating that a small area of medium photic intensity may appear white when its surround is totally unstimulated. If the surround is progressively supplied with increasing intensities of illumination, the brightness of the small area is progressively reduced. With sufficiently intensely stimulated surrounds, the original white may even be changed to black.

Hess and Pretori (1894) made one of the earliest psychophysical investigations of brightness contrast. They used a test field of a 1° square centered on a 10° inducing field. The match field was also a 1° square centered on an adjacent 10° field, all of which was viewed with one eye. The luminance of the match field needed to equate with the test field was found to decrease with increasing luminance of the inducing field. The possibility of complex interactions between the four fields was so great as to make inferences quite uncertain.

One simpler procedure for measuring brightness contrast is to use three target components *A*, *B*, and *C*. *A* and *B* are to be matched; *A* is the standard, *B* the comparison field. If *C* is placed adjacent to the standard *A*, a shift in the comparison intensity will be required for *A* and *B* to match. Thus when the order of the components in the visual field is *CAB*, *C* affects *A*. Thus for *A* and *B* to match, *B* has to be changed in intensity and that change is measured.

Diamond (1953) found that if *C*, the inducing target component, is raised in intensity so that its brightness is greater than *A*, then *A* has to be raised if the original match between *A* and *B* is to be maintained. That is, Diamond started out with *A* and *B* equal in brightness. Then *C*, which was next to *A*, was introduced and raised in intensity until it appeared brighter than *A*. The result was that *B* now appeared brighter than *A*, so *A* had to be raised in intensity to restore the match between *A* and *B* in brightness. The amount by which *A* had to be increased in intensity was the measure of the inducing effect of *C*.

In 1955 Diamond studied the effect of area of the inducing target on the required luminosity of the test field to make it and the match target appear equally bright. His test target was a rectangle. The inducing target was equal in length to the test target but could be made narrower or wider than the test field. The match target was somewhat farther away from the test target than the test target's length. Actually, the image of the test target was placed on the opposite eye, and the posture of the two eyes was controlled by a fused fixation point. As the posture was increased from its narrowest value to its widest, there was a concomitant decrease in the luminance needed for equal brightness of the test and match targets. The amount of the decrease in luminance needed increased with increases in the luminance of the inducing target.

Alpern and David (1959) used four rectangular inducing fields, placed two on each side of the test field. Either two or all four of the inducing targets were used at a time. The match target image was placed on the retina of the opposite eye. They found that the inducing luminances needed for the brightness equation was less with all four of the inducing targets than the sum of the independent measures of two inducing targets at a time. This discrepancy increased as luminance of the inducing targets was decreased and as the separation of the inducing targets from the test target was increased. Alpern (1953) offered some evidence to indicate that inducing targets in the retinal periphery result in a greater contrast effect than those at the center.

Spatial Effects or Temporal Effects?

One of the several effects mentioned in introducing this chapter was intensity. Also, it was pointed out that various experimental studies, by their very nature, could well be introduced into the chapter in more than one place. This is particularly true in deciding whether to classify certain studies as spatial studies, or temporal studies. The descriptions of inhibition and disinhibition that follow is a case in point. They are considered here, although in the original listing, inhibition and disinhibition were given as examples of temporal effects.

Inhibition in the Limulus Eye

Neurophysiologists have provided some information about visual mechanisms that seems to be quite relevant. For many years they have been studying the responses of the elements of the compound eye of the horseshoe crab (Limulus) to controlled photic stimulation. The Limulus eye is made up of a number of units called ommatidia. Each ommatidium is composed of more than one cell but forms a functional unit whose activity can be recorded separately from the activities of other ommatidia. The compound eye is populated by ommatidia lying side by side and the aim of the investigators have largely been to determine how adjacent ommatidia, and even those somewhat separated from each other, affect one another. Separate ommatidia can be stimulated independently by tiny pointlike patches of radiation. This is of quite distinct advantage, for in the vertebrate eye the receptor units synapse with the bipolar cells and these, in turn, with the ganglion cells, synapse before a successful recording site is reached. Hence in the vertebrate eye certain complex interaction processes occur before recording can be accomplished.

In the Limulus, then, the activity of single ommatidia or combinations of them can be studied. It has been found that the activity (or rate of discharge of impulses) of an ommatidium is reduced when adjacent ommatidia are activated. This is of course called inhibition. The activity of the adjacent ommatidia also raises the threshold and reduces the number of impulses discharged when a brief photic pulse is used as the stimulus.

The magnitude of the inhibition, indicated by the decrease in discharge frequency, depends on intensity, area, and configuration of the illumination surrounding the test ommatidium. This was shown by Hartline, Wagner, and Ratliff (1956). Hartline and Ratliff (1958) showed that the inhibitory effects from different ommatidia combine with one another. Thus it can be concluded that inhibition summates and furthermore, that the threshold of inhibitory influence increases with distance between the ommatidia involved.

Disinhibition

Another result, called disinhibition, has been demonstrated. When a spot of photic stimulation activates one ommatidium and then a second spot activates a second ommatidium, the activity of the second ommatidium inhibits the activity of the first one: that is, ommatidium number two slows down the discharge of ommatidium number one. A third spot of photic stimulation can be used to activate a third ommatidium, which is far enough away from ommatidium number one not to affect it greatly but is near enough to ommatidium number two to influence it. The influence consists in a release of number one from some of the initial affect of number two on it. While various complex interactions occur in the Limulus eye, none of them happen to be facilitory. All are inhibitory in one way or another.

The stimulus manipulations made in the disinhibition investigation are reminiscent of those made in the brightness contrast investigation of Diamond (1953, 1955). When Diamond performed his induction experiments, the work of Hartline and Ratliff (1957) had not yet been performed and the concept of disinhibition had not been coined. Although the perceptual (or sensory) effects were clear, the nature of a possible mechanism had not been disclosed.

Disinhibition in the Human Eye

The neurophysiological work on disinhibition induced Mackavey, Bartley, and Casella (1962) to perform human experiments to test for disinhibition. They used the following target arrangement. The match target was imaged on the left retina. The test and the inducing targets were imaged on the right retina. Using the match or standard target in a separate eye removed the standard target from any stray photic effects from the other targets while still keeping it a standard reference for brightness. The inducing target was placed at five different distances from the test target, ranging from 1 to 5°. It was shown that the presence of the inducing target affected the luminance of the test target needed to equate it in brightness with the match target and that this effect was lessened as the inducing target was moved farther away from the test target. The effect became asymptotic at about 4 or 5°. The results seemed quite similar to the Hartline and Ratliff effects in the Limulus. The neural mechanism for the sensory effects is very probably in the retina, although it could have been further along in the optic pathway.

Edges

The distance between two target border processes has a great deal to do with the emergence of object edges[2] in perception. This was measured in threshold experiments. For example, the threshold intensity differences between the two parts of a disk-annulus target decreases as the size of the annulus is increased (its border is shifted farther and farther away from the border of the inner-lying disk). In Figure 8.12 the distance between the two borders is greater in the right-hand target than in the left-hand one. The question, then, is whether area or distance between borders makes the abovementioned difference in threshold. It was long customary to attribute the difference to area. Fry and Bartley (1935) showed that contour processes were responsible.

The first step in this demonstration was use of the target shown in Figure 8.13. There were three stimulus areas, *A*, *B*, and *C*. Areas *B* and *C* were separated by a thin ring, *R*, the size of which varied as it was moved closer to *A* or closer to *C*. Varying the ring size did not affect the constant total area *BC*, lying outside *A*, but it did manipulate a border in the vicinity of *A*. It was supposed that since total area outside *A* was held constant, no shift in the threshold for the emergence of *A* as brighter than *B* would occur if the customary area explanations were to apply. On the other hand, since a border was being varied in distance from the outer border of *A*, a threshold manipulation would occur if the contour process explanation were correct. Experimentation tallied with the contour process expectation. Further manipulations of target conditions were made, and all gave results in line with the idea that two parallel contour processes inhibit each other; that is, they require greater intensity differences on their two sides for the emergence of perceived edges. The same investigators found that nonparallel borders—those at

---

[2] For the sake of clarity, we shall call the bounds of the target its *borders* and the bounds of the visual object its *edges*, thus making clear whether it is target or perception that is being referred to. We shall refer to the intervening process in the nervous system that is responsible for the seeing of objects and their edges as a *contour process*.

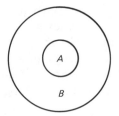

Figure 8.12   Targets made up of a constant central disk area *A* and a surrounding ring area *B* that is manipulated in width.

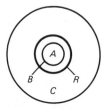 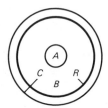

Figure 8.13   Targets made up of a central area *A* and an outer area *B* plus *C* that is constant. The distance of the border of ring *R* from the border of *A* is varied. (Source: G. A. Fry and S. H. Bartley. "The effect of one border in the visual field upon the threshold of another," *Amer. J. Physiol.* 1935, 112, 414–421, Fig. 3.)

right angles to each other—actually resulted in facilitation rather than in inhibition.

TEMPORAL EFFECTS

A variety of perceptual results in vision vary as a function of time. Some of them accrue from a sequence of closely timed presentations. Some of the items in a sequence may overlap or may be spaced apart. Other temporal effects are produced by prolonged continuous stimulation.

Results have been called matacontrast, paracontrast, inhibition, disinhibition, masking, and the like. Some are called adaptation. A great deal depends on the objectives of the experimenter as to whether some of the experiments are considered temporal or spatial.

Temporal Effects on Edges

When the photic radiations reaching the eye from two portions of a target are unequal, the observer usually perceives them as different levels of lightness and these areas may be perceived as having abrupt edges. However, if the target presentation is made in two stages— one area shown before the other—the edges may develop into a blur. If the area presented first is surrounded by the area presented next, the inner area may disappear. The manipulation of the time interval between the presentation of the first target portion and the second produces even additional changes. Thus we may say that timing of stimulation is a crucial factor in the perception of surfaces and edges. For examples of this, we may turn to some experiments of Werner (1935) and Bartley (1939).

Werner presented pairs of targets of many forms varying from circles and disks to irregular and incomplete forms. In one case, for example, a target perceived as a solid black disk when presented alone was briefly presented on a light background (Figure 8.14). In about 150 milliseconds another target centered on the same point in the visual field was presented. When this target was presented alone, it appeared as a black ring. With the 150-millisecond interval elapsing between the presentation of the first and second targets, the disk was never seen; that is, the area within the ring was not black. When the temporal sequences of the targets were reversed, the black disk *was* seen. The timing of the disk-ring succession that eliminated the seeing of the disk is more or less critical. If the rate of succession is slow, the disk will be seen to precede the ring. If it is more rapid, the ring is seen with a darkened inner field. If the rate is still more rapid, the inner field, which might have been expected to be a dark disk, lightens, and it may become lighter in some cases than the light field outside the ring.

It is possible to interchange the intensity relation between disk

Figure 8.14 Werner's figures. The disk and ring are presented in temporal succession, and because their centers are at the same point, the disk occupies the same area as the space within the ring. Under some conditions, when half the ring is presented, only half the disk is seen and then with a tapered surface as indicated. (Source: H. Werner. "Studies in contour, I. Qualitative analyses," *Amer. J. Psychol.,* 1935, 47, 44–46, Figs. 5, 9.)

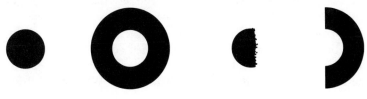

or ring and the ground on which they are made to appear, so that the figures become light and the ground black. In this case the original phenomenon will still occur. That is, the object that ought to have emerged in contrast to the ground will not do so.

It will be noted that the second figure, a ring, had both an inner and an outer edge;[2] whereas the disk, when it exists, of course, has only an outer edge. Since the results differed according to which of the two targets was presented first, they indicate that the outer border of the second target played a part in the outcome. The same results, it may be added, occurred whether both targets were presented to one eye or to separate eyes.

This may be what actually underlay the outcome. When the disk target is presented first but is followed very soon by the ring target, the border contour for the disk does not have time to form. Since the contour process has not formed in the only time given it to do so, the ring simply develops as a ring without the disk ever being seen. At a critical stage in the presentation of the two components of the target the contour process for the second component (the ring) may utilize the decaying contour process for the first component to accentuate its own inner edge, since the direction of the two gradients would be the same. This account is based on the principle originally recognized elsewhere in threshold studies that contour processes must develop and complete themselves before differences in brightness of two areas can be distinguished. Whatever depresses or precludes edge formation precludes the appreciation of the brightness a surface would have.

We may continue with the account by detailing the possible process events when the order of target presentation is reversed. The temporal interval between the presentation of the two targets is not critical. Regardless of how soon the disk target is presented after the ring target, the disk appears as a black surface. That is, if the disk target is presented *before* the contour process for the inner edge of the ring is developed, it is simply forestalled and never completed, and the whole figure is seen as a large disk whose outer edge has time to develop before the presentation of the disk target. This event, by changing the illumination within the ring, obliterates the condition for its continuance.

Bartley's (1939) experiment about to be described had certain features in common with that of Werner. Bartley used a target arrangement that provided for seeing a figure of two parts: a disk that was surrounded by a ring whose inner edge was the outer edge of the disk. The stimulus flux for the disk could be controlled so that a light disk would alternate with a dark one while being surrounded with a gray or only medium-bright ring. When the intensity level of the ring target was raised above the mean value of the two disks, the light phase of the disk alternation became less predominant than the dark phase. When the level of the intensity of the ring target was reduced below the mean, the light phase became predominant. Along with this shift in predominance, a difference in edge properties of the two phases of the disk developed. The predominant phase possessed a sharp edge; the "diminished" phase lacked an edge and became a mere "shadow." The predominant phase seemed to occupy more time, thus taking up most of the cycle.

In order to subordinate the light phase of the disk and to make the dark phase predominant, the intensity of the ring target (when alternation frequencies are low) must exceed not only the Talbot level (Chapter 8, page 205) but also the photic intensity for the light phase of the disk. Increasing the alternation rate reduces the level of the ring target needed until it reaches Talbot level. The light phases of the disk grow less bright as the critical flicker frequency (CFF) is reached. To have the light phase predominate, the experimenter must reverse the target conditions just described.

Dynamic Visual Acuity

The determination of visual acuity as described so far has involved the use of stationary targets, for the attempt has been to ascertain the fundamental spatial relations in the function of the sense cells of the retina. However, visual acuity for moving targets has similarly been studied by Ludvigh and Miller (1953). Visual acuity under the conditions they used is called *dynamic visual acuity.* Ludvigh and Miller's experiment was as follows. The subject, with his head immobilized, viewed a revolving mirror that disclosed a target that was effectively 4 meters from the eye. The rate of revolution of the mirror determined the velocity of the stimulus presentation as it swept past the eye. (Figure 8.15 shows how a revolving mirror provides target motion.) The illumination of the target was held at about 25-foot candles, with a background area that possessed a reflection coefficient of about 85 percent. The angular velocity of the sweep of the radiation beam across the eye was varied from 10 to 170° per second. The total duration of the target presentation was 0.4 second in all cases, regardless of target velocity. The target was a Landolt C whose open portion was positioned randomly from trial to trial in one or the other of eight clockface positions. Figure 8.16 shows the results, which were representable by the equation $y = a + bx^3$, in which a is a measure of static visual acuity. This is, of course, small when static acuity is good. For high values of

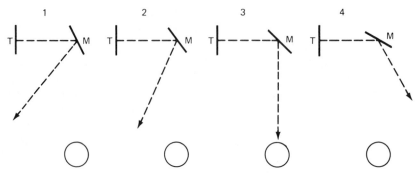

Figure 8.15 How a revolving mirror can pass the radiations from a target across the eye and thus produce the equivalent of a moving target. Each circle is the same eye but at a different instant. From left to right the target is in effect approaching the eye. At third from left it is in full view; at far right it has passed by. M is the revolving mirror. T is the target.

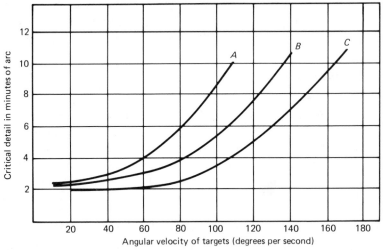

Figure 8.16 Relation between visual acuity and the effective velocity of moving targets for each of the three groups of observers, *A*, *B* and *C*. (Source: E. J. Ludvigh and J. W. Miller. *A Study of Dynamic Visual Acuity*. Joint Proj. Rep. No. 1. Kresge Eye Institute Contr. Nour. 586(00), ONR Proj. Desig. No. 142–023, Bu. Med. Proj. NM 001067.01.01, 1953, Fig. 3.)

angular target velocities, y is chiefly assignable to bx^3, where b is a measure of dynamic acuity. It is small when dynamic acuity does not decline rapidly as angular velocity is increased.

At an angular target velocity of 20° per second, acuity with vertical target motion correlated 0.50 with acuity for horizontal target motion. With angular velocity raised to 80° per second, the correlation rose to 0.72, and for 110° per second it dropped to 0.59. The fact that the dynamic visual acuities in the two directions correlated as well as they did was interpreted to mean that dynamic visual acuity was largely dependent on the efficiency of the overall ocular pursuit mechanism rather than on the strength or behavior of individual muscles as such. The results showed, too, that not all persons with equally good static acuity were similar in dynamic visual acuitites for the various velocities.

Adaptation as a Temporal Effect

Adaptation is the adjustment of the eye and possibly other parts of the visual mechanism to the general photic intensity level it confronts at a given time. Brightness discrimination is the ability of the visual system to distinguish between the various intensity levels involved in a given pattern of photic input. Without these capacities there would be no vision as we know it.

The vertebrate eye and the human eye are capable of responding effectively to an enormous range of intensities of photic impingement. Brightness is the name for the experience that is correlated with intensity or luminosity. Thus brightness is a response term, while intensity and luminosity are impingement terms.

Adaptation and brightness discrimination are closely related. Although it may take a material amount of time perhaps varying from seconds to minutes to adapt completely to a given level of illumination, brightness discrimination requires only a very small fraction of a second to distinguish between and react to differences in intensity of illumination. Photochemically, adaptation and brightness discrimination are taken to be two aspects of the same mechanism at work.

Everyone knows that when we enter an unilluminated or weakly illuminated room, such as a movie theater from the street on a bright sunny day, we cannot see very well. In a few minutes, inability to see diminishes and objects begin to be fairly observable. This is the experiential or visual aspect of *dark adaptation.* An equally well-known occurrence is the same initial inability when we pass from an unilluminated area to an illuminated one, as when leaving the theater and returning to the sunny street. The process in this case is called *light adaptation.* The photochemical processes that go on in the eye are largely responsible for both forms of adaptation.

Since the amount of adaptation is determined by the photic level and the length of time exposed to it, adaptation should be taken into account when attempting to understand visual response.

The individual's perceptions and judgments of the degree of grayness or lightness, for example, are dependent first of all on adaptation level.

There are two ways that photic radiation may reach the eye. It may come directly from an independent source, such as fire, arcs, heated filaments, or glowing gas in fluorescent tubes, or it may reach the eye by way of reflection from surfaces. Radiation reflected from a surface, of course, reaches that surface before coming to the eye and the illumination of the surface in question may be different in intensity than the illumination of other surfaces around it.

There are three ways that photic radiation may reach the eye from scenes. Part of it may come from an *original source*, as mentioned above, be *reflected from specific sources receiving radiation from a general illuminant*, or be reflected from a localized illuminant not cast on all the targets in the scene. It is worthwhile to know that differences in appearances—that is, differences in visual responses—come from these three origins.

As far as the observer or perceiver is concerned, one more factor must be added: the presence of conditions giving rise to perception of *texture* at the reflecting surface. Visual texture can be defined as lack of uniformity in reflectance of a surface, perceived as a physical property of the surface itself. A surface as judged mechanically by touch may have a texture that is not perceived visually, depending on whether the illumination is diffuse or arises from a localized source. Illumination from a localized source is called *specular illumination*. Tactually fine-grain roughness may be seen only as a *matte surface*. On the other hand, visual texture may possess considerable coarseness. Whatever the texture, it is associated with the existence and position of the surface as a visual reality.

Dark Adaptation

The rate of dark adaptation depends on the level of adapatation from which the dark adaptation starts; this is called the *preadaptation* level. Winsor and Clark (1936) showed that rod adaptation for a high preadaptation luminance was slower than for lower levels of preadaptation. Hecht, Haig, and Chase (1937) indicated that both the rod and cone components of adaptation become more and more delayed as predaptation luminances are increased (Figure 8.17). Wald and Clark (1937) showed that the duration of the preadaptation state also affected the rate of dark adaptation. The longer the preadaptation takes (at least up to 10 minutes, let us say), the more delayed the dark adaptation. Mote and Riopelle (1953) and others have obtained similar results. Wald (1954) explained these

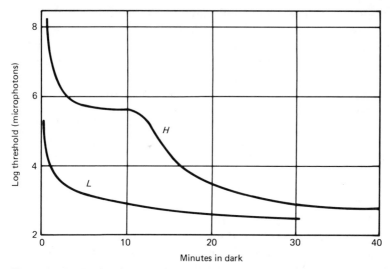

Figure 8.17   Dark-adaptation curves. *H* is the course of dark adaptation starting from a preadapting intensity of 400,000 trolands. *L* starts from 263 trolands.
(Source: S. Hecht, C. Haig, and A. M. Chase. "The influence of light adaptation
on subsequent dark adaptation of the eye," *J. Gen. Physiol.,* 1937, 20, 831–
850. Fig. 2.)

results on a photochemical basis, the description of which is too
involved for presentation here.

   When an eye is adapted to a high intensity (or luminance), it
can detect targets most readily when the fovea is stimulated. That
is, the fovea requires less illumination than the periphery does. On
the other hand, the fovea is much less sensitive than the periphery
when the eye is completely dark adapted. Consequently, the
amounts of dark adaptation for the periphery will manifest wider
ranges than for the fovea.

   Brown, Graham, Leibowitz, and Ranken (1953) followed the
course of dark adaptation for a visual acuity target. They tested a
grating target at various intervals during nonillumination of the eye.
Of course, in visual acuity experiments the fineness of the grating
is a variable, and so in the investigation the level of visual acuity
was an arbitrary matter. The fineness of the grating, for example,
could be set for a visual acuity of 0.5 or 0.25, and then dark adaptation
could be carried out until the striped nature of the target became
visible. Brown and his colleagues found that with wide grating
stripes, resolution was possible via the rods but that with fine stripes
only, the cone portion of the retina was effective. In general, the
higher the visual acuity criterion is, the higher the luminance must

be for successful seeing of detail; however, this luminance is also a function of time allowed for dark adaptation.

When dark adaptation is tested in a neurophysiological preparation such as the eye of the Limulus (the horseshoe crab), the record is of numbers of impulses discharged by the single visual receptor unit. It discharges more and more impulses as the unit is tested after longer and longer intervals without illumination. For example, at 30 seconds, let us say that 4 impulses are discharged; at 5 minutes, 9 impulses; at 10 minutes, 13 impulses; and at 1 hour, 27 impulses (Hartline and McDonald, 1947).

Light Adaptation

Baker (1949) ascertained the threshold increment in luminance *(L)* for a 1° foveal target presented for 20 milliseconds obtained at various times over a period of 15 minutes. He began with observers who had been without photic stimulation (in darkness) for 10 minutes. Light adaptation was so rapid during the first 3 or 4 seconds that he could not measure it by this method. He measured subsequent changes, which in comparison with the first adaptation were small. The pattern of changes was characteristically as follows, regarding light adaptation as depression in sensitivity. After the primary depression there is a rapid recovery that gradually decelerates, reaching a new peak at 2 to 3 minutes after onset. From then on, sensitivity changes slightly to a final level at 10 to 15 minutes.

This is to say, then, that exposure to photic radiation following dark adaptation does not produce a simple effect described as quickly reducing sensitivity to the level suitable for the eye to function in an illuminated environment. The effect is complex. Baker's procedure was to measure the way in which the threshold increment in photic intensity *(I)* varies in a dark-adapted person during exposure to an adapting illumination, the target. The results are not comparable to those using the older methods because they used different measures of sensitivity.

Adaptation is a term applied to changes in other sense modalities as well as in vision. Some of these will be dealt with in Chapter 15 "Perceptual Learning and Change."

THE SPECTRUM AND COLOR EXPERIENCE

Throughout our discussion we have abandoned the copy theory of human perception and have put in its place the idea that certain complex energy patterns impinging on the sense organs induce certain kinds of organismic reactions, one aspect of which is our experiences. We have supposed that our experiences are perfectly unique products of the human organism and copy nothing in the universe.

Nowhere else in all the study of perception is it more necessary to maintain our understanding of the noncopy relations between organisms and environment than in dealing with color experience. The study of the perception of color is much more than dealing with wavelengths in the spectrum of the illuminant, be it sun or incandescent lamp or any other source. The colors we see are in every case a complex end result of several factors: the composition of the illuminant or illuminants, the several reflectances of the visual targets, their spatial relations to each other, the reflectance of the surround or ground, the state of adaptation of the eye, and the body processes, including the activity the organism as a person is carrying on at a given time. Under fundamental and strictly controlled conditions produced for study in the laboratory, the learning that one observer versus another has undergone does not perhaps crucially enter as a factor, but under everyday conditions it does.

Let us take a look at some examples of color phenomena to see what they are like and to determine what has to be considered. The following are some commonplace situations in which color is seen and is of some interest.

1. Food is less palatable under some illuminations than under others. Substances, such as butter, that are ordinarily seen as yellow had a greenish appearance under the illumination of some of the early fluorescent tubes.
2. To be sure of the color of certain materials, we sometimes try to see them in daylight. We know that materials tend to be a different color under artificial illumination but do not know how this color relates to the material's appearance in daylight.
3. To make a colored photograph of a painting on a wall, we do not "shine light" on the painting directly with an unmasked incandescent bulb but set up diffuse illumination. We reflect light onto it from a matte surface, for example. Direct light would produce shiny reflections from some portions of the painting and hence nearly colorless areas in the print. Other parts of the painting would not be lighted well enough.
4. To bring out interesting effects in viewing or photographing colored objects such as china or porcelain, we use direct illumination in order to cause reflections and highlights.

Diffuse illumination would tend to make such objects look dull, flat, and uninteresting.

5. To perceive depth in a scene we must give it some illumination contrast. This means that the illumination we supply must not be diffuse but must come from a single direction. In this way, not only will some portions of the scene be more highly illuminated than others, but shadows will be produced, shadows helpful to an acceptable amount of depth perception.

6. Objects sometimes appear to be different colors in accord with the colors in their surroundings. This is not due primarily to the illuminant. An object appearing blue-green on a white background may appear to be light blue when placed on a black background. On a greenish-yellow (chartreuse) background, it will tend toward a purplish blue. If the background is grayish purple, the object will be brilliant blue.

7. If the illumination of a scene is intense, shadows tend to be dark and objects lying in them are obscured. In such scenes we look *at* the shadows. If we walk up closer, the shadows appear to lighten and we can look *into* them. With a yet closer approach to a shadow, it lightens still more and objects within it are seen still better. Then we may say that we look *through* the shadow: The shadow loses its identity as a shadow, and the low illumination that was the shadow becomes more nearly the illumination level for the scene itself.

8. When we go into dimly illuminated places, the color of objects and surfaces largely disappears. In very dimly illuminated places, even though we may still see well enough to get around, all color is absent.

9. The illumination of a scene definitely controls the viewer's mood, which he or she may attribute to the composition of the scene. For example, outdoor illumination in the afternoon may come from the sun low in the sky, changing the sizes and directions of shadows and other luminous features of the scene and providing for a mood quite different from that at noon.

10. When one looks at a colored object steadily for a moment and then turns away to look at a homogeneous surface, such as the wall of a room, he or she sees the object imaged against the wall. The color of the imaged object, called an afterimage, is different from that of the object first looked at and soon fades and disappears.

Here, then, is a small sample of the countless variety of situations and circumstances in which we see color. These and many others provide many complex questions for those who study color.

The Spectrum

The radiation commonly called light possesses several characteristics that play a role in determining perceptual reaction. Photic radiation is wavelike and usually composed of a wide variety of wavelengths. This combination generally tends to evoke the experience of whiteness. The separation of the components from one another in an orderly array in accord with wavelength produces what we call the *spectrum.*

In the study of color, experimental manipulations may start with spectrally controlled photic sources for targets, in order to determine what is seen, or they may start with experienced situations (confrontation with colors or color patterns) in which the problems are generated by the perceiver. In the latter case, features of photic control needed to produce the phenomena under study are determined secondarily. The color phenomena of possible interest are enormous in number and complexity.

In both approaches, very often impingement specification, instead of supplying wavelength data and other energistic information, is given in response terms. Instead of describing a portion of the spectrum in terms of its wavelength, is too often given in color terms like "the green portion of the spectrum" and "the red end of the spectrum." We suggest that if color terms are to be used in impingement specification, it would be more accurate and helpful to say, "green-producing end of the spectrum" and "red-producing portion of the spectrum." Most often, however, it is preferable to state the wavelength or range of wavelengths that actually apply.

Fundamental Variables

There are three main variables involved in radiation: *wavelength, total energy content,* and *spectral purity.* In simple situations, wavelength goes a long way in determining the perceived hue, redness, greeness, blueness. Total flux largely determines brightness, although certain wavelengths evoke a greater brightness effect than others. Spectral purity is the main determinant of whether a given hue is seen to its fullest extent or more nearly resembles a gray or verges into some other hue. When seen to its fullest extent the hue is spoken of as a fully saturated color. In simple desaturation a color appears more nearly gray. Given hues in normal color vision

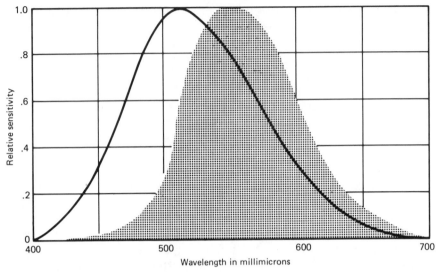

Figure 8.18   Luminosity curves of the human eye. The contour of the solid area represents the sensitivity of the light-adapted eye to various wavelengths. The other curve represents a shift in sensitivity for vision at lower illuminations.

can be produced either by a narrow band of wavelengths (generally spoken of as though only a single wavelength) or by a combination of three particular bands. Normal vision is called trichromatic. (The various defects in color vision that occur in a small percentage of the general population will be dealt with later.)

Not all portions of the color-producing spectrum of radiation are equally effective, that is, wavelengths do not equally affect the sense cells. The diagram of this relative effectiveness is called a *luminosity curve*. In Figure 8.18 there are two luminosity curves; the one bounding the black area is the curve for high levels of radiation, and the other is for low levels. It will be noticed that maximum effectiveness for the high-level (photopic) curve lies in the region of 550 to 560 millimicrons and that the maximum for the other (the scotopic) curve lies at about 510 millimicrons. A shift from one curve to the other occurs as the illumination of a room is lowered, for example. The shift in the relative lightness or brightness of the various hues in a complex scene is called the Purkinje shift.

Color Sources

Some sources of radiation leading to color experiences are: sun, carbon arcs, incandescent lamps, vapor sources such as mercury lamps, and fluorescent tubes. The *array* of wavelengths that any photic radiation source emits is called its spectrum and the spectra of various sources are unlike. Not only is there a variety of wavelengths involved, but also the proportionate amount of energy in the wavelengths in the various sources differ (Figure 8.19).

Some spectra are *continuous*. They contain a more or less complete assortment of wavelengths with no narrow band of wavelengths highly predominant. Other spectra are *discontinuous* and contain prominent narrow bands of wavelengths called lines; ranges of wavelengths are absent. Vapor sources are examples of discontinuous spectra.

So far we have referred to original sources of radiation. Visual stimuli are, of course, not confined to such sources, but include *reflection* from surfaces and the radiation that has been passed through filters, or substances that selectively absorb and transmit various parts of radiation reaching them. Filters are used to obtain desired portions of the *visible spectrum* by eliminating the portions not wanted. The ideal spectrum is the solar spectrum; it is the portion of the complete *electromagnetic array* that contains not only the

Figure 8.19   The approximate relative energy distributions of various sources of radiation within the visible spectrum. *A* is the sun, *B* a mercury arc, *C* a tungsten lamp, and *D* a fluorescent tube. The curves as drawn have no absolute relation to each other; for example, curve *A* could have been set at a different level.

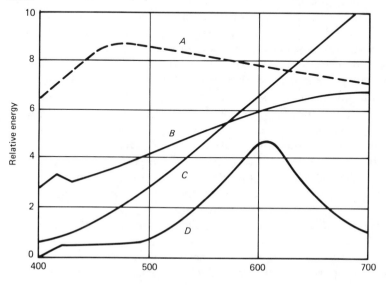

Wavelength in millimicrons

color-producing, ultraviolet, and infrared wavelengths, but also those that make up the band we call radio waves.

Color Filters

The most common filters are used in photography in the form of glass plates. Disk-form filters are slipped on over cameral lenses for various purposes. Sky filters are one type; they filter out short wavelength (blue) and help make clouds more prominent in photographs. Common filters are not highly selective. For filtering out all wavelengths except a desired narrow band of a very few millimicrons, special types of filters are used.

A flexible and precise way to obtain narrow bands of radiation is to use a monochromator, which with a prism or other device helps select a band of the spectrum by refraction. For the most precise control of the very wavelengths and intensities desired, a photic source (a lamp) whose spectrum is known should be used with the monochromator. (The standard illuminant sources are called illuminants *A, B,* and *C.*)

Physical Processes in Photic Radiation

Photic radiation from a source to the eye may involve the processes of *transmission, absorption, reflection, refraction,* or *interference.* These constitute all that happens to radiation once it leaves the source. Some substances *transmit* radiation; it passes through them. Some substances *absorb* photic radiation; radiant energy is transformed within them to other forms, such as heat or mechanical work or chemical processes. Some substances change the direction of the radiation, sending it backward; they *reflect* the radiation. If the radiation reaches the surface of the substance obliquely, the reflection angle has the same value as the incident one. Some substances change the direction of the radiation as it passes through them; this is called *refraction. Diffusion* is reflection by a rough surface or transmission of radiation through a translucent material; in both cases, rays are sent in various directions in a helter-skelter fashion. *Diffraction* is the modification that radiation undergoes in passing along edges of opaque material or through very narrow slits or in being reflected from ruled surfaces (surfaces with parallel lines scratched on them) and producing parallel light- and dark-colored bands.

Interference is the mutual effect of two wave fronts meeting. The effect is partial or total cancellation depending on relative energies and whether the wavelengths are the same or different. In some cases reinforcement instead of cancellation takes place. Interference bands may be set up by different gratings or ruled surfaces. Most of these processes can be manipulated to produce color effects.

COLOR NAMES, SPECIFICATIONS, AND MIXTURES

Number and Names of Colors

Naming colors depends on a number of factors, some of which lie outside an individual's spectral sensitivity as determined by retinal photochemistry. Some peoples of the world have a very scant vocabulary for color-naming. Rivers (1901) tested several primitive tribes and found that certain tribesmen had only three names: one for items we call red, purple, and orange; one for white, yellow, and green; and one for blue, black, and violet. No finer discriminations were apparently called for in the affairs of the tribe. Need seems to be a great determining factor in color-naming, as exemplified by the fact that Eskimos have numerous verbal responses pertaining to snow whereas non-Eskimos have only a few.

The question of how many colors there are and how names are related to color experiences is important in everyday affairs. Evans (1948) pointed out that there are two kinds of color description, quite difficult to distinguish. One set of terms describes color on an absolute basis; it refers to what he calls the "mental color system." The other set depicts differences among colors and applies directly to the amount and direction of shift in hue, saturation, and lightness. Judd (1932) indicated that there are 10 million such distinguishable color differences describable by words. There are far fewer actual color names (the first set). The Maerz and Paul (1951) color dictionary gives less than four thousand, and some of these are only transient names that could be considered synonyms. Thirty-six are single words. A little less than 300 are compound terms consisting of a color name and an adjective.

The Inter-Society Color Council devised a scheme for naming colors that modifies hue names, such as red, yellow, green, blue, purple, olive, brown, and pink, by the adjectives weak, strong, light, and dark. The word "very" is also included. Furthermore, the words pale (light weak), brilliant (light strong), deep (dark strong), vivid (very strong), and dusky (dark weak) are used. Names for intermediate hues, such as yellowish orange, are also used. All told, this system totals up to 319 items, given in terms of the Munsell notations (to be discussed later in this chapter). When one tries to use these names for designating transparent materials, some of the terms have to be changed, obviously, because lighter surface colors run to *white* and the colors of solutions run to *colorless.*

Color Systems

Two fairly well-known systems of color specification involving color samples bear a systematic relation to each other in terms of hue, saturation, and brightness. The first is the Munsell; the second is the Ostwald. In the Munsell (1942) system the three factors varied in the samples are called hue, chroma, and value, which compare roughly to the three variables just mentioned. They are built into a three-dimensional scheme ordinarily called a color solid and having a vertical black-to-white axis. Radiating from this, the hues are arranged in equiangular spacing (see Figure 8.20). Chroma is defined as the horizontal distance from the axis. Munsell published a color atlas containing two sets of colored paper samples or "chips" systematically numbered and arranged in accordance with various sections through the solid, one in the vertical and the other in the horizontal plane. The specification of any test color is given in the form of a numerical statement of where it matches the color solid. The Munsell system as improved in 1943 is the nearest approach to a color solid based on the appearance of surface colors. It must be recognized, however, that such a system has limitations. For example, all colors we perceive are not surface colors, and all surfaces do not act alike; hence all color comparisons we make cannot be made directly by consultation of the atlas.

The Ostwald (1931, 1933) system also employs a color solid in the form of a double cone, that is, two cones base to base (Figure 8.21). In this solid the complementary colors (red, green, blue, yellow, and so on) are placed opposite each other around the circumference of the solid. The axis, running from the apex of one cone to the other, is the black-white axis. A vertical section through the Ostwald solid is in the form of two triangles, base to base, or a diamond.

One of the drawbacks to the Ostwald solid is that is is radially symmetrical. In actuality, not all hues involve equal numbers of steps in saturation and would not be represented by equal distances from the vertical black-white axis. This is aptly illustrated by the Nickerson–Newhall experimental color solid based on the Munsell scheme (Figure 8.20). The main feature of the solid is its demonstration of the inequality of distances from the central axis. Nine different levels of this axis are represented in the construction of the solid and no two of them are similar.

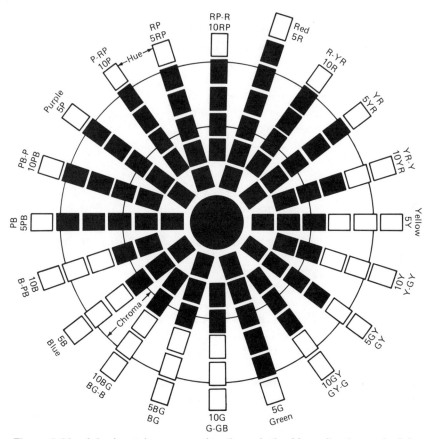

Figure 8.20   A horizontal cross section through the Munsell scheme (solid) of interrelated colors. Although shown here in black and white, the cross section is meant to represent an array of colored samples (rectangles). The Munsell notation 5R, 10R, 5YR, and so on for the various hues radii in the cross section. A second set of labels has been added to make it easier to identify the actual colors, such as red, yellow-red, yellow-red yellow, yellow, and so on. All of the samples in each cross section when colored have the same brightness (value). In the cross section shown the value is 5/. Each cross section is for a different value. Saturation increases along each hue radius, so that the least saturated hues are nearest the central axis of the cross section. It will be noted that the hues do not provide equal numbers of samples (equal steps of saturation). (Source: Courtesy, Munsell Color Company, Inc., Baltimore, MD 21218.)

Color Mixture: Subtractive and Additive Effects

One problem in dealing with color pertains to what to expect when colors are mixed. We find that in color mixture sensory labels are used in place of energistic specifications to describe stimuli. The

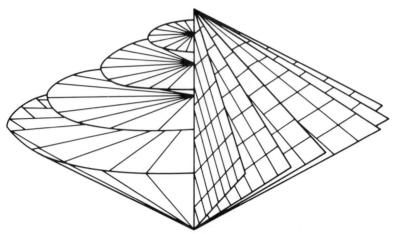

Figure 8.21   The Ostwald color solid. (Source: R. M. Evans. *An Introduction to Color.* New York: Wiley, 1948, Fig. 13.13.)

question is more often "what is the effect of mixing red and green?" than "what is the effect of mixing a certain wavelength (or band of wavelengths) with a certain other wavelength or band of wavelengths?" In familiar rather than energistic language, the following may be said. The effect of a beam of red light with a beam of green light is *additive*—more luminance is given and the result is a brighter beam of light. The result of using pigments is *subtractive*—adding some blue pigment to some yellow pigment does not add luminance. Instead, the combination tends to darken. Furthermore, the result will differ in hue: in this case green. The final color will be that represented by the wavelengths that remain after absorption in the two pigments. This group of wavelengths differs from what is not absorbed by either pigment alone and produces a different color sensation. It is a smaller group of wavelengths and thus is a subtractive effect in luminance.

There has always been considerable interest in *color mixture*, particularly the kind produced by rapidly presenting alternations of different colored surfaces to the eye. This is accomplished by using revolving disks with sectors composed of different colored surfaces. Let us use a disk in which the two sectors can be varied: one is seen as green, the other as red. If this disk is rapidly revolved, the two sectors are not seen individually and the whole disk takes on a new appearance. With the appropriate spectral reflectances— that is, with the proper red and the proper green—the new appearance is gray. It is necessary to adjust the relative proportions of the two sectors so that the gray will be as nearly neutral as possible; otherwise it will be greenish or reddish.

The revolving disk method helps determine the consequences of mixing various pairs of hues. Any two pairs that do not produce gray when mixed are called noncomplementary colors; those that do are called complementary. Red and green are commonly named complementary colors as are blue and yellow. When three hues (three sectors) are chosen so that each has its complementary lying between itself and the third hue, all other hues can be made by mixing the three together in proper proportions. The angular sizes of the sectors required to produce a given result are the crude quantitative measures possible in this form of color mixing.

Color mixing can also be achieved by instrumentation. Double monochromators supply two wavelength bands that can be mixed.

COLOR PHENOMENA

Afterimages

We discuss afterimages now rather than earlier because by studying their production is a way of studying color vision. Some images produced even with nonselected portions of the spectrum are colored and thus can be used for discerning certain things about the relative activities of rods and cones.

Something is seen not only when direct photic input (stimulation) is provided but also shortly afterwards. These after effects, or "after sensations," are usually spoken of as *afterimages.* They are commonly produced by viewing targets of limited angular extents for a few seconds and then either looking at some homogeneous surface (a gray surface, for example) or simply by having the fixated target removed without disturbing fixation and without changing whatever the background (context, surround) had been. The observer sees a new area of the same shape as the previously fixated target. The color and size of the new area depends on several factors. Afterimages are ordinarily not seen in midair but lie on surfaces looked at. The surface on which the afterimage is to be projected can be at a distance from the eye different from that of the original target that is fixated to produce the afterimage. If the new surface is farther away, the afterimage will look bigger than the original target and, correspondingly, if the surface is nearer, the afterimage will be smaller. The size of the afterimage is proportional to the distance of the image's projection. This is *Emmert's law.*

If the target surround and the surface on which the subsequent fixation is directed are neutral gray, the new area (the afterimage) will be complementary to the original target; this new area is called a *complementary afterimage*. It is sometimes erroneously called a *negative afterimage*. But there are *negative afterimages* properly so-called: They are produced in the following manner. If an observer views an intensely luminous patch of light and then turns to a homogeneously gray field, he or she will see a patch either lighter or darker than the field. The lighter patch is called a positive afterimage and the darker one is called a *negative afterimage.*

Afterimages last for sizable fractions of seconds or even for several seconds. They appear and disappear and reappear. The total train of alternations may occupy a number of seconds, during which time they decline in impressiveness.

The microtemporal afterconsequences of photic stimulation may be studied by very briefly exposing a stimulus of relatively high intensity (a fraction of a second) followed by no illumination of either target or surround (a completely "dark" room). Under such conditions a sequence of seven afterimages is often observable. Berry and Imus (1935) listed them as follows:

1. A positive image appearing about $\frac{1}{20}$ of a second after target exposure and lasting for about another $\frac{1}{20}$ of a second.
2. A "negative" or dark period follows.
3. The second positive afterimage, called Bidwell's ghost or the Purkinje image, appears at about $\frac{1}{5}$ second and lasts for that much time.
4. A second dark period follows.
5. The third positive image, which is called the Hess image, appears.
6. A third dark period follows.
7. A fourth, very weak positive phase appears.

McDougall (1904) used a technique that spread the afterimages and the interspersed dark phases out in a spatial array. He used a revolving slit of 2° in angular subtense, which moved in front of a glass surface illuminated briefly from behind. The observer saw a series of light and dark bands in spatial sequense. Some of the bands have been identified, one, for example, as Bidwell's ghost.

Color Adaptation and Conversion

As we deal with color in practical and experimental situations, we are impressed by two apparently diverse principles. Color is seen to be a facile and changeable thing, depending largely on the relationship of one part of the scene to another. Two colors seen as juxtaposed are always different from what they would be were the target simplified so that only one color were seen. Therefore color of a limited target is not fixed in its relationship to the impingement that produces it. On the other hand, colored surfaces do not seem to change much under a wide variety of illuminations. They tend to look somewhat the same in most cases regardless of whether the illumination is artificial or natural (the sun). Although these effects seem diverse and unrelated, they are both due, in part, to the mechanism of color adaptation.

A target seen after the eye's adaptation to a target of a different spectral composition appears to be different from how it would appear without this preexposure. On the other hand, various targets that ordinarily differ in their color may look alike when they are viewed by eyes that have been previously adapted to different wavelengths.

When one's gaze is fixated on a colored area, adaptation of the eye to the area and its immediate surrounds sets in. Though the appearance of the fixated area does not immediately change, the area next viewed, when the eye shifts position, will be affected. This effect depends on the length of the previous fixation, the intensity of stimulation, and the area of the surface viewed. Increasing these factors works toward an increase in the persistence of the effect. Full adaptation occurs quite readily if the viewed target is of moderate intensity and if the eye comes on it from darkness. As fixation on such a target is prolonged, the consequent adaptive effect is more persistent, as demonstrated by the longer time required for adaptation to a new target of low intensity.

In a complex target various portions reflect (or emit) different wavelengths at different luminosity levels. Adaptation to different portions of the target is different; some portions cause adaptation to one part of the spectrum and others to other parts. A shift of the eye or a sudden exchange of targets causes consequences that can be attributed to this differential adaptation.

Let us say that the new target is of the same spatial pattern as the original one, the two differing only in the wavelengths involved in some of their various areas. Areas of the new target that happen to involve the same wavelengths as in the old will evoke reduced response because of previous adaptation. Areas involving new wavelengths will not have been preadapted to these wavelengths; because no preadaptation had occurred, they will evoke strong responses. A whole new set of relationships among the effectiveness of the various areas is produced.

In this shift the spectral composition of the illuminant, as well as the spectral reflectances of the target surfaces, plays a role. In any complex target the outcome is also extremely complex, and only in more recent years has a reasonable understanding of the matter been achieved. This is expressed in Helson's (1964) account, which involves his adaptation level theory. Helson speaks of certain complex phenomena usually discussed in adaptation as "color conversion." The following is Helson's slightly modified statement of Helson and Michels' (1948) earlier statement.

> The principle, based on work with reflecting samples on nonselective surfaces states: In every viewing situation there is established an adaptation level or neutral region such that stimuli with reflectances above this level are tinged with the hue of the source of illumination, stimuli with lower reflectances take the afterimage complementary to the hue of the illuminant, and stimuli with reflectances near AL (adaptation level) are either achromatic or weakly saturated and of uncertain hue. In order that a highly reflecting surface appear achromatic it is necessary that its spectral reflectance be such that, when multiplied by the spectral energy distribution of the illuminant, it yields the specifications of the corresponding achromatic point. But highly reflecting surfaces necessarily depart from this condition toward the hue of the illuminant. According to Equation 15 a stimulus of very low reflectance would be achromatic only if its spectral reflectance, multiplied by the spectral energy distribution of the illuminant, were to yield the chromaticity coordinates of the surround. The reflectance of selective surfaces can depart from this requirement in one of two ways: (1) favoring the dominant wavelength of the illuminant and yielding high reflectance, and (2) favoring other wavelengths, thus causing the color to shift toward the complement of the illuminant. However, this effect alone cannot explain the behavior of nonselective surfaces of low reflectance. The color on such surfaces must be due to the afterimage complementary effect noted with spots of low brightness. The results obtained in the study therefore agree with the principle of color conversion obtained from observations on reflecting surfaces. (Helson, 1964, pp. 169–170.)

An illustration of the operation of color conversion is found in the Land colors (Land, 1959). The Land procedure photographs a scene on black-white film through a long-wave (or "red") filter. Wavelengths in the scene, in the range of 585 to 700 millimicrons, affect the film more than shorter wavelengths. The scene is also photographed through a medium wavelength filter (passing radiation of from 490 to 600 millimicrons). This filter emphasized this band of wavelengths. When positives of these two films are projected on a screen in exact register (occupying exactly the same space on the screen), a reproduction of the original scene in color results when the long-wave positive is projected with illumination coming through the original "red" filter and the medium-wave positive is projected with illumination from a common incandescent lamp with no filter. However, if the red filter for the long-wave positive is replaced by a "green" filter, the colors in the resulting scene are reversed. This is as would be expected from the principle of color conversion.

Helson's explanation is as follows. When positives are made from the two films using the two filters as described above, the long-wave positive reproduces the red-yellow colors of the photographed scene, whereas the middle-wave positive reproduces the green-blue colors in near-white. Supposing the existence of an intermediate adaptation level, the portions of the screen above this level will be viewed as red to yellow, the portions near the level will be colorless, and the portions below the level will show up as various mixtures of the "afterimage complement" or green-blue.

Land supposed that the colors he produced from just two complementaries could not be accounted for by classical explanations of color vision, since normal color vision is supposedly based on three complementaries. Helson's explanation, premised on the idea that adaptation is involved (where Land had rejected it), covers the situation very well. A difference here between Helson's concept of adaptation and many psychologists' conception is that his does not involve the factor of appreciable duration whereas classical adaptation does.

Color Contrast and Induction

In dealing with color effects, one is faced not only with relating photic input to body process and to sensory end result (the color produced) but also with the fact of *spatial adjacency* of various diverse inputs on the retina. Two adjacent areas of the retina provided with different spectral inputs produce effects that are not accounted for by the rules governing the simple relation between wavelength and color end result. The effects are due to adjacency of the two inputs. We are, in more familiar terms, speaking now of color induction and color contrast. A target seen as red looks still redder when adjacent to another target area seen as green. This contrast effect is produced with achromatic targets as well. The processes produce simultaneous contrast, but contrast may occur when the target fixated looks green and is exchanged for one that looks red. The red is redder than otherwise by reason of the exposure to the previous target. Thus since contrast may be of two forms, color induction is of two forms. Successive induction is dependent on adaptation (at least in part) and hence is relevant to the present discussion of adaptation.

Relation of Hue and Saturation to Intensity

The relation of perceived hue to intensity of radiation has been studied by several investigators, including Purdy. Purdy (1931) used a target with two portions, the intensity relations between which bore a ratio of 10 to 1. A large field was matched with a small field that was less intense. In the typical set of results shown in Figure 8.22 the curve shows the amount of discrepancy in wavelength between the two fields that had to be used to make the two hues match. In the extreme left portion of the graph it will be seen that the small matching field had to have a slightly longer wavelength than the test field. As the wavelength for the test field was lengthened, the wavelength for the matching field had to be shortened so as to retain the hue match between the two. At a little above 500 millimicrons the matching field had suddenly to be shifted toward the longer wavelengths. This effect reached a peak in the region of about 525 millimicrons. From there on, the wavelength of the matching field had to be gradually reduced to maintain the hue match. In the region of about 575 millimicrons the two fields matched when their wavelengths were similar. As

Figure 8.22 Change in hue produced by a change in intensity from 1000 to 100 trolands. Targets of these two intensities were matched and a wavelength shift was found necessary to match the hues. (Source: D. M. Purdy, "Spectral hue as a function of intensity," *Amer. J. Psychol.,* 1931, 43, 541–559, Fig. 1.)

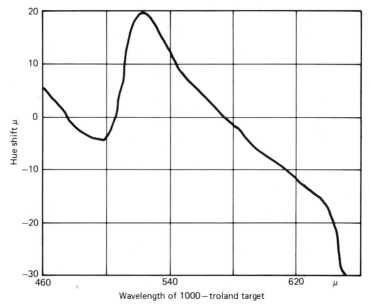

Wavelength of 1000–troland target

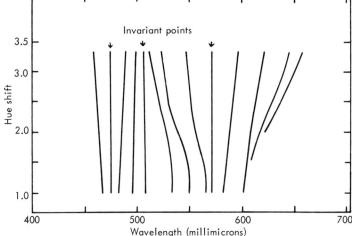

Figure 8.23   A set of curves obtained by Purdy to indicate the relation of constant hue to wavelength and luminance. (Source: L. M. Hurvich and D. Jameson." Some quantitative aspects of an opponent-colors theory. II. Brightness, saturation and hue in normal and dichromatic vision," *J.O.S.A.*, 1955, 45, 602–616, Fig. 9.)

longer and longer wavelengths were compared, the wavelengths of the matching field had to be reduced more and more until, as seen by the graph, the discrepancy became very great.

The results are shown in a different way by Figure 8.23, in which each line represents a constant hue. It will be seen that not all the lines are straight and perpendicular. Many of them shift to the right or left, indicating that the wavelengths represented change as the value of the ordinate of the graph changes (as the luminance changes). At three places along the abscissa (wavelength) there are invariant (stable) points. These same three points are shown in the graph indicated by arrows where the curve is at zero hue shift.

Abney (1913) earlier studied the relation of intensity to hue. He studied a much wider range and came to the conclusion that all hues tend to move toward blue or yellow at high intensities, toward red or green at low intensities. This conclusion is not contradictory to that derived from Purdy's experiment.

Modes of Color Appearance

Colors may be seen in several ways; that is, color may be an aspect of various kinds of perceived situations, which may be divided into five classes. They are generally spoken of as *modes* of perceiving colors and are: (1) the aperture, (2) the illuminant, (3) the illumination, (4) the film, and (5) the object modes of surface and volume.

The *aperture mode* is that in which color is seen without regard to its distance and its being a property of a surface or any object. One of the best illustrations of the appearance of aperture colors is the color seen through some optical instrument, such as a microscope or a spectroscope, in which the field is uniform and not seen as the surface of any object. The same result may be obtained when viewing a spectral target through a cardboard mailing tube.

The *illuminant mode* is assumed when one views a source of photic radiation, such as an incandescent filament, an arc lamp, or the surface of an opal glass window of a lamphouse when illuminated from the side opposite the viewer in a darkroom.

The *illumination mode* is assumed when one detects that the color of a surface is "due to" its illumination or that the illumination of the room is affecting the color of objects in it.

The *film mode* of seeing color is produced, generally, by photic radiation falling on the rapidly moving blades of a fan or an episcotister (a rotating disk with either open or different colored sectors). The film is translucent. One sees not only it but also objects beyond the film.

The two *object modes,* surface and volume, have to do with the perception of the properties of objects. Color seems to be an intrinsic property of the object itself rather than of the light that falls on it. Seeing color as a property of surface is so convincing that at times it takes some peculiar demonstration or explanation to help a person realize that color is a function of illumination as well as of surface properties.

In other cases, for example, in the volume mode of seeing color we do not necessarily see the surfaces of objects as standing out in distinction and are able to look through the objects, as vessels of colored liquids. The color we see is distributed through the liquid and is a three-dimensional affair.

Depending on the mode of viewing, various properties of color emerge.

Properties of Color

When color, particularly a colored surface, is spoken of, a number of properties in addition to hue, brightness, and saturation are included. Some seem to pertain to color the way hue, brightness, and saturation do. Others are effects that do not pertain so much to the color itself as to collateral effects attributed to color. In the list following a number of properties of the first sort are included.

hue	pleasantness or unpleasantness
brightness or lightness	prounouncedness
saturation	area
warmth	location
hardness	

Transparency is another feature attributed to color as a property. This may be so, but it would seem that transparency has more to do with the material that carries the color (color in varnishes as in contrast to color in paints).

Another dubious property of color is *shape*. It is often listed as a color property, as when we say that colors depend on the shape of the object to which they pertain. Here we need to remember an infrequently observed principle: in using the term color, we refer to a perception. Shape is a characteristic seen at the same time that color is seen. They can be said to be two parts of a simple overall perception. It is not proper to use one part of a given response (or perception) to account for another part of the response. If we were free to say that the shape of an object changes its color, we might be able to say that the color has an effect on perceived shape. Neither statement is quite legitimate. For causal explanations, we must go to body processes.

Still other qualities attributed to color are *gloss, luster, sparkle, texture, volume.* Here again, are terms that do not fall into a single category. Gloss refers to an effect produced by the ratio of specular to diffuse reflection of target surface. Specular reflection is reflection that is more pronounced in some direction than others; it is the opposite of diffuse reflection. Therefore it is not a property that pertains to surfaces seen as gray or white or black, as well as to surfaces with a definite hue. Luster is a perceived surface and intensity property; it has not been well defined and its origins are not clearly understood. Texture is not specific to wavelength or to hue but to structural composition of a surface or to the minute variations in texture or a lightness. Other color phenomena will be dealt with in Chapter 11 on perceptual constancies.

Theories of Color Vision

For long over a century, persons interested in vision have produced theories of color vision based on either suppositions or knowledge about the photochemistry of retinal cone pigments and on psychophysical data stemming from relating colors seen to portions of the spectrum used as stimuli. More recently, information regarding *neural processes* in the visual system ("the optic pathway") has been utilized in theory building. Our attention will be given first to the classical *theories of Young and Helmholtz and of Hering.* While there have been numerous theories differing from each other in limited particulars, these two provide a basis for understanding what color theories in general contain and how provisional explanations have been achieved.

Young first presented his color vision theory in 1807, and Helmholtz began his contribution in 1852. The names of the two men are customarily bracketed together as authors of a trichromatic theory. A trichromatic theory states that all the perceivable colors can be obtained from combining three appropriate wavelengths or three bands of wavelengths. It is supposed that there are three fundamental photochemical processes each of which is elicited to some degree by different parts of the spectrum.

Differing from this trichromatic, or three-component, theory, Hering in 1878 and in 1920 believed that there are four primary colors, blue (about 470 millimicrons), green (about 500 millimicrons), yellow (about 570 millimicrons), and red (mixture of red and violet). His sort of theory is known also as an opponent-color theory. Red and green are one pair of opponents; blue and yellow are another pair. In this theory, colors intermediate between the primaries also oppose each other. The primary colors possess important properties not possessed by their intermediates. The primaries do not shift in hue as brightness changes and keep their opposition in producing an achromatic effect (gray) and in simultaneous contrast. The properties of opponent pairs are thought to depend on paired antagonistic photochemical processes, for example, a red-green process, a yellow-blue process, and a white-black process. There are supposedly subprocesses whereby the red opposes green, blue opposes yellow, and so on.

Hering initially characterized the opposing subprocesses as assimilative and dissimilative. Processes for white, red, and yellow were dissimilative; that is, they were breakdown or catabolic processes. Processes for black, green, and blue were build-up or assimilative processes. Intermediate hues were thought to be dependent on the interaction of assimilative-dissimilative components, for example, the reaction of the processes for blue and red to produce violet. This was a kind of opponent-color theory. The present-day version of the *opponent-color theory* is described by Hurvich and Jameson (1955), who developed the first quantitative statement of such a theory.

Granit's Work Relating to Color Theory

The physiological studies of Granit (1947) that began in the 1940s produced information of considerable theoretical significance, although they have not provided data interpretable exclusively by either of the two types of theory just described.

Granit recorded electrical responses, evoked by inputs of different wavelengths, in single or clustered optic nerve fibers and in ganglion cells in the retinas of several species. Microelectrode technique made this possible. In recording from primarily rod-containing eyes, he found that spectral sensitivity curves were broad. They tallied with minor deviations to the absorption curve of visual purple, a rod pigment. Granit called them *scotopic dominator curves.*

In the light-adapted eye of the cat, modulator curves were not obtainable. Instead, Granit found narrow-band curves of sensitivity with maxima at approximately 450, 540, and 610 millimicrons; he called these *modulator curves.* Various animal species differed from each other in the sorts of dominator curves and modulator curves exhibited. The findings tallied with cone-rod eye composition.

Granit described how modulator activities may combine to provide for the human luminosity curve and how hue discrimination and luminosity are brought about.

DeValois' Work in the Lateral Geniculate Body

More recently, DeValois (1960) studied the electrical responses of the lateral geniculate body of the monkey to spectral stimuli. He found cells in the dorsal layers that produced "on" responses and cells in the ventral layers that produced "off" responses. Certain cells in the intermediate layers produced "on–off" responses; these cells responded only to inputs from one eye or the other but not to both. Varying the photic intensity over wide ranges did not shift the responses of "on" cells to "off" responses. Increasing input intensity raised the average number of impulse spikes in the record. Many of the "on" cells were sensitive to only a narrow band of the spectrum. Some cells toward the edges of the lateral geniculate body showed sensitivity to two bands of wavelengths. As the eye was shifted from a dark to light adapted state, the sensitivity peaks shifted, whereas other "on" cells showed no such shift.

Cells that exhibited both "on" and "off" responses exhibited "on" responses to one band of wavelength and "off" to another. For example, a cell may respond during photic input and be quiescent when the input is terminated. If an input of a different part of the spectrum is used, the cell does not respond during input but will respond at the termination of the input. Such a cell is insensitive to inputs of intermediate wavelengths. There seem also to be cells that respond to two wavelengths but differently. They seem also to be cells that respond to two wavelengths but differently. They produce, for example, an "on" response to the short ("blue") end of the spectrum and an "off" response to the yellow-producing portion of the spectrum.

Measurements on the Characteristics of Receptors

Recently, Marks, Dobelle, and MacNichol (1964) recorded difference spectra for single cones in the eyes of human subjects and monkeys. Brown and Wald (1964) did this for the human eye only. Marks and his colleagues found three classes of cones in the eyes of both humans and monkeys. The absorption maxima for photic radiation were at about 445, 535, and 570 millimicrons. The findings of Brown and Wald were quite similar: at 450, 525, and 555 millimicrons, they also made observations on single human rods, showing a maximum of 505 millimicrons.

Marks, et al. summarized their findings in the following way:

1. The primate parafovea contains three kinds of cones, each seeming to have a single predominant pigment.
2. The pigments absorb energy maximally from three distinct regions of the spectrum.
3. The blue receptor is a cone, not a rod. Its absorption maximum is for a shorter wavelength than for rhodopsin found in rods.
4. Cone pigments seem to have the same order of concentration and sensitivity as those found in rods.

Forms of Color Defect

Defective color vision, sometimes called *color blindness* or *anomalous color vision,* is an inherited condition. In color defects, confusion in discriminating and naming of the various target portions that give rise to the normal array of color is manifested. Defects in color perception occur in reference to hue, saturation, and brightness or lightness.

There are three principal forms of color defect. The first is total color blindness, or monochromatism, in which all hues and saturations of them are absent but variations in brightness can be detected. The next condition is partial color blindness or color weakness in which only two distinct hues are perceived regardless of the spectral content of the radiation reaching the eye; this is called *dichromatism.* The third kind of defect is known as *anomalous trichromatism;* it differs least from normal color vision (which is known as *trichromatism,* since radiation from any properly selected three portions of the spectrum can be combined to match a chosen color). In dichromatism, two portions of the spectrum are required to match all colors but the matches vary more from test to test.

There are nine subvarieties of the three principal kinds of color defect, which are so complex as to warrant omission of their description. They are named as follows: (1) typical total color blindness, (2) atypical total color blindness, (3) green blindness (deuteranopia), (4) red blindness (protanopia), (5) absence of blue and yellow perception, (6) weakness for the perception of colors in the short-wave end of the spectrum, (7) green weakness, (8) red weakness, and (9) blue weakness. Some of these forms are exceedingly rare. The most prevalent forms are atypical total color blindness, about 2 percent males and about $\frac{1}{70}$ as many females; green blindness, 1 percent of males and $\frac{1}{10}$ percent of females; red blindness, about 1 percent of males; green weakness, 5 percent of the population; and red weakness, 1 percent of the population.

A great deal of the work on color vision consists in finding out more about the nature of various color defects. Such findings help in the construction of color theories (statements about the understanding of body mechanisms underlying color vision) and in checking on and modifying theories already in existence.

One form of dichromatism is deuteranopia, in which relative spectral luminosity does not differ much from normal vision but in which all colors can be achieved only by mixtures of two primaries, one from one end of the spectrum and one from the other end. Somewhere between these two extremes is a neutral point where hue is best discriminated. Shorter wavelengths give rise to blue, longer wavelengths to yellow. The saturation of the colors increases toward both ends of the spectrum. Yellow, orange, red, and green cannot be discriminated from each other when saturation and brightness are made the same. Blue, violet, and bluish purple are different for the deuteranope only in brightness and saturation but not in actual hue.

Graham and Hsia (1958) determined the absolute luminosity for a subject with normal vision in one eye and mainly deuteranopic vision in the other. Both eyes seemed to be equally sensitive to the part of the spectrum for red, but the color-blind eye was definitely less sensitive for blue and green. By a matching technique the experimenters found that the subject saw only two hues with the defective eye. They matched all wavelengths greater than about 502 millimicrons by presenting a wavelength of 570 millimicrons (yellow) to the normal eye. The shorter wavelengths were matched by a wavelength of 470 millimicrons (blue) presented to the normal eye.

Berger, Graham, and Hsia (1958) found that the luminosity deficits exhibited by this subject held at intensities well above threshold.

Tests for Color Vision

Tests for color defects have been standardized, but they tend to have certain limitations—some owing to their length, some to their failure to deal with all the principal kinds of defects, some to the marked difference between them and the conditions of everyday life in which color defect is significant. A description of all best-known color tests would be too lengthy and complicated for us here.

One form of screening test for color-vision defect is the so-called pseudoisochromatic plate test. The plates are cards covered with various colored dots arranged in random relations except for certain dots that form given figures within the dot field. Subjects with normal color vision see the figures. Subjects with certain defects see the figures on some of the plates but not on others. The earliest of this form of test was the Stilling test produced in Germany in 1875. A Japanese form, the Ishihara test, was produced in 1917. It was meant to detect protanopic and protanomalous defects as well as the deuteranopic and deuteranomalous. A Russian form, the Rabkin test, appeared in 1939, and in 1944 the Dvorine, an American test, came out. In 1955 the H-R-R plates of Hardy, Rand, and Rittler appeared in this country.

In 1943 Farnsworth produced a 100-Hue test that used Munsell color chips to be arranged in order of hue. This is somewhat similar to the old Holmgren yarn test, which involved sorting yarn samples into groups according to hue.

The more precise nature of a subject's color discrimination is determined by instrumentation. The anomaloscope is one form; the most widely used instrumentation is that invented by Nagel in 1898.

A double monochromator may be used, an instrument by which a narrow band of the spectrum can be selected for color observation. One target field can be held constant and the other varied step by step by moving along the spectrum by small amounts. Normal vision detects color differences as small steps are made; with color defectives the steps may be enormous without the emergence of a hue difference.

Temporal Factors in Producing Color

We have already discussed temporal factors in producing visual effects. Here we have temporal factors relative to the production of color, but the procedures used to produce them are those described in the next section on intermittent stimulation.

None of the better known theories of color vision recognize the fact that temporal features of photic input participate in determining the color seen. For these theories temporal factors seem not to exist and the only differential of consequence in the input is wavelength. This is in spite of the fact that for more than a century color has been shown to be producible by whole-spectrum inputs, the inputs that generally produce white or gray.

Fechner (1838) reported color effects from whole-spectrum targets. Benham (1894) devised a top (a spinning disk) half white and half black with some concentric black lines drawn on the white sector. When the disk revolved at about 5 cycles per second under moderate illumination, various weak colored rings appeared.

Much more recently, certain workers have become interested in the role of timing of *intermittency* of stimulus input in the modification of color effects (Bartley and Nelson, 1960; Nelson and Bartley, 1961; Ball, 1964; Ball and Bartley, 1965; Bartley and Ball, 1966; Ball and Bartley, 1966). These authors used stimuli of selected wavelengths. The colors produced were radically changed in hue, saturation, and brightness when intermittent stimuli were substituted for steady stimuli. These experiments were special examples of the technique that first produced the phenomenon Bartley called "brightness enhancement." The only essential difference between Bartley's original studies and these was that his original work employed whole-spectrum ("white") stimuli and his later work employed selected portions of the spectrum (varying from broad bands provided by the common Wratten filters to very narrow bands provided by either a monochromator or special filters).

All these authors insist that any adequate account or theory of the mechanism that produces color must be built on not only the traditional information about receptor photochemistry, but also on the understanding gained from temporal manipulations of stimuli. This is not to be thought strange, for most of the many processes involved in producing color are actually neural rather than photochemical. Since timing is one of the chief factors in the operation of neural systems, timing of the features of stimulus input should be expected to play a causative role in color outcomes.

For example, Ball and Bartley (1965) found that if there are shifts in hue for stimuli at 480 millimicrons, they are toward colors produced by steady stimuli of shorter wavelength (purplish blue, for example). With inputs at 500 millimicrons, the results are variable, depending on PCF (pulse-to-cycle fraction). With stimuli ranging from 510 to 560 millimicrons, the shift is always upward, toward the colors obtained with steady stimulation at longer wavelengths. At 580 millimicrons no hue shift is producible, and with stimuli at 600 to 680 millimicrons, the hue shifts are always downward, toward colors produced by shorter wavelengths. PCFs above 0.25 produce few hue shifts for intermittent stimuli of any wavelength. Thus it is seen that there are two neutral or pivotal points for hue shifts, one at 580 millimicrons and one at 500.

Nelson, Bartley, and Mackavey (1961) applied to the use of pseudoisochromatic plates the findings already obtained in the study of the effects of intermittency on hue shifts. They supposed that using certain rates of intermittency might change color perception in ways that would disenable normal observers from seeing the figures on certain plates. Their experiments substantiated this. More recently, Ball and Bartley (1966) have repeated the study with more precision and have used color-deficient as well as normal observers. At certain rates and with certain PCFs, both normals and color deficients saw figures on the plates less effectively. At certain rates of intermittency, the observers with color defect were able to do better than when steady illumination of the plates was used. The latter fact supports the idea that determination of color vision is partly at loci farther along in the optic pathway than at the receptors, where selective absorption of various photic wavelengths is the definitive factor.

INTERMITTENT STIMULATION

As indicated in the previous section, temporal limitations and special temporal conditions of stimulation are significant in the analysis of brightness discrimination. They consist in (1) variation in duration of single photic pulses, (2) presentation of pairs of pulses whose temporal separation is varied, (3) single trains of pulses containing various numbers of pulses and various temporal separations between the pulses in the trains, and (4) series of trains of pulses with the separation between trains in the series being varied. Of course, in this case the variables already mentioned in (3) are included. Most studies in this kind of experimentation are called flicker experiments or intermittent stimulation.

Although the eye is usually supplied with uniform radiation that continues for some time, it is sometimes presented with a series of short pulses. We use *pulse* here instead of *flash*. A flash is what one sees. A flash does not produce a flash. It is better to say a pulse produces a flash. When the pulse rate is low enough, the observer sees a succession of alternations between light and dark. When the rate is increased, the result is called *flicker.* Experiments with intermittent stimulation are, therefore, often called flicker experiments.

The first end result of significance to us is that when the photic pulse rate is made sufficiently high, the human observer ceases to see flicker or any sort of fluctuation whatever. The point at which the light seen becomes perfectly steady is called the *fusion point.* The pulse rate at the fusion point is called the *critical flicker frequency,* of CFF. Most of the study of intermittent stimulation over the past century has concerned the conditions having to do with CFF.

In addition to pulse rate itself, several other factors—such as the stimulus *intensity,* the *part of the spectrum* used, the retina— have been studied. Figure 8.24 indicates the general relation among stimulus intensity, stimulus area, and CFF. The horizontal axis represents stimulus intensity in logarithmic units. Each curve is for a separate stimulus area, and the values are given in degrees of visual angle (angles of arc on the retina). It will be seen that as area is increased, CFF rises for most intensities. When intensities are extremely low, only the rods are activated, and the results differ from when cones are also involved. The curves flatten out and a different set of CFFs result as intensity is varied. That is, CFF is not always changed as much or in the same direction as when the cone portion of the intensity range is involved. Thus we find that the events in the eye itself are crucial in determining the perceptual outcome. Critical flicker frequency is also manipulated by using different parts of the spectrum.

More than one hundred years ago, Talbot (1834), the father of modern photography, found that there was a simple, fixed, thoroughly dependable relation between brightness that an observer sees and the fraction of the cycles of intermittency occupied by the pulse. Let us say, for example, that the photic pulse itself occupies as much time as the interval between pulses. This gives a one-to-one ratio (50 to 50 percent). Talbot found that the light looked half as bright as it would look if the stimulation were the same intensity and continued throughout the cycle, that is, if it were produced by steady stimulation. He stated that with intermittent stimulation, the perception of steady light produced is as bright as it would be were the same total stimulation distributed evenly throughout the cycle. This is known as *Talbot's law.* Accordingly, if the stimulus part is one-third of the cycle, the brightness will be one-third as great as if the same stimulus were continued through-

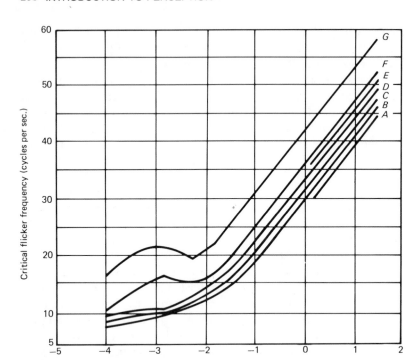

Figure 8.24 Relations among target area, intensity, and critical flicker frequency. Each curve is for a target of different angular subtense. *A* is 51′; *B*, 1°18′; *C*, 1°50′; *D*, 2°44′; *E*, 3°42′; *F*, 5°6′; and *G*, 31°51′. The stimulus and no stimulus phases of the cycle are equal. (Source: S. H. Bartley and J. L. Seibel. "A further study of entoptic stray light," *J. Psychol.*, 1954, 38, 313–319, Fig. 1.)

out the whole cycle. If an experimenter wants to reduce the effective intensity of a target by any amount, he or she can do so by interrupting the light source with a rotating open-sectored disk with an appropriate ratio of blade to open sector.

Brightness Enhancement

The study of the perceptual outcomes from the use of intermittent stimulation has not been wholly confined to pulse rates at and above the fusion point. When pulse rate is very low, the visual result is, of course, a complete alternation between light and dark periods. As pulse rate is increased, the dark period disappears and becomes merely a period less light than the original light period. As pulse rate is further increased, the visual result may be described as a light field (a steady component) and a superimposed fluctuating component. As pulse rate is increased still further, the fluctuating component becomes less amplitudinous and less conspicuous until finally it disappears, leaving only the steady field.

With pulse rates failing to produce steady light—that is, with subfusional pulse rates—the effectiveness of intermittent stimulation as photic pulse rate is progressively reduced varies from the Talbot level to levels even greater than for steady stimulation. The curve in Figure 8.25 representing the effectiveness of intermittent stimulation rises as pulse frequency is reduced. Finally, the curve reaches the point at which steady and intermittent stimulation are the same, shown where the ascending curve reaches the horizontal line in the graph. The increased effectiveness of intermittent stimulation over that of steady stimulation is called *brightness enhancement.*

The principle of enhancement was demonstrated by Brewster (1834) and by Brücke (1864), who used a revolving disk with white and black sectors (Figure 8.26). A small solid white disk was placed on this disk. When certain rates of revolution were used, the glitter of the white sectors rose above the brightness of the white of the small disk. Nowadays, the enhancement phenomenon is also called the *Brücke–Bartley effect.*

Brightness enhancement, then, is a term referring to the increase in brightness that results from an intermittent stimulation.

Figure 8.25 Relation between brightness enhancement and the number of photic pulses delivered per second. At a high rate of intermittency that produces the appearance of a steady light, Talbot's law operates and brightness is at the Talbot level. As rate is decreased, brightness begins to exceed the Talbot level and eventually becomes equal to the brightness produced by steady illumination. As rate is further decreased, brightness transcends the level produced by steady illumination and is called brightness enhancement.

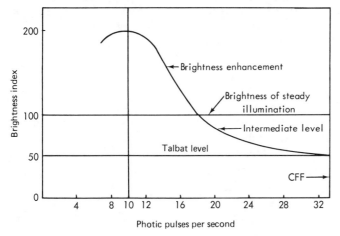

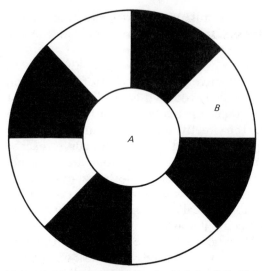

Figure 8.26 Components of a Brücke disk. The inner component *A* is highly reflective, giving the appearance of whiteness. The outer segment *B* consists of alternate light and dark sectors. When the disk is revolved at a certain rate, *B* begins to look brighter than *A*. This is the classical example of what Bartley has called brightness enhancement or the Brücke–Bartley effect.

It is known that other kinds of stimulation produce unexpected levels of brightness and while they may be called examples of brightness enhancement as far as the dictionary definition of enhancement is concerned, calling them so has already given rise to unfortunate confusion between the examples. This is particularly true in discussions attempting to explain the mechanism underlying increases in brightness. In the present discussion of brightness increases, brightness enhancement refers only to the results accruing from intermittent stimulation within the rate range producing a steady component that can be matched with a steady target.

Brightness enhancement was a result obtained when the rate of intermittent stimulation was high enough to enable the perceiver to see an "average" illumination. By the time the rate is reduced from CFF to 10 pulses per second, a considerable steady component of brightness is still involved. The fluctuating (flickering) component is only slight. However, when rates are reduced much further, flicker begins to predominate. Thus what observers see as intermittency rate becomes an alternation of light and dark (flashes and dark intervals), an entirely new visual phenomenon. They are no longer able to make a simple comparison with the steady field of the comparison target.

If perchance the observers are able to select out the brightness of the bright phase in the alternation, they cannot be considered as making a strict continuation of what they were doing when the major brightness component of the target was steady. Thus if the observers find that these rates provide for brightnesses greater than those obtained at higher rates, they move outside the scope of the definition of brightness enhancement.

Brightness increases is also produced by single, short, isolated photic pulses. If one compares the effect of a short pulse to that of continuous radiation of the same intensity, one will find that the pulse effect, the flash, is the brighter. Accordingly, this is technically speaking not to be labeled brightness enhancement.

Neural Mechanism for Brightness Enhancement

Brightness enhancement—the greater brightness produced by intermittent stimulation rather than by steady stimulation—is somewhat paradoxical. It appears to be a case of obtaining more output from less input. We have a good example from which to determine the underlying body mechanism and to provide an explanation of and solution to the puzzle. There seems to be a very satisfactory solution. A full exposition would be quite lengthy and complicated, but a short summary will be given here.

The Alternation of Response Theory

Bartley (1939, 1941) demonstrated in neurophysiological experiments that the channels of the optic pathway can be activated in various temporal groupings. By channels is meant individual circuits from eye to brain. They consist of certain complex chains of neurons in the eye, each of which feeds into a single fiber in the optic nerve and then into a complex circuit in the brain. There are myriads of them all lying parallel to each other. An intense and brief photic stimulus will activate many or all simultaneously. Once activated, they require a certain amount of time to recover before being activatable again. An extended photic stimulus will not hold all the channels into synchrony but will work toward activating the channel population into activity uniform throughout the time the visual system is responding. Hence at no time except at the first instant will the photic input succeed in producing the sensation of a brightness as great as that produced by a brief photic pulse. The complete description of the relation between types of photic input and channel activity, based on a number of neurophysiological and psychophysical studies, is known as the *alternation of response theory.*

A symposium on the "Alternation of Response Theory" occupied the entire January 1971, issue of the *Journal of General Psychology.* This theory was evolved from extended neurophysiological studies of the optic pathway from eye to brain by Bartley and associates. It can be taken as a clear example of how, in general, the visual system begins the perceptual process by coding the input to the retina into neural processes, which when utilized by the central nervous system, result in orderly amounts or kinds of qualitative and quantitative features of visual sensory experience. The alternation of response theory involves both a general statement of how the coding occurs and a specific statement of how it occurs in vision. Since the earlier visual studies that actually led to the theory, the theory has led to studies in other modalities.

For an extended description of perceptual effects of intermittent photic stimulation see Bartley's chapter, "Temporal Features of Input as Crucial Factors in Vision" in *Contributions to Sensory Physiology,* W. D. Neff, ed, New York: Academic Press, 1969.

EYE MOVEMENTS

Eye Movement and the Retinal Image

The earlier presumption in much of the work on and discussion of visual acuity was that the eye is motionless when viewing a stationary target. More recently, it has come to be realized that even with the best of fixation, the eye is not motionless. Tiny oscillations too small to be noticed with the observer's naked eye take place. Thus ways have had to be found to prevent the image from executing tiny oscillations back and forth across the region of the retina on which it was projected.

One way to preclude imperfections of fixation (i.e., unwanted departures from good fixation and tiny, directly unobservable oscillations of the eye) is to use a special kind of target. Pritchard (1961) attached a target to the eye by means of a contact lens on which was mounted a miniature optical system that projected an image on the retina. Thus with every movement of the retina, great or small, the image moved too and the usual spatial disjunction between image and retina was obviated.

Riggs, Ratliff, Cornsweet, and Cornsweet (1953) earlier used a very different device whereby the image remained in a fixed location on the retina regardless of eye movements (Figure 8.27). A photic beam reflected from a mirror attached to a contact lens was projected onto a screen. The beam was then reflected back to the eye through a portion of the contact lens not obscured by the mirror.

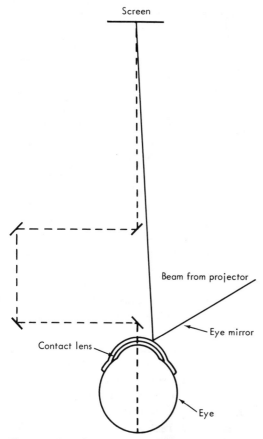

Figure 8.27 Optical arrangement whereby a visual image is maintained on a fixed portion of the retina. (Source: L. A. Riggs, F. Ratliff, J. C. Cornsweet, and T. N. Cornsweet. "The disappearance of steadily fixated test objects," *J.O.S.A.,* 1953, 43, 495–501, Fig. 2.)

The optical system was such that for every movement of the eye a compensating movement of the beam reaching the eye was produced. Thus the net result was that the image remained in the same location on the retina.

Effects of Eye Movement on Visual Acuity

Even in fixation the eye exhibits tiny oscillations; this motion would seem to affect visual acuity. According to Riggs (1965), the movements (1) may be so tiny that they have little effect or (2) may cause a "blurring" of the retinal image much as the jiggling of a camera blurs the resulting negative and print or (3) may "scan" the borders of the target and thus accentuate the differential neural activity beyond that resulting from a static image.

Riggs, Armington, and Ratliff (1954) found that during one second of time a retinal image is carried over about 3 minutes of arc, whereas in 0.10 second the typical excursion is about 25 seconds of arc, just about the angular subtense of a cone. In 0.01 second the typical sweep is 5 seconds of arc. This means that in 0.10 second the movement of the image is less than the separation between adjacent cones in the center of the retina. The critical duration for a visual act in which acuity is crucial is about 0.10 second. Thus during this interval the movement is less than the separation between adjacent cones.

The effect of these movements on visual acuity has been studied in two ways: (1) by ascertaining the instantaneous value of visual acuity by presenting the target for a fixed interval of time and measuring the concurrent eye movement (Ratliff, 1952) and (2) by counteracting or exaggerating the eye movements and determining the consequent effects (Riggs, Ratliff, Cornsweet, and Cornsweet, 1953; Keesey, 1960). Such experiments have shown no evidence that eye movements improve visual acuity; they have shown some evidence to the contrary.

Ratliff (1952), recording fine tremor, larger waves, and slow drifts and abrupt saccades (involuntary eye movements in reading print) showed that the drifts hindered visual acuity. Optically compensating for the eye movement in one case, doubling the effect of eye movement in another, and using the uncompensated condition in a third, Ratliff found that counteracting eye movement produced little effect. When any effect was obtained, it was in the direction of improvement. On the other hand, keeping the image fixed on the retina caused the target to fade from view quite quickly. The condition of optical exaggeration of movement improved the maintenance of vision over extended periods of time.

Keesey (1960) indicated that optically "stopping" the motion of the image had little effect on visual acuity regardless of the presentation time, which he varied from 0.02 to 1.28 seconds. He showed that in each of the two conditions ("stopped" and free-movement images), visual acuity did not improve with presentations beyond 0.2 second. Thus it can be said that eye movements that normally take place during 0.2 second do not have much effect on visual acuity, when measured either by target detection, localization, or resolution. Marshall and Talbot (1942) had supposed that scanning a visual target was necessary to achieve a maximum degree of discrimination.

Reversible perspective figures appear to be good targets for studying eye movements. Such targets are so constructed that as they are viewed they change in their visual characteristics. A question is what changes in the viewer in order that the experience changes. Eye movements may be one of the factors that change.

Flamm and Bergum (1977) continuously recorded eye movements and reversals on film for nine subjects who looked at a central point on a black line drawing of a Necker cube and also on a Rubin vase. They found significantly more reversals of perspective for the Necker cube than for the Rubin vase during 1½-minute test periods. The reversals were unrelated in time to the eye movements made but seemed possibly to be related to the tridimensionality of the figures.

Another recent study (Holcomb, Holcomb, and DeLaPensa, 1977) of eye movements in viewing reversible figures provided a different analysis. In this study it was found that high scanners seemed to be more dependent on eye movements for their reversals; their recognition of the patterns depended on the sequence and location of the eye fixation. This was interpreted to mean that shifts in attention were carried out in the form of large, saccadic eye movements. Low scanners appeared to be able to shift attention internally, that is, by mental restructuring without large eye movements. The authors recognized the possibility that scanning behavior in connection with reversals may be modulated by target complexity.

Chapter 9
The Homeostatic Perceptual System

A COMPREHENSIVE VERSUS TRADITIONAL VIEW

It is not customary for texts on perception to describe a homeostatic perceptual system. The facts that are usually dealt with in homeostasis are generally considered the exclusive domain of physiology, but they are facts about the relation of the organism to its energistic environment and some of them pertain to neural activities and receptors sensitive to physical conditions.

In accord with the way we have defined and thus far described perceptual response, certain aspects of homeostasis seem to fall within the definition of perceptual response. Perhaps one factor that obscures homeostasis from being intimately involved with perceptual responses is that the stimulus conditions lie within the body rather than outside of it.

When the definition of perception was first given in this book, it may not have been clear as to all that perception involved. The emphasis was on the relation of the organism to its energistic surrounds (environment) but the definition was not explicit about the various activities *within* the body. Traditional views imply that the environment is only outside the body so what is about to be discussed in this chapter would seem inappropriate.

To assert that we are a part of Nature has still left us outside in a functional sense. But actually, since the same forces and physical laws operate within us as in space outside us, what we have been calling the environment is, in its energistic respects, within us. It so happens that receptors can and do operate within the body as well as on its surface. The receptors within have to do with maintaining equilibrium in internal conditions, which involves sensitivity to some of the same forces as those outside the body and to which we react. We have come a long way from the time when perception was exclusively a matter of consciousness, and thus some reactions to the environment were yet to lie outside of perception.

Fifty years ago there was a simple definition of perception in the literature—that is, "perception is sensation plus meaning." From then until now various views about perception and sensation have been expressed. However, not until a little more than a decade ago did a radically new concept come into clear expression (Gibson, 1966). This was a tremendous achievement, but it has not yet reached its full meaning in all quarters.

The insight and reasoning that made this possible was the adoption of a new starting point, a form of organismic starting point, which began from a look at the nature of the energistic world and the kinds of demands this makes on the organism as we now see it. Five, identifiable major properties of the energistic universe were recognized and a statement of the human organism's means for meeting these as demands was made (Gibson, 1966). As a logical result, it was seen that the sense mechanisms operating as systems functioned to accomplish the task. The systems were perceptual systems functioning to obtain information regarding the environment.

This outlook, no doubt, despite being well stated, has not been seen as anything new. It functions for some, only as a new set of words. To others, the system idea seems totally arbitrary. And this is no surprise as long as the criteria for classification is thought to reside only in the organism rather than what is demanded by the energistic environment.

PERCEPTION IN HOMEOSTASIS

To complete the outlook on perceptual systems, much remains to be done. All of the demands of coping with the energistic environment are not spelled out by what is stated in current textbooks on perception. The human is *homeothermic;* that is, people are "warm-blooded." This is a major aspect of what is called homeostasis. It so happens that the maintenance of a nearly constant internal temperature involves the nervous system and various internal receptors. This very fact makes it logical that we view the internal thermal maintenance just as we view other sense modality relations between the organism and the environment.

The organism internally must adjust to circumstances. Some of the circumstances meant here are temperature and amount of oxygen, carbon dioxide, and so forth. There are tissues in the body that function as receptors for these conditions, and so the organism's response via these receptors (sense organs) is to be included under the term perception. This is not to go too far afield but rather to recognize fully the unity of the organism in relating to this thing we call Nature. The traditional segmentation of the organism into mind and matter with its associated artificialities is not the scientific outlook on the human.

This chapter, then, is a brief description that at least calls attention to the types of things that go on in the body to relate it to its surrounds. This by no means will be a complete description of what has been and is called homeostasis, for homeostasis involves many things beyond the nervous system, including the endocrine glands. You see, homeostasis is accomplished partly by means other than mediation by receptors.

We are dealing with homeostasis here because there are several sets of definable receptors, for example, those already listed in the chart of the perceptual systems on page 7 that are involved. These receptors have been recognized by anatomists and physiologists for some time. The specific mediating functions of each have been specified separately, but psychologists have not as yet looked on them collectively as a system, let alone a perceptual system. These receptors and their functions may logically be viewed in the same way as any other receptor (or sense organ) system. And if this is done, we have a perfectly logical basis for speaking of a *homeostatic perceptual system.*

RECEPTOR MECHANISMS IN HOMEOSTASIS

The receptors, originally found in the chart on page 8 in Chapter 1, are stated here again, as follows:

1. *The carotid sinus receptors* in the *carotid* artery in the neck are sensitive to chemical conditions and pressure conditions. The chemical conditions pertain to O_2 and CO_2 while the pressure conditions pertain to blood pressure and barometric pressure.

2. *Depressor sensory endings* in the walls of certain intrapericardial vessels and in the pulmonary veins. This is where the regulation of breathing comes into the picture.
3. *Pressor sensory cells* in the vestibular nuclei.
4. *Temperature-sensitive nuclei* in the hypothalamus. In the hypothalamus there are two opposing thermoregulatory centers that initiate coordinated and integrated neural discharges to tissues involved in maintaining a constant body temperature. The hypothalamus centers can be regarded as a thermostat.
5. *Receptors in the tracheobronchial tree* having to do with inflation and deflation of the lungs.

It can be seen without much description that these receptors are sensitive to conditions within the body but are initiated by conditions in the environment or by actions of the body in responding to the environment. It is only by taking these into account that the complete mechanism for the organism's maintaining an overall relation to the environment as a personalistic unity can be portrayed.

We can speak of the human organism as *being* as well as *doing*. In dealing with homeostasis, we are concerned with the types of encounters with the environment, both those that are *imposed* and those that are *obtained* (mentioned in Chapter 2).

Imposed encounters, for example, are exemplified in cases in which external temperatures are high or low. This wide deviation from the optimally maintained internal temperature of the body calls in the one case for getting rid of some body heat, or in the other case for generating body heat.

Imposition leads to action even beyond internal processes themselves, for example, when the brain becomes involved and the individual seeks environmental sources of warmth or cooling. Thus some of the encounters that ensue are *obtained*. In both cases, instant-to-instant relations with the internal and external environment are being involved through the mediation of sense receptors.

Recognition of a homeostatic perception system completes the recognition of the relation of the organism to the rest of the physiochemical universe, "from the ground up" so to speak. We have included this system, not because we have at hand so much experimental material to offer, but to complete the overall outlook with regard to the organism and the world of which it is a part.

REGULATION OF BODY TEMPERATURE

Temperature regulation is an instant-to-instant response to environmental conditions and, at least at times, involves the cerebral cortex and is discriminatory. At such times, it is a form of perceptual response. The regulation of body temperature is better understood when it is thought of as a system of exchanges of heat back and forth between the body and its surrounds. There are four factors in this system: metabolism that produces heat, evaporation that always transfers heat from the body, convection that either takes heat away from or gives heat to the body, and radiation that also may cause the body to lose or gain heat.

The human environment is divided functionally into three different temperature ranges. The upper is called the *range of vasomotor and evaporative regulation* and runs down to about the mid 80° F. Below this, for a distance of about 4° F, there is a *neutral or transitional zone.* Below the transitional zone the range is spoken of as the *cold range* or the *zone of body cooling.* (Winslow, Herrington and Gagge, 1937, and Hardy and Soderstrom, 1938.) These values pertain to unclothed resting subjects and, of course, do not represent environmental temperatures that apply when clothes are worn and active body movement occurs.

In the range of vasomotor and evaporative regulation the blood sent to the skin and superficial tissues increases with environmental temperature. Evaporation from the body also rises, but not in any simple or uniform fashion, with temperature. Skin temperature rises only a little. Body heat loss slowly increases. It turns out that even though a working equilibrium of body temperature is maintained under such environmental conditions, personal comfort diminishes.

In the neutral or transitional zone, heat loss is well adjusted for by shifts of blood to or from peripheral tissues by vasoconstriction and vasodilation. Personal comfort is at its maximum. Perhaps it is some feature of the rate of heat loss that is effective in giving the maximum body comfort. This sort of perception would in a large part be mediated by the temperature sense organs.

Some authorities say that in the cold range no regulation of heat loss occurs. The body loses heat just as any inanimate mass of substance does. If one is cold under such circumstances, he or she must seek a new environment, put on more clothes, become more active physically, or do something that directly changes metabolic rate. Individuals vary greatly in their degree of discomfort under given low-temperature conditions.

Since humidity conditions of the atmosphere alter the rate of evaporation from the human body, humidity also figures in human comfort and in the efficiency with which body temperature regulation is carried on.

An investigation that seems to bear on the role that the temperature sense mechanism plays in body heat regulation is that of Benjamin, Wagner, Ihrig, and Zeit (1956), who cooled a group of canine subjects from 100 to 80° F in 20 minutes by leading the animals' blood from the carotid artery to an outside cooling system and back again. That is, the animals were made to circulate their own blood through an outside cooling system while in a room of normal temperature. This manner of cooling was accomplished without the usual unfavorable symptoms of cardiac fibrillation, shivering, and other shock manifestations. In some cases the temperature was reduced to the point of complete stoppage of the heart. The animals were rewarmed by using the outside system to rewarm their blood. When return from the low temperatures reached a certain point, heart activity returned. When the animals were warmed up to 90° F, they were able to go on from there—that is, they reached their original temperatures without further artificial warming. The point we wish to make is that under ordinary cooling conditions, cooling is accomplished by putting the animal's body in a cool environment. In other words, the body is made to cool from the surface inward. In the technique just described the cooling was accomplished through the blood stream and thus uniformly produced temperature reduction.

It would seem that the second way of cooling in effect bypassed the temperature sense mechanism; that is, cooling was accomplished without activating this mechanism. If so, then the avoidance or omission of shivering and other systemic manifestations could be attributed to this avoidance. The facts suggest, then, that the temperature sense plays the initiating role in activating certain compensatory reactions to cooling. If cooling goes on in spite of the initial compensatory reactions, still more drastic reactions set in. The canine experiment lent evidence to the fact that if cooling bypasses the reaction-initiating system (the temperature sense), it can be accomplished without much, if any, harm to the organism. Obviously, nature unaided could not work this way. If they are to survive, animals must "kick up a fuss" about being subjected to untoward situations. If, on the other hand, the same agency that subjects the organism to the otherwise unfavorable condition avoids activating the alarm mechanism and also takes care that the animal is restored to normal, then the whole procedure goes along reasonably well and in a manner very different from what we should expect from our common-sense background.

NEURAL MECHANISMS FOR TEMPERATURE REGULATION

The neural mechanisms that act to preclude overheating and those that act against chilling are not fully identical. Following destruction of the caudal region of the hypothalamus, exposures to low temperature are not accompanied by somatic changes that prevent fall in body temperature. Muscle tensing, shivering, and so on that are inverted through cerebrospinal channels, are absent, as well as the signs of sympathic activity such as vasoconstriction, piloderection, medullo-adrenal secretion. When a less caudal region is inactivated, exposure to high temperature is not followed by reactions providing for the organism's loss of heat, such as vasodilatation, sweating, and in certain animals, panting and salivation.

The region for the prevention of overheating is above and in front of the optic chiasma, while the region acting against chilling is in the more caudal part of the hypothalamus.

PHYSICAL CONDITIONS AND COMFORT

Winslow, Herrington, and Gagge (1937) studied relations among physiological conditions (such as sweating), physical conditions (temperature and humidity), and the feeling of body comfort (or better still, personal comfort).

The investigators used a five-point scale, varying from very unpleasant to very pleasant, for the subjects to indicate their feelings. It was found that as relative humidity increases, the environmental temperature at which distinct pleasantness is lost drops. The zone of perceptual indifference narrows as relative humidity becomes greater. For example, whereas with dry air the subjects exhibited a temperature range of indifference between 104.5 and 92° F, when relative humidity rose to 50 percent, the indifference range contracted to between 95 and 89.5° F.

THE CORTEX AND HOMEOSTASIS

As already stated, the common impression is that homeostatic regulations are handled in a very different manner from those reactions we call perceptual responses. They are supposedly independent from cortical control that functions in perceiving. Therefore it is pertinent to show that homeostatic regulations are subject to the control of the cerebral cortex.

This was shown in both human and certain subhuman subjects by Russian investigators some time ago. In dogs, they showed that temperature regulations could be conditioned. The positive results in such cases led Slonim and Shcherbakova (1934) to test the matter on humans. Among other things, they tested the body temperature of subjects who were constantly being exposed to cooling in their daily occupational environment. They chose workers who were exposed to inclement weather on railway cars in operating brakes.

One brakeman, for example, showed an increase in metabolism under such conditions but did not show it in town under similar temperature conditions. He was able to spend many hours without suffering from exposure on the runs but could not stand the same conditions in the yards.

A control group's metabolism increased on the outbound rail journey and decreased on the return trip. The conclusions reached by the experimenters was that "congenital subcortical thermo-regulation was insufficient to account for this." What was being shown in this investigation was that cortical influences play a role in metabolism. Cortical impulses enabled the subjects to adjust themselves thermally against the cold when actually necessary, but under less drastic personalistic requirements, metabolism dropped to match. What seems to have occurred related to the subjects' perceptual appreciation of the situation involved.

No doubt, similar variations in metabolism that closely tally with what we recognize as the individual's perceptual orientation than with Fahrenheit levels of a room, could be obtained in present-day perceptual investigations.

This means that *within limits,* the actual thermal conditions of the environment are not as rigidly met as if they were the only factors in the situation. This makes for a thermal equilibrium different from that brought about merely by purely autonomic action.

Chapter 10
The Development of Perception in Infancy and Childhood

Perception is best understood when its development in infancy and childhood is experimentally studied. In fact, the perceptual abilities of the various species in the animal scale also contribute to this understanding. It so happens that lack of space precludes a review of the perceptual capabilities from, let us say, earthworms, mollusks, on to the vertebrates, and to the primates before reaching humans.

Primates seem to have trouble developing perceptual facilities if development has been precluded during infancy. This is attested to by the difficulties in visual performance following experimental confinement in darkness during infancy and by the difficulties encountered by humans when they have been victims of cataracts obstructing vision during the first few years of life. Both apes and humans are unable to perceive the meaning of visual targets for a long time after they have been first rendered able to receive images on their retinas. While the difficulties may be described as features of the learning process, they are nevertheless descriptive of perception under the conditions mentioned.

HUMAN ONTOGENETIC DEVELOPMENT

Human Fetuses

The very earliest response to tactile stimulation is manifested in fetal life, the prebirth stage, of the individual, where such factors as temporal and spatial summation are evidenced. Repeated contacts of the fetus with a light hair are effective when a single contact is not. Contact with a brush containing a number of hairs is effective, when a single hair is not. Different responses are elicited in premature infants by grading impingements, or contacts, from weak to strong. Response is quite consistent from trial to trial and depends on the zone contacted.

The fetus responds to warmth and cold, according to Preyer (1885) and Blanton (1917). Pratt, Nelson, and Sun (1930) found that the responses of newborn infants to stimuli that are colder than the body are more intense than responses to stimuli that are warmer than the body.

Cutaneous pain does not seem to be evokable in the fetus, as is attested by the relative weakness of overt reaction to impingements that cause destruction to skin and underlying tissue. Sometimes no overt response is elicited in premature infants during the first day, even when the impingements draw blood. Carmichael (1934) remarks that in this connection less response is evoked in fetal guinea pigs by such impingements than by contact with a fine hair at the same point.

Taste receptors have been reported to be more widely distributed in the early fetus than in the adult. It has been found that the human infant at birth can distinguish between salt, sour, and bitter as against sweet.

There is some evidence that the auditory receptors of the human fetus can be stimulated under some conditions. For example, it has been reported that a distinct response of a child in the womb was elicited again and again by striking the bathtub in which the mother was seated. A wide range of tones was used to stimulate the child in utero by certain other investigators.

Response indicating distinction between light and dark can be elicited in a 7-month (that is, premature) infant. This is, of course, despite the fact that the optic nerve and other visual structures are not fully mature, even at 9 months, the normal time of birth.

Human Subjects Lacking Visual Form Stimulation from Birth

Understanding perceptual development and change has depended on a number of unique approaches. For example, there is the determination of the characteristics of vision in individuals who from birth were unable to see form on account of cataracts, until later operated on for their removal. Senden's book reporting such cases first appeared in German in 1932. Révész (1950) examined Senden and eliminated the totally unreliable cases, leaving about 22 extending from the years 1810 to 1928. Révész concluded that differeness in object size could be correctly perceived, whereas their identity could not, although the same objects were familiar to the subjects by touch.

HUMAN INFANTS: FANTZ

Fantz (1961) studied human infants by using the activity of the eyes. He supposed that if the subject persistently fixates some forms and not others, he or she must be able to perceive differences among them. The subjects lay on their backs in a crib inside a special chamber of uniform reflectance and illumination. To the ceiling were attached pairs of items (targets) that were exposed to the subject alternately to the right and to the left for certain test periods. The mirrored images were seen on the subject's eyes through a peephole in the ceiling. Therefore it was known when the subject was fixating, or looking at, the item by observing where the images fell on the eyes. If the image fell on the pupil, it was supposed that the item was forming a retinal image and was being looked at by the infant. The time spent fixating each item and looking elsewhere was recorded.

The supposition was, of course, that the visual system of human newborn infants is poorly developed, so that the ability to distinguish complex patterns might not be expected. The first targets used on human infants were equal-sized areas, such as bull's eyes, horizontal strips, checkerboards and two sizes of plain square, a cross and a circle, and two triangles. Thirty infants aged 1 to 15 weeks were tested at weekly intervals. Later, black and white stripes and uniform gray areas were compared. The two targets were equated for overall luminance. After it was found that the infants fixated the striped targets more than the plain ones, quantification was effected by using a series of striped targets containing progressively narrower strips. The conclusion was that with increasing age, the subjects could distinguish targets with narrower and narrower stripes. The infants could distinguish stripes $\frac{1}{64}$ of an inch wide at a viewing distance of 10 inches before reaching 6 months of age. This involves a visual angle of 5 minutes of arc as compared to the normal adult's one minute. At the age of about 1 month the visual angle involved was about one degree or 60 minutes. This poor showing at this age was a long way from what we know as adult vision, but it still represents the capacity to distinguish form.

Later, Fantz (1964) tested 49 infants ranging from 4 days to 6 months in age. They were shown three flat targets the size and shape of a head. One consisted of a stylized black face on a pink background. In the second the features were scrambled, and in the third target the pattern consisted of a solid black area equal to the combined area of the features in either of the other two. In all cases the features were large enough to cover visual angles larger than those known to be used by infants in the earlier experiments. The results, in general, were that the "real" face was fixated most, the scrambled face next, and the other target least. The results were interpreted as showing that in human infants there is a primitive significance in form perception as in chicks.

A third step was made in testing the infants, using a solid sphere and a flat circle, the former being more "interesting" to infants even in the 1-month to 6-month range of age.

Additional Evidence for Form Discrimination in the Newborn

Hershenson, Munsinger, and Kessen (1965) presented neonate humans with pairs of visual targets containing geometric forms differing in the number of turns or angles they contained. Preference for particular forms was interpreted from the number of times fixated. The procedure was somewhat like that of Fantz. Infrared photography was used to record eye positions and fixations. The targets were above the reclining infants at a distance of about 46 centimeters and were 15° to each side of the point viewed when the subject looked straight up. The targets contained either 5, 10, or 20 turns. The infants fixated on the 10-turn targets the most and on the 5-turn targets the least.

The same sort of investigation had previously been conducted on elementary school children and on adults, and no distinction between the two groups was disclosed. The targets contained from 3 to 40 independent turns, and targets containing 10 turns were fixated the most.

It was concluded that the neonates could perceive form and that somewhat the same factors operated against the appreciating of extreme complexity with the older subjects as with the neonates.

Fantz and Miranda (1975) have found that neonates under 7 days of age could discriminate between curved and straight "contours" (target borders). They found that neonates would fixate most targets for a significantly longer period of time when the *outer* borders of the targets were curved rather than straight. Quantitative variables such as reflectance and complexity of target were held constant. They concluded that from birth there is an ability to discriminate that is basic to form perception.

Kessen, Salapatek, and Haith (1972), using corneal-reflection photography, demonstrated that infants ranging from 1 to 4 days of age attended to vertical edges bisecting a blank homogeneous field but not to horizontal edges. Obviously, there is a discrimination for the one and not the other, but reasons or mechanisms underlying this are not clear.

BOWER

Another approach to determining the presence of form and space perception was taken by Bower (1965), who used an operant-conditioning procedure. The response utilized was a turning of the head. The infant lay with his or her head between two pads and by as little as a ½-inch turn to the right or left, a microswitch was activated that operated a recorder. In such a setup, the infant's effort was scant, and even a 2-week old child could provide 400 responses with no noticeable "fatigue."

One of the experiments was meant to determine whether infants can perceive distance and manifest "size constancy" in their behavior. The reinforcement used in the conditioning procedure was provided by the ordinary game of "peekaboo." Each subject was trained to respond only in the presence of a white 12-inch cube located a meter from the eye. We shall call this situation 1, or S_1 (Figure 10.1). Following one hour of this, three new situations were introduced. For S_2 the original 12-inch cube was placed 3 meters away. For S_3 a 36-inch cube was placed at a distance of 1 meter, and for S_4 the 36-inch cube was moved to a distance of 3 meters. All four situations were alternated in a counterbalanced sequence, and the number of responses evoked by each were noted.

S_1, the original conditioned situation, would be expected to evoke the highest number of responses. If the infants were affected by the cube distance and thus perceived distance but did not respond on the basis of "size constancy," situation S_4 should seem more like S_1 than would S_2. The cubes in S_2 and S_4 were at the same distance, but S_4 would produce a retinal image of only one-ninth the area. Were the infants able to discriminate distance but not to respond on the basis of "size constancy," S_3 would produce more responses than S_2, since S_3 involves the same distances as S_1 whereas S_2 does not.

If, however, the infants were able to discriminate distance and

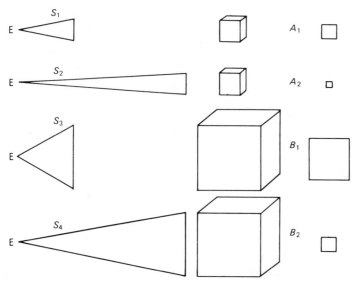

Figure 10.1   Target arrangements used by Bower. S_1, S_2, S_3, and S_4 represent the various situations. The visual angles dependent on cube distance are shown subtended, and the right-hand column of squares indicate the relative sizes of the visual images in the respective situations.

were to exhibit "size constancy," S_1 and S_3 should have evoked about the same number of responses, since they differed from S_1 in one or the other of the major factors. S_2 differed from S_1 in distance and S_3 differed in size; S_4 should have produced the fewest responses, since it differed from S_1 in both size and distance.

The empiricist predictions, according to Bower, would have been as follows: S_4 would elicit at least as many responses as S_3. S_3 would elicit more responses than S_2. Not taking distance factors into account, S_4 should be more effective than S_3. Nativistic predictions would have been the opposite; that is, S_2 would be more effective than S_3 and there would be more responses to S_3 than to S_4.

The experimental results were as follows: S_1 evoked 98 responses; S_2, 58; S_3, 54; and S_4, 22. Bower concluded that the infants did respond on the basis of actual cube size and actual cube distance but not on the size of the retinal image.

The investigation was, of course, not complete at this point. Several factors, such as binocular parallax and motion parallax, had not been prevented from operating. Accordingly, a new group of infants was tested under new conditions: the infants wore a patch over one eye so that binocular parallax could not operate; all that could function was motion parallax and pictorial factors, or "cues." A second group of infants viewed lantern slides copious in pictorial factors but with no basis for either binocular or motion parallax. A third group wore stereoscopic goggles designed expecially for the experiment; the stereograms were of the cube situations; binocular parallax and pictorial factors were present, but motion parallax was precluded.

The results showed that the "monocular" infants behaved just as the unrestricted infants did. In this experiment S_1 produced 101 responses; S_2, 60; and S_3, 53; while S_4 elicited only 22 responses. The group that looked at the slides did very differently. Ninety-four responses were made to S_1, 52 to S_2, 44 to S_3, and 96 to S_4. Bower concluded that the infants responded exclusively to the projected retinal image sizes. The pictorial factors in the slides were seemingly ineffective; otherwise, S_4 could not have been nearly as effective as it was. The behavior of the stereoscope group was like none of the others. Some "size constancy" was interpreted from their behavior but not as much as in the original group, or "monocular," group. Here S_1 evoked 94 responses; S_2, 44; S_3, 40; and S_4, 32.

Bower performed another investigation with young infants, which involved the use of targets varying in their orientation, or slant, with references to the viewer and targets differing in shape. The conditioned target in situation one, or S_1, was a wooden rectangle approximately 10 by 20 inches located 2 meters from the eye and turned 45 degrees from the frontal plane. The target formed a trapezoidal image on the retina. S_2 was the same rectangle at right angles to the line of regard (in the frontal plane). S_3 was a trapezoid placed in the frontal plane. This trapezoid formed the same trapezoidal retinal image as the rectangular target in S_1. S_4 was the same trapezoid turned in the 45 degree position to form a rectangular image.

Bower supposed that if the subjects demonstrated "shape constancy," S_2 would elicit more responses than S_4; S_4 would be about the same as S_3. On the other hand, if retinal image shape were the prime determining factor, S_3 would elicit more responses than S_4 or S_2.

In the experiment the conditioned situation S_1 elicited an average of 51 responses, S_2 45 responses, S_3 an average of only 28.5 responses, and S_4 26 responses. Thus there was no doubt that the infants, between 50 and 60 days old, reponded in accord with the actual shape of the cubes and not with the retinal image shape. There was no statistical difference in the number of responses to S_1 and S_2. "Shape constancy" was demonstrated, and the different orientations of the targets made no discriminatory difference.

This puzzled Bower, and so he made three additional experiments. In the first, the targets varied in image shape and orientation, while target shape remained constant. In the second, target shape varied and so did retinal image shape, while target orientation was constant. In the third, only orientation varied, while target shape and image shape remained fixed.

In the first experiment the infants responded as though the three test situations were the same as the conditioned one; that is, $S_1 = S_2 = S_3 = S_4$. In the second and third experiments the infants showed that variations in target shape, image shape, and orientation can be discriminated. Bower concluded that the infants in the first experiment reacted to target shape (since it was the same in S_1, S_2, S_3, and S_4) as a more salient factor than the target orientations or the retinal image shapes. Bower made a powerful point here, by emphasizing that both the early empiricists and the nativists were wrong in supposing that the perception of simple factors precedes the perception of complex variables.

INTERMODAL PERCEPTION IN EARLY INFANCY

The two dominant modalities for perceiving space external to the body are vision and hearing. Ordinarily these work together; that is, what is heard is seen in the same space frame and vice versa, what is seen, if heard, is heard in the same space frame. This is the basis for ventriloquism.

What can be said about this in early infancy? How young can evidences of this perceptual feature be found? Aronson and Rosenbloom (1971) performed an experiment to test this, using 8 infants ranging in age from 30 to 55 days. In the test the infant was seated in a chair providing for maximal support for both torso and head. The infant was seated facing a window through which the mother could be seen. The mother's voice reached the infant from two loud speakers, one toward each side of the infant. The experiment had two stages. In the first, the speakers were set so that the acoustic intensity was the same for each speaker. This produced for the adults involved the perception of the sound coming from straight ahead, that is, where the mother was seen. During this stage the infants all were calm and apparently relaxed. Stage two consisted in having one speaker volume much higher than the other so, of course, the sound seemed for adults to originate from 90 degrees to the side of the subject, while the mother was still seen in the straight-ahead position. After 15 to 25 seconds, this condition produced dramatic behavioral changes. The subjects all manifested agitation and discomfort, including struggling movements of arms, legs, and body.

As a check, for some of the subjects, this second stage was later repeated, but with the mother not visible. In this case four additional subjects ranging from 28 to 56 days of age were used. These infants did not manifest the disquiet that the previous infants did while their mothers, out of sight, were talking. In addition, the experimenters substituted voices of women, not the children's mothers, in stages 1 and 2. The shift caused changes from calm to distress.

While the study did not tell whether these infants learned this property of perceiving, since they were too old when tested, it undoubtedly did show perceptual discrimination at that stage.

THE VISUAL CLIFF

The Cliff as an Experimental Test Situation

The next type of experiment we turn to is the work with the visual cliff, an apparatus devised by Walk and Gibson (1960), as shown in Figure 10.2.

A huge horizontal plate of heavy glass is supported about 2 feet from the floor. On the underside of half the plate a checkerboard design visible from above is glued. Below the other half the same checkerboard design is placed on the floor. In some instances the

Figure 10.2   The visual cliff. The visual cliff has two figured surfaces and a starting platform. One surface is at platform level, the other is some distance below, for example, at floor level. On the side of the starting platform opposite the figured surface is a glass plate. An infant or animal is coaxed to move onto the plate, but it generally refuses because the surface seen is the figured surface below, visually that of a cliff. Side boards are often used around the whole apparatus at platform level to exclude extraneous visual stimuli.

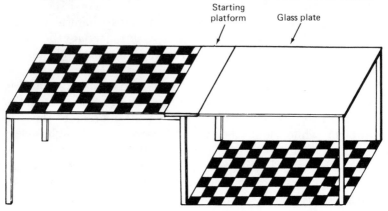

Starting
platform   Glass plate

design may be left free for raising and lowering for certain distances from the floor. Across the plate at the juncture between the two halves is a platform board on which the subject—a small child or a small animal—is placed. As one would expect for adults, the arrangement presents an apparent drop-off cliff on the side of the board where the design is on the floor, and if the two checkerboards were the only surfaces involved, one would expect to fall over the "cliff" if he or she moved off the board on that side. Of course, the glass prevents this, the experimental subject actually being able to move out onto the glass "in midair" with impunity. Enclosing the apparatus precludes the use of familiar objects; for example, the feet and legs of the mother cannot be used as cues for distance.

In this sort of investigation the experimenter relies on the overt behavior of the subject to provide information on the subject's vision. Walk and Gibson used chicks, lambs, kids, rats, turtles, kittens, dogs, and pigs as subjects. In each case the investigators were able to conclude something about the role of vision in the life of the species.

Human Infants on the Visual Cliff

Walk and Gibson (1960) showed that binocular human infants can discriminate depth as soon as they can crawl. Ninety-six percent of the many binocular infants tested crawled to the mother over the shallow side. Some of the infants could be coaxed to crawl over the deep side with certain enticements but not with others. It was found that the infants in the 7- to 9-month age range were more likely to cross the deep side than were those in the 10- to 13-month range. Thus the results showed depth discrimination of all ages tested but a certain variability in behavior when less definite patterns were used in the cliff apparatus.

The experimenters were concerned with whether monocular infants can also make the depth discrimination required in the cliff behavior. The infant used to test monocular vision was a child 10.5 months old. Cancer had necessitated the removal of the child's right eye at the age of 5.5 months. Prior to that, the eye had been blind. The monocular infant was placed in the usual starting position, and in the first trial the child was called from the shallow side and crawled to the mother. In the second trial the mother called from the deep side but the infant crawled off across the shallow side after backing away from the deep side. On subsequent trials the infant refused to crawl off across the deep side, regardless of the coaxing from the mother stationed on the deep side. Behavior was consistent with that of binocular infants and the behavior of most animals placed on the apparatus.

CHILDREN IN LATER STAGES

So much for some of the very beginnings of immediate discriminatory response of the human individual to his or her surrounds. We now turn to some of the individual's developments during later stages. The development of perception as a function of age in the human subject has best been exemplified by the work of Gesell and his colleagues over the past several decades. They particularly studied visual perception in the growing child from birth through the early years.

Gesell, Ilg, and Bullis (1949) gave attention to the perceptual growth of the child by studying five aspects of his or her behavior. The first of these was eye–hand coordination. The neonate was observed to begin at once to deploy the eyes, to move and stop them, which signifies a beginning active endeavor to adapt to the circumstances around the child. This beginning behavior, however, is very crude, incomplete, and ineffective. Pursuit movements of a sort and the ability to fixate come in the first 4 weeks. By 12 weeks the infant can follow an object 180 degrees with blinking, jerky movements. By 16 weeks the infant can retain a toy in the hand, with occasional observation of it. By 24 weeks he or she discriminates between strangers. By 36 weeks the infant feeds himself or herself a cracker. By 48 weeks the infant plays alternately with several toys. By 52 weeks he or she offers toys to another person and enjoys a give and take performance. Although ordinarily thought of in terms other than of perception, all this is a sense-guided type of behavior.

By 2 years the child has freed the eyes from the hands and may inspect objects with the eyes alone. At 2½ years "an object in another child's hand may be seen without regard for the child" himself or herself. At 3½ years the child moves the head close to a magazine page to identify something or may move away and withdraw the head to a greater distance. By 4 years a free and fluid eye–hand relationship is achieved.

This and much more may be said about the typical child, indicating the development of a relation between the child and the environment that involves several achievements: the control of ocular manipulative mechanisms, the manipulation of the child's geometrical relations to his or her surrounds, and the utilization of his or her surrounds to achieve purpose. During this time the very evident early limitations in behavior can be seen to slip away, stage by stage, freeing the child for a more fluid relationship with his or her surrounds. Perception plays a predominate role at all stages.

INTERSENSORY COMPARISON TASKS IN OLDER CHILDREN

One of the methods of evolution has been the development of efficacy in behavior by increased and varied interaction between a limited number of sense modalities rather than a proliferation in the number of sense modalities. As far as the individual is concerned, this can be observed in the early years of life. Examining this is one form of the study of perceptual learning, of which the work of Birch and his colleagues is an instance. Examples of the lack of intersensory cooperation in the animal scale help to make clear what is meant.

Birch and Lefford (1963) cite Abbot's work of many years ago, in which he showed that the frog could not modify a visually controlled response through effects obtained from the pain modality. For example, a frog allowed to strike at a live fly impaled on a rod surrounded by a ring of sharp stakes would continue to try to obtain the fly by thrusting out its tongue even though every thrust resulted in impaling its tongue on the stakes; typically, the frog continues until its tongue is torn to shreds. On the other hand, in the same species the visual response is modifiable by effects received through another sensory channel, that of the sense of taste. This was shown by another experimenter, who demonstrated that the tongue-striking procedure was modified by the taste of a "bitter" catepillar. Birch and Lefford confirmed this by showing that a target coated with quinine will inhibit the striking reaction. Thus these experiments show that visually guided behavior in the frog is not modified by tactual stimulation but is modified by gustatory stimulation. In mammals there seems to be a further advance by way of the more widespread interaction between the senses.

The study of intersensory development made by Birch and Lefford on children consisted in comparisons of the interactions among haptic, kinesthetic, and visual modes of response. By haptic was meant the "complex sensory input obtained by active manual exploration of a test object." Performance of this sort involved tactile, kinesthetic, and surface-movement sensations obtained in manipulating an item such as a block. This was an active performance. What the experimenters meant by kinesthetic sense was the sensory input provided by passive movement of the arm, wrist, elbow, and shoulders.

They studied what they called intersensory equivalence. An item such as a block that was presented visually as an outline form on paper was used as a standard, and the experimenters compared the same and different forms presented haptically as wooden blocks or kinesthetically as grooves traced, while the child's hand held a stylus and was moved in the groove by the experimenter. Thus three comparisons were used: (1) visual–haptic, (2) visual–kinesthetic, and (3) haptic–kinesthetic. Stimuli were paired; the first member of the pair was presented to one sense, the second to the other sense or group of senses. Eight different stimulus forms were used: triangle, square, cross, star, half-circle, circle, diamond, and hexagon.

The subjects were children of both sexes ranging from 5 to 11 years of age. Two kinds of error were determined for each age group. The first were errors of *nonequivalence*, that is, errors made by failing to recognize equivalent forms presented in the intersensory comparisons. The second were errors of *equivalence*, that is, the failures to recognize different forms presented in the intersensory comparisons.

We shall first deal with the errors of nonequivalence. The 5-year-olds averaged 2.3 errors in the visual–haptic comparisons, the number of errors in individual cases ranging from 0 to 11. The 8-year-olds averaged 0.4 errors with a range of 0 to 2.

In the visual–kinesthetic comparisons, the 5-year-olds made an average of 7.9, with a range of 1 to 14 errors. The 11-year-olds made an average of 1.8 errors with a range of 0 to 7.

The average number of errors for the haptic–kinesthetic comparisons at 5 years was 7.9. The range was 1 to 14 errors. The 11-year-olds averaged 1.7 errors with a range of 0 to 6.

The following resulted from the study of errors of equivalence. In the visual–haptic comparisons the 5-year-olds averaged 2.9 errors with a spread of 0 to 11. The 11-year-olds averaged 0.7 errors with a spread of 0 to 3.

In the visual–kinesthetic comparisons the 5-year-old average was 5.7 errors, with a range of 1 to 27. The 11-year-olds averaged 1.4 errors, with a range of 0 to 7 errors.

In the haptic–kinesthetic comparisons the average number of errors for the 5-year-olds was 4.6, with a range of 0 to 15. For the 11-year-olds the average dropped to 0.9 with a range of 0 to 3 errors.

In all cases the curves depicting errors for the various ages had reached an asymptote by the eleventh year.

It was concluded that:

1. The ability to make intersensory comparisons improved with age; the growth curve was a typical logarithmic curve. This tallies with the idea that intersensory functioning is an example of the general law of growth.

2. The fewest errors were made in the visual–haptic comparisons.
3. The visual–kinesthetic and haptic–kinesthetic were about similar in number of errors of nonequivalence. In the errors of equivalence the haptic–kinesthetic comparisons seemed to be less difficult than the visual kinesthetic.
4. The individual differences in performance tended to decrease with age.
5. The comparisons of identical forms were generally more difficult to make than comparisons of nonidentical forms.
6. The performances with preferred and nonpreferred hands were not significantly different.

Birch and Belmont (1964a) compared brain-damaged children with normals in their ability in *intrasensory* and *intersensory* functioning. They found that the two groups were not significantly different in intrasensory functioning but that they did differ in intersensory functioning. The tests were on horizontality, verticality, and object distance in an unilluminated room as against a lighted room. The two groups differed in their behavior in the unilluminated room.

Birch and Belmont (1964b) compared retarded readers with normals in auditory–visual integration and concluded that the retarded readers were less able to succeed in auditory–visual equivalence comparisons than the normal readers.

Still supposing that complex adaptive functions in childhood are dependent on the development of interactions between separate sensory systems, Birch and Belmont (1965) studied auditory–visual integration in brain-damaged and normal children. The subjects were to identify a spatial visual dot pattern that was perceived to be the same as the temporal pattern of taps with which they were presented. The auditory stimuli, the taps, were separated from each other in the pattern by either a half-second or one second. The subjects were 88 brain-damaged children and 220 normals. The range in age of the brain-damaged was from 5 years 7 months to 20 years 10 months. The auditory–visual integrative capacities of the brain-damaged children were found to be significantly below the normals of the same age. The experimenters concluded that the perceptual and perceptual-motor difficulties found in the brain-damaged subjects might stem from disturbed intersensory integration.

TACTUAL LOCALIZATION AND OBJECT SIZE

Another line of investigation on the development of perception is illustrated in the work of Renshaw (1930) and his colleagues on tactual localization, which involved comparisons between blind and sighted children and adults. It was found that sighted children were superior to sighted adults in tactual localization. This was interpreted as due to adults shifting to a dependence on vision in localization. Renshaw and Wherry (1931) found that tactual–kinesthetic localization is superior to visual localization in children from the eighth to the twelfth year, where the difference between the two disappears. During puberty, localization by both means increases and then between the thirteenth and fifteenth years visual localization becomes superior and increases for some years as age increases.

The same shift from prepubertal to postpubertal behavior was interpretable when the studies of Bartley (1953) and Bartley, Clifford, and Calvin (1955) are taken together. Subjects below the age of 10 years performed essentially differently from a college age group when tactual information was used to determine object size. The behavior of the college age group showed the influence of the visual sense modality (see Chapter 8).

Without a doubt, it seems that various types of performance dependent on sensory functioning are not equally difficult and that normally difficulty lessens during childhood development. The performances can be analyzed into those dependent on mainly a single modality and those dependent vary definitely on the participation of several forms of modality information or, as Birch and his colleagues put it, on intersensory organization. This organization shows a traceable development up to about puberty. Various subnormal groups such as the brain-damaged children and the retarded readers show their deficits particularly in the tasks involving intersensory organization.

Intersensory development shows itself not only in tests such as those used by Birch and his colleagues, but in tests of tactual localization and the use of tactual information. Below puberty, tactual information is utilized more nearly without help from the visual mechanism, but from then on visual influences begin to participate even when the information received is only tactual.

PERCEPTION OF QUALITIES OF OBJECTS

Bower (1971) has questioned at what age infants begin to associate specific qualities with the objects they see. He feels that the fact that infants show an ability to discriminate between objects does not tell much as to what the infant knows about the object at various ages—how he or she perceives it.

In one experiment, infants were presented with a box moving toward them. Even 2-week-old infants, who would have had no experience with being hit in the face by a moving object reacted defensively and with distress to this presentation but did not react to the box if it moved away from them. They behaved in the same way toward a projected three-dimensional image of the box. In order to carry this experiment further, newborn infants were presented with projected objects and real objects. The infants would reach out for both, and howl when unable to grasp the projected image while showing no distress when touching the real object. Bower feels this presents evidence for a primitive unity of the senses— that eye–hand interaction is build into the nervous system. Another series of experiments aimed to find out whether a concept of the permanence of objects is also built-in.

The first experiment measured heart rate change as an index of surprise. A screen was moved to cover an object that half the time would have disappeared when the screen was moved away again. If the infant knew the object was still behind the screen when it was covered, its failure to reappear should surprise him or her and increase the heart rate. Infants ages 80 to 100 days were surprised when the object failed to reappear, but not surprised at its still being there. Infants 20 days old exhibited the same response initially, but if the object was occluded by the screen for more than 9 seconds, they would seem to forget about it by showing more surprise at its reappearance than its disappearance.

Tracking movements of infants' eyes were recorded to further explore this effect. This time the screen was stationary but the object was moved so that it disappeared behind the screen and reappeared or failed to reappear. It was found that infants up to 16 weeks old would track the moving object as it disappeared and reappeared and would show the same tracking behavior even when the object stopped in plain view *without disappearing behind the screen.* Further testing showed that an inability to arrest head movement was not a factor. The converse of this effect was then tested. Infants 3 months old watched a toy train move horizontally away from a stationary position to a new position and back again ten times. The train then moved an equal distance in the opposite direction. The infants continued to look for the train in the spot to which it had originally traveled. The conclusion here was that the infants were not watching the train move from place to place but were operating by the rule "object disappears at A, object will reappear at B." Therefore the infant does not identify the moving object with the stopped object.

Another set of experiments tested the effect that various differences in features would have on the infants' perception of objects. An object disappeared behind a screen. Part of the time an object different in size, shape, and color reappeared instead of the original object. Infants close to 22 weeks old tracked the new object, then appeared to look back for the reappearance of the original object. Infants from 6 to 16 weeks tracked either object with no sign of disturbance. In another condition the rate of movement was changed so that the object appearing on the other side of the screen would do so before it should have had time to move across the occluded area. This did not seem to disturb the older infants, but the younger ones would become upset and refuse to track.

These experiments suggested to Bower that the younger infants were so unaffected by the features of objects that they must respond to movement itself rather than to the moving object. Only the infants past 16 weeks had learned that an object "can go from place to place along pathways of movement."

Figure 10.3 Sample photographs from videotape recordings of 2- to 3-week-old infants imitating (a) tongue protrusion, (b) mouth opening, (c) lip protrusion demonstrated by an adult experimenter. (Source: A. N. Meltzoff and M. Keith Moore. "Imitation of facial and manual gestures by human neonates," *Science,* 1977, 198, 75–78, Fig. 1. Copyright © 1977 by the American Association for the Advancement of Science.)

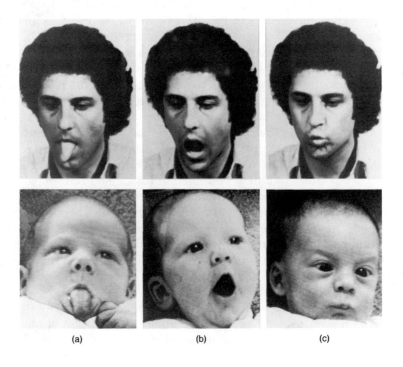

(a)   (b)   (c)

IMITATION

Meltzoff and Moore (1977) reported that infants between 12 and 21 days of age could imitate both facial and manual gestures of an adult. Piaget and others have considered imitations of facial gestures to be an important landmark in infant development. This was thought to occur at 8 to 12 months of age (see Figure 10.3).

Theories as to what this means are a bit complicated and cannot be given here.

In Chapter 15 the matter of development will be given further consideration and the question of whether the principles of perceptual development in infancy and childhood and perceptual learning and change in adults are essentially the same will be asked.

Chapter 11
Perceptual Constancies and Equivalents

In this chapter we shall deal with a fundamental feature of the organism's ability to relate to and cope with the environment. It is something that shows up in all the senses but most saliently in vision. Several words carry the meaning of what is to be considered. They are *constancy, equivalence,* and *identity.* The first is the most used term, but it does not refer to all that is involved. The other two are needed.

The implication of constancy is that something, although different from occasion to occasion remains the same as far as perception is concerned. The implication of equivalence is that a number of external sources of stimulus, although different, end up by providing the sense organ the same pattern. Identification is the perceptual awareness of an object being the same one regardless of its specific sensory attributes, from occasion to occasion. This chapter attempts to depict the way the organism perceptually functions with reference to these matters.

In asking about equivalence, we may inquire as to how different objects provide for the same sensory inputs. In asking about constancy we may inquire as to how it is that a white sheet of paper, for example, looks white in low illumination, as well as at room levels. In asking about identity, we are not asking strictly about constancy or equivalence, but what is required simply for something to be recognized under widely different conditions. Even when a sheet of paper is identified as white under several conditions, is the whiteness of the paper the same in all the cases? Though *whiteness* may be perceived, is it the same in all the cases?

LIGHTNESS OR WHITENESS CONSTANCY

In the discussion of brightness discrimination earlier, much was said that demonstrated lightness constancy. To that discussion, we shall add some examples here. Lightness constancy is to be regarded in terms of the relative weights given two important factors in visual stimulation: (1) the intensity of target illumination by some source of photic radiation and (2) the amount of reflectance of the target itself. We know that the reflectance of a target does not vary as intensity of radiation is varied. That is, a target always reflects a *constant percentage* of the radiation falling on it when intensity is the only variable manipulated. If the property of lightness were dependent on this factor, then the target would look equally light no matter how weak or intense the radiation reaching it. Were lightness to depend on quantity of radiation reaching the target, lightness would vary in keeping with radiation intensity. Lightness does not strictly follow either of these rules. If it followed the first rule strictly, perception would manifest complete "constancy." To the extent that it does not follow the rule, complete constancy is departed from. Some experiments in constancy provide a measure of just how closely complete constancy is approached.

Illumination

Although we shall see that the apprehension of illumination as such is not a necessary factor in producing the kinds of results we are to deal with, it must be recognized that illumination may be involved in various ways in various situations. It must also be recognized that visual results depend in a large measure on the way illumination is involved in a given situation.

There are several ways that illumination may reach the eye. The use of apertures is one. One way to provide an aperture gray is to set up a *hole* arrangement. A screen is provided with a hole that subtends a few degrees of visual angle at the eye. An illumination source is concealed behind the screen. A still better way is to use two rooms, with the hole in the wall between. The illumination falls on some reflecting surface that can send radiation to the observer, as in Figure 11.1. The hole can be seen as an aperture filled in with a certain gray. The light does not seem to come from a definite surface at the plane of the screen, or even at some distance behind the screen, unless the area viewed through the hole is textured, that is, inhomogeneous. If, however, the observer is predisposed toward seeing surfaces, the hole *may* be seen as a surface.

Radiation falls on obstructing surfaces at various angles. These varying *angles of incidence* determine the amount of reflection and, as a result, function for the observer as factors in seeing various degrees of lightness. In addition, the different amounts of reflection from different parts of a surface enable the perceiver to see a third dimension and objects with volume.

Illumination of an area in the visual field may be intermittent, as when one looks at a revolving fan. Its blades intermittently obstruct and permit a view beyond them. Radiation falling on them and reflected to the observer produces what is seen as a film, through which objects are observable beyond. There need be nothing about the visual properties of this film to indicate that it is being produced as is. A sheet of glass with a thin layer of dirt or paint might produce the same visual effect. This ambiguity regarding the nonvisual reality of the situation emphasizes what Ames (1946) has pointed out, namely, that perception possesses the nature of a bet or mere prognostication. In some situations the probability of the bet is high: the likelihood that nonvisual reality will be in accord with the visually perceived reality is high. In other cases the prognostication is poor. If, in the case of the fan, the observer reached out to try to

Figure 11.1 Illumination arrangement to produce an aperture gray. Radiation falls on a surface (the opposite wall of an adjoining room) and is reflected through a hole to the room of the observer whose eye is E. The hole seen as a gray area is now the target on a well-illuminated background, W.

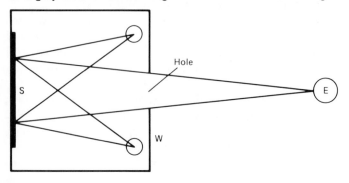

touch it, the poorness of the prognostication would be amply demonstrated, for the individual would get his or her fingers nipped. Visually, the film is perfectly innocuous; tactually, it is a very different matter. Touching the "film" is like touching a buzz saw in motion.

In some respects, interrupted radiation functions essentially the same whether a beam from a radiation source is being interrupted or reflections are interrupted, as in the case of the moving fan blades. The ratio between the period of interruption and the period of transmission or reflection determines the quantity of radiation reaching the eye in a given period and thus determines the lightness or brightness seen. A film, however, is produced only when the radiation source is on the same side of the moving blades as the observer so that there can be reflection.

Constancy and the Perception of Illumination

In Chapter 8 it was pointed out that under some conditions the perceiver is able to make a distinction between the properties of a target surface and the photic illumination it receives. MacLeod (1932, 1940) pointed out that we must not conclude that the perception of illumination as such is an essential condition for the operation of color or lightness constancy. He and a number of other investigators look on the perception of color and lightness constancies and the perception of illumination as two products of some more fundamental factor. Very definite constancy phenomena can be produced that are not dependent on the perception of illumination. His study of brightness constancy in unrecognized shadows (1940) showed this.

Shadows

Illumination may encounter obstructions, in which case shadows are cast. *Shadows* are areas of diminution of illumination within which object lightness constancy tends to be high. Here again, we encounter the need for distinguishing between the observer's ability to *identify* lightness of objects within the area and actually to see the area as having a lightness different from others in the visual field. Equations (matchings) of lightness between the area seen as in shadow and an area seen as outside the shadow are difficult to make. Let a screen be set up in front of the field just implied and let the two areas be viewed through an aperture or separate apertures, and the match at once becomes much less difficult.

Long ago, Hering pointed out that if a black line is drawn around the edge of a shadow, the shadow as such will disappear. The shadow area will take on the appearance of a dark surface. This fact was

244 INTRODUCTION TO PERCEPTION

used by Kardos (1934), who used an encircled shadow with a small disk at its center to show that when the shadow is encircled the disk appears darker, in contradiction to laws of color contrast that would be expected to operate in this situation. He also found that the effect was relatively independent of the area of the field and would occur as easily with a white encircling line as with a dark one. Thus one cannot use the line as a factor in the explanation by saying that it produced a lightness contrast effect. The preferable explanation is that conditions that produce shadows make them operate as special forms of local illumination. Accordingly, the disk shifts toward greater lightness in line with the laws of lightness constancy. When the shadow is turned into a surface, it is seen as darker. Whatever the explanation may be, the change from shadow to surface color in the Kardos experiment is not to be doubted.

MacLeod (1940) repeated Kardos' experiment in the following manner. A circular white line 5 millimeters in width was placed on an upright surface seen as black. A circular shadow was cast so that its penumbra coincided with the line. (A penumbra of a shadow is its tapered or less dark outer border.) In MacLeod's setup the area was seen as a luminous black surface bordered by a white line. The area looked like a piece of velvet or a black hole cut in a surface. When he shifted the surface on which the shadow fell to dispense with the white encircling line, the area simply became a shadow and was not so dark as it was at the beginning.

In the center of the shadow a rotating disk whose two components, "white" and "black," could be manipulated was introduced. Consultation of Figure 11.2 will help to understand the setup. Two disks, C_1 and C_2, are propelled by motors that lie behind screens of low reflectance (black). A is also a low-reflectance surface. E_1 and E_2 are shadowcasters for the radiation source D. The observer is O, and the setup is viewed through aperture F.

When observers were given the chance to observe the visual field produced by the foregoing conditions, they found it quite difficult to say what was what. The shadow cast by E_1 was encircled by the line already mentioned; the shadow cast by E_2 was not. In every case the encircled shadow and its central disk were perceived as definitely darker than the comparison target formed by the shadow of E_2 and its disk. The unencircled shadow was more difficult to localize in distance. In other cases the shadows were seen as being at different distances.

About 60 percent of the 38 observers perceived no special or anomalous illumination. The summary of findings for the experiment as a whole was that (1) a definite difference in lightness was described

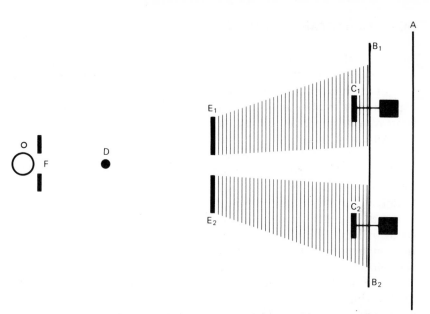

Figure 11.2 MacLeod's arrangement for studying lightness constancy. A is a uniform, low-reflectance surface. B_1 and B_2 are low-reflectance cardboard screens. C_1 and C_2 are color wheels. E_1 and E_2 are shadow-casters. F is an observation window. O is the observer's eye. D is a radiation source. (Source: R. B. MacLeod. "Brightness constancy in unrecognized shadows, *J. Exp. Psychol.*, 1940, 27, 1–22, Fig. 1.)

for the two targets even when neither one of the two shadows was perceived as shadows and (2) a difference remained despite full explanation of the setup to the observers.

It would seem that MacLeod showed that the perception of anomalous illumination conditions does not lie back of all lightness constancy results. MacLeod concluded that the phenomena in question could be handled better by referring them to organization of the visual field and that the concept of "constancy" is of doubtful value in studying such situations as illustrated by the present investigation.

MacLeod's conclusions are in contrast with the usual "cue" explanation of the nature of visual perception. It will be recalled that elsewhere the fallacy of prevalent cue theory has been pointed out, for it consists in using one perception to help explain another when the very same stimulus field is responsible for both of them. Here, in the case at hand, MacLeod has shown that lightness constancy has not depended on the "cue" of illumination.

SIZE AND DISTANCE CONSTANCIES

In size constancy we deal with the ability of the observer to perceive metric size regardless of target distance or other factors. Metric size of target and the awareness of the observer that the object constitutes a smaller and smaller part of the visual field as its distance from him or her increases, must be distinguished.

All visual targets subtend visual angles, small or great. Certain distant large targets subtend the same visual angles as certain near small ones. The visual field need not be structured for an object to be seen at a given distance; but when it is structured the field largely determines the distance at which the object is seen. In keeping with this field structure, we see objects likewise as metrically small or large. To perceive size in this way is something different from noting analytically that the portion of the total visual field occupied by the object is small or large.

An object may be seen as a familiar object, a tree, a playing card, a thimble, and so on. When it is seen as a member of a class of objects whose range in size is rather limited, it is seen also as a large, medium-sized, or small object of its kind. One aspect of the perception of the object is *identification* and the other is *appreciation of size*.

Perception of object size follows one set of laws in an unstructured field and a different set in a structured one. This is to say that when the object in question is the only thing in the visual field, the field contributes nothing to object identification. Hence from the stimulus standpoint, broad field properties cannot be called into use. The only thing that is structured is the small region that constitutes the object itself. This leaves the object to be almost any size. Lack of field structure leaves object location indefinite also. The object may be near or far away. Despite this indefiniteness as far as stimulus contribution is concerned, the observer does not fail to perceive. What has happened is that the organism itself has had to put more into the matter. The organism simply acts as though one of the several alternatives were true. Perception proceeds as though a choice had been made, as though a premise had been used or an assumption had been instantly employed. We do not know what the process actually is. We only know that perception proceeds *as if* the above were true. No marked delay, no antecedent conscious process, takes place. Perception is just as straightforward as though the stimulus situation had furnished all the determinants necessary.

The laws that govern visual perception of size when the field is structured stem from the field itself. The most fundamental and comprehensive description of the visual field is Gibson's texture-gradient concept, which he uses to describe three-dimensional space perception. Here it can be said only that the visual field is conceived as existing as a textured expanse. The texturing of the field is of such character as to determine the distance factor of perceived objects (segregated portions of the field) as well as their direction and size.

Size Constancy and Great Distance

The perceived size of an object does not diminish in keeping with the retinal image of the target as it recedes in the distance. Few persons suppose, however, that the perceived object size does not diminish at all when the target is placed at great distances. At certain distances the target subtends visual angles so small that the object is scarcely visible. It is then that the second of the two aboves mentioned modes of perceiving size comes into prominence. Size now may come to mean the occupation of an insignificant portion of the total visual field; extremely small size and bare visibility may now become synonymous. Before this happens the object might very easily be supposed to be getting smaller. Size constancy is generally thought to break down for targets removed to great distances. This general outlook on size constancy was investigated as follows.

J. J. Gibson (1950) exposed upright stakes in a flat unfurrowed field, one at a time, at various distances. The stakes ranged from 15 to 99 inches in height. A row of comparison stakes was set up at a little distance from the subject at right angles to his line of regard. Each was of a different size, and the stakes were numbered 1 through 15. As a distant test stake was exposed, the observer was to indicate with which of the sample stakes it compared closest in height. The observer could even say "smaller than one" or "taller than 15." No preclusion was made for range in perceived heights.

The trials included different sizes of stakes at different distances in random combinations. Each observer made 150 observations. Averages of the perceptions were computed for the different stake sizes, distances, and observers. Let us look at what the observers did in perceiving a 71-inch stake. At 42 feet the mean perception was 71.9 inches with a standard deviation of 1.8 inches. At 672 feet the mean perception was 75.8 inches with a standard deviation of 7.3 inches. At nearly half a mile (2352 feet) the mean result was 74.9 inches with a standard deviation of 9.8 inches. For four other distances the results were comparable. Since at one-half mile, the 71-inch stake was almost invisible, but was still perceived just about as nearly correctly as stakes much nearer, the question of diminution of size constancy with distance is answered. Distance has essentially little to do with size constancy.

Gibson and Henneman (Gibson, 1950) investigated the perceived size of targets and distances between them in a thoroughly cluttered room. The results indicated that size constancy for objects and constancy for perception of distances between them followed the same principles. Thus it can be said that the same concept of constancy applies to interobject distances and object dimensions. This would tend to lead us to conclude the constancy is a field property rather than simply a *thing* property, thus obviating the need for special explanations for constancy based on some uniqueness in perceiving objects.

Size Perception in an Unstructured Field

As one example of perception in an unstructured field, the following card demonstration is given. If a target comprising a rectangular blank card is the only visual differentiation provided in a dark room, it may be perceived as almost any size. It may be seen as a small rectangle nearby or as a large rectangle far away. Both may produce the same-sized retinal images. Since it is only the retinal image and the contribution of the perceiver himself or herself that determine the perceptual end result, object size is dependent on the *distance* at which the object is *projected* in perception. Size and distance are reciprocal for any fixed retinal image. The observer sees the object as a certain size and a certain distance. All that we can show is that the two are related to each other, as would be expected from the trigonometry involved in target size, target distance, and the retinal image produced. The pivotal factor is retinal image size, for that is the only fixed thing as far as the stimulus is concerned. If a playing card is substituted for the blank card, then one more of the factors becomes determined: The observer "knows" the size of playing cards. Thus with retinal image size fixed and the object size fixed, distance is determined. The object seen can be seen at only one distance, unless it is possible to conceive of giant playing cards and miniature ones. A rare observer may be able to act as though looking at a giant playing card; if so, its distance from the observer is increased. Or the observer may act as though looking at a miniature; if he or she does, its distance is diminished. Nevertheless, the experimenter cannot obtain these results by merely asking all observers to "imagine" that the cards are giants or dwarfs.

We are now ready for another indoor example of size constancy. Holway and Boring (1941) compared two circular targets, one fixed in position and the other posed at various distances. The stationary target was 10 feet from the observer; the movable one varied from 10 to 120 feet. The stationary target was seen as the disk of light the diameter of which was controlled by an iris diaphragm. The movable target was adjusted so as to subtend a visual angle of 1 degree at each position used. The observer's problem was to adjust the stationary target in diameter so that it appeared to be the same size as the movable target whose diameter was kept at 1 degree.

The Holway and Boring investigation approaches the tests for the "law of the visual angle" and the "law of size constancy" by using the stationary target to represent the apparent size of the movable target. The angular subtense (at the eye) of the diameter of the movable target was held at 1°. The movable target was thus made larger and larger as it was moved away from the observer. The diameter of the stationary target was adjusted so that the two targets continued to seem equal in size. This operation should disclose which of the two "laws" or rules operates or whether the results turn out to be a compromise. If the stationary target can remain unchanged in diameter, then the law of the visual angle is demonstrated because both targets, in all cases, subtend the same visual angles (Figure 11.3). If the diameter of the stationary target must be changed as the movable target is placed farther and farther

Figure 11.3 Stimulus conditions in experiment of Holway and Boring (1941).

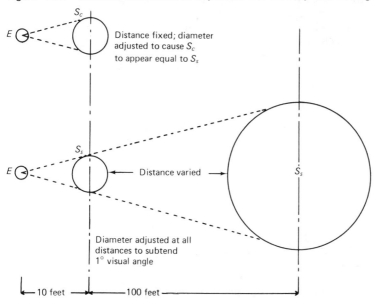

away, then the law of size constancy is demonstrated. Both targets are made equal in size regardless of difference in distance and thus regardless of the visual angle they subtend at the eye.

The two laws represent the opposite extremes that the results could represent. If as in Figure 11.4, the diameter of the comparison target is represented on the vertical axis and the distance of the movable target is represented on the horizontal axis, the relation of the results to the two extremes represented by the laws can be shown. In the figure the horizontal line expresses the law of the visual angle since the movable target is adjusted to subtend constant visual angle regardless of distance. Accordingly, the diameter of the fixed target must remain constant so as to match it, and the line in the graph must be horizontal. The broken sloping line represents the law of size constancy.

Holway and Boring found neither extreme to hold in their study. Four different observing conditions were employed. The results are shown in the four curves in Figure 11.4. The lowest of the four sloping curves represents the results of one-eyed viewing with an artificial pupil and a reduction tunnel to eliminate the operation of certain extraneous field factors.

Obviously, monocular viewing eliminates stereoscopic factors

Figure 11.4 Relation of diameter of comparison target to distance of standard stimulus for the conditions in Holway and Boring's experiment. The diagonal dashed line shows expectations of size constancy. The horizontal dashed line shows expectations according to the law of the visual angle. Curve A is for binocular viewing, B for monocular with natural profile, C for monocular with artifical pupil, and D for monocular with artifical pupil and reduction tunnel. (Source: C. H. Graham. "Visual perception," in S. S. Stevens (ed.), *Handbook of Experimental Psychology.* New York: Wiley, 1951, Fig. 2.)

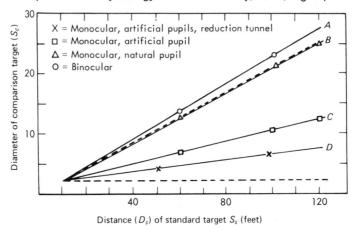

Distance (D_s) of standard target S_s (feet)

and should work toward the perception following the law of visual angle. With binocular viewing, that is, with conditions in which stimulation is least simplified, the law of size constancy is expected to operate most forcefully. In one condition, namely, for unrestricted binocular viewing, the relation went beyond the constancy values (see curve *A*). For monocular viewing with natural pupil *(B)* an approximation to size constancy resulted. Under two conditions, the results were a compromise. The two compromise conditions involved certain limiting viewing conditions, such as monocular viewing with artificial pupil *(C)* and also with reduction tunnel *(D)*.

Hastorf's Investigation

Hastorf (1950) performed a study in size perception that involved two fields of view. One was for binocular vision; the other was for only one eye. The binocular field was such as to give rise to seeing a three-dimensional situation with perspective and objects at several distances. The field for the single eye was completely unilluminated. In the darkness the observer saw only a disk or rectangle of light. The target that produced this could be varied in size. The consequent change in the apparent distance of the disk or rectangle could be indicated by its localization relative to the perceived items in the binocular field. The binocular field comparison items were four posts distributed at intervals of one foot.

The monocular field was a projection screen on which the disk or rectanglular target already mentioned was projected. This screen was at the same distance from the observer as the third post in the binocular field. A Clason projector provided a target that varied in size without developing a consequent blur in contour.

According to the experimenter's instructions, the disk of light in one set of observations represented a Ping-Pong ball and in another set a billiard ball. In two different sets of observations, the rectangle was used, which represented a calling card and an envelope, respectively. In all cases the observers were to set the target (disk or rectangle) at a size necessary for the seen object to be at the distance of post number 3 in the binocular field while using the monocular and the binocular fields at the same time. The supposition was that the binocular field gave three-dimensional perception and could be used as an indicator for the distance át which the object was seen by the one eye using the monocular field. The readings compared pretty well to what would be expected from the visual angles that would have been subtended by the actual objects, that is, billiard ball and Ping-Pong ball. Since these balls are of different sizes, they required different adjustments of the target size.

In the third part of the experiment the size of the target was not at the mean reading given for the Ping-Pong ball. The observer was then asked to locate the distance of the object seen by telling where it was in relation to post number 3. Nothing was said about whether the target in this case was a Ping-Pong ball or a billiard ball, although it was a "billiard ball." The disk was reported beyond post 3, as would have been expected, for the target was too small to be at post 3 if the object was a billiard ball. Implied in the experimentation is the assumption that the observers would still be behaving as if looking at a billiard ball.

Implied in the behavior is the principle that behavior follows certain "assumptions" the observer makes. The investigator felt that he had demonstrated that there is something "assumptive" about perception that heretofore had not been well recognized or demonstrated. While this is not one of the more usual forms of investigation of size constancy, it does involve the continuity and constancy principles.

SHAPE CONSTANCY

The third aspect of constancy is shape, which enables us to identify objects or distinguish them from each other. Shape as pertaining to objects and shape as descriptive of the various regions of the visual field are to be distinguished from each other. For example, we perceive the top of a table as rectangular and say that shape belongs to the table. Rectangularity is ascribed to the table top regardless of its position with regard to us. On the other hand, we know that the "shape" presented to the eye may be any one of an infinite number depending on the table's position. Obviously, perception is involved in distinguishing the shape of the table top from the shape of that portion of the visual field segregated off as table top. Were the perceiving organism unable to make this distinction, it could not react as it does. It might act as though the visual field was a single plane, the frontal plane, with all events occurring within it. Thus if we were to present such an organism with a three-dimensional table top and tip it in various directions one after the other, the organism would not see a single entity being moved about in three-dimensional space but would see a region of a two-dimensional field continually changing shape. If this continually changing of shape were seen as a single entity, it would be credited with being quite elastic or pliable rather than rigid, as we now see table tops to be.

A good place to begin our discussion of shape and shape con-

stancy is with Thouless' (1931) work. His very first study consisted
in presenting observers with a disk target and a square target. One
or the other was placed on a long table and viewed obliquely by
the observer from a fixed viewing position. Obviously, as the position
of the target was shifted farther and farther out along the table, it
was viewed more and more obliquely. Obliqueness of view produces
a retinal image shape different from that of the normal view (at
right angles to the plane of the target). Thouless called the target
the real object, *R*. The resulting retinal image, with its varying shape
in relation to obliqueness of viewing conditions, he called the stimulus object, *S*.

As observers we can deal with targets in two ways: we can
identify them as objects or can deal with some object property, in
this case the property of *perceived shape* as abstracted from identity.
In Thouless' experiment it was obvious to the observers that they
were dealing with a disk and a square at different time so that
the identity of the "real object" was not at issue. Thouless wanted
his observers to indicate the seen shapes as the targets were made
more and more oblique to the eye. (In Figure 11.5 the target obviously subtends a much smaller visual angle at position 3 than at
position 1.)

He had the observers draw the shapes they saw. To indicate
shape, Thouless used a ratio of the short axis (vertical) to the long
axis (horizontal) of the form they observed. Obviously, the shapes
the observers saw in looking at the circular target obliquely were
approximate ellipses. The drawings were measured in terms of the
ratio and found to represent a seen shape (phenomenal shape) some-

Figure 11.5 Thouless' experiment. E is the eye. Items 1, 2, and 3 are the
target positions. Shifting the target from one position to another changes its
effective shape (frontal plane projection) and varies the visual angle subtended
by one dimension.

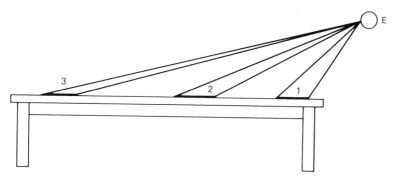

where between the shape of S and the shape of R. This shape Thouless called the phenomenal object, P. To provide a numerical way of expressing the relation of P to R, he used the ratio

$$\frac{\log\ P-\log\ S}{\log\ R-\log\ S}$$

Thouless called this the index of *phenomenal regression*. He labeled the perceptual behavior "phenomenal regression to the real object." This implies that there is some fixed intrinsic entity called the real object and that it has some influence on what is perceived. It is difficult to conceive of the real object meant here as being anything other than either a (1) concept or (2) perceived object to which the perceiver is led to attribute a more ultimate form of reality than the perception of shape referred to the frontal plane. What reaches the eye is a pattern of photic radiation that corresponds to the shape (the geometry of S), whereas R is both a perceptual object and a conceptual one. Thouless is assuming that what ever gives rise to the experience of circularity or squareness, regardless of the angle of viewing the target, is the real object, something that has some uniqueness and indestructibility.

Further Experiments

Some other sorts of investigations involve conditions through which a further look at the idea of real object can be made. Several investigators have used targets in unstructured fields: the targets were luminous and the only observable items in a dark room.

Nelson and Bartley (1956) used three such targets, luminous wire forms, a circle, and two ellipses 4 × 5 inches and 3 × 5 inches. These were oriented in several positions: (1) in the frontal plane, that is, upright; (2) at a 22.5° tilt from the vertical away from the observer; (3) at a 45° tilt; and (4) at a 67.5° tilt. There were 12 different kinds of presentations given in random order. Nelson and Bartley used the same kind of notation as in Thouless' investigation and likewise obtained the data through observers' drawings. The observers, in general, behaved as if they all saw the targets in the frontal plane. That was the stimulus shape. There was no regression. The "real objects" (the targets) in this investigation were not always circles and were not always what Thouless defined as real. One would not know to which real object to refer the data.

It will be remembered here that a target forming the same given retinal image may be an ellipse or a circle, for a tilted circle will involve the same "projection" in the frontal plane (i.e., the same visual angle) as a certain ellipse. Obviously, the observers had no way of "knowing" which was the case in any trial. They could have seen the target as either one for one would have made as much sense as the other. The 24 observers never acted as if they saw tilted circles.

Miller and Bartley (1954) studied circles at various tilts. The field was structured and the targets were cardboard circles and ellipses placed on a tilt board whose limiting edges were hidden by a reduction screen. From this lighted-room experiment the perceptions were much different from those obtained in an unstructured field. The phenomenon that Thouless called "regression to the real object" seemed to be involved. But since there were several "real objects" and since the observer had no way of "knowing" what the targets were like, the concept of real object is not a suitable one.

Perception of Tilt

For reporting on perceptions of tilt we shall consult the findings of Haan and Bartley (1954). In their work the same stimulus conditions were used as in Nelson and Bartley's (1956) study. In this case, however, the observers were asked to report on perceived tilt.

The first thing that can be said about the findings is that most of them lie between the limits expected of a 3 × 5 ellipse and a full circle. But to the question of what is the real object functioning in the experiment there is no sensible answer except to say that whatever the observer sees is real—real to him or her—and that there is no other necessary single reality toward which perception must regress. Here again, we see that the concept of regression to the real object does not apply, and if used at all it has to be confined to Thouless' investigation or a similar one. In this connection it may be stated that in the Nelson and Bartley experiment, telling the observers that the objects were circles at various degrees of tilt, when asking for shape reports, influenced shape very little. Of course, it could not be ascertained how thoroughly the observers were made to "believe" that the targets were "circles," but at least the potential bias was offered, and it did not make much difference in that particular experiment.

Invariance

Invariance is a concept closely related to constancy. Invariance refers to a lawful relationship between two items. It is, in effect, the opposite of irregularity. As one tilts a plane target backward from the vertical or frontal plane position, progressive obliqueness causes the plane to subtend a smaller and smaller visual angle until it subtends virtually none when viewed as merely the thickness of the target. This diminishing vertical dimension is described by the trigonometric function, known as the cosine function.

We have been speaking in "physical" (geometric and trigonometric) terms. In psychology there is a second set of items called the phenomenological (or perceptual). Invariance, then, can be posed in several ways. Is there invariance between physical and perceptual factors, or is there invariance between the two sets of perceptual factors shape and slant? We already know that there is invariance among the geometrical factors.

Let us cite the invariance study of Nelson, Bartley, and Bourassa (1961) on the effect of area characteristics of targets on shape-slant invariance. They believed that there is good reason to suppose that what is seen as shape is influenced by the characteristics of the areas bounded by the borders of the targets. Their data confirmed this.

Koffka's (1930) is the best known statement of the belief that geometry and perceptual processes should tally. Stavrianos' (1945) investigation is the best example to show that they do not tally.

Nelson, Bartley, and Bourassa's (1961) study is a criticism of the idea that humans' perceptual discriminations involve invariance relations similar to those ascribed to the world by Euclidean geometry. In the study, luminous targets were presented in an unilluminated field in which they were the only visible items. Four series of targets differing in internal differentiation (or "texture") were used. Each series contained 20 targets of different inclination and geometrical properties. They varied from a circle to ellipses 5 × 4, 5 × 3, 5 × 2, and 5 × 1 inches. The orientations (or inclinations) were tilted 22.5, 45, and 67.5° from vertical (0°). One series of targets was wire outlines, another series was of untextured surfaces, still another possessed fine textures, and a fourth had course textures.

The task of the 40 observers in part I of the experiment was to reproduce the seen slant of the targets by adjusting a tilt board to match what was seen. In part II the observers were asked to draw the shapes of the objects seen. Shape in the study was defined as the minor–major axis ratios of the drawings.

For the outline targets the invariance was virtually linear for the entire shape-slant continuum. The curves for the other conditions departed from this linearity to different extents, especially in the segments of the curves depicting large slants and small minor–major axis ratios. The departure from linearity was greatest for the course textured targets.

Figure 11.6 depicts the cosine functions for various target shapes

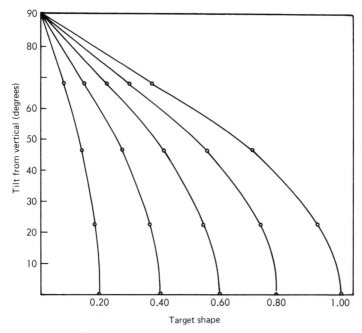

Figure 11.6   Cosine functions of targets for various degrees of inclination. (Source: T. M. Nelson, S. H. Bartley, and C. Bourassa. "The effect of areal characteristics of targets upon shape-slant invariance," *J. Psychol.*, 1961, 52, 479–490, Fig. 1.)

(minor–major axis ratios) indicated on the abscissa. It will be seen that as such targets are tilted from the vertical, each retinal image shape diminishes to zero according to the cosine function via its own parameters. Hence there is a separate and different curve for each target.

When the visual (i.e., perceptual) results are pictured, the relation between shape and slant is not according to the cosine function although it is lawful. The relationship (the invariance) was depicted by an entirely different set of curves (Figure 11.7), as you will note. That is, then, that the family of perceptual curves in Figure 11.7 does not seem to be determined by the variables attributed to the target by Euclidean geometry. One of the influencing factors is the surface characteristics.

We have already mentioned Stavrianos' investigation of shape constancy, or what might be called a test for shape-slant invariance, in which the geometrical and the perceptual factors were not kept separate. Her experiment consisted in having the observer tell which of a group of seven rectangles was seen as a square. The rectangles ranged from taller than wide to wider than tall. The surface carrying

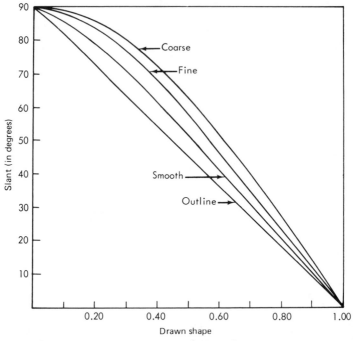

Figure 11.7   Actual relations between target slant and drawn shape. (Source: T. M. Nelson, S. H. Bartley, and C. Bourassa. "The effect of areal characteristics of targets upon shape-slant invariance," *J. Psychol.,* 1961, 52, 479–490, Fig. 1.)

the rectangles varied from vertical to tilted 15, 30, 45, and 55°. The observer was required to adjust a rectangle at his or her right so that its tilt appeared to be the same as the surface carrying the group of rectangles. The observer was also to tell which of the rectangles was seen as a square. As the actual tilt of the standard increased, the comparison target deviated from it progressively in the direction of lesser tilt. Also the error in shape-matching increased as the tilt of the standard increased. With no tilt of the standard, the chosen rectangle was very nearly a square. As tilt became greater, the rectangle chosen as a square became a rectangle with greater and greater height in relation to width. In some respects Stavrianos' experiment showed the same principles as the experiments of the other workers did. However, there was a failure to corroborate some of the expectations made beforehand. One of these was to the effect that a reciprocity would exist between preceived inclination (tilt) and perceived shape. It is not certain that the most appropriate experimental conditions were set up to test this idea, so that failure in strict corroboration is not to be taken as final.

Two recent points of view with regard to the conditions for seeing slant are those of R. B. Freeman (1965a, b, 1966a, b) and Flock (1965). Freeman points out that with monocular viewing, visual slant and shape are a function mainly of linear outline perspective. The greater the magnitude of linear perspective, the greater is the perceived visual slant and the influence on judged shape. Flock believes that the assertion that slant is mainly a function of linear perspective is an oversimplification that does not quite cope with the facts.

Other workers dealing with texture include W. C. Clark and his colleagues (1956a) and Gruber and Clark (1956). Results vary with the conditions used and show that slant can be perceived when texture is absent and that under some conditions texture is less effective for accurate perception of slant than is target outline. All in all, the matter is too complex to allow for a full and adequate description here of the various conditions studied or even for a brief final statement of theoretical conclusions.

COLOR CONSTANCY

Color constancy is the final form of constancy we shall consider. Much of what was said about other forms of constancy applies to color constancy.

General Conditions of Color Attribution

The observer does not always know when he or she sees a surface whether spectral illumination or differential reflection is the cause of its color. The radiation may be from a restricted portion of the spectrum, or the surface of the target may reflect only the restricted band of wavelengths producing the color that is seen.

Cramer (1923) set up a situation that well illustrates this. He papered the walls of a corner of a room to produce a uniform color and then illuminated the walls by a concealed source of nonspectral illumination. The walls then appeared to be illuminated with colored lights somewhat less saturated than the walls themselves. Thus a compromise situation was set up, for a part of the perceived color was attributed to the illumination and a part to the walls.

On a different occasion Cramer projected lantern picture slides on a yellow screen. Houses that would have been seen as white on a white screen retained their original whiteness; that is, the yellow of the house in the scene was attributed to yellow illumination. When the slide was thrown out of focus, the white house lost its object color (its whiteness) and also its three-dimensional appearance. With extreme malfocusing, the scene became simply a cluster of various hues and no object color remained. In another case a blue square appeared as gray when projected onto the yellow screen. This is how it should have appeared, for complementary parts of the spectrum were being mixed. A blue dress of a child, however, was perceived as "blue in yellow illumination."

The Physical Basis of Color Constancy

Each case of reflected radiation—that is, each target surface—possesses a so-called object color. This is its property of modifying the radiation falling on it by means of absorbing some wavelengths and reflecting others. It is a virtually fixed characteristic and plays some role in determining color constancy, although in Cramer's illustrations the role is not great.

If a target is viewed sequentially under two different illuminations or if two identical targets are viewed concurrently under two different illuminations producing two consequent surface-color perceptions, they tend to be similar but not actually identical. This is another way of stating the compromise described in Cramer's first example. The similarity of the perceptions is favored by the identicalness of the target surfaces, while the dissimilarity of the perceptions is favored by the differences in the two illuminations.

Another way of illustrating the influence of the reflectance of the target is to compare the effect of doubling it and the intensity of illumination. When illumination is doubled, little difference is made; when reflectance is doubled, a great difference is made in the color of the surface viewed. In both cases the total radiation leaving the target surface for the eye is the same. Consequently, one cannot expect to alter surface color greatly by spectral changes in illumination unless the changes are extreme in comparison with the spectral sensitivity of the target surface.

A target that appears reddish will be achromatic when illuminated by "green" (the radiation that is the complement of the reflectance of the target), if there is no background associated with it. Let a background that is spectrally nonselective (i.e., "gray") now be used, illuminated by the same "green"; the target will resume its original reddish color. This is a case of simultaneous color contrast. The retinal induction from the illumination is effective in restoring the original color, which was absent when there was no target surround to reflect the green to the eye. This same general effect is supposed to operate to some degree in many other situations where the target reflectance and the illumination are not merely complementary or reciprocal to each other. On the other hand, the same principles in certain cases work in the very opposite direction.

Factors at the Perceptual Level

The investigations that have enabled the most comprehensive outlook on color phenomena, and thus on color constancy, are Helson's (1964). His work argues for a simple underlying mechanism that accounts for the many diverse phenomena of color vision under all conditions. He has been able to conclude that theories of color perception are based on restricted or distorted conditions of investigation when they attribute more or less independence to reflectance and illuminance; disjoin color constancy, color contrast, and adaptation; and attribute different behavior of these mechanisms to surface and film modes of color perception.

Among Helson's conclusions are the following. Targets above the reflectance to which the observer is adapted take the hue of the illuminant. Targets below this adaptation take the hue complementary to the illuminant hue. Targets close to the adaptive reflectance appear either colorless (acromatic) or greatly reduced in saturation. Targets appearing least saturated are near the adaptation reflectance, and this adaptation shifts with reflectance of surrounds. The mere alteration in surrounds changed nearly all the hues he used. The hues that are constant—that will shift toward the illuminant or to the complementary hue—depend on their relation to the reflectance of the surround.

The "Adaptation reflectance," or the achromatic point, is established in accordance with the viewing conditions at the time rather than with daylight illumination, a factor not acting at the time. Helson also asserts that effects often attributed to the "pressure of other objects in the field" or to unspecified organizational factors can likely be attributed to alteration in "adaptation reflectances." brought about by variation in target and surround reflectances.

The question of what actually remains constant under special illumination has received two quite extreme answers. One is that all nonselectively reflective targets remain colorless in nonspectral illumination, and the other is that constancy is zero for targets with selective reflectance in spectral illumination. Some investigations have supported these generalizations but only because they dealt with restricted conditions. Different setups or more pervasive surveys have produced exceptions. Helson states that nonselective targets near the achromatic point remain colorless in nonspectral illumination whereas others do not. Selective targets whose color in daylight is close to the illuminant color, or complementary to it, tend to retain their hue if they are of low reflectance. In come cases nonselectively reflective targets may look colored and some selectively reflective ones may look uncolored in spectral illumination. By an appropriate shift of surround, a target can be shifted from colorless to its complementary color or to the color of the illuminant.

Among the many virtues of Helson's investigations is the fact that he made his manipulations with neutral targets—targets not seen as familiar objects whose "natural" colors lie within a limited range. All the higher level personal factors were eliminated or reduced to an insignificant minimum. Hence we can take his several generalizations as representing the basic process in operation. All other phenomena that appear to be contradictions to these generalizations are only cases in which some higher order process is so strong as to transcend what would be provided when only the basic factors are in operation.

The findings and ideas just described constitute Helson's *adaptation level theory,* which has become so well known in some circles.

EQUIVALENCE IN STIMULUS SITUATIONS

Another basic principle in describing visual space perception is the fact that a number of different situations may produce visually equivalent results. Many examples of this are generally subsumed under the heading of perceptual constancy, but there are others that are not traditionally so classified.

The "law of the visual angle" provides for the equivalent viewing of (or seeing as the same target) an unlimited number of targets differing metrically among themselves and in their orientations and locations relative to the viewer. All the plane targets A, B, C, D, E, in Figure 11.8 and an endless number of others of various sizes and at various distances from the eye will subtend the same visual angle. Unless there is some difference of structure (texture) within the targets or the surrounding visual field, they will be seen as the same object when presented one at a time.

One of the Dartmouth Eye Institute demonstrations showing that what appears to be an interposition may not actually be an interposition also demonstrates a case of equivalence. The lower left-hand part of Figure 11.9 (a modified version of the demonstration) shows three playing cards set up in a row along the line of sight. They can be adjusted sideways and vertically so that all three can be seen, one of them fully and the others partially. This is a

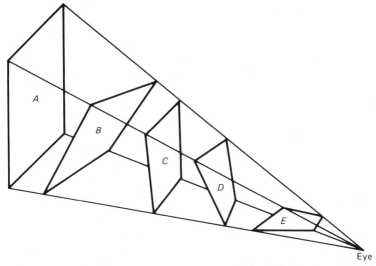

Figure 11.8 Schema showing that an unlimited number of targets may subtend the same visual angles at the eye. The targets here are *A, B, C, D,* and *E.*

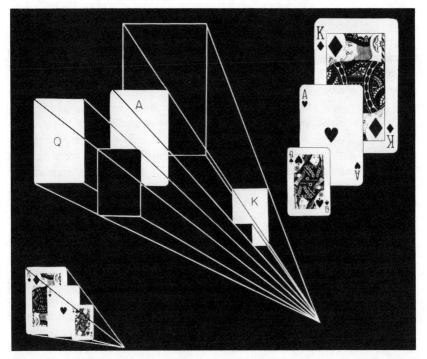

Figure 11.9 Modified Dartmouth Eye Institute demonstration showing interposition and equivalence.

case of interposition (as dealt with earlier in the chapter): In the upper right part of the figure, the queen of spades is nearest the eye and is seen as nearest; next is the ace of hearts and then comes the king of diamonds. Here we have chosen sizes so that the cards all would subtend equal visual angles in the actual situation represented. If these cards were placed directly in line, the queen of spades would just cover the ace of hearts and the king of diamonds. This is shown in the lower left part of the figure.

Our problem is to show that the same (equivalent) visual effect can be produced when there is no interposition, that is, when no part of one card is "covered" by any part of another. The first step is to reposition the cards with respect to the eye. In so doing, we must change their relative sizes so that they, as before, will subtend the same visual angle. The king is now represented as closest to the eye and thus must be the smallest card. The ace is kept in the middistance, and the queen is now farthest away. Of course, as before, they are not directly in line, or else only the king could be seen. The king card is now altered by having its lower left section cut away. Thus when looked at from the represented eye position the ace will now appear to cover the very portion of the king that has been cut away. This is true, of course, only if the two cards are positioned so that the notch in the king card is in line with the upper right portion of the ace card. Using the same principle, the investigator cut away the lower left part of the ace card so as to be in line with the upper right portion of the queen card. Looked at from the represented position (where the visual angle lines converge) the situation will appear to be the same as the original one despite the new positioning and changed sizes of two of the cards. Thus here is a good example of equivalence. The distorted rooms of Ames demonstrate the role of visual angles in the production of equivalences and differences. Ames (1946) showed that an endless series of rooms of various shapes will look like a given rectangular room (a "normal" room) just as long as certain conditions in their construction are satisfied. First examine Figure 11.10. You will notice that the room looks rectilinear and in every way normal, but there seems to be something wrong with the sizes of the faces of the two persons looking through the windows. The person to the left is smaller than the person to the right. This difference would be expected only if one were truly smaller than the other, for the windows of the room appear to be of equal size. The two persons also seem to be equally far away. It is very puzzling why the two persons differ in size, for human faces do not generally, if every, differ as much in size as these do. Let us now turn to the construction of the room.

Figure 11.10   A distorted room with two persons looking in windows. (Source: Drawing from photograph in M. Lawrence, *Studies in Human Behavior.* Princeton, NJ: Princeton University Press, 1949, Fig. 10.)

In Figure 11.11, B is a normal room with two side windows and two back windows. E is the position of the single eye viewing the room. Dotted lines from the eye show the visual angles subtended by the windows and the corners of the room; the lines may be considered also as *lines of direction.* A is the distorted room. The same lines of direction as in B are used for the features of this room. Since the walls in A are in a different position from those in the normal room, the windows have to be of different sizes so as to subtend the same visual angles and to lie in the same directions as they do in the normal room. Note that the back windows are larger than they are in the normal room and that the left window is larger than the right one. The two circles are meant to represent the heads of the people in Figure 11.11. Hence if one person looks in at the right window and the other at the left window, the two heads will be of very different apparent sizes, since the windows are of the same apparent size and the two faces subtend different visual angles. This difference in angular subtense is brought about by a difference in the distances of the two faces from the viewing

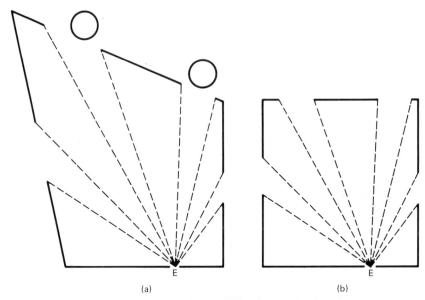

Figure 11.11   Floor plans of a normal rectilinear room (b) and a distorted room (a), the windows in both subtending the same visual angles at the eye (E). The circles represent similar-sized objects that may look unequal in size in this context.

position. Figures 11.10 and 11.11 demonstrate only one of the types of distorted rooms built by Ames.

We have been discussing only lateral distortions—those necessary to make the room appear normal when viewed from a point to the right of center of the near wall—but vertical distortions can also be presented for comparison with the lateral ones. People of equal height standing upright in the room, one against the rear wall on the left and the other against the rear wall on the right, do not look equal in height. In fact, even when the room is photographed the two people do not appear to be equal in height. This is, of course, due to the fact that the person to the left is farther away from the viewer than the partner to the right. The use of distorted rooms for monocular viewing demonstrates exceedingly well the operation of the law of the visual angle.

The basis for the whole set of effects in the distorted-room example is the preclusion of operation of factors other than the law of visual angle. Common situations include other factors, and so when they are eliminated very startling results are achieved. Adopting a single fixed viewpoint allows for presentation of a control situation in which planes or surfaces are viewed at several discernible orientations from the point of viewing. What is seen at first is a room with a back wall in the frontal plane. Moving the target planes does not change the overall appearance, because the visual angles that provided for the perception of a normal rectilinear room in the first viewing are maintained in the new target called the distorted room. All that is necessary to make something look smaller than it would be expected to look, judged from the first viewing, is to place the object farther away from the perceiver; this is most readily done by simply moving one end of the wall of the room farther away (as in Figure 11.11(a)). Thus when an object of fixed size is placed against a feature of the new wall (itself enlarged), that same object looks smaller than it did before. It becomes small for two reasons: (1) the object subtends a smaller visual angle than it would when closer to the viewer and (2) the object is smaller relative to a fixed feature of the viewed scene than would be a second, metrically equivalent object (as a second face). Stated briefly, the visual field was so structured as to *preclude* size constancy for the *test* targets used (the movable, enlargeable walls) and to *promote* size constancy for objects introduced, by following the law of the visual angle.

Rooms properly distorted for binocular viewing have also been made. Since the two eyes view a room from different positions, room form has to be quite different from that for one-eyed viewing. It is not necessary to describe such rooms here, except to say that their walls have to be complexly curved. Such rooms were precalculated in the Ames laboratory and were built by boatbuilders, who were accustomed to fabricating curved surfaces.

Leibowitz, Mitchell, and Angrist (1954) performed an experiment that is relevant. They exposed circles tilted to different extents. With long exposures, the targets looked like tilted circles. With short exposures, they looked like ellipses. The short exposures certainly were examples of perception operating. The longer exposures left time for more processing of the input, and possibly the result could be called a judgment. The short exposure gave a result that followed the law of the retinal image. The longer exposure gave a result that followed the law of shape constancy. Although this was a simple experiment, it brought out some significant points about response.

Chapter 12
Perception of Space

Space is a domain within which the individual is situated and within which he or she moves about. It is a domain within which there are other humans and other animals and inanimate objects. The everyday life of the individual requires effective apprehension of this domain and its contents. So among other things, the individual must be able to perceive the location, size, shape, and motion of objects. This is *space perception.*

Space perception is not a function of vision alone, although vision is rather peculiarly a space sense. Touch and kinestheses enable contact with objects and exploration of their size, shape, and location in a sequential manner. Hearing by way of acoustics enables the detection and identification of objects and events and their locations. But vision provides for an overall apprehension of the space domain in a rather direct way.

However, since several perceptual systems are involved in the perception of space, it has been thought appropriate that one chapter deal specifically with space.

VISION AS A SPACE SENSE

The first thing to note regarding vision is the fact that information from almost a hemisphere of the space domain is given to the visual sense organ at any one instant. Photic radiation is focused through a nodal point in the eyes and the various degrees of intensity of input received from items in space are thus imaged on the retina as a pattern. This pattern, though not a strict copy of the "pattern of externalty," possesses lawful ordinal relations to it. Furthermore, the activity propagated through the optic nerve to the brain is preserved in some lawful way and reflected in the neural input distribution to the visual projection area of the cortex. Not only is a focal pattern represented but also a huge segment of total space, a segment so big that it constitutes a working framework in and of itself. While this framework is made fully functional by means of the motor apparatus of the eyes and the skeletal system, it can be said that space is made meaningful (functional) in terms of vision and what can be imagined (conceptualized) visually. Space experientially is primarily visual space.

BINOCULAR AND MONOCULAR VISION

The way the two eyes work together and the difference between monocular and binocular vision is a major subject in describing space perception. With two eyes, there are two retinas imaging something in the environment. These images may contribute to a single harmonious perception, or potentially they may not. To say the least, the two images are different "views" of the visual scene or encounter. The topic at hand is thus a delineation of the factors involved in various situations with normal and anomalous posturing and functioning of the two eyes.

The two eyes being separated from each other receive inputs from a target from two different vantage points. This results in the formation of somewhat different images on the two eyes when they are fixated on a given target. The nearer the target, the more unlike are these images. Once the target distance exceeds a certain limit, the two images are, in effect, totally alike, and the specific perceptual effects that result from two-eyed seeing vanish.

In other words, when pointing toward near objects, the two eyes *converge*. The greater the convergence, the more dissimilar are the images of the two eyes. With convergence, the images are asymmetrical, and so the study of the effects of asymmetry in retinal images has been of prime importance in what is known as physiological optics—the study of optics as exemplified in the visual system and the visual consequences.

The organism learns on the basis of the orderly relation between retinal images and the properties of the space domain. This learning is the development of experiences of size, location, distance, and the like and the ability to react in effective ways to externality. Hence any condition, artificial (as with lenses) or not, that produces certain retinal images in the two eyes produces the appropriate experience of some three-dimensional scene. For the experimenter to begin to understand vision one must learn what external three-dimensional situations produce what retinal images in the two eyes.

Diagrams to Show Binocular Effects

Diagrams can be drawn to show the various relations between the target and the eyes. The target is generally indicated by a line such as ab in Figure 12.1. The fixation point p is at the center of the line. A line from p to each eye reaches the retina at the fovea and approximately represents the optical axis of the eye; the lines from p to f show the direction in which each eye is pointing. Lines from a and b (the bounds of the target) show where the bounds of the retinal images lie. The distance on a retina between the two lines indicates the size of the retinal image, and the distances of these lines from the foveal line f show whether the image is symmetrical or asymmetrical. Usually, the images are asymmetrical, and the amounts and directions of asymmetry and the differences in the asymmetries of the two retinal images are among the lawful features of information that the visual system utilizes to produce three-dimensional seeing.

Diagram (a) in Figure 12.1 indicates the conditions under which the two eyes are symmetrically convergent on a distant target. The retinal images are small and internally are nearly symmetrical; that is, the portion of the circle falling immediately to the left of fp is nearly equal to the portion falling to the right. In Diagram (a_2) the target is much nearer, and thus the eyes are more greatly converged. The images are larger and asymmetry is far greater. In diagram (b) the target location and orientation to the eyes is asymmetrical, producing some additional characteristics in the retinal images. The sizes of the two images are unequal. The patterns of internal asymmetry of the two eyes are unlike. In diagram (c) the target is fixated but nevertheless the two eyes are not symmetrically related to it in space. Beyond these elemental situations a number of others can be described but it will not be necessary to do so here.

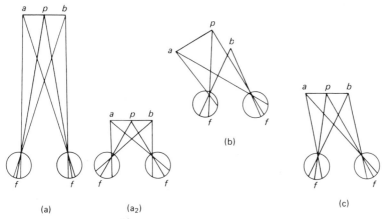

Figure 12.1   The characteristics of retinal images in binocular vision under several conditions.

Retinal Disparity

The points on the two retinas that function to give "single vision" for a given target point are called *corresponding points*. For example, the points on the two retinas that represent the fixation point are corresponding points. While there are many corresponding points on the two retinas for any given fixed posture of the two eyes when they are fixated on a given target point, there are many points on the two retinas that are noncorresponding.

Images from target points that do not fall on corresponding points on the two retinas are said to be *disparate,* and in monocular vision they would result in two different experiences involving two different perceptual directions. Disparities can be of two sorts, vertical and horizontal. It is the horizontal disparities that underlie the stereoscopic perception of third dimension.

Disparities can also be spoken of as crossed and uncrosssed, as shown in Figures 12.2 and 12.3. Figure 12.2(a) shows the separate left and right images of an outdoor scene with the horizon and a roadway leading to it. The vanishing point is labeled *v* for each image. In Figure 12.2(b) the two images are fused, which means that both eyes are fixating on the vanishing point of the road. The two *v*'s fall on corresponding points on the two retinas, in this case the two foveas. It will be noted, however, that certain portions of the rest of the two images do not coincide. Failure to coincide represents disparity. The kind shown in this case is crossed disparity. At the level at which the fixation point is imaged (the vanishing point), disparity is absent, but above and below this disparity begins

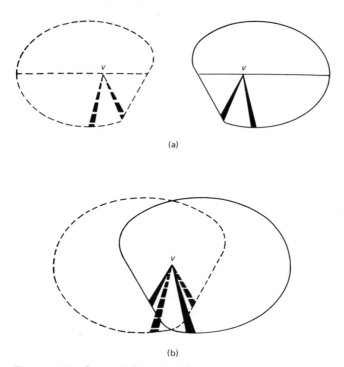

(a)

(b)

Figure 12.2   Crossed disparity. (Source: J. J. Gibson. *The Senses Considered as Perceptual Systems.* New York: Houghton Mifflin, 1966, Fig. 9.14.) (See text for explanation.)

and progressively increases. In this gradient the left eye's image is displaced to the right, and the right eye's image is displaced to the left. This is why the disparity is called crossed disparity.

For fixation on a point nearer than the horizon the portions of the two images at the level of the fixation point will be made to coincide, but there will be disparity above and below this level, as in the previous example. For distances nearer than the fixation point the disparity is crossed (Figure 12.3).

It is apparent from these diagrams that all disparity does not lead to "seeing double" (or diplopia). In both examples the two eyes are converged on some point and a part of the visual field is thus being represented on corresponding portions of the two retinas. The target involved in the fixation is the target that the individual is attending to. Retinal disparities progress from the level of fixation upward and downward. Disparity is the basis for perceiving various distances. On the other hand, when *no* portions of the two retinal images are made to coincide for the targets viewed, there is no

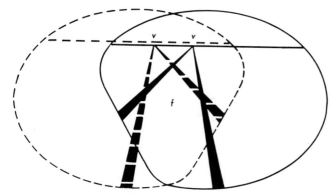

Figure 12.3 Uncrossed and crossed disparity. Uncrossed disparity is produced by target elements beyond *f*, the image of the fixation point. (Source: J. J. Gibson. *The Senses Considered as Perceptual Systems.* Boston: Houghton Mifflin, 1966, Fig. 9.14.)

basis for disparity gradients, no basis for seeing singularly what is being looked at, and double vision occurs.

The topic of double versus single vision is so complex that it cannot be covered here. No single rule can be given to the beginner in understandable terms that would enable him or her to make discrete predictions regarding double vision and merely vision of third dimension. A very common demonstration of double vision can be produced by holding up our index fingers at eye level. One is placed about 5 or 6 inches from the eye and the other at 12 to 15 inches. Looking at the near finger, we see two far fingers, one on either side of the near one but, of course, at a greater distance from the eye. Looking at the far finger, we see the near finger doubled. This sort of result is much different from that of extending our arm outward and then looking at any given point out along it: in no case is any part of the arm seen as double though not all parts are equidistant. In some respects (certain geometrical respects) the two situations are alike, but in others they must be different. They both involve items at different distances, but in one case the items are discrete (the fingers). In the other case, they are parts of a continuum (the arm).

Asymmetry in Retinal Images

Inasmuch as the two eyes converge when they point toward near targets and do not converge when quite distant targets are viewed, students of vision have at times supposed that the kinesthesis that would be involved in positioning the eyes would be a "cue" for the perception of depth, or third dimension. Workers have not been overly successful in providing tangible evidence that convergence, with its consequent kinesthetic innervation, provides a basis for discriminating third dimension and distance.

There is, however, another factor that is brought into play where convergence is varied. Convergence varies the amount of asymmetry of the retinal images. In diagram (a) of Figure 12.4, the two eyes are fixated on a near target and the images of the two eyes, though alike, are internally asymmetrical. Although the eyes are pointing toward the center of the line *ab*, the image of *ap* on the left eye, for example, is larger than the image of *pb* on the same eye. Likewise, the image of *pb* is larger for the right eye than is the image for *ap*. Were the eyes pointed toward a very distant target, this inequality (asymmetry) would be reduced to the vanishing point, as suggested earlier. Thus in keeping with target distance, the images may vary from having considerable asymmetry to having no asymmetry at all.

The fact of decreasing asymmetry for targets farther and farther away can be utilized in producing distance effects, as in museum displays, for example. In such displays there are generally two por-

Figure 12.4 Convergence varies the amount of asymmetry in the retinal images. The target is *apb;* 1–2–3 is the image. In (a) 1–2 is unequal to 2–3; in (b) the two are almost equal.

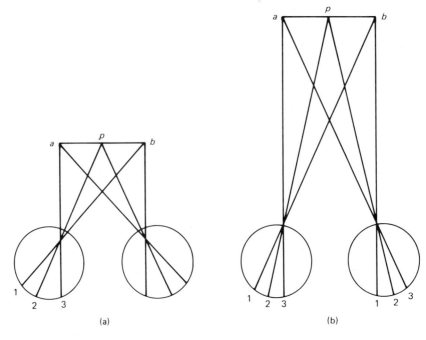

(a)   (b)

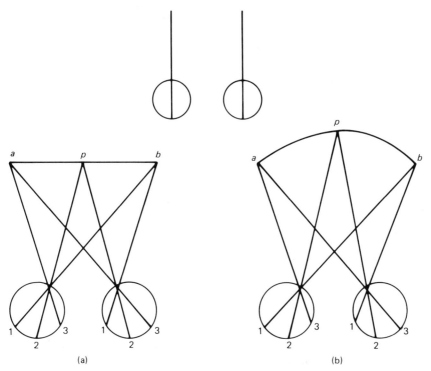

Figure 12.5   Curved (concave) targets tend to produce symmetrical retinal images, even when the targets are near, and thus simulate distant targets. The target is *apb;* 1–2–3 is the image. The retinal images in (b) are much more nearly symmetrical than those in (a).

tions—the midground and the foreground occupied by animals and other objects and a background painted on the wall behind. The background is often flat (not curved), and considerable asymmetry in the visual images of the two eyes is thus already brought about (Figure 12.5). Although what is painted in the background is meant to depict something far away, it does not do so to the fullest extent. The asymmetry brought about by a flat background can be to some degree eliminated by curving it (Figure 12.5(b)). The two portions of the retinal images in Figure 12.5(b) are much more nearly equal—if not totally so—than in Figure 12.5(a). As a consequence, the background produces the kinds of retinal images brought about by viewing distant scenes.

Tilt in the Third Dimension

Another example to show the relation of ocular activity, externality, and visual perception is the viewing a luminous line in a dark room.

The question put to the perceiver is whether the line is vertical or tilts in the third dimension. Actually, when out of the vertical the line may or may not be seen as tilted. The retinal images produced by a vertical-line target (Figure 12.6) are parallel to each other and vertical. Since the two eyes are separated horizontally, the "views" obtained by them converge; that is, they are slightly like side views rather than like views from straight ahead.

If the line target is tipped, the effect on the retinal images is different from what it would be if there were only one eye involved viewing the line from straight in front. With monocular viewing all that would happen to the retinal image would be a foreshortening. If the line were tipped nearly to the horizontal position, the line would become very short, approaching a mere point.

With the slightly sidelike views of the two eyes converging toward the line, however, the retinal images would undergo not only some foreshortening, but also some rotation. Rotation of the two images is in opposite directions from the vertical and is a form of retinal disparity, the stimulus basis for seeing the line as tilted.

Figure 12.6 Positions of retinal images for *ab,* a vertical-line target and a tipped-line target. When the line is vertical, the images are vertical; when the line is tipped away from the eye, the images are rotated laterally outward at the top.

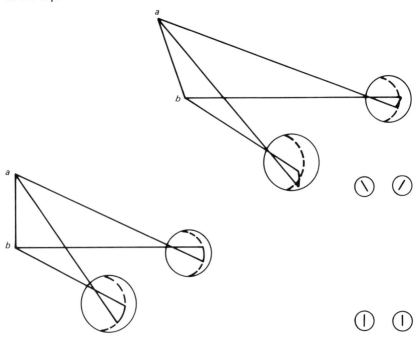

If the line target is a luminous one in a dark field so that there is nothing extraneous to influence the viewer, the line may continue to look vertical even when the target is tilted. Ogle and Ellerbrock (1946) studied the perceptual effects produced by the target situation just described and found that the observer did not always see the line tilted when the target was tilted, at least not unless it was greatly titled. They concluded that the eyes rotated in their orbits to compensate for the rotations of the retinal images. The proper rotations of the eyes prevented the images from falling on points different from those when the line target was vertical, and therefore the target was still seen as vertical. The eyeball rotations just described are called cyclofusional, or cyclotorsional, movements. That the kinesthesis from cyclotorsional movements did not, in itself, become interpreted in some fashion as indicating a change in target position is an example of how insensitive the organism is to actual eye position. This is an argument against the organism's supposed use of convergence as a "cue" for distance.

To preclude the use of binocular vision (i.e., the production and utilization of different images in the two eyes), one may place the luminous line target at a considerable distance from the eyes; the two eyes do not then converge but take up parallel pointing positions with reference to the target.

Stereoscopy

Stereoscopy deals with the principles underlying the production of third dimension in binocular vision. Some visual fields seem three dimensional for reasons other than those we are about to describe. On the other hand, the dissimilarity between the images in the two eyes and the differences in location of the images in the two eyes play decisive roles in the perception of the third dimension.

Figure 12.7 indicates where various points in space are projected onto the retinas of the two eyes when the eyes are in a given position. When the two eyes are fixated on a common point, the images of points nearer to or farther away than the fixation point are located as indicated in the figure. The fixation point is at A, and it is projected on the fovea of each eye. The point beyond the fixation point is C, and it is projected onto the nasal portion of each eye. B, the point nearer than the fixation point, is projected onto the temporal portion of each eye.

The line SS represents a plane that cuts through lines from points A, B, and C. Actually, the line represents the frontal plane. On this line, near points such as B are represented by points b outward from (lateral to) the fixation point at A. Likewise, points

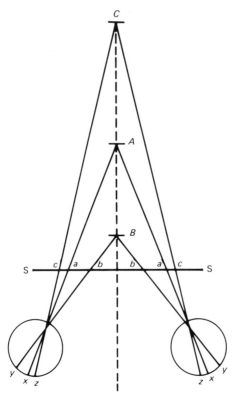

Figure 12.7 How points at various distances are projected onto the retina at various distances from the fovea. Point *A* is at the fixation point. *B* is nearer and *C* is farther away. If one substitutes a stereogram, SS, points *A*, *B*, and *C* would be represented by points *a*, *b*, and *c* on it. Points *a*, *b*, and *c* are projected onto the retina as points *x*, *y*, and *z*.

such as *C* more remote than *A* are represented medial to the point *A* on the plane. These points on the frontal plane then constitute a *plane projection* of the three-dimensional situation *A*, *B*, and *C*.

With this knowledge in mind, we can construct pictures to be viewed through a stereoscope so as to have them perceived in the way, that we wish. A stereoscope is an optical instrument through which a separate target for each eye is viewed. The redirection of the radiation from the targets is such that the targets are seen as a single target with an enhanced third dimension. Before we diagram the optical principle used in the stereoscope, let us examine a couple of stereograms, as shown in Figure 12.8.

In stereogram I the two pictures, or targets, are so constructed that they will be seen as a truncated pyramid with its small portion

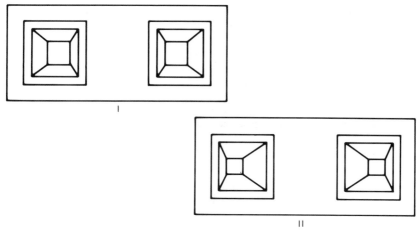

Figure 12.8   Two stereograms. The components in the targets of the top one are so shifted that they will be seen as a truncated pyramid. In the bottom stereogram the shift is in the opposite direction and the targets will be seen as a hallway.

(or apex) toward the viewer. This is because the small squares are shifted toward the center of the target. (The view is indicated by point *B* in Figure 12.7). In stereogram II the opposite is true and the picture is one of a long hallway through which one looks to the doorway at its far end (point *C* in Figure 12.7).

Figure 12.9 indicates the optical principles of the stereoscope. It will be seen that radiation is redirected by the prism lenses P so as to simulate origins different from the actual ones.

Here a rule of thumb is helpful. Parts of the visual field look to be where they would be if the photic flux came straight from them to the eye. This rule is pertinent, for we shall be using lenses, prisms, mirrors, and the like in subsequent examples to change the direction of the flux from what it was as it left the target. This rule is a recognition of the fact that regardless of how many times the flux is redirected between its leaving the target and reaching the eye, no difference is made; only the direction of the flux as it enters the eye counts. In diagraming the flux and its redirection (or refraction), we use the rule by projecting outward from each eye to indicate the direction of flux origin and then by determining where the directions for each eye intersect. The intersection is the point from which the radiation seems to originate. When this rule is applied, we choose the *borders* of a target for use in diagraming. In that way we can illustrate the size and position of the phenomenal object.

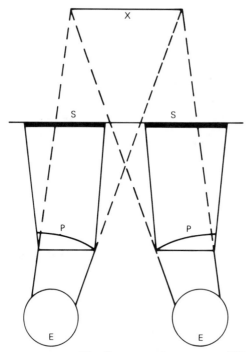

Figure 12.9 The Brewster stereoscope. EE are the eyes of the viewer. PP are the prisms that redirect the radiation from SS, the stereogram items, so as to enter the eyes as if coming from target X. Because the radiation is coming from such a direction and is common for both eyes, a single picture is seen.

In examining the diagram of the stereoscope, we see that the flux is as if it were originating from one target (X) instead of from the two actual ones *(SS)*. Thus the perceived object displays enhanced third dimension. This is accomplished by the fact that the two slightly dissimilar targets are projected onto the retina in a manner similar to the projection of a three-dimensional target viewed from considerable distance.

While the consideration of the visual qualities of objects other than shape, size, and location is not strictly a topic for this chapter, we might mention one such item, an effect brought about in conjunction with the enhancement of apparent third dimension by stereoscopic means. The objects that stand out from each other at the various distinctly different distances change their surface qualities and mechanical character. Targets that are seen as people with bodies of flesh and blood tend to turn into stone-hard objects. What is pliable becomes rigid. This would seem to be some indication of the intimate relation of the widespread effects brought about solely by the manipulations of the forms of the retinal images of the two eyes.

OVERALL SPACE THEORIES

The Point, or Air, Theory

The classical and conventional way of accounting for human visual space perception is to begin with a point and proceed as if all space were made up of an aggregate of such points. This is in line with the old analytical sensation outlook of perception of space as two-dimensional space and made possible by the operation of simple optics because the retina is, in effect, a two-dimensional surface on which two-dimensional space is represented or copied. The third dimension in space gave the conventional theory trouble. The third dimension was not conceived as representable on the retina, since the retina is only a two-dimensional manifold.

To accomplish three-dimensional representation, experiment-ers, resorted to two kinds of factors called "cues." One included the peripheral factors: the convergence of the two eyes and ocular accommodation. Since the amount of convergence is lawfully related to target distance, it was thought that convergence could become a learned cue for distance. Accommodation, or focusing of the eyes, was also expected to be a cue for distance, since accommodation is a muscular effect that varies lawfully as the distance of the target is manipulated.

The second kind of cue was the monocular cue. About seven were usually listed. We shall not discuss them at length, for we have pointed them out previously as examples of using one aspect of perception to explain other concurrent aspects. For interposition and elevation are two commonly given monocular cues (see Figures 12.10 and 12.11). To describe interposition is to describe what the observer sees rather than merely to tell the metric features of the stimulus. If one object is *seen* interposed between the observer and another object, then the object partially covered is seen as farther away. By resorting to these cues, the observer was supposed to build up his or her appreciation of the visual field, as it were, bit by bit. This way of dealing with the relations between stimulus and response provides no initial description of overall field structure whereby to account for the roles played by restricted portions of the visual input.

A number of the so-called cues (or conditions) for seeing the third dimension and for localizing and locating objects are binocular. (They will be dealt with in a later section of the chapter.) However,

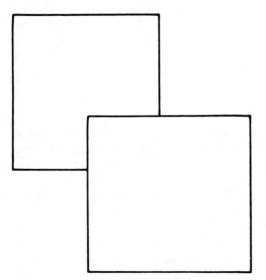

Figure 12.10   Interposition. If an item partially covers another item, the second will be seen as farther away than the first.

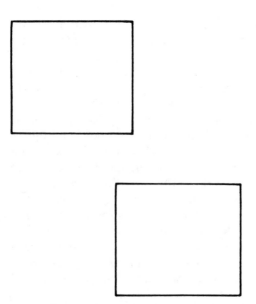

Figure 12.11   Items higher in the visual field are seen as farther away than items below them.

three-dimensional seeing does not depend on the combined use of two eyes as it can be accomplished with one eye. The use of two eyes can even distort it. When of the appropriate sort, the use of two eyes can make three-dimensional seeing more precise for short distances.

The Texture-Gradient Concept

Although the texture-gradient concept of the essential nature of the organism's visually perceived surrounds is implied to some extent in what artists and draftsmen have been doing for centuries, it is a recent development. It is embodied in a book by J. J. Gibson (1950) that describes the nature of the visual world. The concept is an answer to the puzzle experienced by persons who have asked, how is it that the organism can perceive the third dimension? Whereas we know that two dimensions define a plane and can be represented on another plane (such as the receiving surface of the retina), how the third dimension can be represented is an age-old question. It was supposed that seeing three-dimensional space requires a mechanism with three dimensions. The question was posed seriously again and again despite the fact that artists and draftsmen had been representing three-dimensional objects and space relations on two-dimensional surfaces for several centuries.

The first major realization to be made regarding the texture-gradient concept is that the concept implies that all surfaces function as components of a macrotecture of the visual field as a whole. Many surfaces are themselves physically differentiated in some way and are thus seen as textured. In one way or another the whole visual field is textured. The texture possesses various effective characteristics in keeping with the orientation of the surface with reference to the viewer. The surface that lies in the frontal plane provides a virtually undistorted retinal image; that is, there is practically a one-to-one relation between it and the image.

All other surfaces—those lying outside the frontal plane—form tapered textures in the retinal image. The viewer looks at such surfaces obliquely and, as is well known, the farther end of such a surface is geometrically more oblique to the viewer than its near end. For example, as one looks down at the floor near one's feet, the floor lies almost in the frontal plane. As one views the floor farther and farther away from one's feet, obliquity increases. If one looks out along a hallway, the elements of the floor pattern become smaller and smaller. There are, of course, two reasons for the marked tapering of the texture of the retinal image: increasing distance and increasing obliquity of viewing it. The difference between viewing in the frontal plane and viewing an oblique surface is pictured in Figure 12.12. In the figure the two surfaces are marked off in equal spaces by lines running from the surface to the eye. The projected image of the oblique plane (the floor surface) is a tapered texture in the retinal image. Figure 12.13 shows the same sort of situation but as viewed by the perceiver. The one texture is seen as the wall, and the tapered texture is seen as the floor extending from near the viewer to the wall.

The term "perspective" applies to the figure but refers not only to perception but to the techniques the artist and draftsman use to produce the kind of perception we are dealing with here. In fact, the term perspective generally refers to four items: (1) the *target* (the three-dimensional visual field), (2) the *two-dimensional representation* of a three-dimensional visual situation, (3) the *retinal image,* and (4) the *perception.* In common practice, perspective is most used for items 1, 2, and 4. It would be helpful if we made some restriction on our usage of the word, so let us use it only for 4, the perception. Let us use "third dimension" to describe the target (1) and "foreshortening" to describe the arrangement of a

Figure 12.12 Relation between orientation of surfaces to the eye and the texture they present to it. Frontal plane surfaces present a uniform texture when the target field is uniform. The same surfaces oriented obliquely present a graded texture.

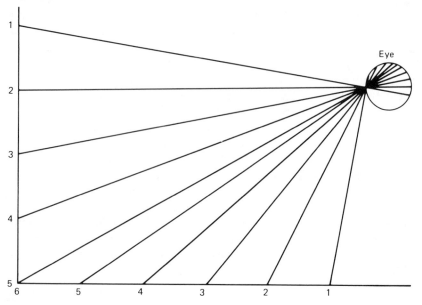

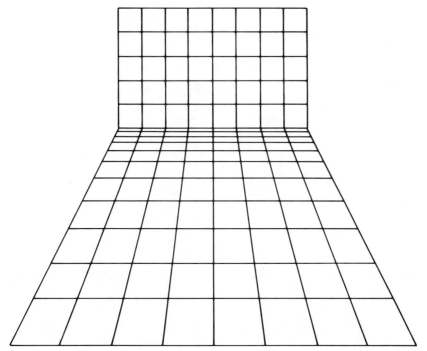

Figure 12.13   The appearance of the surfaces dealt with in Figure 12.12.

three-dimensional object in a two-dimensional representation (2) and the form and composition of the retinal image (3). Thus we see perspective and can produce it by presenting a three-dimensional target or a foreshortened two-dimensional representation of the original target. Both of these presentations produce essentially the same sort of retinal image.

The second major realization involved in the texture-gradient concept is that the visual world of the outdoors is divided by a horizontal line called the horizon. The texture gradients—or the taper of the ground (the field below the horizon) and the sky (the field above the horizon)—run in opposite directions. Faraway positions of the field, both in sky and on land, are of fine texture and the two gradients of texture meet at the horizon.

According to the texture-gradient concept, the elements of vision, the origins in considering visual behavior, are not *points* as in the air theory but *edges, corners,* and so on—that is, the abruptions formed by the junctions of various gradients. Visual objects differ in complex ways by reason of differences in gradients.

In the preceding discussion we have been describing a definite and lawful relation between features of the three-dimensional do-

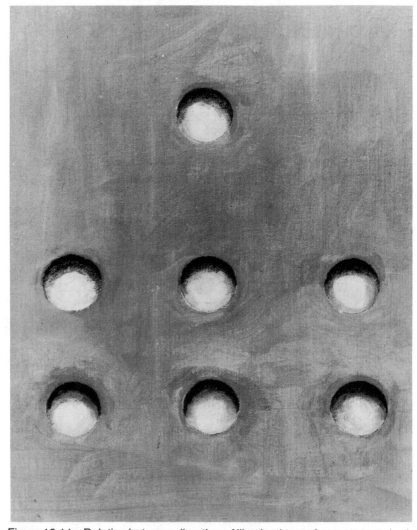

Figure 12.14 Relation between direction of illumination and consequent shadows to the perception of bulges and recesses. Looked at one way the diagram contains recesses; looked at upside down it contains bulges such as those made by rivet heads.

main called space and its representation in geometrical terms on the retina. This description is a sufficient answer to the question of how is it that the organism can appreciate the three-dimensional visual world.

There are still other features besides texture gradient to consider. One is the fact that the organism lives in a world in which photic radiation is not perfectly diffuse but instead is directional.

Although at times we say that the radiation from the sun is quite diffuse, we must recognize that it is directional enough to cast shadows. The sun seems to rise in one direction from us and progress above us across the sky until it sets in the opposite direction; thus photic radiation is, in general, downward rather than upward. Shadows are cast on the earth, on the horizontal plane, and not upward toward the sky. The results of the directionality of radiation become an inherent part of the visual-gradient characteristics. For example, depressions in vertical walls are shaded above and lighted below, a perfectly lawful result that is altered only when for some reason illumination comes from below instead of above. But this seldom occurs except in arrangements made by humans. Figure 12.14 illustrates this principle: Look at the figure right side up and then upside down.

SPECIAL CONDITIONS

Vision with Size Lenses

One means of manipulating the shapes of retinal images, and thus the perception of objects and spatial relations, is by the use of *size lenses*. All the lenses commonly used in everyday affairs are *power lenses*. They focus radiation and form images and consequently are limited for certain experimental purposes dealing with space perception. Used in certain ways, they produce the perception of blur, often contrary to what is needed. Power lenses are of several shapes: biconvex, planoconvex, biconcave, planoconcave, and so on. In every case the two faces of the lens are not parallel or concentric (Figure 12.15).

On the other hand, a lens whose surfaces are parallel or concentric is called a size lens. The simplest is in the form of a plane piece of glass curved about a single axis (Figure 12.16). Since the

Figure 12.15   Various common forms of power lenses.

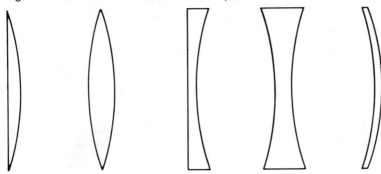

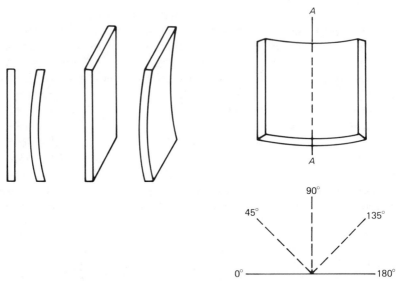

Figure 12.16   The meridional size lens is essentially a curved section of originally plano glass. It does not focus radiation as a power lens does. Its axis
is *AA* and the axis position is designated in degrees from 0 to 180.

lens has a single axis of curvature, it is designated by the meridian
that is used as the axis and is called a meridional size lens. Meridians
are designated in degrees from 0 to 180, beginning with 0° at the
left horizontal (9 o'clock on the face of a clock). The vertical meridian
is 90° and the horizontal meridian (at 3 o'clock) to the right is 180°.
All designations fall within this degree range. A lens formed by
cupping a piece of plano material is called an overall size lens. Meridional size lenses magnify the retinal image in the direction at right
angles to the axis of curvature.

If the meridional size lens is worn in front of one eye, the image
in that eye is magnified in one direction and thus differs from that
in the other eye. The combined retinal pattern for the two eyes
simulates, to some extent, the pattern of some natural three-dimensional target. The natural target is quite different, of course, from
the one actually involved at the time. When an axis-90 size lens is
worn in front of one eye, certain unique perceptual end results
are produced.

The Leaf Room

One of the best target situations for studying space perception with
size lenses is a leaf room, a small room, say a cube of about 7 feet,

open on one end. It is called a leaf room because, typically, it is covered on the inside (ceiling, walls, and floor) with artificial leaves to break up the familiar linear stimulus features produced by corners and edges.

When an observer stands at the open end of a leaf room (Figure 12.17) with an axis-90 lens in front of the right eye, the room's appearance is greatly changed from normal. It no longer appears rectilinear. The back wall is no longer in the frontal plane and its right side is farther away than the left. Although the observer is standing at the midpoint between the two side walls, they no longer appear to be equidistant—from him or her: the wall on the right is much farther away than that on the left. The ceiling slopes upward to the right, and the floor slopes downward to the right. The leaves are larger in the right half of the room than in the left. All these differences are manifestations of a taper toward bigness on the right and littleness on the left.

The use of size lenses in everyday situations indicates the considerable sensory conflict that can be engendered and the personal insecurity that can be evoked. Manipulation of such situations brings out that not only can pure sensory results be obtained but so can other results that could be called emotional and social. Use of the size lens may actually be one potential way of studying personality differences.

The optical features of wearing an axis-90 size lens in front of one eye are depicted in Figure 12.18 showing how wearing the lens produces the perceptual results in the leaf room. The rule of thumb regarding perceived direction is again employed: the image in one eye is elongated, which participates in changing the perceived directions or locations of the limits of the target. The new directions

Figure 12.17   The leafroom as metrically and perceptually seen when an axis-90 size lens is worn in front of an observer's right eye.

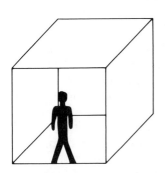 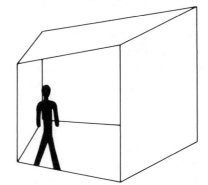

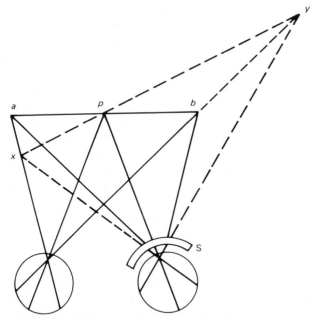

Figure 12.18 The psychooptical principle of the axis-90 size lens worn on the right eye. Target *apb* is seen as *xpy*, since the lens redirects the light in one meridian so as to enlarge the retinal image in that dimension.

are such that the left side of the target *a* is brought closer, to *x*, and the right side *b* is moved farther away than normally, to *y*.

Oblique Size Lenses

If two size lenses are to be worn, they must be rotated to oblique positions—as shown in Figure 12.19—if distortion effects are to be produced. The magnifications are then oppositely oblique in the two retinal images, reminiscent of the oblique tilts of the two line images described on page 276. When one looks at the floor, the perceptual effect of wearing oblique size lenses is to tilt the appearance of the floor either upward or downward. Which it will be depends on whether the axes of the lenses are rotated inward or outward at the top: when the rotation is inward, the tilt is upward; when the rotation is outward, the tilt is downward. The amounts of tilt also depend on the field conditions in general, including the distance of the targets viewed. The farther away the targets are, the less the tilt will be. Instead of tilt, there is a change in apparent size and elevation in relation to the viewer. When size is magnified, motion is increased. When size is diminished, motion is reduced.

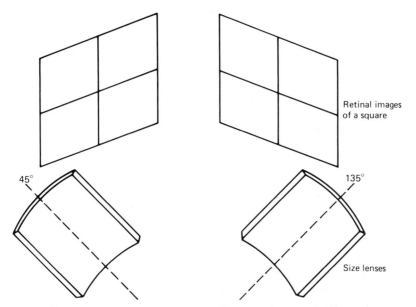

Figure 12.19   Two size lenses worn obliquely distort the retinal images of a square target. (Source: S. H. Bartley. *Beginning Experimental Psychology.* New York: McGraw-Hill, 1950, Fig. 32.)

This effect pertains aptly to water surfaces containing waves. If the observer is in a boat actually affected by waves, he or she expects the boat to be buffeted about in accordance with the size of the waves. If it turns out that the mechanical and visual effects of the waves do not tally, a perceptual conflict is produced. When the waves are smaller than would tally with the buffeting of the boat, the result is very disturbing, because one never expects little waves to toss boats much. Seeing waves larger than would tally with the boat's buffeting is less discomforting, because an observer may be used to standing on solid land while looking at big waves and not being tossed at all. Hence the big wave, little toss situation is natural, whereas the other is highly novel and sometimes productive of uneasiness and motion sickness.

LATERALITY EFFECTS

One of the crucial features in the perception of a visual scene or display—of a picture, photograph, or painting—is called composition. Composition of a two-dimensional display such as a painting, conveys not only the data relative to the separate items in it, but also data regarding space, aesthetic satisfaction, and higher order meanings. One of the factors in composition is the distribution of items in the horizontal dimension, that is, what is contained in the left-hand half of the display or scene versus what is on the right.

Not all visual encounters are three-dimensional. Some are two-dimensional representations of three-dimensional scenes and some are two-dimensional arrangements meant to be seen only as two-dimensional.

Not all displays or scenes are asymmetrical in the horizontal dimension. It is only the asymmetrical ones that will be dealt with here, however. In these, the *third-dimensional* effects based on this left–right asymmetry are among the most crucial.

When these matters are brought to the attention of most workers, they immediately try to explain them, without being aware of the effects. The laterality effects to be discussed here have for some reason not been a prominent, if existent, part of the psychology of space perception. It would appear, however, that they have at least been a part of the intuition of artists for a long time, who composed natural scenes in their paintings.

In reviewing some of the examples that bring out the perceptual principles involved, let us be aware of the fact that two domains are very distinctly involved in the descriptions used and thus two vocabularies are required. One vocabulary has to do with the visual target itself and the other with describing the perceptual responses of the viewer.

Take, for instance, a two-dimensional representation of a natural scene. What is toward the top represents what is farther away. What is partially obscured by a given item is also farther away. So the language that describes space is different in the two-dimensional representation from that in the perception.

One of the simplest ways to begin describing laterality differences is by using pairs of prints or slides of a scene. One member of each pair is the print (or slide representing the scene as photographed. A mirror image of this is produced by flopping the negative and making the second print, or by reversing the single slide in the projector as a comparison. Under such conditions one can select an item in the scene and note the perceptual differences produced in the two displays. The differences in perception are of several kinds—those that concretely pertain to space and those that pertain to higher order meanings.

Wolfflin (1941) and Keller (1942) were early in the study of the laterality factor in vision. Gaffron (1950) also dealt with laterality but did not choose a quantitative aspect of it so that it could be measured.

In 1958 Adair and Bartley studied the perceived distance of

an item as a function of being on the left and being on the right. Their apparatus is shown in Figure 12.20. What you see is a long track on which there is an upright, large target holder. The holder is movable by turning a crank or a knob. You will see a small target

Figure 12.20   Apparatus for comparing prints to determine perceptual distances in them.

holder whose distance from the eye is fixed. The biting board or headrest is not shown. With the headrest, the eye position in relation to the two target holders is fixed. The large target holder carries a large print of a scene, or its mirror image. The stationary small target holder carries the small print of the same scene. The subject (observer) adjusts the distance of the large print so that, to the eye, the item in both prints appears to be the same distance away.

The principle that provides for this result is that items in a large print look farther away than the same items in a small print. To have simply viewed a scene and its mirror image side by side would have given no measurement. The two prints would have become for the moment, left and right halves of a new configuration (display).

For the study, four different combinations of print pairs were used: (1) normal, both prints, (2) large, mirror image, small normal print, (3) large normal, small mirror image print, and (4) mirror image prints for both. They found that what was on the left was seen as nearer.

In 1960 Bartley and DeHardt compared chosen items in scenes to determine the magnitude of the effect of left–right asymmetry on their perceived distances. One of the items was in the foreground, and the other was in the background. Whereas it made a definite difference whether the foreground item was on the left or right half of the scene, the rule did not hold for the background item. It made little or no difference which half of the scene the background item was in.

In 1960 a second study, made by the same authors, some qualifications to the original simple rule were found. In their first study they concluded that whether the item was in the foreground or in the background made a difference. In this present study the large items such as forests or hills in the background were also manipulated so that sometimes these were in the same half of the scene as the original small test items and sometimes they were in the opposite half. In some of the combinations the small test item was in the center of the scene. The scenes used were tabletop mock-ups and provided for such manipulations.

The authors found that lateral position alone did not determine the perceived distance of the small items, but that which half contained the large background items also was a determining factor.

Ranney and Bartley (1963) made a further study of the perceptual effects of left–right asymmetry in the location of items in a scene. The scenes were prints of realistic tabletop arrangements. The test items in them were either a small square or a tall rectangle five times the dimension of the square and the same as the square in width. The standard item was the square at the horizontal center of the scene. The findings led to the following conclusions:

1. The large items appear nearer than small items located in the same position in pictures.
2. The position of a large item in the background plays a role in determining the perceived distance of the test item. It has more weight when the test item is small than when it is large.
3. The test item on the left appears nearer than when on the right when the large item in the background is on the right.

In 1968 Bartley and Winters reviewed the findings that had accumulated to date and made some suggestions aimed at clarifying the vocabularies used to describe two-dimensional visual targets, three-dimensional natural scenes, and features of perception relating to them. The matters reviewed and the caution suggested are too extended to mention here.

Of the number of subjects tested by Bartley and associates, only a very small minority failed to see items on the left nearer than when on the right. The exceptions were not always left-handed persons. No simple relation between eyedness or handedness showed up to account for the few exceptions among the subjects with reference to the distance perception.

One thing to be kept in mind throughout in attempting to interpret or account for the findings is that there is no left without right, nor a right without a left, so whatever the explanation, it must be a holistic or molar one rather than an atomistic one.

The matter of lateral asymmetry in visual perception is dealt with in item 42 in *Perception in Everyday Life*. The role asymmetry plays in providing for higher order meanings is especially brought out in describing Rembrandt's *Return of the Prodigal Son*. Photographs in Figures 12.21 and 12.22 are an example of the laterality effect. In both cases, viewers generally center on the left half and so very different impressions are produced by the two.

Nelson and McDonald (unpublished manuscript) approached the investigation of perception pertaining to when an item is on the left or when it is on the right, in a different way from that of the workers already mentioned. Their subjects inspected 15 pairs of photographs of paintings possessing compositional asymmetry. Both members of the pair were of the same picture but one was a mirror image of the other. The subjects were given one title for each of the 15 pairs and asked to select, in each case, the member of the pair more appropriate for the title. The results tended to confirm the reports of Wolfflin (1941) and Gaffron (1950) that lateral

Figure 12.21   A scene.

Figure 12.22   A mirror image print of the scene in Fig. 12.21.

organization is important to aesthetic appreciation and the statement of Gaffron that objects on the left half of a picture carry more influence than those on the right.

One of the factors Nelson and McDonald attempted to measure, a surprising factor in the study, was apparent depth. Judgments of apparent depth were found to be only moderately related to identification of titles with objects appearing on the left.

SOME OTHER FEATURES OF SPACE PERCEPTION

Front and Back

Harris and Strommen (1974) have asked, "What is the 'front' of a simple geometric form?" They tested 670 college students in three studies for the purpose of defining a set of cues that specify perception of "frontness" and "backness" of objects. In the first study the subjects had to identify the front and back of printed squares to which either one or two circles were attached. In the second study a broader range of geometric forms was used. And in the third study the subjects judged the direction of "imagined" movement of forms used in the first study. The performances indicated that the "front" and "back" are asymmetric opposite sides. The "front" was the side most different from the others and the side toward which the form is imagined to move.

Right Side Up and Upside Down

Braine (1978) points out that visual perception of right side up and upside down are usually made in accord with a spatial framework. She proposes that in addition to the frame work responses, we make some nonframework ones.

She proposes that there are several levels at which orientation information may be processed and that these levels correspond to the stages in the development of the perception of orientation that takes place in individuals from childhood to adulthood. It would seem that the matter is one of the most subtle in all perception. Unfortunately, it cannot be handled within the space we have here but is mentioned nevertheless, because it is highly important in space perception.

For other studies on what is right side up and upside down see the references in Braines's study, noted above.

Ninety-Degree Rotation of the Visual Cliff

In Chapter 10 human performance on a visual cliff was described. In all the examples the visual cliff was a horizontal cliff. Somervill and Somervill (1977) rotated the visual cliff pattern 90° so that the differential pertained to perceiving near and far rather than what is at various levels. This is an ingenious further test with essentially the same target pattern. The question was whether this pattern functioned for the perception of near and far. The authors used nonhuman rather than human subjects—testing 240 newly hatched Leghorn chicks.

The results with the chicks were ambivalent. The study is mentioned here not on the basis of results with such subjects, but as an example of instrumentation for extending our understanding if humans are used.

AUDITORY SPACE PERCEPTION

Externalization of Sound

In Chapter 7 the way that the auditory mechanism might function to provide the apprehension and appreciation of external space was discussed. It was emphasized that the auditory mechanism does not include the facilities that would enable it to take a role in initiating the perception of space as a domain.

One investigation that bears on this point and is appropriate here is the study of the localization of tones produced by earphones. It was found that the resulting tones were localized within or near to the head, which is different from the localization that results when the same tones are produced in the more usual way, that is, by souces at some distance from the ears. In the one case the subject cannot manipulate his or her geometrical relationships to the source, whereas in the other he or she can. This difference may be one factor in producing the perceptual difference in the two cases.

Our chief interest in the fact that sounds produced by external sources may seem to originate *within* the body rather than outside it lies in the demonstration that all sounds do not have to pertain to *externality* even in the sighted. Those who know most about blindness assert that acoustic stimuli are not intrinsically interpreted as being localized *externally* by the congenitally blind. The example of the headphones helps to make this assertion seem more plausible.

In vision, movement of the perceiver and change of optical information from space as a domain go hand in hand in a very direct manner. Persons with hearing but no vision have much less opportunity to relate their sensory experiences to externality. The main thing that the person without vision can do is move his or her head or whole body so as to manipulate intensity and phase relations of acoustic waves, a gross affair compared to the achievements possible with vision. When motor manipulations are to be made by the blind in relation to hearing, they are related to the body as a domain rather than to externality. We would assume that the congentitally blind are not able to get away from the body as a reference. In fact, it would seem that the burden of proof would rest on those who assume that the congentially blind do experience externality.

Localization

Newman (1948) summarized well the nature of sound localization as far as its accuracy is concerned. He pointed out the characteristics as follows:

1. The subject almost never confuses an acoustic source on the right with one on the left.
2. The subject may occasionally report hearing a sound behind when its source is in front or overhead. One may hear a sound as located to the right and in front when its source is to the right and behind.
3. The subject may be confused, in general, when the source is off to one side of the median plane, which is describable by means of a cone whose apex lies at the center of the head (Figure 12.23). Any position on the cone may be con-

Figure 12.23 Cone of confusion in auditory localization. Within the area bounded by the cone two acoustic sources may be confused. (Source: E. B. Newman. "Hearing," in E. G. Boring, H. Langfeld, and H. P. Weld (eds.), *Foundations of Psychology.* New York: Wiley, 1948, Fig. 165.

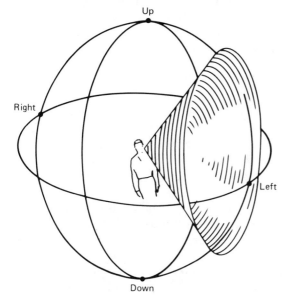

fused with any other position on it. Points on the cone's surface represent both a set of directions and a set of distances (although we are mainly dealing with a set of directions). Hence the opposite sides of the cone represent the extreme amounts of discrepancy in direction between acoustic source and the source heard. Lesser discrepancies are represented by various points within the cone at constant distances from the ear. The cone is the best descriptive device to picture range and combination of positions of two acoustic sources that would tend to be confused with each other, that is, those that would seem to be identical.

Vertical Localization

The localization of sounds in the vertical dimension is very poor in the sighted person when the head and the sound source do not move. The listener must move the head in order to detect the angle of elevation of the source. Wallach (1940) found that if he rotated the head and sound source together in the horizontal plane, the sound seemed to come from above. He called attention to the fact that the only sound sources for which horizontal head rotations usually produce no change in binaural phase and intensity relations are those directly above, and possibly directly below, the listener. Thus we can suspect that the location of sound is keyed to these two factors for hearing, no matter how curious the results in special experimental situations turn out to be. If so, deprivation of opportunity to learn may preclude the development of even some of the most fundamental features of human apprehension—that is, of the experience of an external space domain.

Localization in the Open Air

Most of the work done on hearing, whether on localization or on any other aspect, has been conducted in the laboratory, that is, indoors. Nowadays we have two alternatives to using ordinary rooms with their reverberations that possibly distort results. There are "soundproof" (i.e., acoustic-energy absorbing) rooms and open-air situations.

Stevens and Newman (1936) set up a tall swivel chair on top of a 9-foot ventilator on the roof of a building. This arrangement provided unobstructed space in all directions; even the nearest horizontal surfaces were 12 feet below the observer. The acoustic source was mounted on a 12-foot arm connected to the base of the observer's chair; the arm was counterbalanced and could be shifted noiselessly from one position to another around a complete circle. The stimuli produced tones, a hiss, and a click. For the frequencies between 400 and 4000 cycles the energy level was 60 decibels. The energy level for frequencies beyond this range in either direction was about 30 decibels.

The observer's task was to distinguish between sounds heard from behind and in front of the lateral plane, that is, the vertical plane running through the head from ear to ear. It was found that it was very difficult to make the front–back distinction, and so such reversals were not counted as errors in the investigation. The magnitude of the error was determined as the differences between the reported sound direction and either the lateral direction of the source or the corresponding position in the other quadrant, depending on which was the smaller. For example, if the source was 10° to the right of the straight-ahead position (at 0°), the observer would be considered correct if he or she reported 170° degrees (counting clockwise).

Figure 12.24 indicates the mean of the errors made by two

Figure 12.24   Upper plot indicates the average of errors in degrees of two observers in localizing an acoustic source at various frequencies. The lower plot shows the percentage of confusions between front and near quadrants. (Source: S. S. Stevens and E. B. Newman. "The localization of actual sources of sound," *Amer. J. Psychol.,* 1936, 48, 297–306, Figs. 2, 4.)

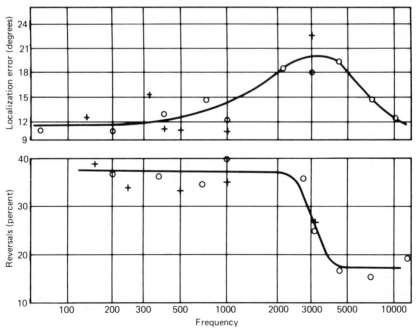

trained observers. The errors for sources of low frequency were quite similar, but in the range of 500 to 3000 cycles the errors became progressively greater. Above about 4000 cycles there was an improvement again, so that at 10,000 cycles localization was almost as accurate as at 1000 cycles.

The maximum error, which peaked at about 3000 cycles, was explained as follows. Low errors at low frequencies were to be expected because of the phase differences in the acoustic waves for the two ears. Phase differences reach their maximum effectiveness at a little over 1500 cycles. The effectiveness of intensity differences reaching the two ears from a source off to one side increases with frequency. Such an intensity differential sets in below 1000 cycles and increases rapidly above 3000 cycles. This would suggest, then, that at 3000 cycles errors should be at a maximum in magnitude because phase difference is too slight at the point to help much as a factor and that differential intensity as a factor for localization has not yet become great enough to help sufficiently.

Figure 12.24 also shows the reversals that were made in the investigation. The frequency range was found to be divided into two quite distinct portions. Above about 3000 cycles the errors were about one-third as frequent as expected by chance. For the lower frequencies the errors were only a little fewer than expected by chance. The effective factor at the higher frequencies was the intensity differential. Phase differences operated for low frequencies. Thus it was concluded that the reduction in reversals was dependent on the ability to use the intensity differential in the two ears.

When a continuous high-frequency source was swung around the observer's head, the tone was less intense when the source was behind than when it was in front. In one part of the investigation the stimuli were varied in frequency from 3000 to 7000 cycles in a random order. This procedure increased the errors of reversal from 18.6 percent in the former procedure to 47 percent. Therefore, the observers must have quite readily developed a personal (or "subjective")standard of intensity in the first procedure.

Hisses and clicks were better localized than tones. Hisses were especially easy to localize. In fact, it was declared to be almost as definite as if one had been looking at the source. As compared to errors of 16.0° for pure tones, the hiss was only 5.6° and the click was 8.0°. The hiss sounded louder when the source was in front of the observer. Also it sounded like *shh*, whereas when the source was behind the observer, it sounded like *sss*. Strangely enough, the intensive and qualitative differences did not rise to awareness in the main part of the investigation. This is a nice example of how certain factors may be operative below clear awareness but never-theless considerable in effect.

Binaural Intensity

One factor aiding the individual to localize sound is the difference in the intensities of the impingements on the two ears. In general, the sound seems to come from a direction toward the side the more intense the stimulation. This relationship has been studied by various investigators, among them Stewart and Hovda (1913), who used two tuning forks in tandem. The stimuli were led to the two ears by tubes of equal diameter and length. One fork was placed about 1 centimeter from the end of one tube. The distance of the other fork from the second tube was varied from 0.20 centimeter to 2.20 centimeters. An intensity ratio of 10 to 1 was needed to shift the apparent direction of the sound source 45°. This ratio is much greater than the one resulting from an acoustic source placed at 45° from the median plane and thus would suggest that intensity is not alone in accounting for the normal accuracy in experiencing the direction of sound sources.

Binaural Phase Difference

Acoustic stimuli originating from a common source to one side or the other of the median plane do not reach the two ears at the same time, and when they do reach the two ears they are slightly out of phase. The higher the frequency, the less is the time involved in the various phases of a given wave. Very high frequencies might well be expected to provide no basis for utilizing phase difference.

Recent investigations have shown that binaural phase difference plays a role but is effective only with pure tonal sources of 1500 cycles per second and below. As was implied, phase difference is reducible to time difference. This was taken advantage of in experiments of Wallach, Newman, and Rosenzweig (1949), in which two click-producing sources, one for each ear, were used. Time differences of as little as 30 to 40 microseconds led to above-chance numbers of reports to one side or another. When the time difference in the click sources was increased to 2 or 3 milliseconds, sound was heard as a double click. With still longer separations, the clicks were heard as fully separate and in widely separate locations.

Reverberation poses certain applications of the principles in-volved in binaural phase differences. It seems, however, that with click-producing sources, the first stimuli to arrive have precedence over the later ones in determining localization.

Stereophonic Localization

Two ears per person and the instrumental facilities of leading into them various acoustic stimuli independently provide tremendous possibilities for manipulation of stimulus conditions. A number of effects quite bizarre to the normal listener have been produced. The discrepancies between what is heard and what exists in a spatial way in the external environment can be overwhelming, to say the least. The problems consist in (1) manipulating the positions of the sound sources, (2) reproducing the acoustic wave patterns set up at various positions with reference to the sound sources, and (3) leading separate end results to the two ears independently.

For example, a dummy listener (mannequin) can be set up with a microphone at each ear. The wave fronts reaching the two ears will be different for a single acoustic source located asymmetrically to them. If what reaches each ear is recorded on a separate tape or separately on a single tape, the result can be played back to a listener. The listener will wear earphones and the two different sound tracks will feed their outputs into the two ears separately. The simplest result would be that the listener would hear a sound coming from off to one side. If two separate sources had been recorded, he or she would hear two sources located at different points. If the source moved, the listener would hear it as very definitely moving. The source could have been produced by an object moving toward the dummy. In that case the listener will hear the object coming toward him or her and will make the appropriate movements to get out of its way. If the original source is rotated around the dummy's head, the listener will hear sound being moved around his or her own head.

Today we have stereophonic recordings of musical compositions, double-track tape recordings of wave fronts picked up from two different positions. The net result is that the listener hears the music as pervading space all about him or her. Instead of being heard as coming from some single direction in front, the listener hears the music as being everywhere. This effect is the nearest thing in audition to what externality is to the person visually.

We pointed out earlier that through optical means, many points in space are represented on the retina from instant to instant. If vision were utilized by only looking through a narrow tube with one eye, no real notion of space such as we know it would develop. Vision in this restrictedly perceived fashion would be somewhat analogous to the way ordinary hearing, by its very nature, is found to be used.

With stereophonic conditions of hearing, sound takes on its maximal spatial properties for the sighted individual. (The effects of stereophonic hearing in the congenitally blind have not been fully explored and reported on in the literature. To test the blind with stereophonic instrumentation would be extremely interesting and possibly very informative.) With stereophonic conditions, one is within the sound field and unable to move in any direction to escape from the sound or lessen its intensity or otherwise avoid or diminish its intrusion on him or her. Like visual space, the sound field becomes an extensional domain, a kind of medium within which the listener exists.

We need not possess stereophonic instruments to experience a moderate amount of this. Much of our auditory experience occurs indoors or in other partially confined spaces rather than in the broad our-of-doors where there are no buildings, hills, or other objects to confine the sound waves and reverberate them. Therefore although we do not produce separate acoustic wave patterns from two different locations, we do receive very complex wave fronts produced by reverberation with the two ears.

For a clearer description refer to Figure 12.25, which indicates that although there is only one original acoustic source (S), the waves strike and are reflected off the walls at various places so that the listener (L) receives acoustic energies from a host of different directions. This adds to the "noisiness" or obtrusiveness of the sound, although the total energy reaching the ears is not any greater than or as great as if the listener were nearer to the source in the open. In the open there would be a whole set of directions from which the acoustic waves would not reach the listener, owing to absence of reverberation. Sound would not seem to come from all around him or her and thus would be unobtrusive. The listener could escape the sound if desired.

Reverberation and Distance

There is a relation between the perceived distance of a sound source and the reverberation component in comparison to the energy that reaches the ear directly from the source. Figure 12.25 would tend to suggest that if a second source were placed closer to the listener than the first source, the major portion of the energy reaching the ear would reach it directly. Only a small amount of energy would reach the ear after being reflected back and forth between the walls. This difference would be represented, then, in the character of the

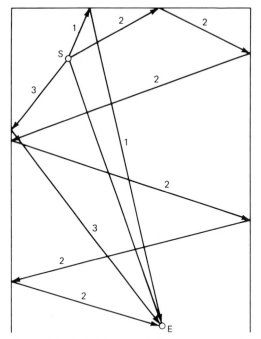

Figure 12.25   S, the acoustic source, reverberates from walls of a room in addition to supplying energy that reaches the listener (E) directly. Each reverberatory wave front is numbered.

wave fronts reaching the ear. Since the relations between reverberation and distance from the ear are lawful ones, they can be learned. Thus part of the basis for hearing a tone as originated far away is to be attributed to its reverberation characteristic rather than wholly to its reduced energy content. Another potential spatial characteristic of sound—its distance—is therefore based on complexity of wave fronts.

False Localization

A conclusion easily arrived at is that the localization of sound sources is very poor. Whereas the usual technique of determining human capacity or sensitivity is to set up simplified experimental situations and to determine thresholds, one may, on the other hand, examine what happens in unsimplified or everyday situations. Several such unsimplified situations described here are meant to illustrate the basis for concluding that sound fails to have strongly compelling spatial qualities or that perceived localization is always primarily dependent on acoustic factors. Sighted persons may at times tend to localize sounds and to become disturbed when no satisfactory localization can be made. The congenitally blind may not be similarly impelled. Our supposition is that if the localization of sound is poor in the sighted, it need not exist at all as a medium for experiencing externality in the congenitally blind.

By false localization is meant hearing a sound as originating from one direction and distance quite different from those of the actual source. Ventriloquism, a complex situation worth considering, is in part the art of producing sounds that are falsely localized. Our purpose is not to present an exposition on ventriloquism but to show that localization of sound is quite poor. The illustrations should indicate that there need be nothing very compelling about a set of sound waves to make the perceiver detect the correct direction and distance of their origin.

In the more usual ventriloquistic situation, the ventriloquist converses with a puppet constructed with movable jaws, which he or she operates. The perceiver experiences listening to two people carrying on a conversation. The words of the puppet are as perceptually realistic as are those of the operator. Since the puppet is in a direction different from the listener, the effect can be described as a false localization of sound when the puppet is perceived to speak.

In other ventriloquistic situations, sounds of the human voice are made to seem to originate at considerable distances from the actual speaker. To do this the operator must change his or her voice as ordinarily heard so as to make it seem like a voice coming from a distance. This is sometimes referred to as "throwing" the voice. It is actually changing the acoustic output as just described and providing a number of visual and other stimulus conditions consistent with the acoustic stimulus produced.

We might generalize as to what is necessary for the success of ventriloquism. The conditions would seem to be:

1. The production of acoustic stimuli at one location and of a character to be heard as coming from another location. This often is accomplished by using two voices from one speaker, one the natural voice and the other a differently sounding one not accompanied by any visual evidences that the real speaker is producing the sound.
2. The production of visual influences that are more potent in localizing the perceived origins of the sound than are the characteristics of the wave fronts as they reach the ear. This is accomplished most easily by use of a puppet, which is visually perceived as a different person. The ventriloquist

need not manipulate the distance characteristics of acoustic wave fronts as much as the visual characteristics of the situation. In all cases there must be something definite to be seen at some location or other, so that a localization can be made. The seen object could be a distant puppet or it could be a wall, just beyond which the sound could seem to originate.

False localization need not involve voices. In fact, it may well involve other familiar sound sources with regard to which the listener may be expected to react in characteristic ways. On one occasion, for example, the author pulled alongside the curb in an old Model T Ford to wait for a friend. It was in the days when streets were still quiet and all that could be heard when he had settled down to wait was a recurrent click at the rate of one every two seconds, pronounced enough to attract his attention and elicit his curiosity. The source of the clicks was quite indefinite except that it seemed to be someplace in the car. When he looked toward the hood, the clicks seemed to come from under it. When he looked down at the floorboards, the clicks came from under them. In general, the clicks sounded like the cooling of some heavy metal object, so he thought they could represent the cooling of the hot engine, but still he was not satisfied of the source. He got out of the car and looked up under the running board toward the engine and transmission. Still, the origin of the clicks was elusive but perceived as being inside the car. He had no doubt that the sound was produced by the car itself.

Failing to localize the specific origin of the clicks, he finally gave up, although when he climbed back into the car the clicks still persisted. He shifted his attention, however, to a couple of children swinging quietly in a porch swing. The houses were set up above the street beyond terraces that rose abruptly from the sidewalk, so the children on the swing were not far away and were above eye level but, of course, were many times as far away from him as were various parts of the car. When he finally noticed a synchrony between the clicks and the pendular motion of the porch swing, he readily deduced that the clicks were made by the friction of the suspension chains of the swing on the screw eyes that supported them. He had finally found the true source of the sound, but it was easy to hear each click originating below the floorboards of the car. He still perceived the sound as originating in an entirely different direction and at a very different distance from the true acoustic source. We could conclude that sound localization is greatly influenced by seen objects rather than more especially by the quality of the sound waves themselves. Visual context is highly effective in localization.

Admittedly, click-producing sources are among the most accurately localized sound producers, but their effects can be easily influenced and manipulated. The fact that localization of the click was not accomplished by anything the listener did—in changing head position, getting out of the car, peering under it, and getting back in—indicates how the process of hearing lacks in intrinsic spatiality, at least on some occasions. Vision is never deficient in anything like this or to the same extent. Sound can seem to come from almost anywhere and at times even from nowhere in particular.

Facial Vision in Auditory Perception

Dallenbach, with his colleagues (Ammons, Worchel, and Dallenbach 1953), studied what has been commonly called *facial vision*. They conducted a number of ingenious experiments indoors and found that (1) audition is the necessary and sufficient condition for the blind person's detection and avoidance of obstacles, (2) pitch is the feature of audition that is involved, and (3) frequencies of 10,000 cycles are necessary for the performance. From these factors it was deduced that anyone who—whether blind or merely blinfolded—possesses normal hearing should be able to learn to detect and avoid obstacles. This took much of the mystery out of facial vision as expressed by some earlier students of the phenomenon. For example, Diderot had called facial vision an amazing ability possessed by only a few of the blind.

Ammons, Worchel, and Dallenbach (1953) addressed themselves to the question of whether the extensive indoor studies at Cornell University on facial vision could be duplicated outdoors under conditions more closely simulating those in which the blind perform in everyday life. A second question had to do with finding out whether blindfolded sighted persons could learn the ability to perceive obstacles.

Their first experiment consisted in determining whether blindfolded subjects with normal or near-normal hearing (group A) could learn to perceive obstacles outdoors and whether this type of subject could learn even with the ears stopped (group B). Both groups of subjects had initial trouble staying on the sidewalk without guidance. Collisions with obstacles were of three kinds: (1) collisions before reporting perception of an obstacle, (2) collisions made after having reported the perception of an obstacle but before being finally sure; (3) collisions made during the time the subject was making final appraisal and was "inching up" to the obstacle.

The subjects of both groups were unable to learn as quickly as subjects in the indoor experiments and their ultimate perceptions were more variable. Perception of obstacles was influenced by wind, sun, and clouds. For example, when walking into the wind, detection of an obstacle was based on the drop in pressure as the obstacle shielded the subject. When walking with the wind, subjects signaled obstacles by reflection of wind from them. Where there was no wind, behavior based on such factors, of course, suffered. When the sun was hot, the presence of obstacles was signaled by temperature changes. Sun shining on various materials caused them to give off detected odors. The net result of the experiment was to show that not only the blindfolded but also subjects with the additional deprivation of a certain amount of hearing could learn to detect obstacles out-of-doors by means undetermined.

The following experiments were made to determine the kind of factors used by the subjects in detecting obstacles in the first experiment. The general conclusions derived from the whole group of experiments were that (1) blindfolded and blindfolded and ear-stopped subjects could learn to detect obstacles, (2) behavior of the latter subjects differed from behavior of subjects blindfolded only, and (3) no single stimulus condition is necessary for obstacle detection. Audition is the principle basis for detection but is "necessary" only in the sense that it is the most reliable and universal of all the factors used. A number of corollaries to these three conclusions were also stated. For example, the "black curtain" or "dark shades" mentioned by some subjects on approaching an obstacle were taken to be imaginal experiences evoked associatedly by auditory stimuli. Subjects helped or hindered by the nighttime experiments fell into groups—those whose performances were bettered were still able to use certain auditory cues when their ears were stopped and thus sought no other cues; those whose performances were impaired sought other factors when, under the conditions of experimentation, the auditory factors were not usable because of the ear blocks. The thermal and olfactory impingements served the subjects well enough in the sunshine but failed them at night when these impingements were absent.

We can see, in the general type of performance just described, what many would call a form of space perception. For us it is another example of the sequential or bit-by-bit sort of perception that enables people to get about in space. Once an obstacle is detected, one next, moves alternately to the right or left so as to determine whether the signals from the obstacle diminish. With this type of feedback, the skilled person can steer himself or herself around the obstacle almost as if it were seen. Of course, varying degrees of skill are to be expected.

Facial vision, then, is another example of the piecemeal detection of the structure of space rather than the apprehension of space as a domain, that is, true space perception. Facial vision could naturally be expected to be more or differently effective in the adventitiously blinded than in the congenitally blind.

Matching Auditory and Visual Perspectives

The other side of the story of sound localization lies in findings made by acoustic engineers in matching picture strips and sound strips for sound movies. It is possible to mismatch these strips in such ways so as to produce the perception of a person talking with

Figure 12.26 Distances from a photographed object (such as a person speaking) that a microphone should be placed, depending on the focal length of the camera lens. The center curve is for a lens of 35-millimeter focal length. Assuming that the pickup is appropriate for this lens when the microphone is at camera distance, one must place the microphone at other distances from the sound source for lenses of other focal lengths. If the focal length is greater than 35 millimeters, this distance is some percentage of the camera distance. The other curves are for sets (stages or scenes) where the sound absorption is either greater or less than average; for these, lenses of 25 and 50 millimeters may be used as reference instead of a 35-millimeter lens. (Source: After J. P. Maxfield. "Some physical factors affecting illusion in sound motion pictures," *J. Acoust. Soc. Amer.,* 1931, 3, 69–80, Figs. 1, 4, 5.)

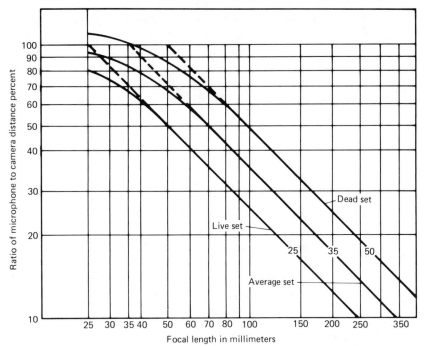

the sound originating at some distant point. In one respect this is an example of a *ventriloquistic situation* such as we have already described. In another respect it shows that the quality of a sound and its perceived distance go hand in hand. If this interrelation was an extremely rigid and sensitive one, the argument for the relative spatial indeterminateness of sound would be negated.

The curious thing about mismatching sound and picture strips on a movie film is that little can be done to bring the phenomenal location of sounds any closer to the listener than the actual acoustic source, generally placed right behind the projection screen. On the other hand, mismatchings that induce hearing sounds as farther away than the visual source can manipulate phenomenal distance quite considerably.

It may be useful to know how sound and picture strips are properly matched. By experimentation, it has been discovered that to equate sound with picture involves the focal length of the camera lens, the relative distance of the microphone from the acoustic source to the camera, and the reverberatory properties of the walls of the room in which the movies are made. Cameras with long, focal length lenses bring distance scenes up close. Microphones quite near the acoustic sources produce stimulus end results perceived as objects nearby. If the walls of the room are highly reverberatory (or live), the percentage of the distance from the acoustic source to the camera at which the microphone must be placed has to be reduced in order to cut down the reverberatory component picked up by the microphone, although the total energy content is increased. The total energy content is not as influential as a stimulus factor for determining perceived distance as is the reverberatory content. The relation among the three factors just mentioned is given in Figure 12.26.

HAPTIC SPACE PERCEPTION

Touch and Kinesthesis as Space Senses

External items can be apprehended by contact as well as by the photic radiation coming from them: this is the sense of touch and pressure. External items may be put into ever differing and new relations to the individual by his or her own motions in space and through practice this activity becomes functionally related to the visual input and response. It must be recognized, however, that both contact and motion provide information *sequentially* (bit by bit) and not as an overall pattern, as in vision through photic input. One imagines contact sequentially. Thus reliving an occasion in tactual or kinesthetic memory is a bit-by-bit affair rather than one having the total appear in an instant. However, as has already been pointed out, kinesthesis may provide for some useful but limited form of unfolding behavior such as tracing a finger maze.

Let us illustrate this by noticing what could be expected of first a sighted person and then a congenitally blind person when asked to imagine a flight of steps. The sighted person can visualize the whole flight all in an instant; it is a total working pattern to him or her. The congenitally blind would at best be expected to respond only by imagining walking up or down the flight of steps. For him or her it would be a sequential affair, not an instantaneous accomplishment in which the "representation" would be a timeless total pattern. Then we could say that space as an overall domain is not a reality to the congenitally blind person in the same way as it is to the sighted person. It is probably not a spatial reality at all, but possibly only a temporal reality.

In Chapter 5, the "Haptic Perceptual System," we dealt with the tactile and kinesthetic senses as they relate to the perception of small objects that can be handled and items that touch the skin. Since the haptic system is not directly a distance sense, what was said there does not focally apply here, for now we are dealing with space external to the body.

THE APPRECIATION OF TIME

The perception of time refers to the evaluation of short intervals as measured in seconds, minutes, and hours and, on the other hand, to longer stretches such as weeks, months, and years. Time is a more abstract matter than space, primarily since the human has no specific time receptors. Time is simply an experience and the individual has no idea of how he or she obtains it. Hence we more appropriately talk about time judgment and time estimations than specific time perceptions. Nevertheless, time is a factor in the physical world duration and pertains to specifying impingements. The estimation of long temporal intervals such as months and years is still a more "abstract" matter.

To humans, in general, time seems to be one of the most obvious features of reality. One cannot think of existence that would be timeless. Time is also a concept that philosophers and physical scientists have long dealt with. It seems in some respects to be something that one directly experience just like experiencing color, size, sounds, and the like, and yet when one tries to consider it in the way other perceptual features are dealt with, it becomes elusive, both logically and empirically.

All of this should not be surprising, since we have no receptors or sense organs for time or duration, as such. As a result, a discussion of time might well be considered out of bounds for this text. In fact, it is omitted in some texts on perception. On the other hand, time is one feature of the environmental universe to which we respond.

Duration is a factor that has already been taken into account in our discussion of experimental method and findings regarding perceptual response to definite *energistic* impingements on receptors.

The question is what mechanisms are involved in what we would call response. Are they sensory mechanisms or are they what we would call cognitive patterns of activity. More probably, the consciousness of time and how we manipulate it in our daily activities is something related indirectly enough to take our categorization of it out of the purely perceptual realm. At least the matter is so subtile and nebulous that we need not discuss it at length in this book.

That body mechanism, mostly neural, are ongoing in their activity and display various sorts of cycles and periodicity is beyond doubt. Furthermore, the fact that some individuals can set the time they want to wake up when they go to sleep—and pretty well succeed— is another feature of human behavior that indicates certain overall activities that can be described in temporal terms, leads many to continue their search for more substantial connections between body process and what we call time. Various biologists have postulated a kind of time clock within the body and have found ways of trying to test it. (Hoagland, 1933, 1935.)

One of the physiological phenomena that has been supposed might provide some evidence of a physiological clock for short intervals, is the electroencephalogram (EEG). The alpha rhythm, a series of waves at 10 per second is prominent in it. In some ways, but not in others, experimentation gave some of the evidence sought. At least there are some known relations between photic input to the retina and the nature of the EEG. We know that certain drugs affect our experience of time, which is to say that certain aspects of what goes on in the body provide, as a total pattern, for our experience of time.

But all of this, though concrete, bypasses the fact that time does not have the class of properties that other experiences have, which we call perceptual. All of this does not locate what we are calling the experience of time in the perceptual category. While we loosely use the term, "perception of time," more strictly we might better say, "the appreciation of time."

Human Chronological Age and Experience of Time

Days, months, and years seem to pass more rapidly as individuals grow older. This is a common observation and has been dealt with by certain authors (Fraisse, 1963).

One of the earlier attempts to explain this was made by Janel in the last century, who suggested that the individual's total chronological age functions as a perceptual frame of reference. At 70 years of age a year would seem much shorter than for a 10 year old, since for the former it represents a much smaller proportion of the total chronological life span. It would seem that this is true both as judged in retrospect and in viewing the future.

Chapter 13
Perception of Movement in the Environment

GENERAL KINDS OF MOVEMENT

The perception of movement pertains to several classes of events. (1) The perception of the person himself or herself moving in the gravitational field, that is, with references to the earth. Here we are not speaking of moving eyes, limbs, or head; we mean the movement of the body as a whole. (2) The perception of movement of the head, or other parts of the body, particularly the limbs. (3) The perception of objects moving in space outside of the body. These may or may not move with reference to the viewer. The first form of movement was dealt with in Chapter 4, "Basic Orientation Perception"; the second, in Chapter 5, "Haptic Perception." The third is the subject of the present chapter and is generally discussed in two categories—real movement and apparent movement. These are forms of visually, tactually, and auditorily perceived movements. Real movement is defined as the case in which something is actually displaced in space, whereas apparent movement, which perceptually may be as "real" or convincing as real movement, is produced by a temporal sequence of stationary presentations (targets). With certain combinations of spacing and timing, the viewer sees or feels or hears a single object moving from one position to another. Movement sometimes is reduced to a mere unclear impression and is called "pure phi," a term clarified later.

VISUAL MOVEMENT

In everyday life, movement of the body, movement of the eyes or head with body still, or movement of objects in the environment do not always occur separately. While the intent of this chapter is to make separations among the kinds of movement and to deal with the occasions when only something in the environment is displaced (moves), certain classifications need to be discussed first.

One of these classifications deals with the net retinal effects of various kinds of encounters. Obviously, not only motions of the objects in the environment but also motions of the body in the environment and motions of the eyes in following objects are being considered.

REAL MOVEMENT

Retinal Image Displacements in Real Movement

It is appropriate to classify the kinds of image displacements that may occur in perceiving real movement, for they are not all of one simple sort. The diagrams in Figure 13.1 show the various essential forms of displacement of images on the retina. The *first* of the five forms is the whole-field image that moves by short jumps across the retina, such as that which occurs in the unwitting jumplike eye movements in reading a line of type. With this form of image displacement, there is no experience of the external environment during these jumps (saccades), hence there is nothing to specify as in motion.

The *second* form of image displacement is the displacement of a portion of the total image, while the image of the field in general is stationary. This is produced when a restricted target is displaced laterally (i.e., in the frontal plane), with the eyes stationary; one experiences the movement of an object in a stable field. This is a very common situation, for example, seeing a bird fly past a window as one is looking out at the scene.

The *third* pattern of retinal change occurs when the eye follows a target that is moving in the frontal plane. The image of the visual field as a whole moves, while that of the pursued target remains

External conditions	Motion of image on retina	Perception of movement
Saccadic eye movements as in reading, visual target motionless	Uniform motion of all parts of overall image	No object movement perceived
Eye motionless, small target moving frontally	Motion of image of restricted target, no motion of overall image	Object motion in frontal plane, rest of world motionless
Eyes pursuing small target moving frontally	Motion of overall image with image of target fixated (pursued)	Only object motion in front plane
Head not turning, body in motion in stable visual environment as riding in train and fixating on horizion	Deformation of overall image, parts representing distant targets stable or more nearly so than closer ones	Perceiver moving in stable world, moving past near objects faster than more distant objects
Eyes motionless, target moving in third dimension	Deformation of overall image, image of restricted target growing or diminishing in size	Object moving toward or away from perceiver in stable world

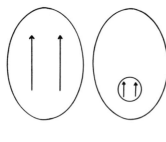

Figure 13.1 Relations among movement of external conditions, retinal images, and what is seen. (Source: After J. J. Gibson. *The Perception of the Visual World.* Boston: Houghton Mifflin, 1950.)

fixed on the retina. If one actually follows the flight of a bird as it goes by in the frontal plane, its image remains fixed on the fovea, while the image of the scene moves across the retina.

The *fourth* kind of retinal change occurs when the head or head and body are moved and nothing is displaced in the external environment. The retinal image of the whole field tends to be deformed. Images of targets close by move across the retina most rapidly. The targets progressively farther and farther away move less and less. Hence there is an internal rearrangement of elements in the target field as a whole. The impression is that of self-movement in a stable world. This is well exemplified as one gazes out the window of a moving train: the horizon is still while objects nearer and nearer move faster and faster.

In the *fifth* kind of retinal change nothing but a restricted target moves in the third dimension. The target image grows or shrinks in size and may change somewhat in shape. The perception is of an object moving in the third dimension while the environment stands still. This is exemplified if the bird flies either toward or away from the observer as he or she watches it.

The displacement of the total image or some part of it occurs in each of the five cases because there is a lawful relation between what happens on the retina and the photically relayed events outside the organism. The adult individual sees what he or she sees partly depending on the changes that occur in the pattern of stimulation on the retina and partly on account of having developed a reaction pattern that is in lawful relation to the positions and motions of other items in the visual field. This reaction pattern stems not only from the motions of other items but from the motions the individual has to execute in dealing with these items.

So far we have been describing the overall changes in the *retinal images* and the overall perceived effects during motion of the field or the observer. We now come to consider the *perceptual features* of seen objects in motion.

Thresholds for Perceiving Motion

The threshold for movement perceived at 9° from the fixation point is about 18 minutes of arc per second. Threshold differences in rate of movement for certain targets near the fixation point turns out to be about 1 to 2 minutes per second. Graham, Baker, Hecht, and Lloyd (1948) obtained a value of 30 seconds of arc per second for the threshold difference in the rate of slow-moving targets and a value of about 100 seconds for fast-moving targets. J. F. Brown (1931) studied the relation of phenomenal (perceived) movement to rate of physical displacement in a field by using an endless broad belt on which variously sized, shaped, and spaced targets were placed from experiment to experiment. Actually, Brown used two such setups, one as a standard and the other as a comparison field. The observer could shift his or her gaze from one to the other, since the targets were placed so that they would not both be visible at the same time.

Velocity of Movement

Brown found that as the physical velocity of a moving square target is increased from 0 to 200 centimeters per second, several kinds of thresholds obtained, including (1) a just perceptible movement, (2) a kind of reversed movement produced when one target moves out of the field as the succeeding target moves in, and (3) a velocity at which the targets become a gray band instead of being distinct items. For the threshold of the first type he found angular velocities of from 2 to 6 minutes of arc per second; the length and width of the field apparently contributed to these values. For the reversed movement (threshold 2), values of 3 to 9° per second were found. The factors producing variation were field dimensions, target sizes, and distances between them on the moving belt. Threshold 3 was obtained at values of 12 to 32° per second.

Various other studies of the perception of velocity have been made. Kennedy, Yessenow, and Wendt (1972) studied the accuracy of perceived movement and whether this could be improved with practice. Little improvement in ability was found. Ekman and Dahlback (1956) attempted a subjective scale of velocity. Later, Mashhaur (1962) did likewise. And in 1966 Rachlin scaled subjective velocity, distance, and duration.

In the experiments about to be described the structure of the stationary and displaced elements of the target were different from those already mentioned. Here it was the question of what factors in the situation were strong in controlling velocity of movement. Delorme and Frigon (1977) used three experiments for the study. In the first, an endless striped belt was moved behind a stable fixation line. In the second, a vertical line moved in front of a stable striped background. In the third, the vertical line was visually pursued. The findings in the three experiments led the authors to conclude that perceived speed increases as a function of the temporal frequency of encounters between the moving target and the elements in its context, at least within limits of target movement and spatial separation of items in the background ("density of encounters").

Brown (1931) reported that speed seems greater in a heterogeneous than in a homogeneous field. Piaget, Feller, and McNear (1958) reported an increase in movement speed when entering a field of reference bars from an empty field. Bonnet (1969) also reported on the effect of background. In that study, overestimation of speed was reported when using a hatched track.

APPARENT MOVEMENT

Apparent movement is the phenomenal movement produced without target displacement. Physical factors such as intensity, position, and timing substitute for the usual displacement. Understanding how these factors operate as substitutes is the main task of studying apparent movement.

There are several forms of apparent movement.

• *Gamma movement.* The perceived radial movement outward from the fixation point when the level of illumination is suddenly raised and the movement in the opposite direction when the illumination is suddenly lowered. Raising and lowering of illumination may take various forms. For example, illumination can be raised from zero value to some finite value or can be changed from some material amount to some greater or lesser amount. Furthermore, the whole field may be involved homogeneously in the raising and lowering of illumination, or the specified change may involve only a restricted portion of the field, which we ordinarily call a restricted *target.* That is, gamma movement can be produced either by varying the level of the whole field or by varying only some part of it.

• *Beta movement.* The perception of lateral movement of a single object from one place to another when two stationary targets are presented in succession. Beta movement is examplified in motion pictures, in electric crossing signals (alternate flashing "lights") for railroads, and in lighted borders of theater marquees. The production of beta movement is dependent on a crucial combination of circumstances. These factors are primarily the proper distance between targets (measured in units of visual angle), the proper time interval between the presentations of the targets, and the proper target intensities.

Some study has been made of these three general factors. Korte (1915), one of the investigators, formulated a loose set of "laws" that have come to be known as Korte's laws. They state that once optimal (i.e., satisfactory or convincing) movement is set up, it may be maintained, even if one of the three foregoing conditions is altered, *if* some compensatory alteration is made in the values of one or both of the other two conditions. Possible alterations are as follows: If distance between targets is increased, the time interval between presentations should be increased ($d \sim t$) in order to maintain good movement. If distance is increased, good movement may be maintained by increasing the intensity of the targets ($d \sim I$). If intensity is increased, the time between presentations should be decreased ($I \sim 1/t$). It is as though a space-intensity combination of brain activity had to be of a certain pattern for apparent movement to be seen. The pattern can best be held nearly constant in form by the kinds of manipulations just specified.

• *Delta movement.* The delta movement is akin to beta movement except that in addition to being a movement in the direction of the sequence in the presentation of two targets, it is finally a backward movement in the reverse direction. Delta movement is produced only when the second target is considerably more intense than the first.

• *Alpha movement.* The apparent movement produced by presenting two parts of a geometrical "illusion" in sequence. One of the most frequently used examples of this is the presentation, one at a time, of the two parts of the Müller–Lyer figure (Figure 13.2). In (a) the whole Müller–Lyer figure is shown. Its right and left portions will be seen as two lines that are unequal in length but are actually metrically equal. When the two parts are presented separately in time and in the positions indicated in (b), the horizontal line portion of the two targets will lengthen or contract depending on which is presented first. The "wings" on the lines "flop" back and forth from one position to the other as the one target follows the other.

The forms of movement thus far mentioned, except one, occur in the frontal plane, being either horizontal or vertical. However, a form of movement that leaves the frontal plane is exemplified in the way the wings in the Müller–Lyer figure behave as they change their lateral positions. The wings pivot as they change from

Figure 13.2 The Müller–Lyer figure used in two parts in rapid succession to illustrate conditions for producing the alpha form of apparent movement.

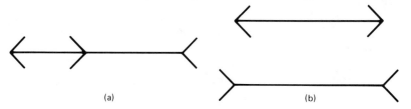

(a)

(b)

one lateral position to the opposite and swing out toward the observer. This behavior may be called *pivotal movement*, for it does not remain in the frontal plane.

Gamma Movement as a Model

Since gamma movement can be taken in many respects as an example of all apparent movement, we shall discuss it more at length. Gamma movement can be used to examine the necessary retinal conditions for movement experience. Therefore let us discuss what happens on the retina when a restricted portion of the visual field is raised in illumination. Figure 13.3 shows the distribution of illumination across the retina when a target of restricted angular subtense is projected on it. The broken-line rectangle represents the distribution of the radiation on the retina as it would be if there were no entopic stray "light" and if the target were mathematically sharply imaged. In contrast, the target supplies illumination outside the image as well as in it. The intensity of the illumination of the retina is tapered from the center of the image to a considerable distance outward and then is rather uniformly distributed from there out to the boundaries of the retina.

It is a general principle in neurophysiology that tissue responds in terms of strength of the impingement on it. The more energetic the impingement, the sooner the measurable response begins. Tissue less strongly impinged on responds only after a greater interval. The interval between the beginning of impingement and the beginning of response is called the latent period. So it may be said that the stronger the stimulation, the shorter will be the latency. As this rule applies here, it could mean that the part of the eye on which the image is projected responds first. Other parts would respond also but only after greater and greater delay depending on the distance from the stimulated area. In other words, the receptors under the image would respond before those radial to it. The re-

Figure 13.3 The pattern of distribution of photic radiation across the retina is tapered and widespread (curve) rather than abrupt and restricted (broken line).

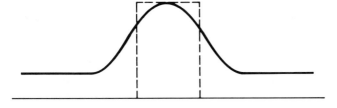

sponse of the eye would be in the form of a spatial sequence with the center of the retina responding first and then the portions successively farther from it.

That such a result is a temporal sequence would be expected to give rise to the experience of movement. Within limits, such a succession is quite like the succession produced by the traverse of an image of a moving target.

Although this description applies to the use of a restricted target, succession in activity in adjacent receptors in the retina can be produced by a uniform illumination over the whole retina. That such a target can produce gamma movement is to be interpreted as meaning that the actual receptors do not all fire off equally rapidly. That is, the rods and cones possibly do not possess the same latency or the central and peripheral parts of the retina may differ in latency on account of the way the elements are connected neurally. Possibly both factors are involved, since we know that the neural hookup in the retina for the more peripheral receptors is different from that of the foveal receptors.

It would seem, then, that even with uniform retinal illumination, the more central portions of the retina would react first. If this is the case, we would expect a temporal succession just as we expected a succession on the basis of relative intensity of stimulation. One step in checking on this assumption would be to see whether, on the basis of relative intensity, we could *reverse* the direction of gamma movement.

Bartley (1936a) was successful in showing that gamma movement can be reversed in direction. His target covered a large portion of the visual field: It was a large opal glass disk over which a number of layers of tissue paper were laid. All layers covered the center of the disk, whereas fewer and fewer layers were involved farther and farther out. When the disk was illuminated from behind, less radiation passed through central sections than through the peripheral ones. The retina therefore received more radiation toward its periphery than on portions toward the center. With the sudden onset of such a pattern of illumination, gamma movement was produced, but it originated at the periphery and moved toward the center of the visual field rather than in the usual way, outward from the center. Of course, at the termination of the stimulus, the movement spread radially outward—the direction opposite to the usual one.

In another experiment Bartley (1936a) used disk targets of varying degrees of angular subtense to check on the then fairly common idea that gamma movement is simply a perceptual aspect of "emergence of figure on ground." Many experimenters of the day had been using targets of small subtense, and it had been found that the edge of the seen object does expand radially as the object emerges into view. It was taken from this that gamma movement of the object border is a function of its phenomenal emergence. Bartley found that when targets of larger angular subtense were used, the gamma movement occurred within the object and the border did not expand radially as it emerged. He drew the conclusion that gamma movement is not a secondary function of the emergence of figure on ground but rather of the spatio-temporal distribution of stimulation of the receptor population. Once the images of target borders are a certain distance out toward the periphery of the retina, the intensity and sensitivity tapers are more gradual and movement is trivial or absent.

One of the arguments of the proponents of a psychological or central theory of the origin of gamma movement is that retinal factors are secondary because gamma movement can be produced just as well by a "black" target on a "light" ground as by a "light" target on a "dark" ground. The argument is that by using a black target, no intensity or only a negligible one is employed in the target and that the rules applying to intensive targets do not hold. It can be shown that the rule of physiology used to explain movement by reason of differences in latency dependent on relative amounts of stimulation holds as well for "dark" as for "light" targets. A withdrawal of radiation in the region of target projection on the retina is greater than for other regions. This withdrawal evokes an off-response in the retina, just as onset of stimulation evokes an on-response. It does not matter whether the object emerges as a black one or a light one; the proper succession of receptor discharge is set up.

Movement in the Third Dimension

In studying gamma movement, Newman (1934) found that under slow rates of reduction or increase of retinal illumination, movement in the third dimension could be produced. This slow rate of transition reduced to the vanishing point the kind of phenomenal movement called gamma movement and produced instead what he called depth movement. Gamma disappeared at about 300 milliseconds and depth movement began with 200 millisecond transitions.

More recently, Bartley and Miller (1954) studied depth movement by varying other factors. They called this movement *adab* movement, since *ad* and *ab* are prefixes meaning toward and away from. A target of a given size was replaced by another one within 0.01 second delay. In some experiments the second target was less intense but of the same size as the first, and in other experiments the second target was of the same intensity but smaller in size. The timing arrangement permitted only the variation of the duration of the second target. At its termination the first target was re-presented.

Adab movement was dependent on the intensity of the second target in relation to the first. In nearly all the conditions eliciting *adab* movement, the weaker the second target, the longer its exposure had to be.

Another factor was the relation of the size of the second target to the size of the first. There was a tendency for the larger targets to require longer exposures to produce *adab* movement. The role played by target size was somewhat complicated, since it involved two factors, a variation in photic flux as size was varied and a shift in retinal image borders. Whereas the first factor would tend to elicit a quicker emergence of the second square, the second factor would operate in the opposite direction, as indicated by the work of earlier investigators who found that contour processes in the retina may work against each other when parallel.

Induced Movement

Another case of movement that differs from those already described is called *induced* movement. Wallach (1959) gives a simple example. If a luminous rectangular target containing a dark object (disk), viewed in a dark room, is slowly moved horizontally to the left or right, the disk is seen to move in the direction opposite to the rectangle. Schiffman (1976) in commenting on this, mentions how in everyday life the moon behind patchy clouds seems to be racing along behind them, whereas it is the clouds that are physically moving.

The Parks Effect

Another movement phenomenon, but one set up by a very different set of conditions, is what might be called the *Parks effect*. It is the effect produced by moving a two-dimensional object horizontally behind a slit in an opaque screen. When the viewer watches the slit he or she sees the object as a whole. If the displacement of the moving object is slow, the horizontal dimensions of the object are increased. When it is moved rapidly they are compressed. The object, of course, is seen as moving. The movement is in the direction of the displacement (Anstis and Atkinson, 1967; Haber and Nathanson, 1968). The issue seems to be how a full figure is seen when at no time is it present. Postretinal storage of serial effects seems to be in operation.

The Pulfrich Phenomenon

Pulfrich (1922) described a visual phenomenon in which the seen path of a moving target was different from what would ordinarily be expected. The phenomenon was produced by observing a pendulum bob with fixation on a point just below the midpart of its excursion. The bob, as any pendulum bob, appears to move in a plane. However, if some sort of filter is placed in front of one eye to reduce the intensity of the target illumination reaching it, the pendulum will no longer appear to move in a plane: its excursion will move in a somewhat elliptical path. As viewed from above, the perceived rotation will be clockwise if the filter is in front of the observer's left eye, counterclockwise if in front of the right eye (Figure 13.4). If the filter reduces the intensity of the input too greatly, the rotational path is obliterated and the bob again moves in a plane.

Figure 13.4   Actual and apparent paths of a pendulum under conditions producing the Pulfrich phenomenon. The pendulum P swings back and forth in path *A*, but when a filter is placed in front of one eye, reducing the luminosity of the target (pendulum and background) for that eye, the pendulum no longer seems to traverse a plane path. It now seems to traverse an elliptical or rotational path *B*. Various experimental conditions can be used to manipulate the magnitude of this effect, called the Pulfrich phenomenon.

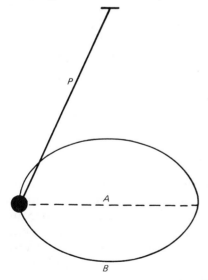

An associate of Pulfrich explained the phenomenon on the basis of reduced stimulation in the eye covered by the filter, increasing the latent time of response in that eye. Whereas corresponding points in the two retinas simultaneously stimulated would react together, the reaction of the points in the filtered eye suffered a delay. This caused a shift in the apparent position of the bob.

Lit (1949) and his associates began to study the phenomenon further. Lit and Hyman (1951) introduced a methodological improvement whereby the seen target was no longer a pendulum bob but rather a dark rod projecting into a horizontal luminous rectangular opening (or field). The rod moved back and forth along the opening, replacing the bob in the original setup. A similar dark rod projected upward into the rectangular field and could be moved in the third dimension (away from the observer) and set so as to appear directly under the oscillating rod at its midexcursion, thus providing a measure of the apparent displacement of the oscillating rod when the observer wore the filter over one eye.

They found that magnitude of the linear velocity of the rod varied with the observation distance while its angular velocity remained the same for all viewing distances. The results were taken to be consistent with the theory and geometric analysis of the phenomenon.

Lit (1959) varied the level of illumination over a range of five logarithmic units and found the precision of depth discrimination to increase twenty-fold. Three different fixations were used and produced different degrees of precision of depth discrimination, except at the very lightest levels of illumination.

Lit (1960) showed that the rod varied in its apparent displacement from the plane of oscillation in accord with oscillation velocity. This result was also taken to be in good agreement with the theory of the Pulfrich phenomenon.

More recent writers (Enright, 1970; Riggs, 1971, and Gregory, 1973) concur essentially on the explanation for the Pulfrich phenomenon already stated.

Perception of Motion of Revolving Plane Targets

One of the most frequently studied targets of the sort referred to here is the trapezoidal window. The Ames trapezoidal window (Ames, 1951) is a plane piece of metal or other material in the form of a trapezoid (Figure 13.5). The mullions of a window are painted on the trapezoid, and thus it has the appearance of a window viewed obliquely. It is pivoted on a vertical axis at about its center and can be rotated by a motor and viewed while in motion. The rate

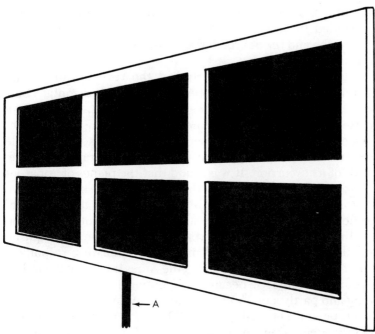

Figure 13.5   The Ames trapezoidal window, consisting simply of a plane sheet of material in the form of a trapezoid with the features of an ordinary window painted on it. This "window" is rotated on a post A. Plain trapezoids are also used to study some of the same effects produced by the simulated window.

of rotation can, of course, be manipulated and used as one of the variables.

While the most common form of the trapezoid used is the one with the window painted on it, the problem of the perceptual results from rotating a plane target can be and has been studied by a plain trapezoid. One of the main things seen as the trapezoid rotates through 360° is that instead of the appearance of a complete rotation, the trapezoid seems to oscillate back and forth.

Day and Power (1965) studied rotary motion in depth, in which the perceptual effect was oscillation instead of complete rotation. They did not confine themselves to the trapezoidal window, or even to a plane trapezoid, but also studied unstructured forms, including an ellipse and three different irregular shapes, as well as a rectangular window. They found that oscillation was seen with all forms used and that the perspective effects in the trapezoidal window do not increase the reversal tendency. The authors reported that their experiments failed to confirm the assumption that misjudgments of orientation are causal.

The outlook of Day and Power on the reversal (or oscillation) effects included the other well-known reversals found in viewing the Necker cube and the Schroeder staircase as well as other motionless targets.

Freeman and Pasnak (1968) studied the reversals in a plain trapezoid in which the linear perspective and the horizontal visual angle subtended by the trapezoid were varied. The amount of angular traverse in the oscillations was measured by a comparison target consisting of a rectangle mounted on a vertical axis and positionable so as to coincide with the apparent position of the trapezoid when at the ends of its excursion. It was found that the planes of apparent reversal were determined both by the amount of linear perspective (the ratio of size of the small end to the large end of the trapezoid) and the horizontal visual angular subtense of the rotating target. Which of the two factors dominated was dependent on the required judgmental task (instructions and means for indicating response)?

Allport and Pettigrew (1957) used the Ames trapezoidal window to test primitive subjects, because perception is partly a product of learning and partly a product of the anatomy and native organization of the species. The authors used 80 observers in four different groups of 20 each. Group A involved urban European boys, group B urban African boys, group C Polela rural African boys, and group D Nogoma rural African boys. The African observers were between the ages of 10 and 14 years as nearly as could be ascertained. Both binocular and monocular viewing were used at two different viewing distances, making, in all, four different conditions.

The pooled results of all four conditions showed a very definite tendency for the urban boys to report the "illusion" more often than the rural boys.

Neurophysiological Experiments

Bartley (1936b) performed certain neurophysiological experiments that were quite parallel to many of the standard perceptual (psychophysical) studies on apparent visual movement. Using an optic setup that would sequentially stimulate two parts of the retina in the rabbit, he recorded from various areas in the cortex. Naturally, he was not able to deal with the rabbit's sensory response but was interested in how various portions of the animal's optic cortex reacted as the timing of the two photic inputs was varied.

He showed that certain cortical points could be found in which the two retinal inputs facilitated each other when applied simultaneously but would nearly eliminate the cortical record when separated slightly in time. When stimulus A later failed to elicit a response of its own, A still augmented the response when A and B were both delivered and reduced the size of B when out of phase with B.

Among the conclusions drawn from the total results was the fact that the interaction between cortical points was more widespread than that between retinal points. This investigation was only a pioneering one, but it did demonstrate the feasibility of making an extensive study of the neural conditions for apparent movement.

Visual Movement and Causality

The perception of movement entails not only the perception of displacement in space, but also a factor of *causality.* Michotte (1946) used a large vertical screen containing a horizontal slot through which two blocks were visible. These could be moved along behind the slot in either direction, at different rates, and in different relation to each other. For example, if B were stationary at mid position along the slot and A moved along toward B and if B began to move away from A as soon as it was touched, the impression was given that A *caused* B to move. Various temporal arrangements of A and B moving were used. Some definitely gave the impression of A *causing* B to move. (See description 38, p. 226 in *Perception in Everyday Life.*)

TACTUAL MOVEMENT

We are now ready to deal with apparent tactual movement. There is no doubt that the visual modality provides for both apparent and real movement by way of its own mechanisms.

Tactile stimuli may traverse the skin surface and be felt as something moving. Of this there is no doubt. The experiences of tactile movement aroused by successions of stationary stimuli have also been reported. Burtt (1917b) reported on results that he labeled tactual illusions of movement. The factors manipulated were temporal intervals between contacts with the skin, durations of contact, and spatial separations between contacts.

He found that, in general, the greater the distance between contacts, the greater was the time interval needed to produce apparent movement. Also, he found that the greater the intensity of contacts, the less time was needed to obtain or maintain movement and that the greater the distance between contacts, the greater their intensities needed to be for movement. Furthermore, when the intensity of the second contact was made greater than that of the first, movement in the reverse direction was sometimes produced. These results followed Korte's laws for visual apparent movement.

Shortening durations of contacts proceeded in the direction of producing the impression of simultaneity or the fusion of the two contacts. Increasing duration of the contacts tended in the direction of producing the experience of tactile movement. Of course, when very great durations were used, impressions of discrete succession of the contacts was produced.

Hulin (1935) varied the separations of his two stimuli from simultaneity up to 300 milliseconds between the ending of the first contact and the beginning of the second. The spatial separations varied from 5 to 150 millimeters. In the many thousands of trials used, about 30 percent yielded some form of apparent movement. The forms of movement were classified into full, end, inner, and bow movement. Taken together these were called optimal movement. Hulin was unable to verify Korte's law for the relation between space and time.

Hulin deduced that there were four principal factors at work to produce the experience reported: pressure irradiation, perseveration and associated factors, visual imagery, and kinesthesis.

Bow Movement

Bow movement is the experience of movement from one place on the skin to another, but instead of the path of the movement being confined to the skin or body, it bows into the air above the skin surface. DeHardt (1961) studied apparent tactual movement, including bow movement. She called the movement perceived as progressing on the skin, "on-skin movement." The other movement perceived (whether actually tactual or not) she called "off-skin movement;" this was the kind others have named bow movement. DeHardt found that the time interval *(TI)* to produce either on-skin or off-skin movement did not have to be inversely related to contact duration *(D)* as was expected. She found that the frequency of obtaining on-skin movement was inversely related to *TI*. The completeness of on-skin movement was also inversely related to *TI*. Both quantity and quality of on-skin movement were greatly dependent on the pliability of the skin tissue. With her longer time intervals, the frequency of off-skin movement was directly related to both time interval and spatial separation between contacts. She also concluded that the experience of off-skin movement is dependent on considerable "time" and "room" and that this movement is the result of exciting appropriate visual images.

Many astute observers who have had the experiences of bow

movement have come to the sure realization that what they were reporting on in bow movement was visualized movement elicited by tactual stimulation. They tended to call it "illusory." Bow movement from tactual stimulation seems to be another case of associative imagery, which we have already described in other connections.

Another difference between bow movement and strictly tactual apparent movement is that bow movement contains none of the true tactual feeling quality, whereas true tactual apparent movement actually *feels* as though something is dragged across the skin.

The two forms of movement elicited tactually bear on what we have already said about the tactual modality not being spatial in the sense that it pertains to space away from the body. The distinction seems to be corroborated by the results we have been discussing, which point toward the conclusion that that which is really tactual is body-confined and that not all experiences elicited by tactual stimuli need be tactual in the strict sense. However, some of them are so intimately connected with the tactual that many observers fail to be aware of the distinction just made.

AUDITORY MOVEMENT

The question of whether the experience of movement elicited by stationary tactual stimuli is actually tactual is the same sort of question to ask in regard to the movement experiences produced by stationary auditory stimuli. It is taken for granted that acoustic sources undergoing physical displacement in space produce genuine auditory movement experiences. We need to consider what happens when using stationary stimuli.

Mathieson (1931) studied phenomenal movement produced by acoustic stimulation producing clicks whose intervals were controlled. She also controlled illumination. The object of the investigation was to determine the compulsory conditions for auditory movement experience after the manner involved in visual experiments. No compulsory conditions were found. With the conditions used, movement experiences were obtained in only 4 percent of the 6000 trials involved. Experiences called movement experiences included all the cases in which some sort of "filling in" took place between the first and second experiences produced by the pair of stimuli. The movement experiences were accomplished by visualization, according to Mathieson. The range of intervals within which movements were found did not tally closely with phenomenal reduction of distance. Conditions of dichotic hearing seemed the most favorable for filling in, or movement. The failure to obtain good movement would seem to be due to the use of click-producing stimuli rather than to some less abrupt and quickly terminating sound sources.

Burtt (1917a) studied what he called auditory illusions of movement. He found a rather definite relation between the duration of stimulation and the interval between exposures needed for the movement experience. If the intensity of the second stimulus was greater than that of the first, the apparent movement was often experienced in the reverse direction. The longer the exposure, the shorter was the optimal interval for producing movement.

Chapter 14
Illusions

The popular name for some perceptual responses is *illusion*. This view is based on the idea that perceptions are copies of what is external to the individual and that an illusion is a "mistaken perception," that is, a mistaken copy of Nature.

According to the scientific view, a perception is a copy of nothing. Objects do not exist except in experience. What does exist in the stimulus world are arrays or patterns of energy impinging on sense organs. Once those impingements are processed by the nervous system, the end results are perceptions that may be in the form of conscious experience or overt reaction, or even something unconscious just as long as the end result is a product of the total organism—as a person.

There is just as lawful a basis for a perception being "illusory" as for it not being at other times.

It should be recognized that a stimulus array that reaches a sense organ is often open to alternate forms of processing. A number of things within the organism determine which alternative will operate to give the final result, the perceptual response. Moreover, factors from more than a single sense modality may be concurrently operating and the weight of one modality may be greater than the other. To call an illusion a mistaken perception is to lead nowhere. It is to imply lawfulness has broken down.

The illusions that have had the most prominent place in textbooks, particularly the early texts, have been the visual ones. The classical examples have been geometrical figures rather than cases found in everyday life situations. They have historical interest and we could bypass them except that they illustrate earlier concepts and some that still linger today. Theories meant to account for illusions have fallen into several classes: (1) eye movement theories, (2) theories regarding limited acuity, (3) theories assuming physiological confusion, (4) empathy theories, (5) pregnance or good figure theories, and (6) perspective theories. We shall not dwell on each of these but may exemplify one.

Harvey Carr (1934) produced an eye movement theory. He believed that in inspecting a geometric figure, the eyes will respond by passing over unfilled space more easily than filled space. Practice reduces the illusory effects by reducing the hesitancy of eye movements. Authors who followed him made his theory untenable, for example, those who studied stabilized images.

Figure 14.1   An open cube similar to the classical reversible cube. Closer inspection shows that it contains an absurdity, a physical impossibility if the cube were literally to represent a three-dimensional structure.

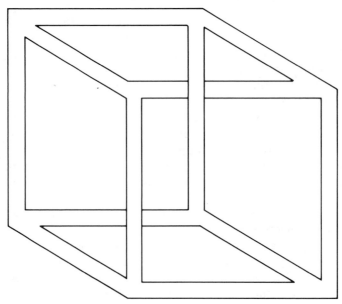

A fundamental question may be asked at this point. Would the geometric figures drawn on a two-dimensional surface be illusory if they were taken to represent something three dimensional?

Another fundamental consideration is that one can construct on a two-dimensional surface a configuration that in the main seems to be a three-dimensional representation but which has features that cannot exist in an actual three-dimensional structure. In other words, it is possible to produce absurdities and monstrosities on paper. They are interesting compositions but contain conflicting elements within them. The absurdities become apparent in some of these constructions; some are fairly simple constructions, such as the example in Figure 14.1, and some are elaborate as in Escher's painting, *Belvedere*, a piece of elaborate architecture.

SOME CLASSICAL ILLUSIONS

Let us examine several classical illusions as seen in Figure 14.2. This simple figure is not usually treated as a three-dimensional representation. It consists of four lines, two horizontal ones, and two lines that tilt from the vertical. Whereas when viewed as a two-dimensional construct, the horizontal lines that are the same in metrical length are seen as unequal and this is the "illusion." If, however, the construction is seen as three dimensional, then the perceptual inequality of the lines is no longer called illusory. The tilted lines are seen as sides of a walk or road and so converge toward a vanishing point. The upper line is now seen as farther away than the lower one and so naturally will be seen as longer than the lower one. It

Figure 14.2   The Ponzo illusion.

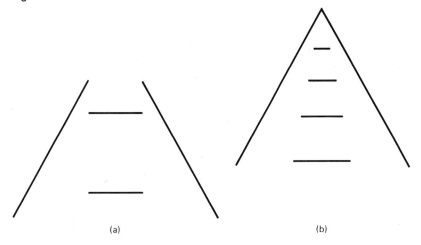

(a)   (b)

covers a larger part of the distance between the two sides of the road. No one would have called the construction an illusion if it had been a picture of a roadway or walk although it would have contained the same essential geometric features.

Not all classical geometric illusions are as easily seen as representing something three dimensional as the Ponzo illusion.

The Poggendorff illusion (Figure 14.3) is a case in point. There are two parallel lines in this figure that seem to be the edges of a parallelogram, or panel. At one side of the panel an oblique line emerges and at the other side, a second oblique line. Metrically, the second line is a "continuation" of the first, but it does not look that way. Thus we have an example of an illusion. If we see the overall configuration as a three-dimensional construct, the two lines are simply two ends of a single line. They represent something in the third dimension, for example, the side of a walk or road. Although they lie in the third dimension, the parallelogram is an upright structure obstructing part of the side of the walk or road represented by the two oblique lines, portions of the road.

In Figure 14.3 the illusion with two variants is shown. One (b) contains only short diagonals that do not seem to be portions of the same line. In (a) the lines are considerably larger and the illusion is largely if not entirely eliminated. The diagonals are more readily seen as something lying in the third dimension—the side of a road, for example. Thus they are parts of a single line. If instead of diagonals, the two lines were made to lie at right angles to the parallels, they would be seen as the two ends of the same line, simply a line obscured by the parallels that are seen as edges of a

Figure 14.3   The Poggendorf illusion.

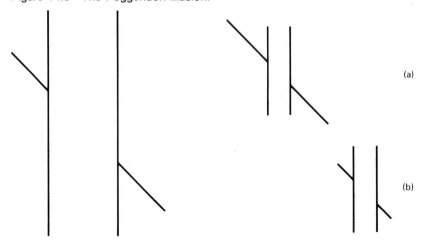

(a)

(b)

solid panel. The two lines would be horizontal and therefore could represent the horizon. So from case to case we may move back and forth from seeing the figure represent something two dimensional to something three dimensional. Through training or through some other factor, we see it one way or another.

There is still another variation that can be made with the figure—the rotation of the whole figure around the axis of regard. This kind of manipulation was made by Anton (1976). He showed that depending on this rotation and on the angle of emergence of the diagonals from the panel (the parallels), there would be some illusion varying from zero to maximum. No recognition was given to the three dimensionality of the figure, however.

In the Ebbinghaus illusion (Figure 14.4) the two inner circles seem unequal. If one attempts to make them equal it is only by a bit of intellectualization, if at all. This is done by assuming the circles are at different distances away. But this is a kind of two-step process rather than a direct reaction to them perceptually.

Now let us get to the *most* commonly referred to illusion— the Müller–Lyer figure (Figure 14.5). Here we have two equal length segments of a horizontal line, but they do not appear equal in length. What can we say in this case? The line with its two metrically equal segments are not the only parts of the figure. At the end of one

Figure 14.4   The Ebbinghaus illusion.

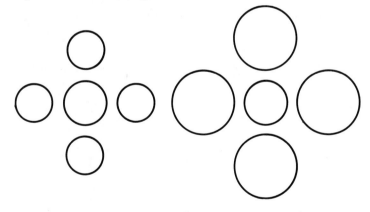

Figure 14.5   The Müller–Lyer illusion.

segment the wings, or short lines, are directed toward the line itself, and at the end of the other segment the wings are directed away from the line. The first thing to recognize is that while the issue or task at hand is supposedly to compare the lengths of the two lines, the perceiver can scarcely perform the task as implied. The viewer is dealing with a configuration that *includes* the wings. They are playing their roles. When one takes a ruler or measuring device and compares the lengths of the lines, the wings are excluded in every sense of the word. If and when the viewer is able to exclude the wings perceptually he or she sees the lines as equal. There is no "mistaken" perception. It is not logically fair to make comparisons between perception and metrical measurements unless the same target limitations apply to both. But this is overlooked in calling the figure an illusion. Among other things, it is a failure to recognize and properly utilize the principles governing configurations. If perception here has given us an illusion, we should better say that perception by its nature is unable in this case to make the selective analysis required. This is different from thinking of perception making mistakes: now and then, not being lawful. The "mistake" is determined by how we conceptualize the matter.

In natural scenes, such as of buildings and rooms, the perpendiculars that represent corners are the analogs of the two linear components of the Müller–Lyer illusion. In a building scene the corners are as in (b) of Figure 14.6. In the room the corners are as in (a). In the first case one is at some distance from such a corner in everyday life, and in the second case one is within the room and the corner is nearby.

Figure 14.6 Components of the Müller–Lyer figure in two natural situations.

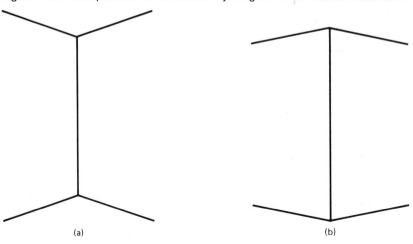

(a)   (b)

THE MOON ILLUSION

The moon illusion, so-called, derives from the fact that the moon at the horizon looks very much larger than when at its zenith in the sky. A number of explanations for this have been given. Here again, it would take undue space to recount all of them. The oldest explanation dates back to the second century, to Ptolemy. His explanation elicits no conviction among the present-day theorists. Whereas Ptolemy said the horizon moon looked farther away than the zenith moon, Boring (1943) found that his subjects reported just the opposite. He went further and varied the subjects' head position in viewing the moon. The illusion was present when the subjects looked at the zenith moon by raising their eyes but not when they lifted their heads and looked directly at it. Boring went even further and had his subjects lie on their backs and look at the zenith moon. In this case when the subjects compared what they said with what they saw in looking at the horizon moon, the zenith moon was larger.

Kaufman and Rock (1962) seemed to negate Boring's work. They had their subjects look through a viewer at an artificial moon at zenith, and another one pointed toward the horizon, and reported that the angle of elevation had only a small effect.

What all these investigators (theorists) were considering was some form of an apparent-distance theory. Kaufman and Rock on the basis of the fact that apparent distance of the moon seems to be influenced by what it is seen against at the horizon, believed that the matter had been settled. Some others have not felt so sure.

Restle (1970) studied the moon illusion and like others, felt he had explained the phenomenon. His theory, too, was that the moon looks small when high in the sky, not because it seems close as some have said, but because of the broad extent of the sky to the horizon. He stated that there is no physical basis for the illusion, therefore it has to be a psychological phenomenon. This is a typical statement that leaves room for the uninitiated to maintain his or her typical mind–body dual causal system.

Nelson and Ladan (1969) studied perception under several field conditions. The impetus for this study was the moon illusion. They reconstructed the natural condition of seeing the moon high in the sky and near the horizon in a laboratory setting. This provided for the study of variables in isolation and in combination. The variables were eye elevation (looking upward and on the horizontal), photic gradients, characteristics of terrain, apparent distance, and movement.

While it has been customary to attempt to account for the illusion by employing single theoretical propositions, it was found that such unifactor theories are not sufficient for explaining the phenomenon. Since Nelson and Ladan's study involved quantitative measurements of illusory effects, they were able to test some of the unitary theories. Although some of them operated in the right direction, no single factor accounted fully for the moon illusion.

The authors found that terrain factors consisting of both texture gradients of space and objects had great influence although not in themselves sufficient explanation of the illusion. Eye elevation and photic gradients produced size effects. The factors that did seem to have an effect in isolation, did not combine in an additive way.

AN ILLUSION IN VISUAL MOVEMENT

If two spotlike sources of illumination are moved together in a dimly or "unlighted" situation, they may not appear to do so. Let us say these two sources are parts of an arrangement that one can hold in the hand and wave quickly back and forth. The bright spot moves over the whole or nearly whole excursion of the hand while the dimmer one may move more slowly and thus not cover the whole excursion. Of course, the results depend on the rate of actual target movement, the relative intensities of the two sources and even other factors. The failure of the dim spot to go along with and keep up with the bright one is quite an unexpected result when first observed. Incidently, I observed this during World War II while in visual research at Dartmouth and for most of the time since had forgotten it until the appearance of a report by Oetting and Oetting (1974). The authors obtained the same results in principle and discussed the causes dealing most with the illusion, including the reaction times to weak stimuli.

AUDITORY AND TACTUAL ILLUSIONS

What some might call auditory and visual illusions were dealt with in the preceding chapter in describing the experience of apparent movement. Custom has called such phenomena "apparent," rather than illusory.

You will recall that we have previously considered false localization of sound and gave an interesting example that led to the discussion of *ventriloquism.*

THE SIZE-WEIGHT ILLUSION

Stevens and Rubin (1970) studied the size-weight illusion by the method of magnitude estimation. The objects varied in volume, weight, and density. Three conclusions were drawn.

1. For a constant volume, perceived heaviness increases as a power function of weight—the greater the volume, the greater the exponent of the power function. These power functions converge in the region of the heaviest weight the subject can lift.
2. For a constant density, perceived heaviness fails to grow as a power function of weight.
3. For a given weight, heaviness decreases as a logarithmic function of volume. The constants of the logarithmic function depend in an orderly way on weight. This study will be seen as a good way to investigate why a pound of feathers seems lighter than a pound of lead.

Colon (1960) found that congenitally blind subjects can experience the size-weight illusion.

Other illusions including some of those presently discussed are dealt with by authors such as Gregory (1973), Swisher and Mandes (1974), Letourneau (1976), Jeager (1975), and Hill (1974).

ILLUSION IN LIFTING WEIGHTS

Davis, Taylor, and Brickett (1977) studied weight illusion that is occasioned by lifting movements. The perceived relative heaviness of lifted objects was found to depend on whether they were lifted vigorously or gently. Objects lifted gently generally felt heavier than those lifted vigorously. The results were discussed in connection with the classical time-order error.

TASTE ILLUSIONS

Certain taste effects can be classed as illusions according to Bartoshuk (1974a), who gives some examples. With reference to the substance, phenylthiocarbomide (PTC), people may be divided into two classes—"tasters" and "nontasters." This difference has been attributed to a simple Mendelian dominance system. It is supposed that the nontasters carry two recessive genes. At first, the sensitivity to PTC was believed to be mediated by saliva. The substance was thought to be rendered tasteless by the saliva of the nontasters. The more recent conclusion is that the effect is unrelated to the saliva. Supposedly nontasters possess one receptor site for bitter taste, while the tasters possess two distinct receptors.

For example, caffeine seems to stimulate both these receptors. Both tasters and nontasters can get a bitter taste from caffeine, but for the nontasters it is far less intense. However, the concentration of caffeine in coffee is so low that the nontasters do not taste the caffeine. So here we have what, under some circumstances, is a very unexpected result and thus "illusory."

Artichokes provide for another unexpected result. For some persons, water tastes sweet after eating artichokes. This illusory effect is an example of one of the adaptation-mediated water tastes. It is now known that water tastes differently depending on the character of the substance that is ingested preceding it. A common example is that water tastes bitter-sour following adaptations to NaCl. The taste one gets from distilled water may come from previous adaptations to NaCl: adaptation is an effect that lingers for many minutes. Water may take on any of the four primary tastes (salt, sour, sweet, or bitter) under the right adaptation conditions.

Bartoshuk mentions a third case in which illusory results may occur. There is a climbing plant found in India, Ceylon, and parts of Africa, that white people have called *Gymnema sylvestre* which natives have believed to be medicinal. The effect of ingesting its leaves is to suppress the taste of sweetness, for example, sugar in one's tea. It not only inhibits sweetness but also bitterness and to some extent saltiness. The leaves themselves taste bitter-salty and the effect in suppressing bitterness and saltiness of other substances is an artifact of cross-adaptation. For proper testing of the adaptation effect the leaves of the plant must be rinsed from the tongue. The effect of one substance on another is different when both substances are in the mouth at the same time from when one precedes the other and has been rinsed from the mouth.

Still another example of an unexpected (illusory) effect was given by Bartoshuk. This time she described the effects of the berries from another African plant (tree). They were called miracle fruit by Europeans. After eating these berries, fruit such as lemons, which are usually very sour, tastes extremely sweet and can be readily eaten with pleasure. The natives used the berries of miracle fruit to change the taste of sour wine and spoiled foods to their original palatability. These miracle fruit plants have been grown in Florida and one company chose to use the substance as another artificial sweetener for coffee, tea, and other foods.

Two unlike theories have been offered for the miracle fruit effect. One proposes it as a sour-suppressor. The other theory proposes that miracle fruit adds sweetness to sour substances. Both theories are a little too complicated to be made clear here.

SUMMARY ON ILLUSIONS

It can be concluded that the perceptual end results called illusions are not examples of unique principles at work, but are cases of the basic principles that apply to other perceptions.

Perceptual response is a result dependent on two sets of factors, the stimulus input (impingement) *and* the neural context into which the input enters. This means that we can expect perceiving to possess alternatives. A reaction to a given pattern of input need not be of only one kind.

Speaking specifically, it can be said that in vision, the organism can treat a two-dimensional display as representing something two dimensional or three dimensional. The consequent perception may be "illusory" or "real." The criteria for this may lie in ineffective motor response or a learned ideational context. The term *conflict* is more applicable to "illusions" than the term, "mistake."

Chapter 15
Perceptual Learning and Change

THE PROBLEM

E. J. Gibson (1963) defined perceptual learning as "any relatively permanent and consistent change in the perception of a stimulus array, following practice or experience with this array." This definition seems to emphasize two things—practice and the relative permanence of the result—and therefore is a statement about perceptual change as seen or dealt with from the learning psychologist's standpoint. If we are to look at the matter from the standpoint of perception, the question is what the organism is prepared to do immediately and what it does as a consequence of a series of confrontments with the new stimulus situation.

Undoubtedly, it will seem that in dealing with perceptual learning we are part of the time showing what the perceptual response to new impingement conditions is in comparison to the old and part of the time demonstrating that the organism can change its perceptual response even to an old set of outside conditions. In any case, the focal consideration is the fact of *perceptual change,* particularly in the fully developed organism.

A fundamental question in this chapter is whether or not the same principles are involved in the modification of perception in adulthood as were involved in the development of perceptual response in the first place.

Perceptual learning, and other modification, involves the participation of the muscle system. This system manipulates the relation of the organism to the environmental conditions (energies) to which the organism must react. With this participation as inescapable, there must be a lawful relation between what muscle systems do and the interpretation given the environment through such senses as vision. This poses the problem of conducting visual perceptual experimentation in such ways as to answer various questions regarding the relation between muscle and visual activities. Or, put another way, it requires the recognition of the possibility that muscle activity is part of the actual visual performance. A pertinent question at this point, then, is whether muscle participation is involved in the same way in bringing about initial perceptual development as in modifying perception later on in adulthood.

INVERSION OF THE RETINAL IMAGE

One of the earliest experimental investigations of perceptual modification and adaptability was that of Stratton (1897), who conducted an investigation in which the relation between the image on the retina and the visual target were reversed. It is well known that with a simple lens system such as the eye, the image of the target is inverted—that is, what is the top of some item in the external world is represented at the bottom in the image. We say the image is upside down. This causes many people to ask why we do not see things upside down, a natural kind of question to ask when we do not realize that the essential feature of image pattern and its relation to externality is *stability* and its *ordinal connection* with externality. By this is meant that the results of responding on the basis of a retinal image must always turn out the same. This property of stability can best be illustrated by our relation to the gravitational system. If sometimes when you stepped off the edge of a platform you fell downward and other times you just kept on walking out into space and at still other times something else happened, you could not function at all. This is the same way with the visual image, its position on the retina and its shape and size and its movements across the retina. They must always lead to the same successful motor reaction as a response. When the various internal parts of the image are considered, this stability of relation is spoken of as ordinal stability. The question is what happens when stability is disturbed. If disturbance were variable and ever changing, little or nothing could be learned by it. So when a change is to be made for experimental purposes, it must generally be a stable kind of change.

Stratton had his subject wear a lens system on one eye that inverted the already upside-down image. The other eye was kept blindfolded. Thus he provided a wholly *new* but stable set of relations between image and externality for his subject, who now "saw" objects in a new way. When the subject reached for something, he or she reached in the wrong direction. When he or she heard sounds, the subject heard them coming from the wrong direction. Wearing the lens greatly disrupted the auditory motor behavior as well as the visual. Accomplishing the simplest acts involved a great deal of fumbling and grasping. Placing food in the mouth was difficult but only when he or she relied on visual sense for guidance. With the experimental eye closed, the subject could rely on kinesthesis with no conflict. The disorientation continued for three days before it abated, and at the end of eight days a new visuomotor coordination became fairly effective. But, on removal of the lens, disorientation was again set up. It disappeared, however, more quickly than the disruption on first wearing the lens.

Snyder and Pronko (1952) performed the same general investigation. The lenses were worn for 30 days. One conclusion of this investigation was the difference between the "natural" characteristic of perception and its characteristic under critical and analytical conditions. For example, when toward the latter part of the investigation a subject was asked whether a given scene looked upside down, the mere asking of the question abruptly changed how things looked. What looked all right (right side up) the instant before now began to look upside down. He or she stated that when it was recalled how the scene had looked before wearing the glasses, the subject had to say that it now looked upside down. He or she had been unaware of it and had not given a thought to the question of right side upness or upside downness.

The requirement for normal effective perception seems to be harmonious interaction among the various modalities of response. If they are in harmony, the scene looks all right and is right side up; if not, various forms of perceptual anomaly and trouble set in.

THE EFFECT OF PROLONGED WEARING OF SIZE LENSES

In recent years a second kind of change in retinal image relation to externality was instituted as an experimental tool. Manipulation with the use of size lenses was made at the Dartmouth Eye Institute. An axis-90 meridional size lens worn in front of one eye distorts the appearance of certain environments in certain ways. Wearing size lenses therefore constitutes one set of conditions in which perception is altered. The most relevant question is whether during prolonged wearing of the lens, initial distortions in the visual field slowly or finally disappear. That is, can the visual mechanism adapt to the new conditions and enable the wearer to see things as he or she did prior to wearing the lens? This question was studied by Burian (1943).

Wearing an axis-90 lens in front of one eye not only distorts the field but causes discomfort, in general, such as eyestrain and nervous tension. The ambient wearer has to make motor adjustments owing to the conflict between where things look to be and where they are reached for or where one steps. One feels insecure, especially in precarious situations such as in traffic. The disruption in visual perception is not as complete as it was in the Stratton and Snyder–Pronko experiments but nevertheless is real and crucial.

Burian used three subjects all of whom wore the size lens all through their waking hours for from eight to fourteen days. The original effects gradually wore off, although environments lacking the usual features of rectilinear perspective found in rooms with edges of doors, windows, tables, walls, floors, and ceilings still posed problems.

The longer the lens was worn, the less noticeable were the distortions in the visual field and finally disappeared and remained absent as long as the environment contained abundant features of linear perspective. The change in image size produced by the lens showed some reduction, after wearing the lens, but was not obliterated even when perception improved. Hence it was not considered likely that the disappearance of perceptual distortion was to be attributed solely to peripheral factors but rather included central factors, often spoken of as psychological.

When the lenses were removed from the subjects' eyes, there was shift in the location of objects but in a direction opposite to the shift produced when the lenses were first worn. The effect lingered for from one to three days. With precise measuring instruments, some effect could be demonstrated for a week or ten days after lens removal.

LEARNING IN FORM PERCEPTION

Reafference and Exafference

Holst and Mittelstadt (1950) concluded from their work on animals that the role of body movement in vision is of two kinds: (1) one involved when movements are self-produced (active movement) and

(2) one when movements are produced by an outside agent (passive movement). The changes in sensory stimulation that stem from active movement were called *reafference* and those consequent on passive movement *exafference*. For an animal to orient itself effectively in space, it must be able to distinguish between the two sorts of input and to utilize them differently. This means that changes in the visual target that are associated with active movement are dealt with differently from changes in the same target that are associated with passive movement. This sounds plausible enough and most anyone would assent to the surface meaning of the statement. But there is more to the matter than appears on the surface. The focal question is whether the animal can learn equally well under conditions of exafference and reafference, or whether it would be possible to learn at all under exafference.

Experiments with Prisms

A way to test the problem just posed is to require subjects to wear prisms before one eye while occluding the other. This changes the relation between externality and the spatial information provided by the retinal image.

One sort of investigation conducted by Held and Schlank (1959) was based on the fact that the effective location of visual targets can be altered by interposing a prism between them and the perceiver. If the perceiver is asked to point to or reach for the object seen, he or she will mispoint or misreach. Helmholtz many years ago asserted that, with practice, the perceiver under such conditions can learn to reach in more nearly the right direction or the right amount. Furthermore, when the original conditions are reinstated, the perceiver finds himself or herself again in trouble. One misreaches in the direction opposite to ones misreaching under the original conditions. The classical interpretation has been that the perceiver comes to recognize the error and consequently corrects for it. Held doubted this interpretation. He supposed that a single basic mechanism underlies both the *acquisition* of skill in the first place and *adaptation* to changes in the stimulus situation later on. He felt that simply an error-correcting mechanism could scarcely account for developing the skilled performance in the first place. The experiments of Held and his co-workers are numerous so we can describe only a few of them here.

Held and Schlank (1959) performed the following experiment. Using an apparatus consisting of a light box with upper and lower compartments, subjects marked the apparent location of a target contained in the upper compartment (Figure 15.1). The image of

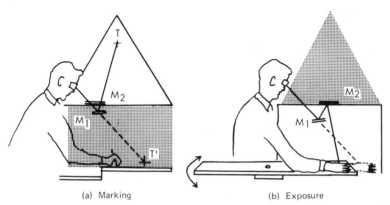

(a) Marking   (b) Exposure

Figure 15.1 Held and Schlank's experiment using a prism to change the apparent location of the visual target. (Source: R. Held and M. Schlank. "Adaptation to disarranged eye–hand coordination in the distance dimension," *Amer. J. Psychol.,* 1959, 72, 603–605, Fig. 1.)

the target was reflected to the eye by a fully reflecting mirror below the half-silvered mirror that formed the partition between the two compartments. The hand was in the lower compartment, and whether it or the target was visible depended on which compartment was illuminated. A biting board secured the subject's head in a fixed position. In the first part of the task the subject saw not his or her hand but only the target. In the next part of the task the subject saw his or her hand at an increased optical distance owing to the combined optical action of the two mirrors. This apparent increase in distance was about three inches at the level of the marking surface. One form of movement was made through the subject's own efforts (active movement). In the other, the experimenter moved the swiveled cradle supporting the arm and hand (passive movement). The question then was how much, if any, adaptation (compensatory or corrective adjustment) would occur by virtue of either type of movement.

The compensatory shift following active arm movement was significant in amount and in the right direction, whereas the change with passive movement was essentially zero. Thus the results of the investigation supported the Holst–Mittelstadt *reafference* hypothesis.

The question of what conditions are required to achieve full compensation for visual arrangement of the environment was considered by Held and Bossom (1961). They were also concerned with whether the same principle seemed to hold for compensation for errors (adaptation) as have been shown to be involved in the development of perception in the first place. Riesen and Aarons (1959) found that gross bodily movements under natural conditions of exposure were needed for the development of perception in their experimental animals.

Held and Bossom seated their subjects in a revolving chair that could be rotated by leg movements. The position of the subject's head was fixed by a bite-board which rotated around the same axis as the subject's body. A drum 5 feet in diameter was mounted so as to be revolvable around the same axis as the subject, with its midlevel at the subject's eye level. Targets located inside the drum were a luminous vertical 2-inch slit and a vertical line when room illumination was used. The view of the line was restricted so as not to include any information relating to direction based on drum position or other visual cues. During target exposure the subject wore goggles that eliminated all but 60° of the central field of each eye. Each eye viewed this field through a 20-diopter prism that caused an 11° lateral deviation of the field.

Two experimental conditions were used. *Preactivity* of self-produced movement was provided by having the subject, wearing the prisms, walk along a path lined with trees and an occasional building. Equivalent *passive* movement was provided by having the subject pushed along the same path in a wheelchair.

In experiment I, 15 subjects were given two one-hour pretest activity trials of walking along the path. In one trial they wore base-right prisms, in the other base-left prisms. At least one day separated the trials. As a result, these subjects compensated for a little more than 10 percent of the prism-induced errors when tested in the chair-drum setup. The subjects with passive motion manifested negative, nonsignificant amounts of shift.

In experiment 2, 15 subjects walked 11 to 21 hours distributed over four days of pretest activity. Eight of the 15 attained full compensation for the prism-produced distortions of the visual field. The other subjects did not reach full compensation by the end of the four days. Two subjects run with passive pretest exposure manifested no significant compensation even with the four-day exposure.

The investigators believed that the similarity of exposure times needed for *adaptation* (compensation) to the rearrangement and for *development* of effective perception in the first place is to be interpreted as evidence for an identical mechanism involved in both.

Whereas in Held and Bossom's study full compensation for *rearrangement* of the visual environment such as produced by wearing prisms was tested, the question of the nature and consequences of *disarrangement* of the environment was entertained in the following study. The conditions that had been used in *re*arrangement involved the subject's exposure to transformations in the relation between motor output and sensory feedback in an isomorphic, continuous, and time-independent manner. In other words, an essentially lawful connection was maintained between the movements made and their effective consequences. In *dis*arrangement a fundamentally different set of conditions was used in which no fixed and stable connections between body movements and their consequences existed. This can be illustrated in other situations. For example, when the individual is in weightlessness, he or she may flail the arms, make stepping movements, and do all sorts of things and find that there is an unpredictable relation between his or her movements and their consequences.

Such conditions are not attainable for most experimenters, however; but there are laboratory setups in which discrepancies between perceived object positions and where the objects can be successfully reached for are varied during pretest exposure. These conditions are achieved by using *rotary prisms*. A rotary prism is an optical system of two wedge prisms whose mutual relations can be suddenly changed at any time or amount or changed slowly in a sequential pattern decided by the experimenter. For example, when two equal wedge prisms are placed with their bases opposite, their combined refractive effect is zero. When their bases are together, their effects add and are maximum. So if by some means one prism is rotated in relation to the other, which is held in a fixed position, the amount of perceived shift in the position of target is varied. Using such an optical arrangement, we find that there is no fixed relation between the reafferent effect of muscle activity and the seen position of the target. The authors suspected that after some exposure to such conditions, the ability of the subject to use reafference might become impaired, which would be evidenced in increased ambiguity in response to relevant sensory signals.

Held and Freedman (1963) used *dis*arrangement. They used a prism of variable power whose maximum was 40 diopters. Otherwise, their general setup was the same as for testing simple *re*arrangement. Although the rotation of the prisms went through fixed cycles during testing, the variation in the positions of the marks showed no covariation with the cycles, indicating that no learning of the cycles was taking place.

The reduction in the accuracy of the markings indicated that the eye–hand control system was being degraded in the dimension specific to the time-varying factor of the prism strength. Eight subjects were later tested for the difference between the effects of *passive* and *active* movement conditions. It was found that the same degrading of test behavior did not result from the passive movement conditions. This seemed to show that *active* movement under *dis*arrangement conditions brings about the degradation. Passive movement is neither an aid to compensatory achievement in rearrangement nor a means of degradation of eye–hand control in conditions of disarrangement.

Two Types of Adaptation to an Optically Rotated Field

The experiments on adaptation to optically rearranged visual fields far from tell the whole story. Accordingly, certain other experiments were made. It seemed from the well-known results of first Wundt (1898) and then J. J. Gibson (1933) that viewing certain targets was a process that in itself produced changes in the viewer. Gibson reported several experiments of this sort. The effect of parallel lines looking curved through wedge prisms tended to diminish, if not totally disappear, on extended viewing. When the prisms were removed, the straight lines of the target again appeared curved but in the opposite direction. The same effect was noticed when a subject viewed a target with a line tilted slightly off the vertical. Soon it might tend to look vertical, but then if a vertical line were presented, it looked tilted but in the opposite direction. This type of experiment was the forerunner of the study of figural aftereffects by Köhler and Wallach (1944). Since such effects differ from those mentioned in the previous section, there seem to be two types of adaptation.

Mikaelian and Held (1964) studied these by studying the *aftereffects* of viewing environments through prisms that rotated the retinal images 20°. In experiment I the pretest environment was a long hallway. One group of subjects performed active movements while wearing the prisms. The other group was given passive experience in the same pathway in the hall. These latter subjects failed to achieve full and exact compensation as tested by adjusting a line to the vertical and by making equivalent shifts in the egocentric location of the two target points. The subjects who made active movements achieved full and exact compensations.

In experiment 2 the subjects were placed in a figured environment in which gridlike patterns of straight lines were involved. Active exposure to this environment while wearing prisms resulted in the same shifts as for the first environment. There were no shifts produced, however, for passive movement in the environment.

The results confirmed the criteria that the workers had outlined in the beginning for distinguishing aftereffects produced as a result of wearing prisms in a normal environment and under Gibson's conditions. The aftereffects produced by prisms were of the following:

1. They reached a magnitude equivalent to the rotation of the visual field produced by wearing the prisms.
2. They required self–produced movement (active movement) of the wearer of the prisms.
3. They showed up not only as an apparent tilting of the line target but also in the egocentric location of single tested points in the field remote from the line.

Gibson's aftereffect was suggested as not exceeding 2 or 3° tilt and not requiring any active movement of the observer and occurring without accompanying shifts in the subjective location of points in the visual field.

Held and Mikaelian (1964) went still further. They faced the suggestion that passive movement (being moved by wheelchair) failed to produce results typical of active movement situations because "need" was lacking in the passive movement. They examined results produced when instead of being moved by someone else pushing the wheelchair, the subjects propelled the chair themselves. The investigation showed that the subjects who propelled themselves by wheelchair manifested little, if any, compensation for the prism effect despite their *need* to deal with directional errors and to take advantage of the information.

FELT POSITION OF BODY PART IN REACHING RESPONSE

Several investigators have believed that adaptation to target rearrangement accrues from a change in the felt position of the body parts relative to each other. This view is based on the fact that the changed direction of reaching for visual targets, after seeing the optically displaced hand, shows up when the subject points to nonvisible targets (sound sources). This generalized adaptation including nonvisible targets is said to result from a proprioceptive change underlying the felt position of the reaching arm.

While this may seem plausible for certain limited sets of findings, Efstathiou, Bauer, Greene, and Held (1967) believe they have shown that such an interpretation is not in line with the following experiments they conducted. Some years ago it was shown (Scholl, 1926) that the adaptation in reaching for a visible target by one hand is also evident in reaching for a nonvisible target, for example, reaching for the other, unseen hand. The Efstathiou experiment sought to test these two forms of adaptation under fully comparable conditions.

Reaching for a visible target was checked by having the subject mark on a sheet of paper, while not seeing his or her hand, the perceived location of the virtual images of four points seen with both eyes through a fully reflecting mirror. To the viewer the points appeared to lie on the table surface about perpendicular to his or her line of sight (frontal plane). The viewer's visual field was restricted to the target area by lenseless goggles.

Reaching for the nonvisible hand was tested by having the viewer mark on the same surface, with eyes occluded (blindfolded), the perceived positions of the index finger of the hand. This finger was placed successively on each of the positions on pins protruding from the underside of the table where the contralateral finger touched one pin at a time. Throughout the experiment the viewer's head was held stationary by a bite-board.

In all, they performed three different experiments in this investigation. The amount of the shift varied with the type of target. The results suggest two independent forms of reaching: one based on equating arm movements and possible head orientations toward a target and the other based on the felt position of the arm. The first is changed by adaptation. The second is unaltered and tends to limit the shifts resulting from the first.

Visual Adaptation When No Part of Body Is Seen

McLaughlin, Rifkin, and Webster (1966) showed that when an observer looks at a visual target through prisms, adaptive changes occur even when no part of the body is seen as a visual reference. They stated that these changes stem from "a change in judgment of the direction of gaze," an oculomotor change arising from two secondary prismatic effects—the asymmetry of the visual scene and the apparent rotation about the vertical axis of a plane surface such as a wall in front of the observer. They stated that the first effect is responsible for the remaining and major part. The first factor is not aided by eye-movement activity.

The procedure used a target that was a luminous 3-centimeter line, 0.3 centimeter in width viewed from a point 33 centimeters away. The observer's head was held fixed by a biting board with dental impression. Without prisms the target appeared straight ahead. The track and target were mounted on a vertical plywood panel. Only the target was visible when the room was unilluminated. With the usual room illumination, the observer could also see the pointer and right hand. Other features of the visual field were occluded from view. A prism was then placed in front of each eye, producing an angular deviation of about 11° to the right. The observers made their own settings with their right hands.

In the unilluminated room the observer was asked to set the pointer straight ahead (setting 1). Then, when the target was illuminated, the observer was again asked to set the pointer straight ahead (setting 2). For the next setting the pointer was set so that its tip was directly beneath the target (setting 3). Following this a 5-second adaptive exposure was provided. Then, settings 2 and 3 and the adaptive exposures were repeated 15 times, omitting the final adaptive exposure.

In a single experimental period, four different adaptive conditions were used. In (a) the visual target was merely viewed in the unilluminated room. In (b) the hand was removed from the pointer, the room was illuminated, and the pointer was set directly beneath the line. Under this condition the pointer and the panel were visible and the tip of the pointer was fixated. In (c) the conditions of (b) prevailed but the pointer was moved back and forth while its tip was fixated. In (d) the observer kept his or her hand on the pointer and could see hand, pointer, and target. In this condition the observer was told to set the pointer directly beneath the target. Before each of the adaptive periods, three to five minutes of eye–hand activity with the prisms omitted were given.

The results were summarized essentially as follows:

1. When a small target viewed through prisms is the only thing visible, a small adaptive oculomotor change occurs. That is, the perceived position of the target is not deviated as much as the value of the prism would indicate. There is also a proprioceptive compensation, which the experimenters attributed to a "cognitive effect" stemming from previous knowledge of the "true" position of the target. The oculomotor effect (compensation) is attributed to the asymmetry of the visual field seen through the prisms.
2. When an illuminated surround is used, there is large adaptive oculomotor effect and a small proprioceptive change in the opposite (nonadaptive direction).
3. When oculomotor activity occurs, the oculomotor adaptive effect is not increased.
4. When reafference (muscle activity) necessary for adapting to visual displacement by prisms was found, the investigators, it is suggested, were dealing mostly with proprioceptive adaptive changes. On the other hand, when adaptation resulting without reafference was found, those investigators were dealing mostly with oculomotor adaption.

Immediate Perceptual "Correction"

Rock, Goldberg, and Mack (1966) showed that when a target is viewed through prisms, an immediate "correction" of the visual displacement occurs. Objects appear to lie closer to the "true" direction than the direction that would be expected from the optics of the prisms.

In their experiment a luminous spot was the target in an unilluminated room. Its position could be adjusted vertically or horizontally by the observer. The observer was brought blindfolded into the room and his or her head position was fixed by a biting board. After removal of the blindfold, he or she was asked to adjust the spot so that it looked straight ahead. Then prisms were placed in front of the eyes and the observer was again asked to adjust the spot so that it appeared to be straight ahead. Twenty-diopter prisms were used. From these, it was expected that the new location would be about 11° from the position determined with naked eyes. Following this, the room lights were turned on and the observer was again asked to position the spot. The difference between the preceding position and the one now indicated was taken as the measure of the correction effect.

Eradication of Confusion in Perception

Initially confusable items of sensory input may become distinguishable with practice. This shift is another form of perceptual learning or change. Two opposing views have given rise to specific investigations to account for this. Gibson and Gibson (1955) called them the *differentiation view* and the *enrichment view*. The former says that practice functions to reduce generalization among the items of input, to increase precision of discrimination of the variables present, and to detect relevant variables or distinctive aspects not previously detected. This view requires a new concept of stimulation since it holds that effective stimuli for perception are changed by the learning process.

The enrichment view quite differently emphasizes *addition* to perceptual features by the process of association.

The study of factors for or against discriminability does not always include the demonstration of learning within the study itself. Learning sometimes becomes an idea to explain the results of the study.

Liberman and his colleagues (1961) measured the discriminability of the acoustic differences within and between phoneme boundaries and compared the results with acoustic differences in inputs not perceived as speech. The subjects discriminated better across phoneme boundaries than in the middle of a phoneme class. The results with the control inputs disclosed no superiority in discriminability in the region corresponding to the phoneme boundary. The conclusion was that the increase in discrimination at the phoneme boundary is the result of learning, which is an "acquired distinctiveness" from long practice in attaching phoneme labels. Other experimenters have obtained similar results.

Pick (1965) wanted to determine whether in discriminating standard from comparison figures the subject comes to identify the absolute features of the standard figures or the features of variation distinguishing it from the comparison figures. The first is called *prototype learning*, the second *transformation learning*. Her study included both visual and tactual presentations. She compared the subject's transfer of the original discrimination to one of two tasks involving a response either to the absolute features of the original , standard or to the dimensions of variation among the presentations. When standard and comparison were presented simultaneously, transformation learning seemed to occur in both visual and tactual tasks. With successive presentations (studied only in touch), the difference between the two required responses disappeared. It was expected that succesive presentations would be more conducive to learning the absolute features of the stimulus presentations.

E. J. Gibson and colleagues (1962) believed that a skilled reader would visually discriminate letter groups constructed in accordance with the rules of spelling-to-sound correspondence better than groups only partially of this sort or not at all. They presented appropriate letter groups tachistoscopically. In a try-out group of 121 subjects, greater discrimination resulted for the pronounceable letter combinations than for the unpronounceable ones. In a later experiment, their subjects reproduced more accurately letter combinations that could be pronounced than the other letter combinations. In a third experiment, essentially the same results were obtained with tachistoscopic presentations whose discriminations were demonstrated by matching their perceptions with items in a multiple-choice list.

Learning in the Perception of Slant

Freeman (1966b) studied the learning of visual slant. He found that the effectiveness of cues to slant may be modified by differential reinforcement or by instructions. In the experimental conditions used there were probably only two possible cues to slant, the major–minor axis ratio of the retinal image and perspective. All other binocular cues and extreme monocular cues were eliminated. In spite of this, large errors of judgment occurred in slant-matching as a function of the physical size of the plane rectangles used as targets. Freeman attributed preexperimental error to the greater perspective weight (or cue) to the larger targets and to the relevance of the perspective cue required of the observers. He gave reinforcement when the observer's responses corresponded with the physical slant of the targets. In as many as half the trials, positive reinforcement was given for a "greater slant" response in which the perspective cue of the more slanted target was less than that of the less slanted target. In other trials the opposite situation response was reinforced. The major–minor axis ratio of the retinal image tallied nearly perfectly with the experimental reinforcement. The results supported the prediction of his cue-relevance theory.

SPLIT-BRAIN INVESTIGATIONS

"Split-brain" investigations consist in determining an animal's sensory behavior following the transection of the neural connections between the two cerebral hemispheres. This sort of operation might be expected to incapacitate the subject since it produces a radical change in the functional anatomy of the nervous system. It separates (splits) the two gross structures that ordinarily work together to achieve a unitary (or consistent) behavioral result. Such radical interference with the nervous system would be expected to have crucial effects on perception, altering and reducing the organism's abilities. The question then is to determine what postoperational perceptual response is like and what sorts of adaptation and improvement can be brought about by practice.

The actual behavioral results of split-brain operations have not turned out to be as anticipated but have been most instructive. The first finding was that an animal with a split brain can function quite effectively. Some stimulation reaches both hemispheres when no control is put on sensory input, and thus ordinary circumstances do not test what a single hemisphere can do. Experimentation consisted in delivering sensory input to only a single hemisphere. It was found that, in many respects, successful response could be elicited.

It was then found that response learned by one cerebral hemisphere was not transferred to the other one. For example, visual targets whose images were so placed on the retina as to activate areas feeding into only one hemisphere were used as the original stimulus material. When a discriminatory response was learned under such conditions, the animal was tested by having the target imaged on retinal areas feeding into the other hemisphere. The response in the second case showed no advantage of the previous learning in the first hemisphere. The correct response had to be learned, just as the response using the first hemisphere.

Experiments with other modalities such as touch were conducted and yielded the same sort of result. Surface texture was used as the differential feature; the animal had to learn to choose between two textures on the two pedals that could be operated to obtain food. Whereas an intact animal could perform with the second paw what had been learned by using the first paw, cutting the corpus callosum—separating the two hemispheres—made this impossible. Such experiments were performed on cats and monkeys, and it was concluded that the two hemispheres are required in these species for integrating the two halves of the visual field and for integrating inputs from the two opposite limbs.

Split-brain operations were finally performed on humans. This was first contemplated for severe epileptic patients. The evidence from work on animals that such an operation might very likely do away with the intense epileptic seizures made the risk morally justifiable. The expectation was realized and, in ordinary situations, little if any degradation in behavior could be noticed.

As already pointed out, in everyday situations no control is exercised on which hemisphere receives a given kind of information. Both hemispheres, even in a split-brain patient, generally receive information in the usual ambient situations. Therefore it was necessary to subject split-brain patients to controlled experimental situations to test behavior stemming from the action of a single hemisphere. Gazzaniga, Bogen, and Sperry (1963, 1965) were the first to experiment with split-brain subjects after operations to cure epileptic seizures.

The first finding obtained from the first case was that the operation disconnecting the two hemispheres had cured the seizures. The second finding was that the patients were left with two "minds." The meaning of this statement will shortly become apparent. Another finding was that the left hemisphere provided the subject with the ability to speak. The other hemisphere provided all the behavior of the left hemisphere except speech.

In one experiment the subject was seated in front of two screens transilluminated from the rear and separated from each other by 4 inches. Midway between the two was a fixation point. The first test in the series pertained to pattern discrimination in which a pattern was to be chosen from five others appearing on cards on the table in front of the subject. The item to be chosen from the cards was briefly presented on one or the other or both of the screens. Generally, a new set of cards was used for each trial. One of the cards contained the item that was flashed, one was blank, and the other three contained incorrect items. The materials used were geometrical forms, words, and short phrases. In some trials the subject was to make a verbal response, in others only a manual one. The task, in each trial, was to pick out the item most like or identical to the item presented.

The right hand responded with nearly perfect accuracy to all right screen presentations and only at a chance level to those on the left. The performance of the left hand to left-screen presentations was two and a half times better than chance. The left hand seldom made responses to right-field presentations and those that were made were only at a chance level of correctness. With left-screen presentations, the subject when questioned denied having seen anything and often even seemed puzzled that the questions had been asked. This was in spite of having made the correct manual retrieval response.

For the trials in which the presentations were made on both screens, each hand made its correct response, just as when the presentation was on its own screen alone. No conflict of any sort appeared. Verbal recognition continued to be specific to right-screen stimuli.

A different sort of visual presentation apparatus was used for another set of tests so constructed that separate discrimination tests could be provided for each hand. Each half-field was composed of two small screens on which small figures could be presented. Four normals and four split-brain subjects were compared in the relative amounts of time required to make discriminations. In normals the hand took about 40 percent longer to discriminate its own half-field when simultaneous presentations of both half-fields were given. The split-brain subjects showed no difference in response latency whether only one or both half-fields were presented. This seemed to indicate that the split-brain subjects were not involved in a kind of interference characteristic of the normals. One patient, for example, was tested in his ability to draw with the right and left hands. The patient was righthanded and never had had occasion to draw with his left hand before the operation. The test was started with the right hand and with verbal instructions to get the left hand to perform in the experiment. After some familiarity with the procedure a shift was made to the left hand by a demonstration from the experimenter and instructions to "do this." The use of the two hands was alternated with three minutes allowed for each drawing. A kind of anomalous activity of the left hand was observed a number of times. The hand would tighten and go out of control toward the end of the three-minute effort. It would swing upward to a position above the left shoulder.

In a later experiment the object to be drawn was a Necker cube. The right hand was given the task of drawing it, after a demonstration by the experimenter of drawing two overlapping squares and connecting their corners. This task seemed to be impossible for the right hand. Immediately after this failure, the left hand drew the complete cube without using the demonstrated technique. The right hand could construct only simple figures and only after considerable practice.

When the task was to construct standard patterns with blocks with the free use of both hands, the patient was usually unable to achieve the goal, largely because the right hand would try to assist the left and in so doing would undo the effective accomplishments of the left hand.

The behaviors dependent on other sense modalities were also tested. It was found that areas on the left side of the body, not cross-localized by the right hand, were unable to evoke a correct verbal response regarding which of two presentations felt hotter or colder. But if a warm or cool glass of water were provided and the subject was asked to select the proper glass of water from two others, he or she was able to do very well. If the task was made intermanual, the performance dropped to the chance level. The areas on the head or face taken to be bilaterally represented in the nervous system were quite capable in thermal discrimination expressed either verbally or manually. The same mapping of bilateral and unilateral areas found to function for touch and temperature seemed to function for pain-producing stimuli.

To test the ability to perceive position (the kinesthetic sense), the experimenter placed the joints at the wrist, elbow, shoulder, knee, and ankle in specific positions and asked the blindfolded patient to state the position in which the distal part of the limb was pointing. For the right hand and foot there was no difficulty manifested, but the patient was completely unable to describe the positions displayed by the fingers, wrist, and toes on the left side of the body. The sense of position of the left shoulder was retained but for the elbow it was variable.

BILATERAL TRANSFER IN TACTUAL DISCRIMINATION

The literature contains a number of studies of bilateral transfer of training, that is, the learning of a sensory or motor response in a given body region through practice in a contralateral region. Such studies generally involve a complex interplay of sensory modalities, militating against determining whether the observed effects came from improvement in a sensory or motor function or a change in the person's orientation to the task.

Ton (1973) assumed clearer insight in such problems could be gained from studying response in a single sensory modality. He chose to study transfer of training in tactile two-point threshold discrimination. Certain earlier studies were made on this problem but they involved shortcomings such as application of stimulation by hand. Length of application was only roughly controlled. Control groups were not used, nor was statistical analysis of results applied. In Ton's study these shortcomings were eliminated. He used the method of constant stimuli and the range and number of interstimulus values were guided by Ruch's (1955) work and by data from a pilot study. The study showed that changes in the two-point tactual threshold are transferred from one arm to the other.

Chapter 16
Perceptions Related
to People and Abstract
Qualities

We live in a world of people. It is other people who evoke some of the individual's most subtly based perceptual reactions. While no new basic laws enter, the factors function in ways that call for special consideration.

While we speak of personal interrelations as social, what is social and what is not social is often difficult to distinguish. People influence us while present and while out of sight and hearing. The world of people possesses institutions and rules to live by and scales of value. All of this affects our perception.

In discussing social perception, we shall only be able to deal with selected matters, and it will be difficult, if not impossible, to provide a fair picture of all that is called social perception in a single chapter, such as this.

When we deal with what is to be called social, we are in a very complex situation as in contrast to when we were largely considering quite direct relations between focal energistic features of the environment and the responses that ensue. The organism's activity was classed as perceptual on the basis of this definable relationship.

Individuals did differ somewhat among themselves, and it was recognized that this difference in response was based on learning and other factors in internal organization. But when we come to something that is to be called social, we apply a label (social) and sooner or later, if not immediately, we begin to include many kinds of indirect factors. However, to omit the influences of people on each other as a category worth our attention would be to omit a great many features of perception. Not all texts on perception give much space, if any, to social perception.

We shall first sample the study of social perception as it was several decades ago.

A SET OF ASSUMPTIONS IN SOCIAL PERCEPTION

Allport (1955) listed six propositions found in the study of social perception as he saw it. They are: (1) that bodily need determines, within limits, what a subject will perceive; (2) that reward and punishment are also factors in determining what a subject will perceive and that they greatly influence thresholds at which items will be recognized; (3) that values represented in the personality of the perceiver tend to determine thresholds of recognition; (4) that the size perceptions evoked by stimuli are in line with the social value connotations involved; (5) that the personality features of the perceiver predispose him or her to perceive in a manner consistent with such features; and (6) that overt recognition reactions to personally disturbing stimuli have a longer latency than do reactions to neutral material, that this material tends to be misperceived in radical ways, and that it evokes autonomic reactions at thresholds below overt recognition thresholds.

The immediately following examples are of studies pertaining to Allport's categorizations. While it can be assumed that bodily needs will play a role in determining what and how a person perceives, this does not in itself put the perceiving into the social category.

Reward and Punishment

The study of Proshansky and Murphy (1942) dealt with the influence of rewards and punishment on perception; the perception of the lengths of lines and the magnitudes of weights were investigated. Rewards and punishment in the case were devices to impose values on certain stimulus presentations they would not have otherwise. The experimenters imposed symbolic values or properties on visual targets that under ordinary circumstances would not possess such properties.

A pretraining sequence of two sessions per week lasted for five weeks, during which time several lines of different length were presented to the subjects. The same thing was done with weights that subjects lifted. After the pretraining period series was concluded, a second period, or training period, was begun. It lasted seven weeks, with two sessions per week. In this part of the study the subjects were instructed not to make any overt response but were simply to observe. During this training period a reward was given for each long line and heavy weight shown to the subjects. For each short line and light weight the subjects were punished— previous rewards were taken away. For the stimuli of intermediate physical value, reward and punishment were interspersed an equal number of times at random. A third period in the study consisted in the subjects again reporting their perceptions of length and weight, respectively, as the stimuli were presented. In this period, only the intermediate stimuli were presented. The object of the investigation was to see what influence the second period had on the third.

For the control subjects the first of the three periods was the same as for the experimental subjects. In the second, or training period, the control subjects were neither rewarded nor punished but were simply presented with the lines and weights. In the third period the two groups, the control and the experimental, responded differently. The control group showed no significant differences in perception in this period from perception in the first period. The experimental group, on the contrary, did show significant shifts in perception in the direction of perceiving the lines and weights of intermediate magnitude as similar to those that were always rewarded in the second period.

The Individual's Value System

Certain social psychologists maintain that the values of the individual tend to influence the duration thresholds at which materials related to these values are recognized. Postman, Bruner, and McGinnies (1948) gave the Allport–Vernon study of values to 25 subjects, obtaining their scores on the six value categories: religious, political, social, aesthetic, economic, and theoretical. The subjects were given 36 words by tachistoscope, with each set of six words related to one of the six categories. The exposure times were at first very short and became increasingly longer until the words were correctly perceived. It was found that subjects responded correctly to shorter exposure of words belonging to the high–value categories. This, of course, was in line with the investigators' expectations.

The authors analyzed the nature of the incorrect responses made by the subjects and grouped them as follows. The response words representing the same value category as the stimulus words themselves were called "covaluant responses"; the responses that represented an opposite meaning were called "contravaluant responses"; certain other responses were called "nonsense responses." Stimulus words in categories of high value to the subjects evoked more covaluant responses than stimulus words in less value areas. Stimulus words in low-value areas evoked more contravaluant and nonsense responses.

The same kinds of results were obtained in a similar study by Vanderplas and Blake (1940), in which the variable was the intensity of the sound of spoken words; consequently, the principle has, in a way, been demonstrated in hearing as well as in vision.

Perceived Magnitude and Value

The perceived size of an object is changed when size has some relevance to some need of the perceiver. The kind of evidence that is adduced for such a conclusion was first obtained by Bruner and Goodman (1947) by the following equipment. They used 10-year-olds to report on perceived sizes of coins by use of a spot of light whose size could be altered to match that of the coins seen in a different part of the visual field. A knob varying the size of an iris diaphragm was the means of varying the light spot. The coins used were pennies, nickles, dimes, quarters, and half-dollars. The perceived sizes of all the coins were enhanced. The magnitudes of the overestimation increased for successive coin denominations up to the 25-cent piece, and then dropped somewhat for the 50-cent piece. A control group was given cardboard disks to use as standards instead of the coins. With these, there was essentially no overestimation. The values clustered around true size for each coin.

A further comparison was made by using two groups of subjects, one from "poor" homes, the other from "rich" homes. The poor children "overestimated" the coins definitely more than did the rich children. When on another occasion the children were asked to imagine the size of coins, the poor children overestimated them. The exaggerations reported by the rich children occurred only for the half-dollar. Carter and Schooler (1949) redid the Bruner–Goodman study and failed to confirm the original findings except in the nonperceptual task of remembering coin sizes.

Ashley, Harper, and Runyan (1951) also repeated Bruner and Goodman's experiment, putting their subjects into different socio-economic categories by hypnosis. Their subjects were adults, to some of whom was suggested (by the experimenters) while in the hypnotic states that they were "poor" and to others that they were "rich." While still in the hypnotic state, the subjects were put through the process of reporting on perceived coin sizes. The results confirmed the findings of Bruner and Goodman. As a control, the reports of the same subjects before hypnosis were used. The subjects saw the coins as substantially their sizes. Not only were actual coins accentuated in size in the hypnotic series but so were slugs, whose metals were variously described as lead, silver, white gold, and platinum. They were accentuated in keeping with the value of the metal suggested and the suggested economic status of the subjects. Even remembered sizes of coins bore relation to value.

It is extremely difficult to evaluate such experiments and their results, since we do not know what goes on in hypnosis. Were we to think of hypnotic subjects as merely in a peculiar state of pleasing the hypnotist and thus being under his control, then the behavior that turned out to be in line with his or her knowledge and expectations could not be used to support the kind of hypothesis implied in the experiment.

Another investigation in which social context has determined the nature of resulting perception is the study of Bruner and Postman (1948) that investigated the role of symbolism (value, again) in influencing visual perception of size. These authors used disk targets. One set bore a dollar sign, another a swastika, and a third a supposedly neutral symbol—a square with its two diagonals marked across it. The symbols were of equal size and were contained within a circle. The targets themselves varied from three-quarters of an inch to half an inch in diameter. The task of the subjects was to adjust the size of a circular disk of light seen elsewhere in the visual field until it appeared equal in size to the symbol-bearing disk. It was supposed that the subjects were oriented differently toward the symbols—positively toward the dollar mark and negatively toward the swastika. Ten subjects were presented the neutral and positive targets and ten were presented the neutral and negative targets. Each subject made 48 trials, one-half with the neutral and one-half with the other targets.

The three symbols made differences in the perceived sizes of the disks. The disks with the dollar sign were perceived as largest, those with the swastika the next largest, and those with the square the smallest. This was true regardless of the various literal sizes of the disks.

If the patterns as symbols were to have made a difference in perceived disk size, one might have supposed that symbols toward which some distinct attitude is held might merely heighten perceived size. The most exacting critic might feel that there is a shadow of a doubt left in the experiment with reference to the sheer visual attributes of the three target configurations as geometrical forms. Both the dollar sign and the swastika are open forms, whereas a square with its diagonals is a closed form. What would have happened were the diagonals alone used for the neutral symbol? This might be submitted to test. On the other hand, we should not be so conventionally and rigidly oriented toward attributing vision to geometrical determinants alone as to refuse to believe that the symbolic character of a visual pattern has something to do with its perceived size.

Klein, Schlesinger, and Meister (1951) performed their own version of the Bruner–Postman experiment on the perceived size of symbolic targets. Their results did not represent a single marked tendency for all subjects but rather a set of consistent individual differences. It was interpreted that the size enhancement does not flow directly from some broad specified need but in the way that the specific individual is organized to deal with his or her needs.

Lambert, Solomon, and Watson (1949) set up a token-reward situation in which, by a conditioning process, poker chips that had no special value to begin with were used to obtain natural rewards. Their perceived size was retested and found to be greater than it was before the reward role was developed.

Although these experiments do not rule out the possibility of geometrical designs having a spatial influence of their own on the perceived size of the disk targets on which they are inscribed, they do indicate that there is something that the individual perceiver contributes to his or her perceptions. This contribution shows up in perceived size, making it decidedly different from what would be expected were perception stimulus-bound. Although we do not know the mechanisms underlying its expression, the contribution has connection enough with what is otherwise expressed as "personality," "personal needs," or "personal values" to be attributed to these entities in certain specific situations. Of course, as a result, broad generalizations regarding perception are then made in such forms as "personal needs influence the sizes of perceived objects," for example. This does not mean that perception is fickle and that the ordinary psychophysical experiments on perceived size are to be discarded. The findings demonstrate that the differences obtained in the "social situations" and in conventional laboratory experimentation are the products of very different sets of conditions. Our understanding of perception ought to encompass both of these extremes of circumstance.

The use of the concept of need in explaining behavioral results is open to some criticism inasmuch as there are no criteria for determining what needs are and which ones are operating in a given subject in a given case. The concept of *need* is in as much need of verification as is the perceptual behavior under study. Without criteria for establishment of needs, anyone is at liberty to state a need at any time. The term should have more than a mere commonsense meaning. Even food deprivation is not always an ironclad need. Length of time since last food intake may, in a statistical way, seem to serve. But when results vary considerably, what is going to be the interpretation? We are not denying that some concept of need might be scientifically valid and useful, but that, certainly, the term *need* cannot be made an explanation in an indiscriminate way. It can be said, in general, that the term has not been used carefully enough in many cases.

Nelson and Lechelt (1968) performed an experiment on children's discrimination of number that is an outcome of the previous studies on the discrimination of size as affected by socioeconomic status. They chose to study number (of items) rather than size and set up the following hypotheses.

1. Reliable differences will not occur in the perception of number (numerosity) between low and high socioeconomic children on the basis of monetary value when the number of items (coins, slugs) looked at does not exceed some critical number.
2. Actual monetary value of the coins will produce a numerosity bias in a given direction when a critical number of viewed items is exceeded.
3. Low socioeconomic children will differ progressively from the high socioeconomic children as the items of monetary value go beyond the ability of the sensory pathway to discriminate. This difference will be one of overestimation.
4. No differences will result between the two groups of children when slugs are viewed under any condition.

Actually, one factor the investigators saw in the situation of number estimation was a distinction between results determined primarily by the sensory mechanism and its limits and the results obtained when the limits of the sensory mechanism to discriminate number were exceeded. With numbers of items viewed beyond this critical limit, motivational factors could enter in.

Forty third-grade children in the city schools of Edmonton,

Canada, were used, of ages ranging from 7 years 9 months to 9 years 5 months, with a mean of 8 years 6 months. The children were first given a questionnaire, in the attempt of the experimenters to define and distinguish between high and low "need." The pupils were considered equally familiar with "value" aside from their socioeconomic status. New Canadian dimes and aluminum blanks (slugs) were shown on a black velvet surface.

It was found that when the number of items exceeded five, the low socioeconomic children's estimations exceeded the estimations of the high socioeconomic group when the items were dimes. This difference grew as the number of dimes was increased from six to twelve. No difference was found in the estimates of the two groups when slugs were used or when the number of items was five or less.

Personality Characteristics and Autisms

It is said that the personality features of an individual predispose him or her to apprehend objects and situations in ways relevant to these features.

Schafer and Murphy (1943) made the following study to disclose the autistic nature of perception. They used an ambiguous figure-ground target in which human faces could be perceived. To form the targets, circles were bisected by an irregular line so devised that either the right-hand or left-hand portion taken alone could be seen as a face unambiguously. With the two portions of the circle taken together, the target as a whole was ambiguous. The right-hand portion could be seen as a face, the left-hand as the ground field; or at other instants the left-hand position could be seen as figure (i.e., as face), the right-hand portion as ground field.

The investigation used two such ambiguous targets, in which, of course, a total of four faces was involved. The four face targets could be shown singly and were first shown that way in random order. From the experimenters' point of view the targets were two pairs of faces; from the subjects' point of view, they were seen as four distinctly different faces. Each target presentation was made by a Whipple tachistoscope for an exposure of one-third second. The subjects were told that they would see faces in the exposures to be made, and before each target was presented the subjects were given a name to associate with each face they would see. The object was to learn the faces and their names. Finally, the two portions of the circle were put together, and then collateral conditions were manipulated to see whether the subjects could be predisposed to see one rather than the other of the two faces elicitable by the target. The subjects were told that when they saw either of two specified faces of the four, they would be rewarded by 2 or 4 cents and that each time they saw either of the other two of the four faces, they would be deprived of 2 or 4 cents. In each trial the subjects were told how much they had won or lost, and in accord with this they were to take from a pile of pennies the right amount or put back into the pile what was owed.

Five subjects were used and all acquired the same set or bias in favor of seeing the rewarded faces for the first 16 presentations, after which the perceptual process underwent what the authors called a process of consolidation. This process depended on factors within the perceivers other than those controlled by the initial reward-and-punishment experiences. A control subject also acquired a set for two faces in the pretraining period.

Rock and Fleck (1950) obtained negative results in their experiments with reward and punishment with figure-ground stimuli. They found that their two-face components had a novel appearance when put together.

As is usual, when two different investigations of the same matter turn out oppositely, we have to suspect differences in method of instruction, material used, or the subjects themselves. Actually, differences in subjects is one of the chief concerns of the social psychologist. The fact that Schafer and Murphy obtained their positive results under the conditions, as well as they can be understood, leads us to the conclusion that rewards and punishments play a role in perception, such as in determining what will be seen as figure and what will be seen as ground. Often what is ground and what is figure are taken to be largely controlled by structural factors. We know that this is not so in all cases. There are those in which there is ambiguity, as in the targets of the experiments just cited. Schafer and Murphy have shown that organismic contributions are crucial in determining figure and ground in such cases. Not only reward and punishment are influential but autistic factors as well.

Disturbing Stimuli and Two Orders of Response

Postman, Bruner, and McGinnies (1948) produced a very frustrating situation for a group of subjects who were given a series of three-word sentences by means of a modified Dodge tachistoscope. The subjects were to report "what they saw, or what they thought they saw." This request is a typically phrased one, owing to the tendency of the naïve subject to omit descriptions of perceived items with which considerable doubt is associated. It will be recalled, in this connection, that we earlier discussed the attribute of relative certainty in the perceiving process.

Each of the sentences was presented for various durations, some so brief that scarcely anything at all was seen, others long enough so that the three words were comprehended. Stated in other terms, each sentence was presented once for a duration of 0.03 second shorter than "threshold," once for 0.02 second shorter, and twice for 0.01 second longer. Steps of 0.01 second in duration were added trial by trial until all three words were recognized.

The procedure for the first nine sentences of the total eighteen was the same for both the control group and the experimental group. At the completion of this part of the investigation the experimental group was put into a perceptually frustrating situation. In other words, the subjects were called on to do the impossible and were badgered in various ways by the experimenters as the study progressed from this point.

A black-and-white reproduction of a highly complex painting was shown to the members of this group. The subjects were instructed that they were going to be shown something that they were to describe fully. The instructions were delivered in a very serious tone. The picture was exposed at a low illumination for only 0.01 second. None of the subjects could make out anything of the exposure except to discern a few vague contours and shadows. Remarks were made by the experimenters calculated to embarrass and belittle the observers for not being able to see something definite and detailed. During the ten or twelve trials the picture was shown, even the health of each subject's eyes, as well as the state of his or her mind were brought into question. Control subjects were shown the same picture, but under favorable circumstances, including a 30-second exposure. During this time these subjects were given the same task as the experimental group.

The performances of the two groups were compared in terms of what was called threshold performances. If one word was perceived correctly out of the three, a one-word threshold was said to have been reached; if two words, a two-word threshold; if three, then a three-word threshold.

The control group improved but the experimental group did not. Not only did it not improve but the sort of words the experimental group perceived from the material presented had some very illuminating characteristics. The words perceived pertained to the needs and curious circumstances in which the subjects found themselves.

McGinnies (1949) used a list of 18 words that were presented one at a time tachistoscopically to 16 subjects, eight male and eight female. The words were presented for increasing durations, step by step, until they were recognized. In each trial the subject reported what he or she thought the word was. Eleven words were neutral and seven were critical. The latter were socially disapproved words, for example, whore, raped, bitch. Galvanic skin response was recorded in each trial. Duration thresholds for recognition of the critical words were greater than for the neutral ones. The galvanic skin responses to the words before they were fully recognized were greater for the critical than for the neutral words. The "misperceptions" (or misjudgments) for the critical words were less similar to the "right perceptions" than for the neutral words.

It is as though a form of recognition occurs below what is called the recognition threshold, but it is such that possibly overt evasion can result. What we are talking about really is a lie detector test. Whereas overt *evasion* can occur in verbal behavior, it cannot occur in the autonomic responses, such as the galvanic skin reaction. Studies using the theory of signal detection (already discussed in Chapter 3) would be very appropriate here. Instead of specifically naming some factor that influenced results, the broad category of *response bias* would be the first step in analyzing results.

Howes and Solomon (1950, 1951) suggested another factor that might be involved in experiments such as McGinnies' study. One factor was a word frequency explanation. It is known that some words are used more frequently than others in our language. These words used more frequently by subjects might have a lower threshold. A still more potent factor in the situation might be the subjects' unwillingness to state what they think they saw, if it is simply a "tabooed" word.

Ericksen (1963) and others have followed up the type of work in the previous studies and have related the results to personality characteristics of the subject. He found that some subjects showed higher thresholds for anxiety-arousing material, while others showed lower thresholds. This led him to use the terms repressors and sensitizers, respectively.

OTHER TERMS IN SOCIAL PERCEPTION

Among the many terms that have been coined, or given a unique treatment in the area of social response, are *selection, accentuation,* and *fixation.* They have been invented by certain authors and then taken up by others. What is meant by selection may vary, but at least in some cases it refers to the lowering of thresholds for "objects of distinct personal reference to the individual." Accentuation has to do with the appearance of objects as brighter, larger, and so on than would be expected in the classical matching experiment. Fixation is the term given to the persistence and preferential retention of certain modes of perceptual response.

A host of other terms have arisen in connection with the idea of perception being selective and accentuational. For example, there are such terms as dominance, normalization, assimilation, vigilance, primitivation, compromise formation, schematization, hierarchy of thresholds, and degrees of personal relevance, value resonance, selective sensitization, not to mention others, all of which are meant to have some technical meaning. One of these is *perceptual defense.* Other terms that go with it are *preperception* and *subception.* The first is merely a term that has been used by critics in describing the implications of the idea of perceptual defense. The second (subception) is a term that was seriously used by McCleary and Lazarus (1949) in accounting for the kind of results they obtained. In their investigation they obtained discriminatory galvanic skin responses to words with shorter exposures than they were required for conscious recognition of the words themselves. McGinnies (1949) describes such things as conditioned avoidance. Whereas there is no objection to having terms to indicate processes that occur within the organism and underlie the perceptual end result, it is important to know in what category these processes are supposed to take place. Are they neural or are they going to be in terms of still other hypothetical entities whose existence is as much in need of establishment as the processes to be explained? The tendency to build premise on premise, each as hypothetical as the next, is all too often practiced in the more subtle areas of psychology.

Perceptual defense implies some sort of discrimination that precedes the discrimination that we call perception. To be on the defense, in the ordinary meaning of the term, is first to be able to determine what is threatening and what is not and, then, as a second step, to do whatever is required—for instance, in the case of reacting to words, to reject the threatening ones perceptually or to treat them differently. Bruner and Postman (1947, 1948) among others are aware of the implication of using two steps to account for perception and that the mechanism carrying out the first step is about equivalent to having a little person within the perceiver himself or herself. They state the matter in a dramatic way, saying that the experiments "suggest to the guileless investigator the image of the superego peering through a Judas eye, scanning incoming percepts in order to decide which shall be permitted into consciousness."

An investigation was carried out by Bricker and Chapanis, (1953) in which they used guessed responses to nonsense words presented tachistoscopically. After the first two wrong guesses, fewer trials than needed by chance were found to be required to perceive the words "correctly." They used a very simple and convincing interpretation for their findings. It was merely that what is incorrectly perceived under the conditions of the experiment conveys some information. They state that information conveyed prior to recognition comes from partial aspects within the stimulus target. Thus they attempted to bypass the notion of subception, although it is not easily understood as to how they thought this was accomplished.

Certain other writers also reject the notion of subception. Perhaps the term itself does not sound suitable. Howes (1954) declares that with certain fairly reasonable assumptions, such data as those of McCleary and Lazarus (1949) can be predicted better on the basis of *probability theory* than by subception. We have indicated that subception does not need to mean just one thing. It has to do with a set of processes, whatever they are, that goes on prior to the emergence of the end result we call perception. It is simply a way of labeling the antecedent processes rather than of couching them in personalistic or psychoanalytic terms and looking to processes on some level of functioning different from perception for the roles required to provide the end result. Undoubtedly, chance plays a role; chance here being but a fortuitous concatenation of circumstances. Surely, however, there is more to it than mere fortuitousness. When one uses probability theory to explain something, he or she had better inspect the assumptions to see the nature of the *loading* they contain. The loading may contain the same elements that were rejected in the theory that probability is supposed to supplant.

In 1962 Zajonc had his subjects learn a line of "paired associates." Stimulus and response words were paired in the following combinations: taboo-taboo, taboo-neutral, neutral-taboo, and neutral-neutral. Following the learning period, Zajonc measured the duration threshold for recognition of the stimulus words, by having the subjects respond with the response word instead of the stimulus word just learned as an associate. By this procedure he could separate out possible *perceptual defense* effect from what he called response bias.

Bruner (1951) and Bruner and Postman (1947) have more to say about perceptual defense and the matter that some call subception. They suppose that the subject begins to recognize the generic characteristics of the stimulus, prior to complete recognition. In certain defensive perceptions the subject often negates the nature of the actual stimulus in his or her response. This, they say, looks like a paradox at first. In order that the subject repress or negate a stimulus, the subject, it would seem, must first recognize the stimulus for what it is. Bruner and Postman believe that this paradox can be obliterated if we do not restrict the definition of recognition to a single type of report—namely, a veridical one—and if we do not insist that all responses about which we talk depend on prior recognition (see Bruner, 1951).

Now let us see how these cautions are to work. The authors say that to a stimulus there can be tripped off a constellation of response tendencies, among which veridical responding is only one. Others may be tripped off as well and be very effectual in leading to other responses. Each of the possible tendencies is said to have its own threshold. This is determined both by the stimulus and the directive state of the organism. The directive state is otherwise labeled as the differential availability of the responses in the organism's total repertory. They believe that to make this idea work the threshold of affective avoidance is often lower than for veridical report, although it may be the other way around in some cases. When so, "correct" recognition must take place prior to affective response.

Bruner and Postman (1947) assumed that recognition requires a process of interconnection between an incoming "stimulus" and a "trace." The matter, they say, can be stated in stimulus–response terms by saying that an incoming stimulus, in order to evoke a recognition response, must develop a connection with some response mechanism. The next assumption is that not all traces are equally "available to the development of the connection with response processes." Deprivation, punishment, disuse, and the past history of the organism might be factors leading to this relative unavailability. They also include need states and states of expectancy in accounting for availability.

Bruner and Postman say that when a stimulus is in line with the prevailing state of the organism, it is recognized more readily. Put into our language—all impingements are dealt with by the organism in ways dependent on what is occurring in the organism at the instant. Some impingements will be quite ineffective in evoking perceptual response. Some impingements will be reacted to without delay (i.e., with minimal latency); others will be slowly reacted to. Some impingements can be utilized in the internal ongoing process and will evoke perceptions of familiar objects, whereas in the great majority of other instances the impingements would not evoke such perceptions at all. Hence we have two problems: the quickness of response and the kind of response. If the internal state of the organism is "not favorable," a much more intense or long-lasting impingement will be required to evoke any response.

We all agree with Bruner and his colleagues that from start to finish there is something hierarchical about the processes that are involved in developing what comes out as an experiential perception or as an overt act of recognition or choice. Just as long as we hold to envisaging these factors in other than perceptual terms and thus to keeping away from language that should be confined to describing the perceptions themselves, we are on the proper path. The terms we shall have to utilize, although they may not as yet be used by neurophysiologists, will ultimately fit into their understandings.

Broadbent and Gregory (1967) believe that it is clear that the emotionality with reference to words has an effect that is not explained by a constant bias against them in the response machinery. Words may sometimes receive a positive and sometimes a negative bias on account of transient states of mood, hence simple experimental procedures to test simpler notions about the matter are not competent.

Erdelyi (1974), in his article "A new look at the new look," reformulates the perceptual defense-vigilance effect into information processing terms. The reformulation considers the effect to be a special case of selectivity in cognitive processing. Erdelyi's article is a very valuable one, surveying the questions of response, perception, and related topics that have to do with the processing of input and so is relevant to much that needs to be considered in pondering the nature of social perception.

The Honi Phenomenon

A phenomenon that can well be considered to have a social origin is the Honi phenomenon. In Chapter 12 the nature of the distorted rooms devised by Ames at the Dartmouth Eye Institute was described and the results were explained. The Honi phenomenon is simply an unexpected deviation from the usual response. A few years ago a woman observer saw the face of her husband at the one window and the face of a stranger at the other. The size change, as usual, was reported for the face of the stranger, but not for her husband. In 1952 Wittreich made a study of this phenomenon that has come to be called the Honi phenomenon, after the family nickname of the woman observer just mentioned.

Wittreich performed two experiments. The first involved ten married couples, providing twenty observers. Six of the couples had been married less than a year, the others for two to ten years. Distorted rooms of two sizes were used. Viewing was monocular in all cases. In using the small room, each observer was asked to describe (1) the room, (2) the hands of the experimenter that were put through the two windows, (3) the marble that rolled across the floor, giving the appearance of rolling uphill, (4) the two cases of two people showing their heads at the two windows (one case with two strangers, the other with the spouse as one of the two people).

The experiment with the large room was somewhat similar. Among the ways it differed was to have the observed persons walk across the room after first having been seen standing in their respective corners.

In the small room experiment, six of the twenty observers reported a difference between the appearance of the spouses and the strangers. This difference was in the expected direction. In the large room experiment, seven of the twenty reported a difference in the expected direction. At no time was the spouse reported as changed in appearance more than the strangers. One member of all the couples married less than a year manifested the phenomenon in one or the other of the two rooms. Only one of the observers married more than a year reported the phenomenon.

The criterion for the Honi phenomenon in the large room where the observed persons walked from the corner to the center of the back wall was that little or no distance had to be covered before he or she became normal in appearance. The magnitude of the difference in the distance walked by the spouse and the stranger was used to portray the strength of the Honi effect.

Whereas the small room served to show whether or not the Honi phenomenon would appear, the experiment with the large room was an attempt to quantify results. In the second room the differences obtained in the appearance of spouses and strangers were significant. The attempt to relate the strength of the Honi phenomenon to length of marriage failed, however. No explicit explanation was offered for the results.

Other Studies on Social Perception

Whereas most, if not all, the preceding studies have tried to test responses that could be called indirect and abstract relationships to other people in general, some studies have to do with perception in situations of direct confrontation with other people or their portraits. The following studies represent this latter approach.

Sappenfield (1977) had his subjects sort photographs according to what was called openness (PO) and perceived trustworthiness (PT) in one study and in a second study to respond to Shastrum's personal orientation inventory.

He interpreted his results to indicate that trustworthiness was, while openness was not, perceived as definitely as were certain other personal characteristics studied earlier. Sappenfield (1971) had studied attractiveness, similarity to self, similarity to the ideal personality, intelligence and hostility. In those tests males and females came out about the same.

If the present text were involving subhuman studies as well as human, the well-known work of Harlow and his associates on surrogate mothers would be included in this chapter. That work shows how the exercise of certain perceptual systems in infancy (largely haptic) has a great deal to do with the animals' relations to others in later years and how social perception is structured in adult life.

Two interesting and instructive human examples of the principles demonstrated in Harlow's monkeys are given in Bartley's *Perception in Everyday Life*, pp. 116–120. The one parallel between the monkey and human examples is clear. It is not often that an investigator wishing to make this clear comparison could have the opportunity to do so. The other example is an example of how perception is altered by continence, that is, avoidance of sexual relations between spouses.

There is a plethora of studies that deal with what authors call social perception, but on close inspection it is often not perception that is at issue—it is cognition, judgment, attitude, understanding and the like. The studies are valuable in themselves. They do test and bring out something about human nature or human behavior, but despite the authors' implication that perception is being isolated and studied, the studies do not all focus on perception.

The indeterminate nature of the general area is what has led us to give this chapter its present title.

Chapter 17
Special Perceptual States

We are concerned in this chapter, as elsewhere, with the interactions between the organism and the environment. Up to this point we have not dealt with all general patterns of this interaction. So far we have been dealing with active environments and various forms of definite and active response stemming from them. We have yet to consider what the organism does when stimulation is withdrawn or is greatly reduced and also to describe what the individual can do to reduce activity to a minimum as if producing a detachment from the environment. We want to consider such matters simply from the standpoint of understanding human perception and not with the motivation that leads individuals to enter the aforementioned states.

The prominent terms to be found in this chapter are *sensory deprivation, isolation, transcendental meditation, biofeedback, systematic relaxation,* and *alcoholism.*

The perceptual states we wish to consider are of two kinds— what the organism does when considerable stimulation is withheld from it and what happens incidentally when the individual takes steps to become detached in certain ways from the environment.

Some of this detachment is definitely intended and in other respects is incidental. In certain addictions it is partially the one and partially the other. Since we are considering unusual environment–organism relations we shall have something to report on alcoholism. The question has come up as to whether alcoholism is or is not partially determined by the pecularity of the individual's nervous system as well as by the other more usually supposed factors, such as amount of alcohol imbibed and stressful conditions met by the imbiber (see Figure 17.1).

In essence, most of the states involved here are not new. For example, meditation has been practiced in the Orient for a long, long time. It has been characteristic for a large portion of the world to seek withdrawal from the cares and excitement and the vigorous activities of everyday life by achieving forms of tranquility, the experiences of which those who practice meditation have come to value highly and to interpret in a religious way. In contrast, we are more familiar with a style of life in which personal fulfillment is sought in the opposite way, by devices that, among which, include orgies and drugs.

We are becoming better acquainted with the techniques of the Orient that have been bypassed so long and are now utilizing them to some degree and are interpreting them in naturalistic ways.

Human existence can tend in either of two directions: toward excitement or toward calm. In the one there is tension, in the other there is a "letting go" or release from tension. There are intentional ways at arriving at the latter, and these differ quite significantly. Some are labeled as meditation and some as relaxation, for example, Jacobsonian relaxation.

Figure 17.1   Special perceptual conditions.

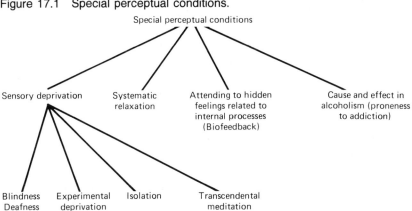

Our interest here in these various states rests on the supposition that they are definite departures from the usual as far as perception is concerned. It so happens, however, that they are not traditionally mentioned in textbook discussions of perception.

SENSORY DEPRIVATION

Apparently, when the term sensory deprivation is used, the reference is to the environment. However, it is only under special circumstances that the individual's environment is devoid of many kinds of stimuli. Even to think of it as capable of being greatly impoverished is not typical. But of recent years the problem has arisen as to what happens when the environment is emptied as much as possible of the energistic events to which the human being is structured to react. What does it mean for the human to be in such a vacuum (or near vacuum)?

Deprivation may be either of two kinds: the kind in which the environment is emptied of stimuli or the kind that results from some sensory capacity, such as blindness or deafness or a combination of both. These latter forms of deprivation are long-term, whereas the experimental emptying of the environment of stimuli is temporary. The sensory deprivation that has come to be studied is the kind of degree that can be produced in the laboratory and the duration of which can be determined. Often it is only a matter of hours or a few days.

The topic of sensory deprivation logically contains within it the condition called *isolation*. This is the situation in which all of the elements of stimulation for the individual but the social ones are present. The topic of sensory deprivation likewise includes conditions the individual himself or herself creates, the most prominent example being transcendental meditation.

The hypothesis that an organism requires not only stimulation (i.e., sensory impingement) but a quite varied input has been presented in recent years and has been tested by a number of investigators. This outlook has come to include the expectation that perceptual disorganization is one result of sensory deprivation. Such disorganization might include hallucinations on the one hand and curious or unusual interpretations of sensory inputs on the other.

Single-Modality Sensory Deprivation

Zubek, Flye, and Aftanas (1964) placed 16 subjects, in pairs, in a room for a week. The only deprivation was visual (darkness). There were no restrictions on movement, conversation, or use of a radio.

From measurements before and after they found a significant increase in tactual acuity. Likewise, they found a significant increase in thermal and pain sensitivity. In all three forms of sensitivity there was a more or less gradual return to normal during a seven-day period following deprivation.

Zubek, Flye, and Willows (1964) also made a study of a seven-day exposure to diffuse homogeneous illumination. The experiments showed a significant increase in thermal and pain sensitivity. The increase persisted for two days for heat and one day for pain.

In a third study, Duda and Zubek (1965) tested 15 subjects with regard to auditory sensitivity before and after a week's stay in darkness. For this they used five tonal frequencies, 100, 300, 1000, 5000, and 9000. The absolute thresholds for these frequencies was not altered. They then used an auditory flutter technique using white noise (with a pulse-to-cycle ratio of .90. The AFF (auditory flutter fusion) rose during the seven days and remained at the final attained level for one day following deprivation, and dropped to near normal on the second day.

The terminal study (Schulte and Zubek, 1967) had to do with ascertaining whether olfaction was effected by visual deprivation. Using a certain concentration of benzene as an olfactory stimulus, the investigators found that seven days of darkness increase olfaction sensitivity, but during the first two days following darkness there was an "overswing" to reduced sensitivity. After this the sensitivity gradually returned toward normal, but by five days had not quite reached it.

For gustation, sensitivity to different substances were unlike. For NaCl and sucrose the sensitivity increased significantly with after effects lasting a day. Sensitivity to HCl and quinine was not changed significantly during the darkness, but a trend for HCl sensitivity occurred right after deprivation. It was concluded that this difference between reaction to the substances ingested was caused by the concentrations used.

Nagatsuka (1965) on the other hand did find that a one-day deprivation produced a 36 percent rise in sensitivity to quinine.

Milstein and Zubek (1967) found that sensitivity in a tactual fusion task showed progressive improvement with duration of visual deprivation. Bross and Zubek (1975) reported that a week's auditory deprivation produced a significant component in visual performance as measured by critical flicker frequency (CFF).

Bross and Zubek (1976) studied the effect of one week's auditory deprivation on cutaneous sensitivity. In addition to reduction in auditory stimulation, the illumination of the room was reduced to a low level. Tactile fusion measured by a "flicker" technique developed by Shewchuk and Zubek in 1960 showed improvement from the deprivation. The measure was called critical frequency of percussion (CFP).

Broad Experimental Sensory Deprivation

Experimental sensory deprivation came alive in the following studies. Bexton, 1953; Bexton, Heron, and Scott, 1954; Doane, 1955; Doane, Mahatoo, Heron, and Scott, 1959; Hebb, Heath, and Stuart, 1954; Heron, Doane, and Scott, 1956; Scott, 1954; Scott, Bexton, Heron, and Doane, 1959. The conditions used in the original studies at McGill (Bexton et al., Heron et al., Scott et al.) were as follows. Male college students were hired to lie in comfortable beds as long as they could (about three or four days). The beds were in lighted, semisoundproof cubicles 8 × 4 × 6 feet that had been fitted with a window for observation from outside the room. The subjects wore translucent goggles that admitted illumination but precluded form vision. Except when eating or going to the lavatory, they wore cotton gloves and had their arms in cardboard cylinders from the elbow to beyond the fingertips. Auditory perception was greatly limited by the continuous hum of the earphones in their foam rubber pillows, which provided the only intercommunication between subject and experimenter who was always present outside the cubicle, day and night. Although the subjects were informed that they should call for anything they needed, they were not informed of the time of day or night.

The subjects usually spent the early part of their isolation by sleeping. As time wore on, they slept less and seemed eager for stimulation. Their overt behavior consisted of talking and singing to themselves and tapping the cardboard cylinders together or using them to explore the interior of the cubicle. They became restless and their movements became random.

Considerable emotional lability was manifested. During their stay the subjects were given certain tests, about which they remarked more freely than when tested outside the cubicle. Most subjects reported elation during the early part of isolation, but this changed to irritability, which increased toward the end.

When the subjects terminated their isolation and came out and had their goggles and gloves removed, they seemed dazed. They mentioned some disturbance in visual perception usually for a minute or two. They had difficulty in focusing; things looked two-dimensional; color seemed enhanced. Some reported confusion; some, mild nausea; some, headaches. In some cases the symptoms continued for 24 hours.

The phenomena reported as pertaining to the period within

the cubicle included inability to concentrate on any topic, inability to conduct organized thinking, lapses into uncontrolled daydreaming, and emergence of "blank periods." From tests administered in some of the studies, such functions as number-series completion, word making, and digit-symbol substitution were impaired. Tests on figural aftereffects, size constancy, tactual form perception, and spatial orientation showed that some subjects were not affected, but the overall results could be interpreted as evidencing the deterioration of cognition and motivation. A major consequence of deprivation was the emergence of hallucinations. Some referred to "having dreams while awake." The hallucinations involved audition as well as vision. Feelings of "otherness" and "bodily strangeness" were also common.

The results including both the tests and the hallucinations led the investigators to conclude that limiting the environment gave quite direct evidence of a form of dependence on the environment not previously realized. Subsequent studies in other laboratories differed somewhat in certain findings, but the conditions of experimentation were also different.

The early experiments reporting hallucinations, made it seem that given little or no sensory input the organism is freed from the kind of direction that the external environment provides and the internal machinery is left to act on its own. This would mean that the individual would see and hear things that are not present.

Hallucinations are generally thought of as the result of excitation of the central nervous system, but they stem from two very different origins. One is sensory deprivation. This is a known *external* origin. The other origin is provided by drugs. Whatever the drug, this is an *internal* condition. Since hallucinations are examples of activity, they should be explained as to why they occur without external stimulation.

The shortcut explanation we might tend to suggest is that when a system such as the central nervous system is not given sensory input, it is not only in a contextual vacuum, but is freed from certain constraints and begins to act in accordance with a kind of momentum of its own, giving rise to experience, in part, induced by this momentum and, in part, by the very slight sensory inputs still contained in the deprivation situation. It would seem that the stimulus world has a stabilizing influence on central nervous activities, and devoid of this, a certain amount of disorganization may tend to emerge in hallucinating activity.

The British neurologist, Hughlings Jackson, had a perceptual-release theory that has since been updated by Jolyon West (see Siegal, 1977). The hypothesis states that normal memories are suppressed from expression by a gating mechanism that has to do with the influx of outside data. New data inhibit the emergence and the awareness of previous inputs. However, if new input is greatly decreased while awareness still remains, the older "material" is released and functions as hallucinations, dreams, or fantasies.

We are not, however, free to think in terms of absolute deprivation, for not all experimental situations reduced the input conditions to zero. Many studies merely reduce the input and leave some stimulation. So we get varied reports from different studies. Even so, we do have enough to go on in describing the organism at times perceiving itself and its surrounds in what we may call fantastic terms. It is as if we could label perception as something *inventive,* producing from within itself experiences that are assigned to the subject's external surroundings and having the qualities of realism that characterize perception under normal conditions.

It happens that not all of the experiences reported in the studies have been given the same name. Some have been called hallucinations, some images, and others "reported sensations." These "reported sensations" have been of one or the other of two kinds— reported visual sensations (RVS) or reported auditory sensations (RAS). It was Murphy, Myers, and Smith (1963) who used these two terms.

Brownfield (1965) compiled 25 different terms found in the literature used more or less synonymously for the experimental conditions we are generalizing as sensory deprivation. In this list sensory deprivation was, of course, one of these items. It has been pointed out that none of these terms, as defined in the dictionary, adequately describe the majority of the conditions in the experiments being referred to.

Zuckerman (1969) summarized the various kinds of findings reported, indicating the hypotheses supported and not supported. A few of these reported and supported generalizations follow.

1. Most subjects who are told to report their visual experiences during experimental isolation, do so mostly during the first few hours of isolation. When postisolation reports are called for, it appears that the phenomena show up only after a 24-hour period.
2. RVS's appearance is facilitated by the reclining position.
3. RVS's progress from simple unstructured, meaningless sensations to more complex, structured, and meaningful ones.
4. RVS's are most likely to occur as dream phenomena when in low arousal states.
5. RVS's differ from drug induced hallucinations. In sensory deprivation the reports produced are visual while psychotic

hallucinations are mostly auditory. Although psychotic hallucinations involve dimensionality, belief of the subject, arousal, and dynamic significance, sensory deprivation hallucinations are rarely of this kind.

A great deal needs to be done before we can have a well-rounded outlook on sensory deprivation, but we need to know more about what the organism does when external stimulation is not present as well as when it is.

Isolation

Isolation is a particular kind of sensory deprivation. Total sensory deprivation can be produced only under careful laboratory conditions, if at all. Life outside the laboratory, however, sometimes is such as to constitute partial deprivation. Much of this we call *isolation*, and examples follow.

Some years ago Admiral Richard Byrd spent six months alone in the Antartic confined to a small hut buried in the snow. This was a voluntary stint he conceived to achieve peace and to allow him to think about things without being disturbed by outside sources.

He found the polar night, with scarcely a sound from outside his quarters, anything but desirable. His initial and intended peacefulness turned into just the opposite. He soon was impressed by the physical hazards of carbon monoxide poisoning and the awful cold and the possibility of his quarters collapsing from the accumulating weight of snow and ice. So fear was with him for some time. But this changed into apathy so that he was hardly able to carry on the simple routines of daily existence. He lay in bed hallucinating and going over and over all kinds of bizarre imaginings.

Another significant result as far as we are concerned was that he developed the convincing feeling that he was part of a broad unstructured universe. That is, his perception of himself lost structure and, had he been like the Eastern yogis, Admiral Byrd would have called this a deeply religious experience, being at one with God.

What has just been reported about Byrd is not unique, for we can read about the experiences of the ancients who went out into the deserts for fasts of many days and came back to report their experiences. Curiously enough, this reduction of personality structure was a religious experience and, according to the fasters, opened them up to new understandings. They believed that their understandings were something that transcended those of everyday life and should be heeded by their fellow countrymen.

Curious effects of isolation from human contact have been reported by those who have made transatlantic voyages alone.

Milder forms of isolation have been undertaken by other individuals and they, too, report definite changes in the way their surroundings were perceived and in their cognitive outlook.

The following example of voluntary isolation is different from that of Admiral Byrd. In this case the individual did not undergo bodily confinement nor were the visual and auditory stimuli reduced to a minimum. He chose only to be a hermit in a cabin in a remote spot in the mountains near Hot Springs, Arkansas. Here he was able to "do what he wanted without interruption." He was spared the interruptions and distractions of telephone, radio, television, and the presence of other humans "yak-yaking" around him. His only human contacts were his sister and brother-in-law who visited him once a week but brought no news from the "outside," except news of close friends and family.

To begin with, he followed a schedule of writing in the morning, reminiscing in the afternoon, and reading in the evening, and during the day took long walks.

His first trouble came in being unable to sleep well. He could only sleep in short snatches, spending a great deal of time in a state between full sleep and waking. He also got up in the mornings feeling tired and this tiredness increased day by day.

One of the main devices he used to advantage was the involvement of the sensory systems as much as possible.

There are such individuals as hermits and we seldom, if ever, hear any reports from them as to the nature of their existence. It will be noted, however, that, typically, they have animals with them—dogs, donkeys, and other domesticated animals with which they can and do interact. It seems quite characteristic for all individuals who live in isolation to have pets.

The foregoing description regarding isolation is meant to point out what happens to normal people under certain restricted stimulus conditions. Isolation is a state in which new objects come into existence in the individual's experience of what is real. He or she sees strange new creatures that the nondeprived would not see. Depending on his or her initial outlook on life and the age in which he or she lives, the individual interprets these creatures as gods, devils, emissaries of the devil or the divine.

Kayak Disease

A specific form of isolation or sensory deprivation exists in "Kayak disease." Kayak disease is a nontechnical term often given to the behavior of an individual in the following situation.

An Eskimo will often go out in a kayak to hunt seals. The result about to be described may occur on a day on which the sea and the sky are hardly distinguishable. All around him is visual uniformity. It is a particular kind of Ganzfeld. The Eskimo's task is to sit motionless if possible, even for hours, so as to simulate something lifeless and not to scare away the seals. What actually happens in this case is that instead of remaining alert and ready to spear the seal that may come near, he develops a kind of stonewall immobility and his attention dwindles to near nothing and he becomes unaware of anything and everything around him. In that state he is said to have Kayak disease.

TRANSCENDENTAL MEDITATION

Transcendental meditation is practiced for its own sake and also constitutes part of Yoga. Apparently, Yoga consists of three components: a form of muscular exercise, a form of meditation, and a philosophy for rationalizing these and interpreting the results, mainly including the experiences of the practioner. We shall bypass the muscular exercises at this point and describe "meditation." Transcendental meditation exists in several specific forms depending on where in the Orient it was developed and practiced. I shall describe it only in a very general way, thus some of the features of meditation familiar to the reader may not be mentioned. In essence, meditation is a form of controlling attention, for example, by concentrating on or visualizing some spot on the body and by relating the imagination to one's breathing. For example, one may be asked to count to ten and then to repeat this again and again. In so doing, the individual relates the counting to the respiratory cycles, naming a number as he or she slowly exhales.

Thus, in any case the exhalation phase of the respiratory cycle is the letdown or relaxation phase. One often droops the shoulders and makes other physical alterations form a postural part of relaxing, which in some contexts is a part of "sighing."

If this routine is continued in a quiet room without external distraction, the subject loses awareness of his or her surroundings and attention narrows to the spot or object he or she is imagining. If one is simply imagining a spot, the "visual" field also becomes very simple, diffuse, and homogenous. There are certain hypnogogic-like experiences that sometimes occur under some conditions but these need not be discussed here. What seems to happen is a kind of relaxation and a shift in measurable internal processes such as heart rate, brain wave rates, and blood pressure. These latter are taken by researchers as evidences that the meditation state is different from the ordinary waking state or hypnotic state.

Various forms of *meditation* achieve about the same result. Little or nothing is said about relaxation in describing the state, but relaxation is evidently one of the incidental accomplishments, and on this account the meditation and relaxation procedures we consider in this next section have a big factor in common. No single description will cover all varieties of transcendental meditation, but another example may add to the understanding of what is involved.

In one form the subject is placed in a situation where he or she is alone but a guru may peep in from time to time. The subject is given a very simple but possibly difficult task to accomplish. For example, he or she is in the dark with eyes closed and is to imagine a spot on his or her upper lip. The subject is to keep looking at this continuously, or as nearly continuously as possible. Or he or she may be asked to look at an imaginary spot of light on the abdomen, let us say at the position of his navel. The subject may begin with this spot and slowly have it spread until it fills the whole imagined visual field. Or the subject may begin with imagining the whole field homogeneously lighted up and proceed until the light contracts into a tiny spot and vanishes. A practiced subject may end a session in an intended trance.

Regardless of the specific modes of meditation practiced by various peoples, they all are techniques whereby the attention is narrowed to some particular focus and held for extended periods. As a consequence, many of the same aspects of bodily functioning are changed as in systematic relaxation. The differences have mainly to do with the theoretical, health-seeking, or religious purposes involved. These differences tend at first sight to mask what is actually taking place in the individual. We are interested in the changes in the individual, primarily alterations in his or her perceptual stance. Transcendental meditation is an area that is remote from the everyday living of many people and therefore what is said about the topic appears to be little more than empty words. Nevertheless, meditation and the effects it produces could well be an appropriate part of sophisticated people's understanding of themselves as human beings. In such a state their perceptions are different or many forms are virtually absent and from this their cognitive outlooks undergo change.

Piggins and Morgan (1977) discuss the effects of two conditions that are the essential components of most meditation procedures, namely, steady visual fixation and a repetitous auditory input, such as a click or a regularly repeated multisyllabic word. They found that clicks tend to group themselves and the words undergo profound changes. Warren and Gregory (1958) call this the verbal transformation effect.

This transformation can occur in situations far from transcendental meditation. I remember that when I was studying perception in college, the students were asked to sit and look quietly and steadily look at their motionless thumbs. It did not take long before the thumb changed its appearance and became a surprisingly funny looking object. So it is no wonder that extended procedures where viewing and attention are held as constant as possible result in profound perceptual alterations.

Younger, Adriance, and Berger (1975) wondered whether some of the time spent in meditation might not be actually spent in sleeping. To test this, they recorded electroencephalograms (EEGs) and DC electrooculograms (EOGs) during the meditation of experimental subjects. Records scored blind indicated that six of the eight spent portions of their meditation periods in sleep as evidenced by the electrical records. This would seem to be a likely result. Jacobson (1957) denies his technique produces sleep during relaxation sessions. The fact that sleep may occur is not evidence that meditation is nothing but sleep. It is fortunate that the instrumental records show the difference between the two states.

SYSTEMATIC RELAXATION

Thus far we have seen what happens when the individual is in more or less a stimulus vacuum. We have also seen that the individual can, by certain self-applied procedures, put himself or herself into a perceptual state very different from normal. In these procedures one of the major factors is withdrawal from the usual attention-getting everyday affairs and focusing the attention on certain repetitive acts. In the usual descriptions of the endeavors little or nothing is said regarding body states such as tension of muscles, but the procedures are certainly tension-relieving.

Now we come to special procedures whereby extreme relaxation of many or all the muscle groups of the body can be achieved— a state wherein the individual is surely in a unique condition not only regarding muscles, but also regarding the way he or she reacts to sensory inputs. A well-known technique was introduced by Edmund Jacobson many years ago for clinical purposes. Our interest here is getting to realize the organism's possibilities in relaxation.

Tension

Much of the usual reference to kinesthesis is rather indirect. One of the more familiar forms of reference pertains to muscular tension. What is called tension has several aspects. Sometimes it is called personal tension or nervous tension. Tension is, on the one hand, a kind of experience that has to do with one's own state and relation to his or her surrounds, particularly with the task demands and, on the other hand, tension is a stated or implied muscular or neural condition.

In the limbs and in some other members, skeletal muscles are arranged in pairs and may act either against each other or in reciprocity. In movement, muscle pairs act in some degree of reciprocity. When one member of the pair contracts, the other relaxes and elongates. This opposition may be in the form of easy going reciprocity or a tug of war. Reciprocity may occur in many temporal patterns to produce the many forms of skeletal movement of which we know the human subject to be capable. Tension in muscle is not only more or less phasic (producing motion) but is also residual. Motor responses do not occur and complete themselves but last on as residual tensions.

The state of tension in various muscle groups may vary from a minimum during sleep to a maximum under high excitement when awake. Part of this may be spoken of as tonus necessary for the maintenance of posture and other action against gravity, and part of it may be excessive.

Irradiation, the progressive involvement of more and more musculature during the performance of a prolonged task, is one expression of tension. This may happen, for example, in writing a long letter. The writer starts out by using only the restricted musculature that is needed to move a pen but ends up by using arm, neck, back, and so on.

Muscle tonus and tension are involved in helping to sustain the excitation level of the cortex. Freeman (1948), who has given a great deal of attention to muscle tension and motor activity, calls the peripheral input from the muscle a backlash and credits it with the task of maintaining alertness. Kinesthesis, then, can be seen to play a role in personal alertness.

Not only does muscular activity, including muscular tension, send a sustaining innervation into the central nervous system, but it also produces the feeling of effort. When a task is difficult, there is likely to be a greater fraction of the total activity spent in excess tension than when the task is easy. When there is little diversion into this ineffective sidetrack called tension, the task *feels* easy; when tension is at its height, the task *feels* difficult.

Relaxation

The question of the relation of muscle state to alertness, sleeplessness, and other special conditions of the individual is not clearly understood. Edmund Jacobson (1957), who concerned himself with the medical aspects of tension taught people to relax their muscles and found that the relaxed muscular state is conductive to personal tranquility and the alleviation of anxiety and to good health. Jacobson obtained concrete evidences for both the relaxed and the tense muscular states by recording muscle action potentials.

An essential feature of Jacobson's teaching of progressive relaxation is to get his patient-trainees to become aware of tensions in particular muscle groups of the body one at a time.

If one bends the hand backward at the wrist one does so, of course, by contracting muscles lying in the back of the forearm. One would expect the tension in this muscle group to be felt, but this is not immediately so. What is felt is tension at the wrist, which Jacobson terms strain. But until the person becomes aware of the tension in the muscles just indicated, one cannot learn to relax them. Training to become aware of tension in specific muscles is carried out from group to group throughout the body, and once awareness of tension has been achieved, relaxation can be produced at will on future occasions. Jacobson's systematic relaxation brings about a very different mode of relationship with the stimulus world. The individual in utilizing the systematic relaxation procedures, encounters certain experiential results. In addition, one may move into a routine that is essentially the routine of transcendental meditation. One may put himself or herself into a comfortable position, either seated in a chair or reclining, and may repeat to himself or herself the words "relax," or "let go."

Such variants are understood to exist by Jacobson, who warns against any procedure that could be called self-hypnosis. As far as we are concerned here, the fact that these variants can exist is a demonstration relevant to what we are trying to describe—namely, that the various major procedures whether they be yoga, transcendental meditation, autogenic training, or Jacobsonian relaxation all have something in common. And although they differ in certain assumptions and involve unlike routine details, these procedures owe their success to getting the individual in a state of calm. This state has muscular relaxation as a major and indispensible feature.

In this state of muscular relaxation an individual's perceptual world is a far different one from the one experienced in everyday life. In its extremes, there is a feeling of having withdrawn from the world of worry and concern. Visual imagery, for example, retreats from the usual complexity to less and less structure. The very lack of muscular tension is one of the factors, it would seem, that allows the individual to sink into that "oneness with the universe," mentioned earlier.

Although reporting here on systematic relaxation does not provide the reader with laboratory experiments of fine detail, nevertheless, it refers to a very real and essential feature of the human organism—the ability to arrive at states in which the perceptual information seeking and processing mechanism is pretty much calmed down.

Although from some standpoints it may seem that relaxation has little to do with perception, this is not the case, for here we are dealing with a sense modality—namely, the kinesthetic sense—and with the condition the individual can get into when kinesthetic input to the central nervous system is reduced to a low ebb. This changes one's perception of one's body and in turn changes even his or her perception of the external environment. While the clinical aspect of relaxation has usually been emphasized and studied and reported on, its perceptual aspect is no less important from the standpoint of understanding the human organism.

As in outright sensory deprivation, relaxation is an altered state of the individual and changes in both the testable body processes, and the individual's perceptual relations to the environment can be expected. It so happens that this area has not as yet been as fully studied in the laboratory as it might. However, the special conditions we have been dealing with in systematic relaxation needed to be included to round out our understanding of perception.

BIOFEEDBACK AND PERCEPTION

Biofeedback is one aspect of what occurs where instrumentation is used to mirror psychophysiological processes of which the individual is normally unaware, and consequently these processes may be voluntarily brought under control. Biofeedback is used to give a person immediate information about his or her own biological conditions, such as brain-wave activity, galvanic skin response, heart rate, muscle tension, blood pressure, and the like.

In sessions in which biofeedback is involved the individual pays attention to himself or herself in order to detect certain feelings that correlate with the monitoring instrumentation. While this procedure has come mainly to have clinical importance and utilization in certain circles, it is a form of self-perception, and in being what it is, biofeedback is a special form of perception. This form was not recognized until very recently. It is an outgrowth of the insights and research of Neal Miller and his associates who have been interested in showing certain unsuspected characteristics of the autonomic nervous system (see Miller, 1971).

BIOFEEDBACK EXPERIMENTS

Green, Walters, Green, and Murphy (1971) have described a biofeedback technique for producing what they call deep relaxation. A brief look at this technique to compare or contrast some of its features and accomplishments with those of Jacobson is worthwhile here.

Muscle in complete rest does not display the electrical potentials ordinarily recordable from it.

The feedback technique consists in using electrical instrumentation, whereby through electrodes placed on the muscle group involved, a visible record can be obtained of the discharging motor units for the subject to see. The subject is instructed to try to reduce the discharge rate. For example, in some procedures a cut-off rate is chosen by the experimenter and when firing is below that rate a continuous sound is heard, or a light appears. When the rate is above, all is quiet, or no light shows. The task of the subject is to make the sound or light be on continuously. Apparently, the subject is able to detect a subtle feeling of some sort in the one condition that differs from the other. Once the subject is at least vaguely aware of this, he or she works to make the needed feeling continuous.

It is claimed that individuals in a few minutes can achieve periods of zero firing. Before the feedback system was used the experimenters were unable to get any of their subjects to this state in a short time. Now in one experiment, 7 out of 21 of the subjects achieved this state within 20 minutes.

The next example involves the control of "brain waves." Brain waves are the recordable electrical potentials that occur in the brain and are recordable from placing electrodes on the scalp. The wave pattern that sometimes stands out over others is a relatively simple frequency of about 10 per second. It is called the *alpha rhythm.* Obviously, here is a neural activity of which the subject knows nothing. Characteristically, trains of alpha waves alternately appear and disappear.

Presumably, there is something characteristic of bodily state when alpha waves are occurring and which is absent when alpha waves are not occurring. Kamiya (1971) wondered whether a person could be made aware of internal states. He set out to answer this question by designing an experiment using alpha waves as an indicator. Kamiya began with a single subject placed in a quiet, darkened room. During this stay the subject's brain waves were monitored from an adjacent room. He was told that he would hear a bell ring now and then, part of the time when he was in state A (when alpha waves were appearing) and at other times when he was in state B (when no alpha waves were appearing). Each time the subject heard the bell he or she was to guess in which of the two states he or she was. The subject of course, was told whether he or she was right or wrong.

During the first day's experiment the subject was right about 50 percent of the time which is the percentage expected by mere chance. During the second day he was right 65 percent of the time. His score rose to 85 percent on the third day. On the fourth day he made a perfect score, being correct the 400 times without an error. As a further test the subject was to indicate which of the two states he was in when asked, when there was no bell used.

Following this, the possibility of eye position affecting the results was tested. It was found that every time the subject raised his eyes, an alpha burst resulted. So a test series was run with the subject instructed to keep looking straight ahead. This run produced a score of only 80 percent correct. Yet with more practice he achieved a perfect score.

The same tests were tried on a series of other subjects and most of them did well, too. The investigators were insightful enough to suppose that a conditioned introspective response is finally set up in the experiment, so now subjects were asked to describe the differences in the way they felt in the two states, A and B. All the subjects were able to make descriptive distinctions. In state A, the state with the alpha waves, the description was typically of "letting the mind wander." Kamija concluded that when the subjects had learned to discriminate the two states with a perfect score, they were able to control their "minds" to the extent of being able to institute and maintain either state at will.

Later, a different method was devised at the Langley Porter Neuropsychiatric Institute in San Francisco. The method involves the use of an electronic device with an electrode on the scalp that sounds a tone when alpha waves are occurring.

The subjects in this experiment were placed in a sound-deadened room and asked to try to keep the tone sounding continuously. The subjects were told that certain mental states were required to do this. No overt muscular movements were permitted. At the end of each minute the subjects were told the percentage of time they had been able to sustain the tone. Later, the subjects were required to see to what extent they could suppress the tone. After 40 of the one-minute tests, eight out of ten subjects were able to control the tone—that is, having it sound or not, according to instructions. The subjects reported on their mental states while suppressing the tone and on sustaining it. Alpha waves were found to occur during a kind of state devoid of visual imagery, and it was this state that the subject began to detect and tried to maintain as continuously as possible.

Other laboratories have also studied the production and suppression of alpha waves.

The relevance of the biofeedback techniques to what has been described about transcendental meditation lies in the fact that the reports of the subjects in the alpha state closely resemble those of Yoga and Zen meditation states. It was also found that subjects who were experienced Zen meditators learned to control their alpha waves much more quickly than other subjects.

The use of the biofeedback technique has spread quite rapidly in the past few years and many writers, both popular and technical, have described it as a demonstration of mind-over-body process, down to the last detail. What we have already said about biofeedback technique may simply lead readers to concur and think in the same outmoded way, using the traditional terms, *mind* and *body* as the two categories into which all cause-and-effect phenomena are put. It will be helpful to review our comments in Chapters 1 and 2 about cause and effect and emergent phenomena versus the one cause-and-effect system, the energistic system.

A good discussion of *awareness* is given by Hilgard (1971) which bears nicely on behaviorism and other forms of psychological outlook and is relevant here.

Awareness in the biofeedback experiments is perceptual awareness and is a form of concern in the discussion of perception.

PERCEPTION IN ALCOHOLISM

In this section we are taking a specific example of perception in connection with drug usage. This category, if dealt with fully, would include the cases related to narcotics, to psychedelics, and, of course, to alcohol. The relation of the individual and drugs is broad and many aspects of it are not relevant to our purposes here. We have occasion and space at this time only for reporting on some experimental findings in regard to alcoholics and alcoholism.

The public outlook on alcoholics has changed over the years. There was a time when alcoholics were simply drunks, possibly nèer-do-well. We were made to understand that alcoholics were people who were sick.

Some experimental findings now suggest that alcoholics are individuals who are perceptually different from other people even when not under the influence of liquor at the time. These effects could be chronic residuals of the excessive use of alcohol or they could indicate that, even to begin with, some people are different from others in ways that dispose them to addiction and thus they get into the group we call alcoholics.

Getting drunk, or even the limited use of alcohol, is often thought indispensible for "having a good time." In other words, there are times that alcohol is used to relieve tension and to forget one's troubles. While this may be admitted, the impression given to certain experimenters regarding alcohol usage is that perceptual deficits may exist in certain people and that alcohol is used to compensate for these deficits.

This brings up the question of how to define alcoholism. Is it the state we find in persons addicted to alcohol? Or is it some condition that can be identified that makes some persons tend to become excessive and compulsive users and cravers for alcohol in the first place? Any way we look at the matter it seems to pose this double-barreled question. In either case we are dealing with some sort of special perceptual condition.

We shall briefly report on some findings and conclusions in this area. Nelson, Sinha, and Olson (1978) found that chronic alcoholics, tested when sober, show greatly inferior short-term memory for hue. This deficit persists even when hue memory is corrected for age. And it is greater for advanced alcoholics than for early ones. This deficit does not seem to be localized in any particular part of the color space, and this along with other findings in the literature led the authors to suppose that the deficit they found reflects generalized damage to the nervous pathways mediating color.

Jacobson, VanDyke, Sternback, and Brethauer (1976) tested 402 males and 160 females in a hospital for alcoholics on the rod-and-frame test. When their performance was compared with normals and psychiatric patients, it was found that alcoholics were definitely more field dependent than the others. They also found some statistically significant sex differences.

Nelson and Swartz (1971) studied perceptual conflict in alcoholics by making a comparison of their behavior with nonalcoholics in the study of Nelson and Vasold (1965), which manipulated object surface independently of edge. This was done by using positive and negative photographic prints of 20 common objects, presented under time-controlled exposure (see Figure 17.2). The time taken to recognize these objects was used as a measure of recognition difficulty.

The difference between negative and the usual positive prints lies in the fact that surface characteristics are altered from the usual without changing edge. The negative prints thus constitute conflicting information, because surface conditions are not consistent with those of edge or outline.

Not all objects present the same degree of difficulty in recognition. The more complex objects seem to be identified on the basis of surface characteristics that contain gradients of lightness or visual texture.

The subjects used in Nelson and Swartz's study were 30 unselected outpatients of a clinic for alcoholics. Alcoholics, like normals, were found to have more difficulty in recognizing negatives than positives (prints); that is, they required a longer exposure time for the negatives. This difficulty increased with complexity. In all but two of the 20 pairs of prints, the difficulty for the negative print was greater than for the positive. The data showed that the alcoholics absolutely and relatively were less able to process conflicting information than Nelson and Vasold's normals.

Apparently, alcoholics have difficulty in processing information pertaining to objects in general. This is increased when the target contains features in conflict with the viewer's habitual relations to the visual world. Since this and all of the foregoing reports regarding alcoholics had to do with tests on sober subjects, what was being dealt with was an internal condition not produced by alcohol imbibed at the time of testing.

Nelson and Swartz ask a question regarding the inferior ability to process the information relating to surface properties in general, which is worsened when the target confronted possesses surface features in conflict with the individual's habitual assumptions about the visual world. They ask whether this is a result of physiological damage from the excessive use of alcohol or whether it is a result of an inherent condition in some individuals predisposing the seeking of alcohol to bring relief. The investigators suggest the latter view. This is a novel view of the alcoholic, but nevertheless represents something important for investigators to entertain and investigate.

Alcohol Levels During Tests

Various studies since 1940 have suggested that levels of alcohol that impair perceptual and psychomotor skills also diminish awareness of impairment. (Jeffinek and McFarland, 1940; Wallgren and Barry, 1970.) However, the experimental findings on awareness differ.

Since many of the assessments of alcohol effects on the subject's awareness of performance have come from postexperimental interviews or other factors biasing the results, Lubin (1977) undertook to check on awareness. His data support the idea that alcohol impairs both performance and performance awareness: the study included spurious feedback cues and it was found that these were increasingly effective with higher levels of alcohol.

Such studies may seem unnecessary since many people have been satisfied that alcohol is effective in reducing the speed and accuracy of performance. But the main thrust here has been to

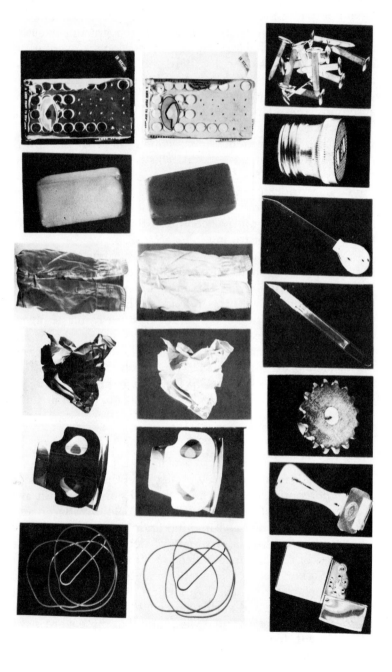

Figure 17.2 Positive and negative prints. (Source: Thomas M. Nelson and Paul C. Vasold. "Dependence of object identification upon edge and surface," *Percept. & Mot. Skills*, 1965, 20, 537–546, Fig. 1. Copyright © by Southern Universities Press, 1965.)

see whether certain ideas of this sort can be confirmed. Lubin's study showed that the individuals under the influence of alcohol at the time not only perform more poorly but are unaware of the deficit in their performance.

A study of perception of distorted auditory messages was made by Nelson, Sinha, and Deegan (recent personal communication, 1978). In this study 44 university students of both sexes ranging from 19 to 45 years were tested. Four groups varying in amount of alcohol consumed (corrected for body weight) listened to taped messages. The authors measured what they called recognition and attention in messages exhibiting standardized degrees of distortion.

Alcohol consumption was found to affect both attention and recognition adversely; the higher the blood alcohol content, the lower was the efficiency of performance. They found no support for popular suggestions that drugs enhance perceptual and cognitive functions. They did warn that the findings cannot be safely generalized to include chronic users of alcohol, for alcoholics might possibly employ compensatory cognitive strategies enabling more accurate perception of verbal material than otherwise.

What is involved in this area is a kind of special perceptual state. It has become increasingly obvious to some that the matter is far from simple. First of all, studies have shown that subjects under the influence of alcohol do perceive differently from sober persons. Secondly, advanced alcoholics do more poorly than those who have been classed as alcoholics for a shorter time. This is, of course, seen by some as an effect of the prolonged excessive use of alcohol. Thirdly, the suggestion is made that certain individuals possess body process characteristics that predispose them to use alcohol excessively. As to perception, these individuals would be in a special class. Whatever future findings ensue, the general area we have been discussing here involves special perceptual conditions.

MODES OF ENCOUNTER

In discussing special perceptual conditions, we have dealt with (1) differences in relation of the organism to the surrounds and (2) differences in the internal states of the organism itself. We have made no more than a brief excursion into the possibilities in the area. And there are possibly different ways of describing the various categories we have included. The following account is an example.

Swartz (1969) pointed out two modes of "encounter"—the *particulate* mode and the *transcendent* mode. To hear such a word as "transcendent" may seem to indicate that we are dealing with a concern totally alien and unmentionable in experimental psychology, but such is not necessarily the case.

The particulate mode is one in which human experience deals with objects in their specificity. In the transcendent mode the person is in phenomenal union with his or her world. In this mode, experience (consciousness) pertains to broad qualities and conditions *as* qualities and conditions and the subject–object relation has diminished to the vanishing point.

This concept is not as new as it may seem. We have already found Admiral Byrd in that condition alone in the Antarctic. But we do not have to go that far to find other examples. It would seem that in states of ecstacy that some people experience, the individual's consciousness could be aptly described as a state in which specific details of his or her ordinary relation to things are largely absent. The experience is of oneness with something bigger than the self. In pointing this out, Swartz refers to what Maslow (1962) describes as "peak-experience," or to the "I-Thou" encounter of Buber (1958). Subject–object relations are absent or nearly so. The important consideration is the human's experienced state of being.

Language becomes paralyzed in any attempt to describe transcendent encounter, but it does not take much to demonstrate the validity of the encounter as a form of human experience. As far as we are concerned here, it is only necessary to point out this fact.

Recognizing the transcendent state helps to round out the description of the human and thus our description of perception.

References

Abney, W. de W. *Researches in Colour Vision.* (London: McKay, 1913).

Abraham, O. "Zur psychologischen Akustik von Wellenlänge und Schwerin-gungszahl," *Zf. F. Sinnesphysiol.,* 51 (1920), 121–152.

Adair, H. J., and S. H. Bartley. "Nearness as a function of lateral orientation in pictures," *Percept. & Mot. Skills,* 8 (1958), 135–141.

Alexander, S. J., M. Cotzin, C. J. Hill, E. A. Ricciuti, and G. R. Wendt. "The effect of variation of time intervals between accelerations upon sickness rates," *J. Psychol.,* 19 (1945), 49–62.

Alexeenko, N. Y. "Directional hearing, effect of unilateral change of same direction," *Science,* 167 (1970), 1009–1010.

Allport, F. *Theories of Perception and the Concept of Structure* (New York: Wiley, 1955).

Allport, G. W., and T. F. Pettigrew. "Cultural influence on the perception of movement: The trapezoidal illusion among Zulus," *J. Abnorm. Soc. Psychol.,* 55 (1957), 104–113.

Alpern, M. "Metacontrast," *J.O.S.A.,* 43 (1953), 648–657.

Alpern, M., and H. David. "The additivity of contrast in the human eye," *J. Gen. Psychol.,* 43 (1959), 109–126.

Ames, A., Jr. "Visual perception and the rotating trapezoidal window," *Psychol. Mono.,* 65, no. 324 (1951).

Ames, A., Jr. "Binocular vision as affected by relations between uniocular stimulus patterns in commonplace environments," *Amer. J. Psychol.*, 59 (1946), 333–357.

Ammons, C. H., P. Worchel, and K. M. Dallenbach. "Facial vision: The perception of obstacles out of doors by blindfolded and blindfolded deafened subjects," *Amer. J. Psychol.*, 66 (1953), 519–553.

Anstis, S. M., and J. Atkinson. "Distortions in moving figures viewed through a stationary slit," *Amer. J. Psychol.*, 80 (1967), 572–586.

Anton, B. S. "Poggendorf illusion as a function of orientation of transversal and paralled lines," *Percept. & Mot. Skills,"* 43 (1976), 83–90.

Apkarian-Stielau, P., and J. M. Loomis. "A comparison of tactile and visual form perception," *Percept. & Psychophysics*, 18 (5), (1975), 362–368.

Aronson, E., and S. Rosenbloom. "Space perception in early infancy: Perception with a common auditory visual space," *Science*, 172 (1971), 1161–1163.

Ashley, W. R., R. S. Harper, and D. L. Runyan. "The perceived size of coins in normal and hypnotically induced income states," *Amer. J. Psychol.*, 64 (1951), 564–572.

Aubert, H. "Die Bewegungsempfindung," *Arch. Ges. Physiol.*, 39 (1886), 347–370.

Bach-y-Rita, R. *Brain Mechanisms in Sensory Substitution* (New York; Academic Press, 1972).

Baker, H. D. "The course of foveal light adaptation measured by the threshold intensity increment," *J.O.S.A.*, 39 (1949), 172–179.

Ball, R. J. "An investigation of chromatic brightness enhancement tendencies," *Amer. J. Optom., Arch. Amer. Acad. Optom.*, 41 (1964), 333–361.

Ball, R. J., and S. H. Bartley. "Effects of temporal manipulation of photic stimulation of perceived brightness, hue, and saturation," *Amer. J. Optom., Arch. Amer. Acad. Optom.*, 42 (1965), 573–581.

Ball, R. J., and S. H. Bartley. "Further investigations of color perception under temporal manipulation of photic stimulation," *Amer. J. Optom., Arch. Amer. Acad, Optom.*, 43 (1966), 419–430.

Bartley, S. H. "The comparative distribution of light in the stimulus and on the retina," *J. Comp. Psychol.*, 19 (1935), 149–154.

Bartley, S. H. "Relation of retinal illumination to the experience of movement," *J. Exp. Psychol.*, 19 (1936a), 475–485.

Bartley, S. H. "Temporal and spatial summation of extrinsic impulses with intrinsic activity of the cortex," *J. cell. comp. Physiol.*, 8 (1936b), 41–62.

Bartley, S. H. "Some effects of intermittent photic stimulation," *J. Exp. Psychol.*, 25 (1939), 462–480.

Bartley, S. H. *Vision: A Study of Its Basis* (Princeton, NJ: Van Nostrand, 1941).

Bartley, S. H. "The perception of size or distance based on tactile and kinesthetic data," *J. Psychol.*, 36 (1953), 401–408.

Bartley, S. H. "Some comparisons between print size, object position, and object size in producing phenomenal distance," *J. Psychol.*, 48 (1959), 347–351.

Bartley, S. H. "Temporal Features of Input as Crucial Factors in Vision," in W. D. Neff, ed., *Contributions to Sensory Physiology* (New York: Academic Press, 1969).

Bartley, S. H. and H. J. Adair. "Comparisons of phenomenal distance in photographs of various sizes," *J. Psychol.* 47 (1959), 289–295.

Bartley, S. H., and R. J. Ball. "Changes in brightness index, saturation, and hue produced by luminance-wavelength-temporal interaction," *J.O.S.A.*, 56 (1966), 695–699.

Bartley, S. H., L. T. Clifford, and A. D. Calvin. "Effect of visual imagery on tactual and kinesthetic space perception," *Percept. & Mot. Skills*, 5 (1955), 177–184.

Bartley, S. H., and D. DeHardt. "A further factor in determining nearness as a function of lateral orientation in pictures," *J. Psychol.*, 50 (1960), 53–57.

Bartley, S. H., and D. DeHardt. "Phenomenal distance in scenes with independent manipulation of major and minor items," *J. Psychol.*, 50 (1960), 315–322.

Bartley, S. H., and G. A. Fry. "An indirect method for measuring stray light within the human eye," *J.O.S.A.*, 24 (1934), 342–347.

Bartley, S. H., and J. W. Miller. "Some circumstances surrounding apparent movement in the line of regard," *J. Psychol.*, 38 (1954), 453–456.

Bartley, S. H., and T. M. Nelson. "Certain chromatic and brightness changes associated with rate of intermittency of photo stimulation," *J. Psychol.*, 50 (1960), 323–332.

Bartley, S. H., and R. Thompson. "A further study of horizontal asymmetry in the perception of pictures," *Percept. & Mot. Skills*, 9 (1959), 135–138.

Bartley, S. H., and R. W. Winters. "Target structure and visual distance," *J. Psychol.*, 70 (1968), 267–278.

Bartoshuk, L. M. "Taste illusions: Some demonstrations," *Annals of the New York Academy of Sciences*, 237 (1974a), 279–285.

Bartoshuk, L. M. "NaCl thresholds in man: Thresholds for water taste or NaCl taste?" *Journal of Comparative & Physio. Psy.*, 87 (1974b), 310–325.

Basler, A. "Über die Verschmelzung der Warmeempfingung bie rhythmisch esfolgenden Reizen," *Arch. f. Biol.*, 71 (1920), 1–18.

Beebe-Center, J. G. "Standards for use of the gust scale," *J. Phychol.*, 28 (1949), 411–419.

Beebe-Center, J.G., and D. Waddell. "A general psychological scale of taste," *J. Psychol.*, 26 (1948), 517–524.

Beecher, H. K. *Measurement of Subjective Responses* (New York: Oxford University Press 1959).

Beidler, L. M. "Biophysical approaches to taste," *Amer. Sci.* (Winter 1961), 421–431.

Békésy, G. von. "Über die Hörsamkeit der Ein- und Asschwingvorgänge mit Berücksichtigung der Raumakustic," *Ann. Physik.*, 16 (1933), 844–860.

Békésy, G. von. "The variation of phase along the basilar membrane with sinusoidal vibrations," *J. Acoust. Soc. Amer.*, 19 (1947), 542–560.

Békésy, G. von. "Similarities between hearing and skin sensations," *Psychol. Rev.*, 66 (1959), 1–22.

Békésy, G. von. "Taste theories and chemical stimulation of single papillae," *J. Applied Physiol.*, 21 (1966), 1–9.

Benham, C. E. "The artificial spectrum top," *Nature*, 51 (1894), 200.

Benjamin, H. B., M. Wagner, H. K. Ihrig, and W. Zeit. "Hypothermia by internal cooling," *Science*, 123 (1956), 1128–1129.

Berger, E., C. H. Graham, and Y. Hsia. "Some visual functions of a unilaterally colorblind person. I. Critical fusion frequency in various spectral regions," *J.O.S.A.*, 48 (1958), 614–622.

Berlyne, D. E. "Attention to change," *Brit. J. Psych.*, 42 (1951), 269–278.

Berlyne, D. E. "Attention," in E. Canterette and M. Friedman, eds., *Handbook of Perception*, Vol. 1 (New York: Academic Press, 1973).

Berry, W., and H. Imus. "Quantitative aspects of the flight of colors," *Amer. J. Psychol.*, 47 (1935), 449–457.

Bever, T. G., J. R. Lackner, and R. Kirk. "The underlying structures of sentences and the primary units of immediate speech processing," *Percept. & Psychophysics*, 5(4) (1969), 225–234.

Bexton, W. H. "Some effects of perceptual isolation on human subjects," doctoral dissertation, McGill University, 1953.

Bexton, W. R., W. Heron, and R. H. Scott. "Effects of decreased variation in the sensory environment," *Canad. J. Psychol.*, 8 (1954), 70–76.

Birch, H. G., and L. Belmont. "Auditory-visual integration in retarded readers," *Amer. J. Orthopsychiat.*, 34 (1964a), 852–861.

Birch, H. G., and L. Belmont. "Perceptual analysis and sensory integration in brain-damaged persons," *J. Genet. Psychol.*, 105 (1964b), 173–179.

Birch, H. G., and L. Belmont. "Auditory visual integration in brain-damaged and normal children," *Devel. Med. Child Neurol.*, 7 (1965), 135–144.

Birch, H. G., and A. Lefford. "Intersensory development in children," *Mono. Soc. Res. Child Devel.*, 1963, 28, no. 5.

Bishop, G. H. "Responses to electrical stimulation of single sensory units of skin." *J. Neurophysiol.*, 6 (1943), 361–382.

Bishop, G. H. "The peripheral unit for pain," *J. Neurophysiol.*, 7 (1944), 71–80.

Bishop, G. H. "Neural mechanisms of cutaneous sense," *Physiol. Rev.*, 26 (1946), 77–102.

Bishop, G. H. "Relation of pain sensory threshold to forms of mechanical stimulator," *J. Neurophysiol.*, 12 (1949), 51–57.

Blanton, M. G. "The behavior of the human infant during the first thirty days of life," *Psychol. Rev.*, 24 (1917), 456–483.

Blix, M. "Experimentelle Beiträge zur Losung der Frage über die specifische Energie der Hautnerven," *Zeit. fur Biol.*, 20 (1884), 141–156.

Bloch, A. M. "Expériences sur la vision," *Paris Soc. Biol. Mem.*, 37 (1885), 493–495.

Blondel, A., and J. Rey. "Sur la perception des limuniniére bréves á la limite de leur portée," *J. de Phys.*, 1 (1911), 530–550.

Bonnet, C. "Perceived velocity and its relation to the length of the track," *Studies Psychol.*, 11 (1969), 148–149.

Boring, E. G. "The moon illusion," *Amer. J. Physics*, 11 (1943), 55–60.

Boring, E. G., and S. S. Stevens. "The nature of tonal brightness," *Proc. Nat'l Acad. Sci.*, 22 (1936), 514–521.

Borst, J. M. "The use of spectrograms for speech analysis and synthesis," *J. Audio. Eng. Soc.*, 4 (1956), 14–23.

Bower, T. G. R. "Stimulus variables determining space perception in infants," *Science*, 149 (1965), 88–89.

Bower, T. G. R. "The object world of the infant," *Sci. Amer.*, 225 (1971), 30–38.

Boynton, R. M., J. M. Enoch, and W. R. Bush. "Physical measures of stray light in excised eyes," *J.O.S.A.*, 44 (1954), 879–886.

Braine, L. G. "A new slant on orientation perception," *Amer. Psychol.*, 33 (1) (1978), 10–22.

Brewster, D. "On the influence of successive impulses of light upon the retina," *Phil. Mag.*, 4, 3rd series (1834), 241–245.

Bricker, P. D., and A. Chapanis. "Do incorrectly perceived tachistoscopic stimuli convey some information?" *Psychol. Rev.*, 60 (1953), 181–188.

Brindley, G. S. "The Bunsen–Roscoe law for the human eye and very short durations," *J. Physiol.*, 118 (1952), 135–139.

Broadbent, D. E. *Perception and Communication* (New York: Pergamon Press, 1958).

Broadbent, D. E. and M. Gregory. "Perception of Emotionally Toned Words," *Nature*, 215 (1967), 518–584.

Bross, M., and J. P. Zubek. "Effects of auditory deprivation on visual resolving power," *Canad. J. Psychol.*, 29 (1975), 340–347.

Bross, M., and J. P. Zubek. "Effects of auditory deprivation on cutaneous sensitivity," *Percept. & Mot. Skills*, 42 (1976), 1219–1226.

Brown, J. F. "The thresholds for visual movement," *Psychol. Forsch.*, 14 (1931), 249–268.

Brown, J. F. "The visual perception of velocity," *Psych. Forsch.*, 14 (1931), 199–232.

Brown, J. L., C. H. Graham, H. Leibowitz, and H. B. Ranken. "Luminance thresholds for the resolution of visual detail during dark adaptation," *J.O.S.A.*, 43 (1953), 197–202.

Brown, P. K., and G. Wald. "Visual pigments in single rods and cones in the human retina," *Science*, 144 (1964), 145–151.

Brownfield, C. H. *Isolation: Clinical and Experimental Approaches* (New York: Random House, 1965).

Brücke, E. "Über den Nutzeffekt intermittierender Netzhautreizungen," *S. -B. K. Akad. Wiss. Wein. Math-Nat. Kl.*, 49 (2) (1864), 128–153.

Bruner, J. S. "Personality dynamics and the process of perceiving," in R. R. Blake and G. V. Ramsey, eds., *Perception: An Approach to Personality* (New York: Ronald Press, 1951).

Bruner, J. S., and C. C. Goodman. "Value and need as organizing factors in perception," *J. Abnorm. Soc. Psychol.*, 42 (1947), 33–44.

Bruner, J. S., and L. Postman. "Emotional selectivity in perception and reaction," *J. Personal.*, 16 (1947), 69–77.

Bruner, J. S., and L. Postman. "Symbolic value as an organizing factor in perception," *J. Soc. Psychol.*, 27 (1948), 203–208.

Bryden, M. P. "Tachistoscopic recognition of non-alphabetical material," *Canad. J. Psych.*, 14 (1961), 78–86.

Bryden, M. P. "The role of post-exposure eye movements in tachistoscopic perception," *Canad. J. Psych.*, 15 (1961), 220–225.

Buber, M., *I and Thou* (New York: Scribner, 1958).

Bürck, W., P. Kotowski, and H. Lichte. "Der Aufbau des Tonhöhenbewusst-seins," *Elek. Nachr. -Techn.*, 12 (1935), 326–333.

Burian, H. M. "Influence of prolonged wearing of meridional size lenses on spatial localization," *Arch. Ophthalmol.*, 30 (1943), 654–666.

Burtt, H. E., "Auditory illusion of movement: A preliminary study," *J. Exp. Psychol.*, 2 (1917a), 63–75.

Burtt, H. E. "Tactual illusions of movement." *J. Exp. Psychol.*, 2 (1917b), 371–385.

Cagan, R. H. "Chemostimulatory protein, A new type of stimulus," *Science*, 18 (1973), 32–35.

Carmichael, L. "An experimental study in the prenatal guinea pig of the origin and development of reflexes and patterns of behavior in relation to the stimulation of specific receptor areas during the period of active fetal life," *Genet. Psychol. Mono.*, 16 (1934), 337–491.

Carr, H. *An Introduction to Space Perception* (New York: McKay, 1934).

Carter, L. and E. Schooler. "Value, need and other factors in perception," *Psychol. Rev.*, 56 (1949), 200–208.

Clark, D., H. Hough, and H. G. Wolff. "Experimental studies on headache," *Arch. Neurol. Psychiat.*, 35 (1936), 1054–1069.

Clark, W. C., A. H. Smith, and A. Rabe. "Retinal gradients of outline distortion and binocularily disparity as stimulus for slant," *Canad. J. Psychology*, 10 (1956), 77–81.

Cohen, W. "Spatial and textural characteristics of the Ganzfeld," *Amer. J. Psychology*, 70 (1957), 403–410.

Cole, R. E., and A. L. Diamond. "Amount of surround and test inducing separation in simultaneous brightness contrast," *Percept. & Psychophysics*, 9 (1971), 125–128.

Colon, F. "The size weight illusion in blind persons," unpublished master's thesis, Michigan State University, 1960.

Cornsweet, T. N. *Visual Perception* (New York: Academic Press, 1970).

Cramer, T. "Über die Beziehung des Zwischenmediums zu den Transformations und Kontrasterscheinungen," *Zf. f. Sinnesphysiol.*, 54 (1923), 215–242.

Crovitz, H. F., and W. Daves. "Tendencies to eye movement and perceptual accuracy," *J. Exp. Psychology*, 63, 5 (1962), 495–498.

Cutsforth, T. D. *The Blind in School and Society* (New York: American Foundation for the Blind, 1951).

Dallenbach, K. M. "The temperature spots and end organs." *Amer. J. Psychol.*, 39 (1927), 402–427.

Davis, C. M., M. Taylor, and P. Brickett. "A weight illusion produced by lifting movements," *Percept. & Mot. Skills*, 44 (1977), 299–305.

Day, R. H., and R. P. Power. "Apparent reversal (oscillation) of rotary motion in depth: An investigation and general theory," *Psychol. Rev.*, 72 (1965), 117–127.

DeHardt, D. C. "An investigation of tactual apparent movement," doctoral dissertation, Michigan State University, 1961.

DeLattre, P. C., C. Liberman and F. S. Cooper. "Acoustic loci and transitional cues for consonants." *J. Acoust. Soc. Amer.*, 27 (1955), 769–773.

Delorme, A., and J. Y. Frigon. "Influence of temporal frequency on perceived movement," *Percept. & Mot. Skills*, 45 (1977), 39–50.

Desor, J. A., and G. K. Beauchamp. "The human capacity to transmit olfactory information," *Percept. & Psychophysics*, 16 (1974), 551–556.

Deutsch, J. A., and D. Deutsch. *Physiological Psychology* (Homewood, IL: Dorsey Press, 1966).

DeValois, R. "Color vision mechanisms in the monkey, Part II," *J. Gen. Physiol.*, 43 (1960), 115–128.

Diamond, A. L. "Foveal simultaneous brightness contrast as a function of inducing- and test-field luminances," *J. Exp. Psychol.*, 45 (1953), 304–314.

Diamond, A. L. "Foveal simultaneous contrast as a function of inducing-field area," *J. Exp. Psychol.*, 50 (1955), 144–152.

Doane, B. K. "Changes in visual function with perceptual isolation," doctoral dissertation, McGill University, 1955.

Doane, B. K., W. Mahatoo, W. Heron, and T. H. Scott. "Changes in perceptual function after isolation," *Canad. J. Psychol.*, 13 (1959), 210–219.

Dodge, R. "Habituation to rotation," *J. Exp. Psychol.*, 6 (1923), 1–35.

Duda, P. D., and J. P. Zubek. "Auditory sensitivity after prolonged visual deprivation," *Psychonomic Science*, 3 (8) (1965), 359–360.

Dwyer, W. O., and C. S. White. "Peripheral area-intensity reciprocity in visual latency," *Vis. Res.*, 14 (1974), 971–974.

Dzendolet, E., and H. L. Meiselman. "Gustatory quality changes as a function of solution concentrations," *Percept. and Psychophysics*, 2 (1967), 29–33.

Edmonds, J. D., and W. O. Dwyer. "Peripheral area-intensity relations in scotopic visual reaction time," *Amer. J. Optom. & Physiol. Optics*, 54(2) (1977), 104–106.

Efstathiou, A., J. Bauer, M. Greene, and R. Held. "Altered reaching following adaptation to optical displacement of the hand," *J. Exp. Psychol.*, 73 (1967), 113–120.

Ekman, G., and G. Dahlback. *A Subjective Scale of Velocity*. Psych. Lab. Rep. No. 31, University of Stockholm, Sweden, 1956.

Enright, J. T. "Distinctions of apparent velocity," *Science*, 168 (1970), 464–467.

Erdelyi, M. H. "A new look at a new look: Perceptual defense and vigilance," *Psychol. Rev.*, 8(1) (1974), 1–25.

Ericksen, C. W. "Perception and personality," in J. W. Wekman and R. W. Keine, eds., *Concepts of Personality* (Chicago: Aldine, 1963).

Evans, R. M. *An Introduction to Color* (New York: Wiley, 1948).

Fantz, R. L. "The origin of form perception," *Sci. Amer.*, 204 (1961), 66–72.

Fantz, R. L. "Visual experience in infants. Decreased attention to familiar patterns relative to novel ones," *Science*, 145 (1964), 668–670.

Fantz, R. L., and S. B. Miranda. "Newborn infant attention to form of contour," *Child Development*, 46 (1975), 224–228.

Farnsworth, D. "Farnsworth–Munsell 100-hue and dichotomous test for color vision," *J.O.S.A.*, 33 (1943), 568–578.

Fechner, C. T. "Über eine Scheibe zur Ergengung subjectiver Farben," *Ann. Physik.*, 45, 2nd series (1838), 227–232.

Fechner, G. *Elements of Psychophysics*, trans. H. E. Adler (New York: Holt, Rinehart and Winston, 1966).

Findley, A. E. "Further studies of Henning's system of olfactory qualities," *Amer. J. Psychol.*, 35 (1924), 436–445.

Fischer, M. H. "Die Regulationsfunktionen des menschlichen Labyrinthes und die Zuzammenhänge mit verwandten Funktionen," *Ergebn. Physiol.*, 27 (1928), 209–237.

Fisher, B. M. "The relationship of size of surrounding field to visual acuity in the fovea," *J. Exp. Psychol.*, 23 (1938), 215–238.

Flamm, L. E., and B. O. Bergum. "Reversible perspective figures and eye movements," *Percept. & Mot. Skills*, 44(3) (1977), 1015–1019.

Fletcher, H. "Loudness, pitch, and timbre of musical tones and their relation to intensity, frequency, and overtone structure," *J. Acoust. Soc. Amer.*, 6 (1934), 59–69.

Flock, H. R. "Optical texture and linear perspective as stimuli for slant perception," *Psych. Rev.*, 72(6) (1965), 505–514.

Flock, H. R., and E. Freidberg. "Perceived angle of incidence and achromatic surface color," *Percept. & Psychophysics*, 8 (1970), 251–256.

Flock, H. R., and K. Noguchi. "An experimental test of Jameson and Hurvich's theory of brightness contrast," *Percept. & Psychophysics*, 8 (1970), 129–136.

Forgus, R. H., and L. E. Malamed. *Perception: A Cognitive Approach*, 2nd ed. (New York: McGraw-Hill, 1976).

Fraisse, P. *The Psychology of Time.* (New York: Harper & Row, 1963).

Fraisse, P., and G. MacMurray. "Étude génétique du sénile visuel de perception pour quatre catégories de stimuli," *Année Psychol.*, 60 (1960), 1–9.

Freeman, G. L. *The Energetics of Human Behavior* (Ithaca, NY: Cornell University Press, 1948).

Freeman, R. B., Jr. Ecological optics and visual slant, *Psychol. Rev.*, 72(6) (1965), 501–504.

Freeman, R. B., Jr. *Threshold Visual Slant as a Function of Stimulus Shape and Retinal Perspective*, Pennsylvania State University, Dept. of Psychol. Res. Bull. No. 35, October, 1965.

Freeman, R. B., Jr. "Absolute threshold for visual slant: the effect of stimulus size and retinal perspective," *J. Exp. Psychol.*, 71 (1966a), 170–176.

Freeman, R. B., Jr. "Effect of size on visual slant," *J. Exp. Psych.*, 71 (1966b), 96–103.

Freeman, R. B., Jr. and R. Pasnak. "Perspective determinants of the rotating trapezoid illusion," *J. Exp. Psychol.*, 76 (1 pt 1), (1968), 94–101.

Frey, M. von, Beiträge zur Sinnesphysiologie de Haut," *Ber. ges. Wiss.*, 49 (1897), 462–468.

Fry, G. A., and S. H. Bartley. "The effect of one border in the visual field upon the threshold of another," *Amer. J. Physiol.*, 112 (1935), 414–421.

Fry, G. A., and P. W. Cobb. "A new method for determining the blurredness of the retinal image," *Trans. Acad. Ophthalmol. Otolaryngol.* (1935), 1–6.

Gad, J., and H. Goldschneider. "Über die Summation von Hautreizen," *Ztschr. F. klin. Med. Berlin*, 20 (1892), 337–373.

Gaffron, M. "Right and left in pictures," *Art. Quart.*, 13 (1950), 312–331.

Gagge, A. P., L. P. Herrington, and C. E. A. Winslow. "Thermal interchanges between the human body and its atmospheric environment," *Amer. J. Hygiene*, 26 (1937), 84–103.

Gazzaniga, M. S., J. E. Bogen, and R. W. Sperry. "Laterality effects in somesthesis following commissurotomy in man," *Neuropsychologia*, 1 (1963), 209–215.

Gazzaniga, M. S., J. E. Bogen, and R. W. Sperry. "Observations on visual perception after disconnexion of the cerebral hemispheres in man, Part II," *Brain*, 88 (1965), 221–236.

Geldard, F. A. *The Human Senses* (New York: Wiley, 1953).

Gessell, A., F. L. Ilg, and G. E. Bullis. *Vision, Its Development in Infant and Child* (New York: Harper & Row, 1949).

Gibson, E. J. "Perceptual learning," *Ann. Rev. Psychol.*, 14 (1963), 29–56.

Gibson, E. J., A. D. Pick, H. Osser, and M. Hammond. "The role of grapheme-phoneme correspondence in the perception of words," *Amer. J. Psychol.*, 75 (1962), 554–570.

Gibson, J. J. "Adaptation, after-effect, and contrast in perception of curved lines," *J. Exp. Psychol.*, 16 (1933), 1–31.

Gibson, J. J. *The Perception of the Visual World* (Boston: Houghton Mifflin, 1950).

Gibson, J. J. "The concept of the stimulus in psychology," *Amer. Psychology*, 15 (1960), 694–703.

Gibson, J. J. "Observations on active touch," *Psychol. Rev.*, 69 (1962), 477–491.

Gibson, J. J. *The Senses Considered as Perceptual Systems* (Boston: Houghton Mifflin, 1966).

Gibson, J. J., and E. J. Gibson. "Perceptual learning: Differentiation or enrichment," *Psychol. Rev.*, 62 (1955), 32–41.

Gibson, J. J., and D. Waddell. "Homogeneous retinal stimulation and visual perception," *Am. J. Psychol.*, 65 (1952), 263–270.

Goldscheider, A. "Beiträge zur Lehre von der Hautsensibilität," *Zsch. Klin. Med.*, 74 (1911), 270–296.

Goldscheider, A. "Weitere Mitteilungen zur Physiologie der Sinnesnerven der Haut," *Pflug, Arch. Ges. Physiol.*, 168 (1917), 36–88.

Graham, C. H., K. E. Baker, M. Hecht, and V. V. Lloyd. "Factors influencing thresholds for monocular parallax," *J. Exp. Psychol.*, 38 (1948), 205–223.

Graham, C. H., R. H. Brown, and F. A. Mote, Jr. "The relation of size of stimulus and intensity in the human eye. I. Intensity thresholds for white light," *J. Exp. Psychol.*, 24 (1939), 555–573.

Graham, C. H. and Y. Hsia. "Color defect and color theory," *Science*, 127 (1958), 675–682.

Granit, R. *Sensory Mechanisms of the Retina* (London: Oxford University Press, 1947).

Graybiel, A., W. A. Kerr, and S. H. Bartley. "Stimulus thresholds of the semicircular canals as a function of angular acceleration," *Amer. J. Psychol.*, 61 (1948), 21–36.

Green, D. M., and J. A. Swets. *Signal Detection Theory and Psychophysics* (New York: Wiley, 1966).

Green, E. E., E. D. Walters, A. M. Green, and G. Murphy. "Voluntary control of internal states: Psychological and physiological, in T. H. Barber, et al., eds., *Biofeedback and Self-Control* (New York: Aldine, 1971).

Gregory, R. L. *Eye and Brain*, 2nd ed. (New York: World University Library, 1973).

Gregory, R. L. *Eye and Brain*, 3rd ed. (New York: Holt, Rinehart and Winston, 1971).

Gruber, H. E., and W. C. Clark. "Perception of slanted surfaces," *Percept. & Mot. Skills*, 6 (1956), 97–106.

Guilford, J. P., and E. M. Lovewell. "Touch spots and the intensity of the stimulus," *J. Gen. Psychol.*, 15 (1936), 149–159.

Haan, E. L., and S. H. Bartley. "The apparent orientation of a luminous figure in darkness," *Amer. J. Psychol.*, 67 (1954), 500–508.

Haber, R. N., and L. S. Nathanson. "Post retinal storage? Some further observations on Park's camel as seen through the eye of a needle," *Percept. & Psychophysics*, 3 (1968), 349–355.

Hahn, H. Die psychophysicischen Konstant und Variablen des Temperatursinnes. *Zf. f. Sinnesphysiol.*, 60 (1930), 198–232.

Hahn, H., and H. Günther. "Über de Reize und die Reizbedingungen des Geschmackssinnes," *Pflug. Arch. Ges. Physiol.*, 231 (1932), 48–67.

Hardy, J. D., and C. F. Soderstrom. "Heat loss from the nude body and blood flow at temperatures of 22 degrees C. to 35 degrees C.," *J. Nutrition*, 16 (1938), 493–510.

Harper, H. W., J. R. Jay, and R. P. Erickson. "Chemically evoked sensations from single taste papillae," *Physiology & Behavior*, 1 (1966), 319–325.

Harris, L. J., and E. A. Strommen. "What is the 'front' of a simple geometric form?" *Percept. & Psychophysics*, 15(3) (1974), 571–580.

Hartline, H. K., and P. R. McDonald. "Light and dark adaptation of single photoreceptor elements in the eye of Limulus." *J. Cell. Comp. Physiol.*, 30 (1947), 225–253.

Hartline, H. K., and F. Ratliff. "Inhibitory interaction of receptor units in the eye of the Limulus," *J. Gen. Physiol.*, 40 (1957), 357–376.

Hartline, H. K., and F. Ratliff. "Spatial summation of inhibitory influences in the eye of the Limulus and the mutual interaction of receptor units," *J. Gen. Physiol.*, 41 (1958), 1049–1066.

Hartline, H. K., H. G. Wagner, and F. Ratliff. "Inhibition in the eye of the Limulus," *J. Gen. Physiol.*, 39 (1956), 651–673.

Hastorf, A. H. "The influence of suggestion on the relationship between stimulus size and perceived distance," *J. Psychol.*, 29 (1950), 195–217.

Hazzard, F. W. "A descriptive account of odors," *J. Exp. Psychol.*, 13 (1930), 297–331.

Head, H. *Studies in Neurology* (London: Oxford University Press, 1920).

Hebb, D. O., E. S. Heath, and E. A. Stuart. "Experimental deafness," *Canad. J. Psychol.*, 8 (1954), 152.

Hecht, S., C. Haig, and A. M. Chase. "The influence of light adaptation on subsequent dark adaptation of the eye," *J. Gen. Physiol.*, 20 (1937), 831–850.

Hecht, S., and E. U. Mintz. "Visibility of single lines at various illuminations and the retinal basis of visual resolution." *J. Gen. Physiol.*, 39 (1939), 593–612.

Hecht, S., and C. D. Verrijp. "The influence of intensity, color, and retinal location on the fusion frequency of intermittent illumination," *Proc. Nat'l Acad. Sci.*, 19 (1933), 522–535.

Heinbecker, P., G. H. Bishop, and J. O'Leary. "Analysis of sensation in terms of the nerve impulse," *Arch. Neurol. Psychiat.*, 31 (1934), 34–53.

Held, R., and J. Bossom. "Neonatal deprivation and adult rearrangement," *J. Comp. Physiol.*, 54 (1961), 33–37.

Held, R., and S. J. Freedman. "Plasticity in human sensorimotor control," *Science*, 142 (1963), 455–462.

Held, R., and H. Mikaelian. "Motor sensory feedback versus need in adaptation to rearrangement," *Percept. & Mot. Skills*, 18 (1964), 685–688.

Held, R., and M. Schlank. "Adaptation to disarranged eye–hand coordination in the distance dimension," *Amer. J. Psychol.*, 72 (1959), 603–605.

Heller, M. A. "Body locus and form perception," *Percept. & Mot. Skills*, 45(1) (1977), 267–270.

Helmholtz, H. L. F. von. "On the theory of compound colours," *Phil. Mag.*, 4 (1852), 519–534.

Helson, H., *Adaptation-Level Theory* (New York: Harper & Row, 1964).

Helson, H., and S. M. King. "The tau effect: An example of psychological relativity," *J. Exp. Psychol.*, 14 (1931), 202–217.

Helson, H., and W. C. Michels. "The effect of adaptation on achromaticity," *J.O.S.A.*, 38 (1948), 1025–1032.

Henning, H. "Die Qualitätenreihe des Geschmacks," *Zf. f. Psychol.*, 74 (1916), 203–219.

Hensel, H. "Temperaturempfindung und intercutane Wärmbewegung," *Arch. Ges. Physiol.*, 252 (1950), 165–215.

Hensel, H., and K. Bowman. "Afferent impulses in cutaneous sensory nerves in human subjects," *J. Neurophysiol.*, 23 (1960), 564–578.

Hensel, H., and Y. Zotterman. "The response of mechanoreceptors to therman stimulation," *J. Physiol.*, 115 (1951), 16–24.

Hering, E. *Zur Lehre vom Lichtsinne* (Vienna: Carl Gerald's Son, 1878).

Hering, E. *Grundzüge der Lehre vom Lichtsinne* (Berlin: Springer, 1920).

Hermann, J. "Gesamterlebnisse bei Gerüchen," *Neue Psychol. Stud.*, 1 (1926), 473–506.

Heron, W., B. K. Doane, and T. H. Scott, "Visual disturbances after prolonged perceptual isolation," *Canad. J. Psychol.*, 10 (1956), 13–18.

Hershenson, M., H. Munsinger, and W. Kessen. "Preference for shapes of intermediate variability in the newborn human," *Science*, 147 (1965), 630–631.

Hess, C., and H. Pretorie. "Messende Untersuchungen Über die Gesetzmässigkeit des simultanen Helligkeitskontrastes," *Graefes Arch. Ophthalmol.*, 40 (1894), 1–24.

Hilgard, E. R. "Altered states of awareness," in T. Barber, et al., eds., *Biofeedback and Self-Control* (Chicago: Aldine 1971).

Hill, A. L. "Examination of Passey's assimilation theory of the Poggendorf Illusion," *Percept. & Mot. Skills*, 38 (1974), 27–35.

Hoagland, H. "The physiological control of judgments of duration: Evidence for a chemical clock," *J. Gen. Psy.*, 9 (1933), 267–287.

Hoagland, H. *Pacemakers in Relation to Aspects of Behavior* (New York: MacMillan, 1935).

Hochberg, J. E. "Perception, I. Color and Shape, II. Space and Motor, in J. W. Kling, and L. A. Riggs, eds., *Woodworth & Schosberg, Exper. Psychol.* (New York: Holt, Rinehart and Winston) 1 (1971), 395–550.

Hochberg, J. E., W. Treibel, and G. Seaman. "Color adaptation under conditions of homogeneous stimulation (Ganzfeld)," *J. Exp. Psychol.*, 41 (1951), 153–159.

Holcomb, J. H., H. A. Holcomb, and A. DeLaPensa. "Selective attention and eye movements while viewing reversible figures," *Percept. & Mot. Skills*, 44 (1977), 632–644.

Holst, E. von, and H. Mittelstadt. "Das Reafferenzprinzip," *Naturwiss.*, 37 (1950), 464–476.

Holt-Hansen, K. "Extraordinary experiences during crossmodality perception." *Percept. & Mot. Skills*, 43 (1976), 1023–1027.

Holway, A. H.,, and E. G. Boring. "Determinants of apparent visual size with distance variant," *Amer. J. Psychol.*, 54 (1941), 21–37.

Howes, D. "A statistical theory of the phenomenon of subception," *Psychol. Rev.*, 61 (1954), 99–110.

Howes, D., and R. L. Solomon. "A note on McGinnies' emotionality and perceptual defense," *Psychol. Rev.*, 57 (1950), 229–234.

Howes, D., and R. L. Solomon. "Visual duration threshold as a function of work probability," *J. Exp. Psychol.*, (1951), 401–410.

Hulin, W. S. "The effect on tactual localization of movement during stimulation," *J. Exp. Psychol.*, 18 (1935), 97–105.

Hurvich, L. M., and D. Jameson. "Some quantitative aspects of an opponent-colors theory. II. Brightness, saturation, and hue in normal and dichromatic vision," *J.O.S.A.*, 45 (1955), 602–616.

Jacobson, E. *You Must Relax*, 4th ed. (New York: McGraw-Hill, 1957).

Jacobson, George R., Ann VanDyke, Theodore G. Sternback, and Russel

Brethauer. "Field dependence among male and female alcoholics. II. Norms for the rod and frame test," *Percept. & Mot. Skills*, 43 (1976), 399–402.

James, William *Psychology, Briefer Course* (New York: Holt, Rinehart and Winston, 1892).

Jeager, T. "Effect of changes in line-length on apparent shape-length and depth in the Müller–Lyer illusion," *Percept. & Mot. Skills*, 41 (1975), 79–84.

Jellinek, E. M., and R. A. McFarland. "Analysis of psychological experiments on the effects of alcohol," *Quart. J. Stud. Alcohol.*, 1 (1940), 272–371.

Jenkins, W. L. "Studies in thermal sensitivity," *J. Exp. Psychol.*, (1938), 21, 164–177; 22, 178–185; 23, 411–416, 415–461, 464–572.

Jones, M. H. "Second pain: fact or artifact?" *Science*, 124 (1956), 442–443.

Judd, D. B. "Chromaticity sensibility to stimulus difference," *J.O.S.A.*, 22 (1932), 72–108.

Kamiya, J. "Operant control of the Alpha rhythm and some of its reported effects on consciousness," in T. H. Barber, et al., eds., *Biofeedback and Self-Control* (New York: Aldine, 1971).

Kardos, L. "Ding und Schatten," *Zf. f. Psychol.*, Supp. 23 (1934), 184.

Karn, H. W. "Area and intensity-time relation in the fovea," *J. Gen. Psychol.*, 14 (1936), 360–369.

Kaufman, L., and I. Rock. "The moon illusion," *Sci. Amer.*, 207 (1962), 120–130.

Keesey, U. T. "Effects of involuntary eye movements on visual acuity," *J.O.S.A.*, 50 (1960), 769–774.

Keller, R. "The right–left problem in art," *Ciba Symposia*, 3 (1942), 1139.

Kennedy, R. S., M. D. Yessenow, and G. R. Wendt. "Magnitude estimation of visual velocity," *J. Psychol.*, 82 (1972), 133–144.

Kenshalo, D. R., T. Decker, and A. Hamilton. "Spatial summation on the forehead, forearm, and back produced by radiant and conducted heat," *J. Comp. Physiol.*, 63 (1967), 510–515.

Kenshalo, D. R., and J. P. Nafe. "Cutaneous vascular system as a model temperature receptor," *Percept. & Mot. Skills*, 17 (1963), 257–258.

Kenshalo, D. R., J. P. Nafe, and B. Brooks, "Variations in thermal sensitivity," *Science*, 134 (1961), 104–105.

Kenshalo, D. R., and H. A. Scott. "Temporal course of thermal adaptation," *Science*, 151 (1966), 1095–1096.

Kessen, W., P. Salapatek, and M. Haith, "The visual response of the newborn to linear contour," *Exp. Child. Psychol.*, 13 (1972), 9–20.

Kimura, K., and L. M. Beidler. "Microelectrode study of taste buds of the rat," *Amer. J. Physiol.*, 187 (1956), 610.

Klein, G. S., H. J. Schlesinger, and D. Meister. "The effect of personal values on perception: An experimental critique," *Psychol. Rev.*, 58 (1951), 96–112.

Koffka, K. "Some problems of space perception," in Carl Murchison, ed., *Psychologies of 1930* (Worcester, MA: Clark University Press, 1930).

Köhler, W., and H. Wallach. "Figural after-effects, An investigation of visual processes," *Proc. Amer. Phil. Soc.*, 88 (1944), 269–357.

Korte, A. "Kinematoscopische Untersuchungen," *Zt. f. Psychol.*, 72 (1915), 193–296.

Kries, J. von. "Über die Funktion der Netzhautstäbschen," *Z. Psychol. Physio. Sinnesorgane*, 9 (1895), 81–123.

Kuhn, T. S. *The Structure of Scientific Revolutions*, 2nd ed., (Chicago: University of Chicago Press, 1970).

Ladan, C. J., and T. M. Nelson. "Quantitative aspects of thermal flicker fusion," (personal communication, 1971).

Ladefoged, P., and D. E. Broadbent. "Perception of sequence in auditory events," *Quart. J. exp. Psychol.*, 2 (1960), 162–170.

Lambert, W. W., R. L. Solomon, and P. D. Watson. "Reinforcement and extinction as factors in size estimation," *J. Exp. Psychol.*, 39 (1949), 637–641.

Land, E. H. "Experiments in color vision," *Sci. Amer.*, 200 (1959), 84–99.

Landau, A. A., and R. S. Ragor. "Effect of 'apparent' instruction on brightness judgement," *J. Exp. Psychol.*, 68 (1964), 80–84.

Leibowitz, H., E. Mitchell, and N. Angrist. "Exposure duration in the perception of shape," *Science*, 120 (1954), 400.

Letourneau, J. E. "Effects of training in design on magnitude of the Müller–Lyer illusion," *Percept. & Mot. Skills*, 42 (1976), 119–124.

Lewis, D. R. "Psychological scales of taste," *J. Psychol.*, 26 (1948), 437–446.

Liberman, A. M. "Results of research on speech perception," *J. Acoust. Soc. Amer.*, 29 (1957), 117–123.

Liberman, A. M., F. S. Cooper, K. S. Harris, and P. F. MacNeilage. "A motor theory of speech perception," *Proc. Speech Comm. Seminar* (Stockholm, Royal Institute of Technology, 1962).

Liberman, A. M., P. DeLattre, and F. S. Cooper. "The role of selected stimulus variables in the perception of unvoiced stop consonants," *Amer. J. Psychol.*, 65 (1952), 497–516.

Liberman, A. M., P. C. DeLattre, L. J. Gerstman, and F. S. Cooper. "Tempo of frequency change as a cue for distinguishing classes of speech sounds," *J. Exp. Psychol.*, 52 (1956), 127–137.

Liberman, A. M., K. S. Harris, P. Eimas, L. Licker, and J. Bastian. "An effect of learning on speech perception. The discrimination of durations of silence with and without phonemic significance," *Lang. Speech*, 4 (1961), 175–195.

Liberman, A. M., K. S. Harris, J. Kinney, and H. Lane. "The discrimination of relative onset time of the components of certain speech and non-speech patterns," *J. Exp. Psychol.* 61 (1961), 379–388.

Licklider, J. R. C. "Basic correlates of the auditory stimulus," in S. S. Stevens, ed., *Handbook of Experimental Psychology*, (New York: Wiley, 1951).

Lippold, O. C. L., J. G. Nichols, and J. W. T. Redfearn. "A study of the afferent discharge produced by coating a mammalian muscle spindle," *J. Physiol.*, 153 (1960), 218–231.

Lit, A. "The magnitude of the Pulfrich stereo-phenomenon as a function of binocular differences of intensity at various levels of illumination," *Amer. J. Psychol.*, 62 (1949), 159–181.

Lit, A. "The effect of fixation conditions on depth discrimination thresholds at scotopic and photopic illuminance levels." *J. Exp. Psychol.*, 58 (1959), 476–481.

Lit, A. "The magnitude of the Pulfrich stereo-phenomenon as a function of target velocity," *J. Exp. Psychol.*, 59 (1960), 165–175.

Lit, A., and A. Hyman. "The magnitude of the Pulfrich stereo-phenomenon as a function of distance of observation." *Amer. J. Optom., Arch. Amer. Acad. Optom.*, 122 (1951), 1–17.

Lubin, Robert A. "Influence of alcohol upon performance and performance awareness," *Percept. & Mot. Skills*, 45 (1977), 303–310.

Luckiesh, M. *Light, Vision, and Seeing* (Princeton, NJ: Van Nostrand, 1944).

Ludvigh, E. J., and J. W. Miller. *A Study of Dynamic Visual Acuity*, Joint Proj. Rep. No. 1, Kresge Eye Institute Contr. Nonr. 586 (00), ONR Proj. Desig. No. 142–023, BuMed Proj. NM 001067.01.01, 1953.

Mac Donald, M. K. "An experimental study of Henning's prism of olfactory qualities," *Amer. J. Psychol.*, 33 (1922), 535–553.

Mach, E. *The Analysis of Sensations* 5th ed. (Trans. by S. Waterlow) La Salle, Il.: Open Court Pub. Co. 1914.

Mackavey, W. R. "Spatial brightness changes in Koffka's ring," *J. Exp. Psychol.*, 82 (1969), 405–490.

Mackavey, W. R., S. H. Bartley, and C. Casella. "Disinhibition in the human visual system," *J.O.S.A.*, 52 (1962), 85–88.

MacLeod, R. B. "An experimental investigation of brightness constancy," *Arch. Psychol.*, 135 (1932), 102.

MacLeod, R. B. "Brightness constancy in unrecognized shadows," *J. Exp. Psychol.*, 27 (1940), 1–22.

Maerz, A., and M. R. Paul. *A Dictionary of Color*, 2nd ed. (New York: McGraw-Hill, 1951).

Mann, C. W., and N. H. Berry. *The Perception of the Postural Vertical. II. Visual Factors*, Pensacola, FL, Joint Rep. No. 5, Tulane University and USN. School of Aviation Med., 1949.

Mann, C. W., and J. H. Dauterive, Jr. *The perception of the postural vertical. I. The modification of non-labyrinthine cues*, Pensacola, FL, Joint Rep. No. 4, Tulane University and USN. School of Aviation Med., 1949.

Marks, L. E. "Spatial summation in the warmth sense," in H. R. Moskowitz, et al., eds., *Sensation and Measurement: Papers in Honor of S. S. Stevens*, (Dordrecht, Holland: Reidel, 1974), pp 369–378.

Marks, L. E., and J. C. Stevens. "Perceived cold and skin temperature as functions of stimulation level and duration," *Amer. J. Psychol.*, 85(3) (1972), 407–419.

Marks, L. E., and J. C. Stevens. "Spatial summation of warmth: Influence of duration and configuration of the stimulus," *Amer. J. Psychol.*, 86(2) (1973), 251–267.

Marks, W. B., W. H. Dobelle, and E. F. MacNichol. "Visual pigments of single primate cones," *Science*, 143 (1964), 1181–1183.

Marler, P. R., and W. J. Hamilton. *Mechanisms of Animal Behavior* (New York: Wiley, 1966).

Marshall, W. H., and S. A. Talbot. "Recent evidence for neural mechanisms in vision leading to a general theory of sensory acuity," in H. Klüver, ed., *Biological Symposia* (Tempe, AZ: Jaques Cattell Press, 1942).

Mashhaur, M. M. "On the validity of scales derived by ratio and magnitude estimation," *Psychol. Lab. Report*, University of Stockholm, Sweden, 1962.

Maslow, A. H. *Toward a Psychology of Being* (Princeton, NJ: Van Nostrand, 1962).

Mathieson, A. "Apparent movement in auditory perception," *Psychol. Mono.*, University of Iowa Studies in Psychol., 14 (1931), 74–131.

Maxfield, J. P. "Some physical factors affecting illusion in sound motion pictures," *J. Acoust. Soc. Amer.*, 3 (1931), 69–80.

Mayzner, M. S. "Visual information processing of alphabet inputs," *Psychol. Mono. Supplements*, 4(13) (1972), 239–243.

Mayzner, M. S., and M. E. Tresselt. "Visual information processing with sequential inputs: A general model for sequential blanking, displacement and over printing phenomena." *Annals. of the New York Acad. of Sci.*, 169 (1970), 599–618.

McBurney, D. H., and V. B. Collings. *Introduction of Sensation and Perception* (Englewood Cliffs, NJ: Prentice-Hall, 1977).

McCleary, R. A., and R. S. Lazarus. "Autonomic discrimination without awareness," *J. Personnel*, 18 (1949), 171–179.

McDougall, W. "The sensations excited by a single momentary stimulation of the eye," *Brit. J. Psychol.*, 1 (1904), 78–113.

McGinnies, E. "Emotionality and perceptual defense," *Psychol. Rev.*, 56 (1949), 244–251.

McLaughlin, S. C., K. I. Rifkin, and R. G. Webster. "Oculomotor adaptation to wedge prisms with no part of the body seen," *Percept. & Psychophysics*, 1 (1966), 452–453.

Meltzoff, A. N., and M. K. Moore. "Imitation of facial and manual gestures by human neonates," *Sci.*, 198 (1977), 75–78.

Melzack, R. "Phantom limbs," *Psychology Today* (Oct. 1970).

Michotte, A. *La Perception de la Causalité*, Brussels: Louvain Institute, Superior de La Philosophie, 1946).

Mikaelian, H., and R. Held. "Two types of adaptation to an optically-rotated visual field," *Amer. J. Psychol.*, 77 (1964), 257–263.

Miller, G. A. *Psychology: The Science of Mental Life* (New York: Harper & Row, 1962).

Miller, G. A., and W. G. Taylor. "The perception of repeated bursts of noise," *J. Acoust. Soc. of Amer.*, 20 (1948), 171–182.

Miller, J. W., and S. H. Bartley. "A study of object shape as influenced by instrumental magnification," *J. Gen. Psychol.*, 50 (1954), 141–146.

Miller, N. "Learning of visceral and glandular responses," in T. Barber, et al., eds., *Biofeedback and Self-Control* (Chicago, Aldine, 1971).

Milstein, S. L., and J. P. Zubek. "Temporal changes in cutaneous sensitivity during prolonged visual deprivation," *Canad. J. Psychol.*, 21 (1967), 337–345.

Mote, F. A., and A. J. Riopelle. "The effect of varying the intensity and the duration of pre-exposure upon subsequent dark adaptation in the human eye," *J. Comp. physiol. Psychol.*, 46 (1953), 49–55.

Munsell Book of Color (Baltimore, MD: Munsell Color Co., 1942).

Murphy, D. B., T. I. Myers, and S. Smith. *Reported visual sensations as a function of sustained sensory deprivation and social isolation*, Pioneer III, Draft Research Report, Hum RRO, U.S. Army Leadership Human Research Unit (Monteray, CA: Nov. 1963).

Nafe, J. P. "Pressure, pain, and temperature senses," in Carl Murchison, ed., *A Handbook of General Experimental Psychology* (Worcester, MA: Clark University Press, 1938).

Nafe, J. B., and K. S. Wagoner. "The nature of pressure adaptation," *J. Gen. Psychol.*, 25 (1941), 323–351.

Nagatsuka, Y. "Studies in sensory deprivation III, Part 2, Effects of sensory deprivation upon perceptual functions," *Tohoku Psychologica Folia*, 23 (1965), 56–59.

Neisser, Ulric. *Cognitive Psychology* (New York: Appleton-Century-Crofts, 1967).

Nelson, T. M., and S. H. Bartley. "The perception of form in an unstructured field," *J. Gen. Psychol.*, 54 (1956), 57–63.

Nelson, T. M., and S. H. Bartley. "The role of PCF in temporal manipulation of color," *J. Psychol.*, 52 (1961), 457–477.

Nelson, T. M., S. H. Bartley, and C. Bourassa. "The effect of areal characteristics of targets upon shape-slant invariance," *J. Psychol.*, 52 (1961), 479–490.

Nelson, T. M., S. H. Bartley, C. M. Bourassa, and R. J. Ball. "Symposium on alternation of response," *J. Gen. Psychol.*, 84 (1971), 3–177.

Nelson, T. M., S. H. Bartley, and W. Mackavey. "Responses to certain pseudoisochromatic charts viewed in intermittent illuminance," *Percept. & Mot. Skills*, 13 (1961), 227–231.

Nelson, T. M., and C. Ladan. "Size perception under several field conditions," *Amer. J. Optom. & Archives of AAO*, 46 (June 1969), 418–425.

Nelson, T. M., and C. Ladan. "Affective descriptions of spatial arrangements which vary in hue, brightness and surface quality." Unpublished manuscript.

Nelson, T. M., and E. C. Lechelt. "Nativistic, empirical, and motivation variables and children's response to number," submitted to the Canad. Psychological Assn., 1968.

Nelson, T. M., B. K. Sinha, and R. Deegan, "Perception of distorted auditory messages reduced by alcohol impairment" (personal communication, 1978).

Nelson, T. M., B. K. Sinha, and W. M. Olson. "Short term memory for hue in chronic alcoholics," *Brit. J. Addiction*, (1978).

Nelson, T. M., and P. Swartz. "Perceptual conflict and alcoholics," *Percept. & Mot. Skills*, 33 (1971), 1023–1028.

Nelson, T. M., and P. Vasold. "The dependence of object identification upon edge and surface," *Percept. & Mot. Skills*, 20 (1965), 537–546.

Newman, E. B. "Versuche über das Gamma-Phänomen," *Psychol. Forsch.*, 19 (1934), 102–121.

Newman, E. B. "Hearing," in E. G. Boring, H. Langfeld, and H. P. Weld, eds., *Foundations of Psychology* (New York: Wiley, 1948).

O'Connor, J. D., L. J. Gerstman, A. M. Liberman, P. C. DeLattre, and F. S. Cooper. "Acoustic cues for the perception of initial /w, j, r, 1/ in English," *Word*, 13 (1957), 24–43.

Oetting, S. R., and E. R. Oetting, "Preliminary observations on a visual perception illusion," *Percept. & Mot. Skills*, 39 (1974), 1290.

Ogle, K. N., and V. J. Ellerbrock, "Cyclofusional movements," *Arch, Ophthalmol.*, 36 (1946), 700–735.

O'Mahoney, M. "The interstimulus interval for taste. L. The effeciency expectoration and mouth rinsing for clearing the mouth of salt residuals," *Perception*, 1 (1972a), 209–215.

O'Mahoney, M. "The interstimulus interval for taste. 2. Salt taste sensitivity drifts and the effects on intensity scaling and threshold measurement," *Perception*, 1 (1972b), 1, 217–222.

O'Mahoney, M. "Taste specificity for chemical stimulation of single papillae, toward an explanation of disparate results." *Percept. & Mot. Skills*, 37 (1973a), 677–678.

O'Mahoney, M. "Ascending series thresholds for NaCl effect of mouth rinsing," *I.R.C.S. Med. Science*, Rep. No. 73-3, 39-2-5 (1973b).

O'Mahoney, M. "Qualitative descriptions of low concentration of sodium chloride solutions," *Brit. J. Psychol.*, 64, (4) (1973c), 601–606.

Ostwald, W. *Color Science* (London: Windsor and Newton, Part I, 1931: Part II, 1933).

Parinaud, H. *La Vision* (Paris: Doin, 1898).

Passey, G. E., and F. E. Guedry, Jr. *The Perception of the Postural Vertical. III. Adaptation Effects in Four Planes*, Pensacola, FL, Joint Rep. No. 6, Tulane University and USN. School of Aviation Medicine, 1949.

Penfield, W. G. "A contribution to the mechanisms of intercranial pain," in C. A. Patten, A. N., Frantz, and C. C. Hare, eds., *Sensation: Its Mechanisms and Disturbances* (Baltimore: Williams & Wilkins, 1935).

Pfaffmann, C. "Taste and smell," in S. S. Stevens, ed., *Handbook of Experimental Psychology* (New York: Wiley, 1951).

Pfaffmann, C. "Gustatory nerve impulses in rat, cat, and rabbit," *J. Neurophysiol.*, 18 (1955), 429–440.

Pfaffmann, C. "The sense of taste," in V. E. Hall, ed., *Handbook of Physiology*, Vol. I, Sect. 1. (Washington, DC: American Physiological Society, 1959).

Piaget, J., Y. Feller, and E. McNear. "Essai sur la perception des vitesses chez l'enfant et chez l' adult," *Arch. Psychol. Geneve*, 36 (1958), 253–327.

Pick, A. D. "Improvement of visual and tactual form discrimination," *J. Exp. Psychol.*, 69 (1965), 331–339.

Piggins, D., and D. Morgan. "Note upon steady visual fixation and repeated auditory stimulatives in meditation and in the laboratory," *Percept. & Mot. Skills*, 44 (1977), 357–358.

Piper, H. "Über die Abhängigkeit des Reizwertes leuchtender Objekte von ihren Flächen," *Winkelgrossen*, 32 (1903), 98–112.

Pitblado, C., and C. R. Mirabile. "Relationship between visual orientation and susceptibility to motion sickness," *Percept. & Mot. Skills*, 44 (1977), 267–273.

Postman, L., J. S. Bruner, and E. McGinnies. "Personal values as selective in perception," *J. Abnorm. Soc. Psychol.*, 42 (1948), 142–154.

Pratt, K. C., A. K. Nelson, and K. H. Sun. "The behavior of the newborn infant," *Ohio State University Studies, Contrib. to Psychol.*, No. 10 (1930).

Preyer, W. *Spécielle Physiologie des Embryo* (Leipzig: Grieben, 1885).

Pritchard, R. M. "Stabilized images on the retina," *Sci. Amer.*, 204 (1961), 72–78.

Proshansky, H., and G. Murphy. "The effects of reward and punishment on perception," *J. Psychol.*, 13 (1942), 295–305.

Prytulak, Lubomir. "Critique of S. S. Stevens' theory of measurement scale classification," *Percept. & Mot. Skills*, 41 (1975), 3–28.

Pulfrich, C. "Die Stereoskopie im Dienste der isochromen und heterochromen Photometrie," *Naturwiss.*, 10 (1922), 553–564, 569–574, 596–601, 714–722, 735–743, 751–761.

Pulgram, E. "Introduction to the Spectography of Speech (London: Gravenhage, Moulton, 1959).

Purdy, D. M. "Spectral hue as a function of intensity," *Amer. J. Psychol.*, 43 (1931), 541–559.

Purdy, D. McL. "Vision" in E. G. Boring, H. S. Langfeld and H. P. Weld, eds. *Psychology*, New York: Wiley, 1935.

Rachlin, H. C. "Scaling subjective velocity, distance, and duration," *Percept. & Psychophysics*, 1(2) (1966), 77–82.

Ranney, J. E., and S. H. Bartley. "A further study of determinants of phenomenal distance in plane targets perceived as three-dimensional scenes," *J. Psychol.*, 56 (1963), 19–27.

Ratliff, F. "The role of physiological nystagmus in monocular acuity," *J. Exp. Psychol.*, 43 (1952), 163–172.

Renshaw, S., and R. J. Wherry. "Studies on cutaneous localization. III. The age of onset of ocular dominance," *J. Genet. Psychol.*, 39 (1931), 493–496.

Renshaw, S., R. J. Wherry, and J. C. Newlin. "Cutaneous localization in congenitally blind versus seeing children and adults," *J. Genet. Psychol.*, 38 (1930), 239–248.

Restle, F. "Moon illusion explained on the basis of relative size," *Science*, 167 (1970), 1092–1096.

Révész, G. *Psychology and Art of the Blind*, (London: McKay, 1950).

Riccó, A. "Realizazione fra it minimo angolo visuale e l'intensita luminosa," *Memorie della Riga Academia di Science, lettere, ed arti in modena*, 17 (1877), 47–160.

Riesen, A. H., and L. Aarons. "Visual movement and intensity discrimination in cats after early deprivation of pattern vision," *J. Comp. Physiol. Psychol.*, 52 (1959), 142–149.

Riggs, L. A. "Visual acuity," in C. H. Graham, ed., *Vision and Visual Perception* (New York: Wiley, 1965).

Riggs, L. A. "Vision," in J. W. Kling and L. A. Riggs, eds., *Experimental psychology*, 3rd ed. (New York: Holt, Rinehart and Winston, 1971).

Riggs, L. A., J. C. Armington, and F. Ratliff. "Motions of the retinal image during fixation," *J.O.S.A.*, 44 (1954), 315–321.

Riggs, L. A., F. Ratliff, J. C. Cornsweet, and T. N. Cornsweet. "The disappearance of steadily fixated visual test objects," *J.O.S.A.*, 43 (1953), 495–501.

Rivers, W. H. R. "Primitive color vision," *Pop. Sci. Monthly*, 59 (1901), 44–58.

Rock, I., and F. S. Fleck. "A re-examination of the effect of momentary reward and punishment on figure-ground perception," *J. Exp. Psychol.*, 40 (1950), 766–776.

Rock, I., J. Goldberg, and A. Mack, "Immediate correction and adaptation based on viewing a prismatically displaced scene," *Percept. & Psychophysics*, 1 (1966), 351–358.

Rose, J. E., and V. B. Mountcastle. "Touch and kinesthesis," in J. Field, H. W. Magoun, and V. E. Hall, eds., *Handbook of Physiology* (Washington, DC: American Physiological Soc., 1959).

Rossi, A. M., and P. E. Nathan. "Research on alcoholism: nomothetic or idiographis," *Proc. 77th Ann. Convention of Amer. Psychol. Assn.*, 4 (Part I) (1969), 317–318.

Ruch, T. C. "Somatic sensation," in J. F. Fulton, ed., *A Textbook of Physiology* (Philadelphia: Saunders, 1955).

Rudolph, H. J. *Attention and Interest Factors in Advertising* (New York: Funk & Wagnalls, 1947).

Sanders, A. "The selective process in the functional visual field." *Institute for Perception, RVU-TNO Saesterberg*, (The Netherlands, 1963).

Sappenfield, B. R. "Social desirability, the halo effect, and stereotypical perception in person perception and self-perception," *Percept. & Mot. Skills*, 33 (1971), 683–689.

Sappenfield, B. R. "Perception of openness, trustworthiness, and other characteristics in facial photographs," *Percept. & Mot. Skills*, 45 (1977), 195–200.

Schafer, R., and G. Murphy. "The role of autism in a visual figure ground relationship," *J. Exp. Psychol.*, 32 (1943), 335–343.

Schiffman, H. R. *Sensation and Perception* (New York: Wiley, 1976).

Scholl, K. Das räumliche Zuzammernarbeiten von Auge und Hand, *Deut. Z. Nervenheilbk.*, 91 (1926), 280–303.

Schulte, W., and J. P. Zubek. "Change in olfactory and gustatory sensitivity after prolonged visual deprivation," *Canad. J. Psychol.*, 21 (1967), 337–345.

Schultze, M. "Zur Anatomie und Pysiologie der Reina," *Arch. Mikr. Anat.*, 2 (1886), 175–286.

Scott, T. H. "Intellectual efforts of perceptual isolation," doctoral dissertation, McGill University, 1954.

Scott, T. H., W. H. Bexton, W. Heron, and B. K. Doane. "Cognitive effects of perceptual isolation," *Canad. J. Psychol.*, 13 (1959), 200–209.

Schwartz, A. S., A. J. Perey, and A. Azulay. "Further analysis of active and passive touch in pattern discrimination," *Bull. Psychonomic Soc.*, 6(1) (1975), 7–9.

Senden, M. von. *Raum- und Gestaltauffassung bei operierten Blindgeborenen vor und nach Operation* (Leipzig: Barth, 1932).

Shewchuk, L. A. and John P. Zubek, "A technique of intermittant stimulation for measurement of tactual sensitivity: approaches and preliminary results." *Canad. J. Psychol.*, 14 (1960), 29–37.

Shlaer, S. "The relation between visual acuity and illumination." *J. Gen. Physiol.*, 21 (1937), 185–209.

Siegal, R. K. "Hallucinations," *Sci. Amer.*, 237(4) (1977), 132–140.

Sinclair, David C. *Cutaneous Sensation* (London: Oxford University Press, 1967).

Skramlik, E. von. "Über die Lokalization der Empfindung bei den niederen Sinnen," *Zf. f. Sinnesphysiol.*, 56 (1925), 69–140.

Slonim, A. D., and O. P. Shcherbakova. *Metabolism in Primates*, Bull. VIEM, 8(9), 17, 1934.

Somerville, C. Z., and J. W. Somerville. "Vertical vs. Horizontal Presentations in the Visual Cliff Apparatus," *Percept. & Mot. Skills*, 45(1) (1977), 18–19.

Snyder, F. W., and N. H. Pronko. *Vision with Spatial Inversion* (Wichita, KS: University of Wichita Press, 1952).

Stavrianos, B. K. "The relation of shape perception to explicit judgments of inclination," *Arch. Psychol.*, (No. 296) (1945).

Steinhardt, J. "Intensity discrimination in the human eye. I. The relation of $\Delta I/I$ to intensity," *J. Gen. Physiol.*, 20 (1936), 185–209.

Stelmack, R. M., and W. J. Leckett. "The effect of artificial pupil size on recognition threshold," *Percept. & Mot. Skills*, 39 (1974), 739–742.

Stevens, J. C., E. R. Adair, and L. E. Marks. "Pain, discomfort and warmth as functions of thermal intensity," in *Physiological and Behavioral Temperature Regulation* (Springfield, IL: Thomas, 1970).

Stevens, J. C., and W. P. Banks. "Spatial summation in relation to speed of reaction to radiant stimulation," *Int. J. Biometeor.*, 15(2–4) (1971), 111–114.

Stevens, J. C., and L. E. Marks. "Apparent warmth as a function of thermal irradiation," *Percept. & Psychophysics*, 2(12) (1967), 613–619.

Stevens, J. C., and L. E. Marks. "Spatial summation and the dynamics of warm sensation," *Percept. & Psychophysics*, 9(5) (1971), 391–398.

Stevens, J. C., L. E. Marks, and P. Gagge. "The quantilative assessment of thermal discomfort," *Environmental Res.*, 2(3) (1969), 149–165.

Stevens, J. C., and L. L. Rubin. "Psychophysical scales of apparent heaviness and the size-weight illusion," *Percept. & Psychophysics.*, 8(4) (1970), 225–230.

Stevens, S. S. "Tonal density," *J. Exp. Psychol.*, 17 (1934a), 585–592.

Stevens, S. S. "The volume and intensity of tones, *Amer. J. Psychol.*, 46 (1934b), 397–408.

Stevens, S. S. "A scale for the measurement of a psychological magnitude: Loudness," *Psychol. Rev.*, 43 (1936), 405–416.

Stevens, S. S. "To honor Fechner and repeal his law," *Science*, 133 (1960), 80–86.

Stevens, S. S. "On the psychophysical law," *Psychol. Rev.*, 64 (1967), 153–181.

Stevens, S. S. and Davis, H. *Hearing: Its Psychology and Physiology*, New York: Wiley, 1938.

Stevens, S. S., and A. G. Ekdahl. "The relation of pitch to the duration of a tone," *J. Acoust. Soc. Amer.*, 10 (1939), 255.

Stevens, S. S., and E. B. Newman. "The localization of actual sources of sound," *Amer. J. Psychol.*, 48 (1936), 297–306.

Stevens, S. S., J. Volkmann, and E. B. Newman. "A scale for the measurement of psychological magnitude: Pitch," *J. Acoust. Soc. Amer.*, 8 (1937), 185–190.

Stewart, G. W., and O. Hovda. "The intensity factor in binaural localization: an extension of Weber's law," *Psychol. Rev.* 25 (1913), 242–251.

Stratton, G. M. "Vision without inversion of the retinal image," *Psychol. Rev.*, 4 (1897), 341–360, 463–481.

Swartz, Paul. Perceptual Conflict and Alcoholics in Symposium: Perception & Alcoholism, *Department of Psychol. Univ. of Alberta and Div. of Alcoholism, Alberta Dept. of Public Health* (Alberta, Canada, 1968).

Swartz, P. "Modes of Encounter," *Psychol. Reports*, 24 (1969), 683–690.

Swisher, C. W., and E. Mandes. "Müller–Lyer illusion decrement as related to adaptation preceding negative aftereffect: correlation and analysis." *Percept. & Mot. Skills*, 39 (1974), 377–378.

Talbot, H. F. "Experiments on light," *Phil. Trans. Roy. Soc.*, London, 3 (1834), 298.

Taus, R. H., J. C. Stevens, and L. E. Marks. "Spatial location of warmth," *Percept. & Psychophysics*, 17(2) (1975), 194–196.

Teghtsoonian, R., and M. Teghtsoonian. "The effects of size and distance on magnitude estimations of apparent size," *Amer. J. Psychol.*, 83 (1970), 601–612.

Thouless, R. H. "Phenomenal regression to the real object," *Brit. J. Psychol.*, 1931, 21 (Part I), 339–359: 22 (Part II), 1–30.

Thunberg, T. "Untersuchungen über die bei Einer Einzelmen Momentanen Haut Reizung Aufretenden swei Stechenden Empfindung," *Skand. Arch. Physiol.*, 12 (1902), 399–442.

Ton, W. H. "Bilateral practice and tactural discrimination," *Percept. & Mot. Skills*, 37 (1973), 639–642.

Tussing, L. "Perceptual fluctuations of illusions as possible physical fatigue effect," *J. Exp. Psychol.*, 29 (1941), 85–87.

Uttal, William R. *The Psychobiology of Sensory Coding*, New York: Harper & Row, 1973.

Vanderplas, J. M., and R. R. Blake. "Selective sensitization in auditory perception," *J. Personal.*, 18 (1940), 252–266.

Vernon, M. D. *Perception Through Experience* (London: Methuen, 1970).

Vierling, J. S., and I. Rock. "Variations of olfactory sensitivity to exaltolide during the menstrual cycle," *J. Appl. Physiology*, 22 (1967), 311–315.

Wald, G. "On the mechanism of the visual threshold and visual adaptation," *Science*, 119 (1954), 887–982.

Wald, G., and A. B. Clark. "Visual adaptation and the chemistry of the rods," *J. Gen. Physiol.*, 21 (1937), 93–105.

Walk, R. D., and E. J. Gibson. "The 'visual cliff,' " *Sci. Amer.*, 202 (1960) 64–72.

Wallach, H. "The role of head movements and vestibular and visual cues in sound localization," *J. Exp. Psychol.*, 27 (1940), 339–368.

Wallach, H. "The perception of motion," *Sci. Amer.*, 201(1) (1959), 56–60.

Wallach, H., E. B. Newman, and M. R. Rosenzweig. "The precedence effect in sound localization," *Amer. J. Psychol.*, 62 (1949), 315–336.

Wallgren, H., and H. Barry. *Actions of Alcohol: Biochemical, Physiological and Psychological Aspects*, XIV (Amsterdam. The Netherlands: Elsevier, 1970), 400 pp.

Warren, R. M. "Restoration of missing speech sounds," *Science*, 167 (3917) (1970), 392–393.

Warren, R. M., and R. L. Gregory. "An analogue of the reversible figure," *Amer. J. Psychol.*, 71 (1958), 612.

Warren, R. M., C. J. Obusek, and J. M. Acknoff, "Auditory Induction: Perceptual synthesis of absent sounds," *Science*, 176 (1972), 1149–1151.

Warren, R. M., and R. P. Warren. "Auditory illusions and confusions," *Sci. Amer.*, 223(6) (1970), 30–36.

Wegel, R. L., and C. E. Lane. "The auditory masking of one pure tone by another and its probable relation to the dynamics of the inner ear," *Phys. Rev.*, 23 (1924), 266–285.

Wendt, G. R. "Vestibular functions," in S. S. Stevens, ed., *Handbook of Experimental Psychology* (New York: Wiley, 1951).

Wenzel, B. M. "Differential sensitivity in olfaction," *J. Exp. Psychol.*, 39 (1949), 124–143.

Wenzel, B. M. "Chemoreception," in E. C. Carterette and M. P. Friedman, eds., *Handbook of Perception*, Vol. III (New York: Academic Press, 1973).

Werner, H. "Studies in contour. I. Qualitative analyses," *Amer. J. Psychol.*, 47 (1935), 40–64.

Wever, E. G., and C. W. Bray. "The nature of the acoustic response: The relation between sound frequency and frequency of impulses in the auditory nerve," *J. Exp. Psychol.*, 13 (1930), 373–387.

White, B. W., F. A. Saunders, L. Scadden, P. Bach-y-Rita, and C. C. Collins. "Seeing with the skin," *Percept. & Psychophysics*, 7(1) (1970), 23–27.

Wilcox, W. W. "The basis of the dependence of visual acuity on illumination," *Proc. Nat'l. Acad. Sci.*, 18 (1932), 47–56.

Wing, C. W., Jr., and G. E. Passey. *Perception of the Postural Vertical. XI. The Visual Vertical Under Conflicting Visual and Acceleration Factors*, Pensacola, FL, Joint Rept. No. 20, Tulane University and USN. School of Aviation Med., 1950.

Winsor, C. P. and A. B. Clark "The measurement and analysis of color adaptation phenomena," *Proc. Roy. Soc.*, London 155 (1934), 49–87.

Winslow; C. E. A., L. P. Herrington, and A. P. Gagge. "Relations between atmospheric conditions, physiological reactions, and sensations of pleasantness," *Amer. J. Hygiene,* 26 (1937), 103–115.

Witkin, H. A., and S. E. Asch. "Studies in space orientation. III. Perception of the upright in absence of a visual field," *J. Exp. Psychol.,* 38, (1948a), 603–614.

Witkin, H. A., and S. E. Asch. "Studies in space orientation. IV. Further experiments on perception of the upright with displaced visual fields," *J. Exp. Psychol.,* 38, (1948b), 762–782.

Witkin, H. A., H. B. Lewis, M. Hertzman, K. Machover, P. P. Meissner, and S. S. Wapner. *Personality Through Perception* (New York: Harper & Row, 1954).

Witt, I., and H. Hensel. "Afferente Impulse aus der Extremitätenhaut der Katze bei thermischer und mechanischer Reizung, *Pflug. Arch. ges. Physiol.,* 268 (1959), 582–596.

Wittreich, W. J. "The Honi phenomenon: A case of selective perceptual distortion," *J. Abnorm. Soc. Psychol.,* 47 (1952), 705–712.

Wolfflin, H. "Ueber das Rechts and Links in Bilde," *Gedanken zur Kungstgeschichte,* Basil (1941).

Woodworth, R. S., and H. Schlosberg. *Experimental Psychology,* rev. ed. (New York: Holt, Rinehart and Winston, 1954).

Worrall, N., and D. E. Firth. "Figure orientation effects amount of Müller–Lyer illusion." *Percept. & Mot. Skills,* 38(1) (1974), 161–162.

Worschel, P., and K. M. Dallenbach. "The vestibular sensitivity of deaf-blind subjects," *Amer. J. Psychol.,* 61 (1948), 94–98.

Wright, G. H. "The latency of sensation of warmth to radiation," *J. Physiol.,* London, 112 (1951) 344–358.

Wundt, W. "Zur theorie der räumlichen Gesichtswahmehmungen, *Phil. Stud.,* 14 (1898), 11.

Young, T. "On the theory of light and colours," in *Lectures on Natural Philosophy,* Vol. II (London: Savage, 1807).

Younger, J., W. Adriance, and R. J. Berger. "Sleep during transcendental meditation," *Percept. & Mot. Skills,* 40 (1975), 953–954.

Zajonc, R. B. "Response suppression in perceptual defense," *J. Exp. Psychol.,* 64 (1962), 206–214.

Zigler, M. J., and R. Barrett. "A further contribution to the tactual perception of form," *J. Exp. Psychol.,* 10 (1927), 184–192.

Zotterman, Y. "Studies in the peripheral nervous mechanism of pain," *Acta Med. Scand.,* 80 (1933), 185–242.

Zubek, J. P., J. Flye, and M. Aftanas. "Cutaneous sensitivity after prolonged visual deprivation," *Science,* 144 (1964), 1591–1593.

Zubek, J. P., J. Flye, and D. Willows. "Change in cutaneous sensitivity after prolonged exposure to unpatterned light," *Psychomic Sci.,* 1 (1964), 283–284.

Zuckerman, M. "Hallucinations, reported sensations, and images," in J. P. Zubek, ed., *Sensory deprivation: Fifteen years' research* (New York: Appleton-Century-Crofts, 1969).

Zwaardemaker, H. *L'Odorat.* (Paris: Doin, 1925).

Index of Authors

Index of Subjects

Adaptation
  color, 190
  contrast, 190
  dark, 176 ff.
  level, 262
  light, 178
  perceptual "correction," 357
  reaching response, 355
  reflectance, 261
  to rotated field, 354
  temporal, 175
Alcoholism, 382, 399
Anguish, 83
Alphabets, phonetic, 133 ff.
Atomism, 4
Attention
  fields of, 19
Audition
  auditory thresholds, 116
  combination tones, 125
  consonance, 125
  directional effects, 124
  dissonance, 125
  hearing loss, 117
  overtones, 124
Autisms, 372

Behavior, 12
Biofeedback, 382, 386, 397
Brightness
  contrast and induction, 165
  enhancement, 206, 209
  target diameter, 163

Coding, 21
Coldness, 70
  paradoxical, 72–73
Color
  adaptation, 190
  contrast, 193
  defect, 200
  filters, 184
  after images, 189

mixtures, 185, 187
modes of appearances, 195
names, 185
properties, 196
receptors, 200
sources, 182
systems, 186
temporal factors, 203
theories, 197
Conflict, 2
Constancy
  color, 259, 260
  distance, 247
  lightness, 241
  perceptual, 240 ff.
  shape, 252
  size, 246 ff.
  whiteness, 241
Cosine function, 256–257
Critical flicker frequency, 39
Cross modality matching, 35
Cube
  reversible, 18

Deafness
  partial, 141 ff.
Decibel, 113 ff.
Decision axis, 28
Development
  Bower, 226
  Fantz, 224
  human fetuses, 223
  imitation, 239
  intermodal perception, 229, 233
  object qualities, 236
  object size, 235
  subjects lacking vision, 222
  tactual localization, 235
  visual cliff, 230 ff.
Disinhibition, 168
Disparity
  retinal, 271